- ELECTRIC CARS- P.
- LEOPOLD + LOEB MUR
-. MANY <u>AAA</u> WORKE
    COMMIE PARTY- P. 40

- CIO = COMMITTEE ON INDUSTRIAL ORGANIZATION
- CIO LEADERSHIP LARGELY COMMIES- P. 84, 101-102,
    118,

P-USA SUPPORTED JAP/AMERICAN RELOCATION CAMPS- P. 90
COMMIES HAD "CLASS BIAS" TOWARD THE
    WEALTHY- P 94
- COMMIE SUPPORT FOR FDR'S 1944 ELECTION - P. 99

- THE CIO-PAC WAS THE VERY 1ST PAC IN
    US HISTORY- P. 104; See P. 100-101,

- BIRTH OF THE "PROGRESSIVE PARTY"- P. 144

- SMITH ACT- DEFINED- P. 150, 205-206, 217,
AUTHOR APPROVES OF SOVIET TAKEOVER OF
CZECHOSLOVKIA - P. 167

BERNIE SANDERS [INDEPENDENT SOCIALIST] -P. 189

- FEINBERG LAW- DEFINED - P. 205

- Author considers his help in dismantling the McCarran Act the outstanding achievement of his professional life - p. 193

- Reason why "under god" was added to the pledge of allegiance - p. 198

- Author's thoughts on Stalin's 1930's-1940's purges p 212-213

- Author has no doubts concerning "The Rosenbergs" innocence. p. 250

- Author believed the USSR "intervened" in Hungary but did not "invade" - p. 243

- Lee Harvey Oswald shouted out to reporters "get hold of Abt to ~~be~~ be my lawyer -!" p. 251

- Justice Douglas gives most articulate statement why our gov't should not penalize or punish one for being a communist saying that communism embraces a broad range of ideas... p. 260-261
  see also p. 281,

- Author's view on capitalism - p. 302 ff

— FINAL NOTE ON POSSIBLE SUCCESS OF
SOCIALISM BY THE AUTHOR P. 302
— HOWARD FAST: p. 155, 191,

Advocate and Activist

ALP = AMERICAN LABOR PARTY

IPP = INDEPENDENT PROGRESSIVE PARTY - p. 156, 161,

CI = COMMUNIST INTERNATIONAL - p. 195.

JOHN APT
→ see P. 144
1) SISTER = MARION ; MARION'S SON = JOHNNY - P. 95
2) WIFE = JESSICA → see P. 144
3) BROTHER IN LAW = ARTIE [ARTHUR] BACHRACH P. 94
4) JUDY : JESSICA'S ADOPTED DAUGHTER - P. 97
5) DAVID : JESSICA'S SON - P. 97

Advocate
and Activist

Memoirs of an American
Communist Lawyer

— JOINS CP-USA IN 1934   P. 39-40
— RECRUITED INTO CP-USA BY HAL WARE P. 102
— BECAME CP-USA GENERAL COUNSEL [FOR >30 YEARS]
IN 1951, P. 219, 238

John J. Abt
with **Michael Myerson**

UNIVERSITY OF ILLINOIS PRESS
Urbana and Chicago

This book is printed on acid-free paper.

Library of Congress Cataloging-in-Publication Data

Abt, John J. → 1904 — 1991
    Advocate and activist : memoirs of an American communist lawyer /
John J. Abt with Michael Myerson.
        p.   cm.
    Includes index.
    ISBN 0-252-02030-8 (acid-free paper)
    1. Abt, John J. 2. Lawyers—United States—Biography.
3. Communists—United States—Biography. I. Myerson, Michael,
1940-   . II. Title.
KF373.A28A32   1994
349.73'092—dc20
[B]
[347.30092]
[B]   92-47040
                                                              CIP

Contents

Foreword by Margaret Burnham

I first came to know John Abt through a young child's eyes. Forty years ago, when two hundred miles was a considerable distance to travel, especially in the slow and sometimey cars that seemed to be my father's preference, a trip to Kent, Connecticut, where John and his wife, Jessica, had a log cabin, was a major production. We would all pile in, cranky children who'd been forced to give up long-made plans to do nothing in the city for a mandatory ride to nowheresville and adults eagerly anticipating the country respite.

Invariably, there would be a stop here and there to lift the hood and check things or to consult the maps and, if necessary—and it always was—rechart. No matter how well-laid our plans, night would always fall before our arrival, so that the car would have to carefully inch out every yard of the last few miles. Finally, the big old house would be in front of us, and we'd see John and Jessica beneath the yellow porch light, both smiling deeply, relieved we'd arrived and glad for our presence. The porch led into a warm kitchen with a big wood stove, and the table would be set for the meal we should have eaten hours earlier. We children would be fed and led to bed, while the adults stretched their limbs and minds around the huge stone fireplace, their laughter circling up to where we lay on the second floor, trying to accustom ourselves to the night sounds of the country.

It was John's nature to make the children feel that we were his special guests. He kept close track of our comings and goings in school and always insisted that we share our music with him. He'd have us pick up a project from one Kent visit to the next, pressing fall leaves, catching frogs or Monarchs. He could hardly have known it then, but John awakened us to more than the sweetness of the country during those visits. The animated adult conversation seemed to us nonstop, and as guests debated the topics of the day, we would listen, absorbing the intensity of both their political commitments and their deep respect for one another.

* * *

John Abt was the only lawyer I ever knew as a child, and certainly then, I knew nothing of his life's work. What I saw was the private space of an enormously complex and brilliant man. In pulling together the private and the public self of this monumental figure, this memoir records some of the darkest moments in our country's history. But as well, it describes what I witnessed as a child—the tender friendships and loyalties that helped sustain a besieged and reviled movement.

Here is the life of one of America's very finest advocates—a story of bravery, courage, intelligence, and perseverances. It is the lonely story of how one man stood up while most of the bar and bench ran for cover. John Abt's representation of the Communist party and its members took him into hundreds of hostile courtrooms around the country. Repeatedly, he went to Washington to urge an increasingly repressive Supreme Court to uphold the Bill of Rights. He stood by the side of hundreds of witnesses and defendants whose lives and reputations were being mowed down by an unbounded and unprecedented hysteria. A principal architect of the Smith Act defense, he was as well, for more than two decades, the central legal strategist of the Party's response to the Internal Security Act of 1950, which created the Subversive Activities Control Board, and the Communist control Act of 1954, which declared that the Communist party "should be outlawed" and provided that the Party was not "entitled to . . . the rights" created by U.S. laws.

It is a challenge, today, to fathom the horrific personal and political devastation of the McCarthy-Truman years. Almost every state slavishly followed the lead of national repressive legislation and set up legislative committees investigating "un-American" activities. By 1951, about 150 municipalities had passed antisubversive ordinances and a number were requiring loyalty tests of public employees. In the 1950s, more than 13 million Americans were required to respond in some way to the huge network of private and public loyalty and security programs.

Moreover, the victims of McCarthyism often endured their ordeal without legal assistance, for the bar, its members fearful of being tainted, had vanished. Typical was the advice one lawyer gave his government employee client who had to undergo a loyalty hearing and wished to avoid a second one: "Drop your Negro friends and express no views whatsoever on any programs which are not generally accepted as conservative." Nor were there public interest legal organizations such as exist today to defend these civil liberties victims. The ACLU, far from defending the Bill of Rights, was a full partner in the Red Scare. For example, it voted to reject as members anyone whose "devotion to civil liberties" was "qualified by adherence to Communist . . . doctrine."

It was in this desolate climate of intense fear, where virtually all eyes were closed to civil liberties principles, that John Abt plied his trade as a constitutional lawyer. Long before other progressive lawyers were on the scene—and long after they had left for other, more lucrative endeavors—John defended the legal existence of the Communist party. From its inception in the 1950s until it was ultimately eliminated in 1973, he fought to outlaw the Subversive Activities Control Board. He challenged the actions of state authorities in New York, Minnesota, and Connecticut in seeking to ban the Communist party's electoral efforts. Representing thousands of individual clients, he appeared before school boards, union bodies, HUAC, and the Supreme Court.

* * *

John Abt's work stretched well into the 1970s. Personally, it was my great fortune to renew the friendship I had had with him as a child when, in 1970, we worked together on Angela Davis's case. At the time of her arrest Angela had heard of, but did not know, John, and one could hardly imagine two more different people. Between these two brilliantly opinionated political animals, it fell to me to squeeze out some common ground. At one point early in the legal proceedings, when the state of New York sought to extradite Angela to California, John had crafted a carefully nuanced statutory and constitutional argument why extradition should be denied. But Angela— sensing that the statutory issues were a lost cause in this highly political case—wanted the argument in court to be, simply, that the extradition of her from one state to another was akin to the treatment afforded fugitive slaves. John resisted, all the more because the judge before whom he had to make the argument was African-American, and Angela insisted, in part because she underestimated the importance of the legal tools at her disposal. Ultimately, both were satisfied when John wove a comment about fugitive slaves into his otherwise traditional argument.

In the course of John's representation of Angela Davis in New

York, I learned from a master how to construct a legal defense to a political prosecution. His accumulated wisdom over so many years of political cases caused him to counsel restraint—both political and legal—in our defense, and this strategy proved critical in the long run. It was John who, in 1970, shaped Angela Davis's early case and thereby lay the seeds for her ultimate victory.

* * *

Before it can be said that the cold war is truly over, there must be a full accounting of the travesty visited upon our country during the McCarthy era. We must come to know the depths of the personal suffering endured by millions of Americans, the legacy left by the vicious battering the Constitution underwent, and, as well, the heroic efforts of the few who refused to remain silent but who chose, instead, to live the good life, the brave life, and the honorable life. John Abt, an unsung hero, takes us along the path to recreating life in that darkest moment in our history.

Introduction by Michael Myerson

For my generation, the assassination of President John F. Kennedy on November 22, 1963, was perhaps the defining moment. Any adult who was alive then can tell you where they were and what they were doing when they heard the news. Like everyone else, I closely followed each news development that fateful weekend from my apartment in Berkeley, California. When, just before his own murder, the accused assassin, Lee Harvey Oswald, told the press that he wanted John Abt to represent him, I vaguely recalled that this was the lawyer representing the Communist party in a raft of litigation before the Supreme Court, trying to reverse the legal consequences of the McCarthy years.

Eight years later, I was living in New York and had met John on a couple of social occasions at homes of mutual friends. I was active in the Angela Davis support campaign, when she was arrested on a federal fugitive warrant and John became her co-counsel in fighting extradition to California. As the result of a *Ramparts* magazine interview I'd made with Angela, I became a minor player and hostile prosecution witness in the trial of David Poindexter, who was arrested with her. During that experience, I began to get to know John. Or at least, I thought so.

But I rarely saw him after that. I'd sit across from him at an occasional meeting or exchange pleasantries at a reception or holiday party. Then in 1986, my friend Gil Green came to me on John's behalf. Gil was an old pal of John's, who had also been a client during his years in Leavenworth Penitentiary on a Smith Act conviction. John's wife, Jessica Smith, had recently died, and John was having some difficulty coping. Gil suggested, partially for therapeutic reasons but also because of John's enormous accomplishments, that he write his life story. John reluctantly went for the idea but, then in his eighties, said that he needed someone to help compile his memoirs. Gil asked if I was available.

I declined. I was then national director of a peace organization and buried in more work than I could adequately handle. I made several alternative suggestions. One, Marc Mishler, a young attorney in Albany, New York, within driving distance from John's summer place, spent some time interviewing John, filling in a number of blanks from an abbreviated oral history John had given to the Communist party's archives. But for a combination of reasons, the project stalled.

By the end of 1989, I let it be known that I was leaving my job in the peace movement and entertaining the idea of returning to California. Gil Green, on the excuse that he wanted to keep me in New York, again raised the idea of "doing John's book."

From our first discussions, John let me know that this would not be easy. Never given to keeping papers, the few he'd held onto were thrown out after Jessica's death. Moreover, John had outlived most of his closest friends and co-workers, so not many of his contemporaries were available for interviews. Finally, John's own personality and professional training mitigated against autobiography. As he tells in these memoirs, his father often expounded on the difference between objectively appraising one's self-worth and vanity, which is little more than self-promotion. "People," John writes, "who truly appreciate themselves have no need to seek from others reassurance that they are what they are—or flattery to beguile themselves into believing they are something better."

It was his sense of actual self-worth that allowed John, for over half a century, to submerge his own views and brilliant legal skills to those of the strong-willed personalities whom he served—Jerome Frank, Senator Robert LaFollette, Jr., Robert Jackson, Sidney Hillman, Henry Wallace, and the leaders of the Communist Party USA. For most of his career, John was a political operative as well as legal counsel, and his contributions, bestowed in anonymity, were usually credited to these public figures.

Moreover, John's entire career as a lawyer was in just such circumstances, acting not as an individual luminary—a Melvin Belli or F. Lee Bailey or William Kunstler, say—but on behalf of an institution or organization, a government agency or political party. And whether as an attorney for the government or defense counsel for the Communist party under legal assault by the same government, John

needed to be absolutely discreet. Raised to be a "gentleman" in the
ambiance of Chicago's affluent Freud Hill, discretion came easily to
him.

This discretion, public modesty, and self-appreciation served him
well not only in his long career but also in a rich private life filled
with loving friends and family. Admirable attributes though they be
in general, however, they are not necessarily helpful in compiling
one's memoirs. On any number of occasions, I had to remind him,
"John, if you are going to tell your life's story, you must talk about
your life."

I had a good deal of help in getting him to do so. I am thankful to
the anonymous souls from the Communist party's history unit who
took that initial stab at an oral history with John, as well as to Marc
Mishler for his follow-up interviews. These sent me to a number of
other sources. For several months I received help from the staffs of
the Columbia University Oral History program, the New York Public
Library, and the Tamiment Institute Library at New York University.
The research department of the Amalgamated Clothing and Textile
Workers' Union allowed me to inspect the papers of the union and of
Sidney Hillman, which are housed at Cornell University's New York
State School of Industrial and Labor Relations. The staff of the Mar-
tin P. Catherwood Library in Ithaca was most helpful.

In these memoirs, every quote from John's colleagues—Jerome
Frank, Beanie Baldwin, Rexford Tugwell, etc.—that refers to the
source's oral history is to be found in the Columbia University Oral
History program. Quotations from published works cite the book's title (or cite the case, in instances of legal briefs and arguments) without publishing history, to make for easier reading. Sidney Hillman's
speeches, sometimes quoted herein, are located either in the Catherwood Library or in John's personal files. In all cases, they are speeches John wrote for Hillman. All other quotes are from John's notes or
recollection.

Loaded with an armful of questions from this research, I filled up
another armful from interviews with the following friends, colleagues, and family members of John's: Vita Barsky, Dorothy Burnham, Margaret Burnham, Harold Cammer, George Crockett, Angela
Davis, Elizabeth Dodson, Judy Ware Dodson, John Gates, Gil Green,
Vincent Hallinan, Vivian Hallinan, Dorothy Healey, Esther Jackson,
James Jackson, Ruth Jett, Charles Kramer, Charlene Mitchell, Thelma Dale Perkins, Allen Rosenberg, Phyllis Silverman, Jeffrey
Schwartz, and Telford Taylor. With both armfuls of questions, I spent
over 120 hours taping and noting John's responses, which make up

the body of this volume. Later, Vita Barsky, Gil Green, Judy Dodson, and Laura Myerson read the manuscript in draft and made helpful suggestions. I am grateful to all of them for the time and courtesy they uniformly extended. In addition, Laura Myerson, Morton Schillinger, and Peter Schillinger, each in different ways, helped bring me into the twentieth century, if not the twenty-first, by introducing me to the personal computer.

This is John's book, not mine. I emphasize this because John was wary of the project in the beginning. Not only for the reasons already mentioned, but he was concerned that I not impose my own views on the book. The things he learned were often told to him in confidence, and as a lawyer he was uncommonly scrupulous in observing confidences. He knew that by training and temperament, I was more given to outspokenness. Not that we disagreed on much. We shared many, perhaps most, of the same criticisms of the Communist party leadership, but he knew I was more likely to give voice to them beyond the confines of a few intimates. He was particularly concerned that I refrain from doing so in this book. I have been diligent in respecting his concerns. Often in the course of recording him or taking notes, he would indicate that I should turn off the machine, that what he was about to say was off the record. On a few occasions I appealed to him to include this or that and he usually declined. There is nothing in this book that John did not want included.

The first draft of the manuscript was completed in June 1991, just days before John was to leave for his summer home upstate. I had given him sections of the manuscript as I finished them. I drafted "May Day Child" nearly a year earlier, with the idea of lending a distinct "voice" to the book. John was not fully comfortable with the style I developed and made a number of specific suggestions for changes, which I eventually incorporated. But we agreed that rather than get bogged down in rewriting, I would simply record, digest, and edit what he said for the rest of the book, at the end of which we would go through it, page by page. John gave me liberty to include occasional literary references or turns of phrase of my own, but basically what you read in this book are John's words. The exception is "Losses," when John, anxious to complete the draft before leaving the city for the summer, told me, "Michael, please put these thoughts and ideas down on paper in your own words. Give me something to accept or edit." A couple of weeks later, he phoned to say that he was especially pleased with these final pages and was inclined to accept them "as is." The original manuscript was one-third larger than the finished product. I told John that he had to make substantial cuts to meet the publisher's mandate. He hoped to spend the last part of the summer in this endeavor. I tentatively agreed to visit him in Copake, to discuss possible cuts. On August 6, 1991, John suffered a massive stroke and died two days later. It fell to me to complete the book on my own.

In Moscow, just eleven days after John's death, the defense minister and KGB chief led an aborted coup d'etat against the Soviet president, Mikhail Gorbachev, which, upon unraveling, led to the disintegration of the USSR itself. The coup attempt, and the backhanded support it received from U.S. Communist leader Gus Hall, accelerated in the Communist Party USA a debate that had begun two years earlier. This culminated in the party's twenty-fifth national convention in December 1992, which saw Hall and his supporters win a pyrrhic victory, the price being the decimation of the organization. John's closest remaining comrades, among them Gil Green and Charlene Mitchell, together with Angela Davis, Herbert Aptheker, Louis Weinstock, and other well-known party figures, were denounced and removed from all leadership positions.

At the end of this book, John mentions the crisis of socialism in his last years and says that "in this sense only, I'm glad that Jessica is not around to witness it. It would have simply broken her heart." One can only conjecture how John would have reacted to the end of the Soviet Union, and to the U.S. party, as he knew it. I believe he would have been greatly saddened but not terribly surprised. A few months before his death, he had "finally tackled," as he put it, *Let History Judge,* Roy Medvedev's massive and seminal study of Stalin and Stalinism. He told me the experience was "disturbing, but also cleansing," that just a few years before, he would never have read Medvedev, a dissident in the Brezhnev years. The book explained and put into perspective some things he hadn't understood, John said, and some things he denied to himself. The refusal of his own party to come to grips with the failure of the Stalinist model of socialism in Europe preordained its own death. "The party is finished," John said.

He took no joy in this conclusion. His entire political life—nearly six decades—was spent in the Communist Party USA, and to the end, he never regretted his choices. A number of leading attorneys tell me that had John "played his cards" differently, he could have gone onto the U.S. Supreme Court or Court of Appeals. They cite his "pedigree," his legal acumen—including more than a dozen victorious arguments before the Supreme Court—and the caliber of his colleagues in the New Deal and the war years, many of whom themselves were appointed to these highest courts. But John was happy with his own life and his own choice of friends. He believed to his dying days that, though the authoritarian model of socialism proved not to be viable, the future for U.S. capitalism was hardly rosy, triumphant cheers to the contrary notwithstanding. John felt that eventually, and through struggle, people would find a just alternative to the present order, built as it is upon wars and plunder abroad and racism and an obscene disparity between rich and poor at home. Whatever crimes were committed by Stalinist governments—and he took no comfort in having supported what he later called "the indefensible"—John's life was devoted to defending and extending democracy in the United States. He was justifiably though quietly proud of his contributions. None did it better.

Note to the Reader by John J. Abt

The reader who is expecting dramatic revelations as to the identity of members of what came to be known during the McCarthy period witch-hunts as "the Ware Group"—members of the Party who held positions in the Roosevelt administration—will be disappointed. Throughout this memoir, I will identify no members of the Communist Party, including those now deceased, except insofar as they themselves have so identified themselves. I have arrived at this approach after long consideration. In my own case, even though I had been named as a Party member when I was in the government and afterwards, and although I served as general counsel for the Communist party for some thirty-plus years, it was not until my eightieth birthday, a half century after joining, that I felt free to publicly identify myself as such. I had no personal fear of acknowledging my membership. But my many friends and associates, past and present, in or out of the government, would have been uncomfortable, perhaps embarrassed, perhaps have felt it necessary to defend their friendship or end it, and—at various points in these past fifty years—been themselves under pressure or in danger from the government.

One of my dearest friends, also a Communist, said to me some years ago: "John, if you outlive me and are asked to speak at my funeral or memorial service, I want you to say that I lived and I died a member of the Communist party." As it happens, I did outlive him and his son asked me to speak at his memorial meeting. I told the son that I'd be most honored and happy to speak and then told him of his father's request and my agreement and that I intended to carry out my agreement. The son became terribly disturbed and upset and pleaded with me not to do so—he was a lawyer himself with contacts in the federal government. My deceased friend, like myself, had been identified before congressional committees, grand juries, and in the press as a Communist. But that I would publicly confirm this at his father's memorial was causing such distress for the son. After careful thought, I decided it was more important to avoid causing harm or embarrassment to the living than to keep my agreement with the dead. So I did not mention my late friend's membership in the Communist party when I spoke.

As I said when I announced my membership at a banquet in honor of my eightieth birthday, "It seems to me a rather sad commentary on the state of the freedom of political association in this country that I had to wait for half a century after the event before I felt free, publicly and proudly, to confirm a fact which anyone who knows anything at all about me has assumed to be true for lo, these many years." What is commonplace, even mundane, in Italy and Finland and Japan and Brazil—membership in a political party that advocates socialism as a higher form of organization for society—unfortunately still today carries associations of something alien or dangerous here in the bastion of the "free world."

Advocate and Activist

1

May Day Child

On April 1, 1904, my mother returned home from a brief shopping expedition to be greeted by my sister, Marion, then a precocious five-year-old, who called out excitedly, "Mommy, mommy, the stork brought the baby while you were out!" Then, as the story has been endlessly recounted, Marion announced, "April Fool." I arrived on the scene exactly one month later, on May 1, fortunately while mother was at home with an obstetrician in attendance. I have sometimes wondered whether there could be a link between my choice of May 1 as a birthday and the subsequent events that shaped my life as a labor and left-wing lawyer.

At the dawn of the twentieth century, Chicago was the heart of American industry and the home of American labor. Exactly eighteen years before I was born, on May 1, 1886, nearly forty thousand workers walked out on strike in support of the eight-hour workday. What unfolded in the next seventy-two hours was as traumatic for the city as what occurred a decade before when Mrs. O'Leary's famous cow reportedly kicked over a lantern. Scores of thousands of more workers joined in the strike, and the city fathers reacted in panic. On the evening of May 4, as thousands gathered in Haymarket Square, the center of the packinghouse district, a bomb exploded in the midst of a crowd of police officers, killing seven of them. The police immediately opened fire and shot round after round into the crowd, killing several workers and wounding two hundred. While subsequent evidence indicates that the bomb was the work of an agent provocateur, the police arrested seven leading radicals who were later tried, convicted, and hanged. It is in memory of these, the Haymarket Martyrs as they are known to labor historians, that workers from Moscow to Montevideo march to celebrate on my birthday.

Not that my childhood circumstances could by any stretch of the imagination be described as proletarian. My paternal grandmother was a Hart and my grandfather, Levi Abt, a founder of the leading men's clothing manufacturer, Hart, Abt and Marx. Subsequently, out of revulsion to the alcoholism of one of the Hart members of the firm, my straight-laced grandfather left to establish another company, and the original partnership became Hart, Schaffner and Marx.

My German-born paternal grandparents had come to this country around 1848, young Jews in search of freedom and fortune. While Grandpa Abt's new firm, L. Abt and Sons, never achieved the great success of Hart, Schaffner and Marx, he must have done reasonably well in his new venture. He was able to send my father, Jacob, to Yale, where he graduated in 1890, and his twin brother, my uncle Isaac, to Johns Hopkins and Rush Medical School. Isaac was the first Chicago doctor, perhaps the first American doctor, to specialize in pediatrics and was the author of an encyclopedia, *Abt's Pediatrics*, which was the standard work on the subject. (Years later, Dr. Benjamin Spock, sitting next to me at a political conference, told me, "That's a great name in pediatrics.")

My maternal grandfather, Adolph Shire, was in the tobacco business, with a cigar store in the Loop, Chicago's downtown business district. The store perished in the Chicago Fire, but grandpa recovered from the disaster. In retirement before my birth, he spent his days sitting at Slaughter and Company, the stockbrokers, watching his investments. He was a lovely, gentle man, self-educated but widely read. He taught me chess and first introduced me to the classics of literature—Dickens, Balzac, Thackeray, and so on.

Young idealists just out of college—my mother, Mildred Shire, went to University of Chicago—my parents came under the influence of Jane Addams and spent much time at Hull-House. As it happened, Hull-House was a center of support for the burgeoning textile workers' union in Chicago, particularly during their strike of 1910, when forty thousand clothing workers took to the street, sparked by a group of sixteen women. Their demands were for a closed (union) shop and the establishment of a mechanism to settle grievances. The object of the strike was Hart, Schaffner and Marx. After four months of bitter struggle, an agreement signed by the firm and the United Garment Workers' Union established a three-person arbitration board. The company named its representative, the union named its lawyer, Clarence Darrow, and the third person never was selected. Most notable for the future course of the union was the emergence of Sidney Hillman, Jacob Potofsky, and Frank Rosenblum as rank-and-file activists from the Hart, Schaffner and Marx shop floor. These three would eventually become the national leaders of the union for the next half century.

My grandfather had by that time left the Hart, Schaffner and Marx firm, and my father, as I say, was involved in settlement house work. But their sympathies were clearly with the company. Meantime, Jane Addams's colleagues at Hull-House, Frances Crane Lillie (the very wealthy heiress to Crane Plumbing) and Ellen Starr, sparked community support—together with local figures like Carl Sandburg and faculty members at the University of Chicago—for the poor Jewish sweatshop workers. At home there was talk of "good doers."

Under the guidance of Ellen Starr, my parents helped establish a counterpart of Hull-House in a Jewish community "back of the yards." This was the Maxwell Street Settlement at which my father was head resident and my mother a teacher of bilingual (Yiddish-English) education to recent immigrants from eastern Europe and Russia. They were by now deeply in love and married. Faced with the responsibility of marriage and a prospective family, father left settlement work and entered my grandfather's wholesale clothing business. The years at Maxwell Street Settlement remained happy memories, and when Marion came along in 1898 they gave her the middle name of Maxwell. (Years later, father wrote a weekly column—in fact ghostwritten by Marion—in the Fairchild publication *Men's Wear* called "Maladies of the Needle Trades" under the name "Dr. Max Wells.")

Our family life was very happy indeed. My parents were far from rich, at least not in comparison with some of their really wealthy relatives and friends. But we were certainly comfortable. Father was by no means an extravagant man, and money-making ranked low on his order of priorities. Family finances were never discussed in the presence of the children, and I don't remember ever being denied a material wish for lack of the means to satisfy it. Father was fond of quoting Charles Lamb to the effect that "money is like fish—if kept for more than two days, it stinks." I never knew my parents to quarrel or exchange a mean word. And they were most loving to each other and to us. Marion and I used to congratulate ourselves on how wise we had been in our choice of parents.

Father, however, was unhappy working in the firm. He hated the business aspects of the job, particularly the loneliness of sales trips downstate, and to Wisconsin, Michigan, and other states. He left L.

Abt and Sons to become president of the Chicago Wholesale Cloth-
iers' Association, whose principle function was to keep the Chicago
men's clothing market nonunion. In 1914, the Amalgamated Clothing Workers' Union (ACWU) was founded as an independent industrial union in a breakaway from the United Garment Workers, the
AFL affiliate. Under the leadership of Sidney Hillman, the ACWU constitution contained a "revolutionary" preamble that spoke of the "constant and unceasing struggle being waged" between labor and capital. Hillman was regarded in our family as something of an evil spirit,
to be evoked as a parental warning, e.g., "John, if you don't eat your
spinach, Sidney Hillman will get you." My early memories include
nights, when a strike was in progress, spent at the living room window, waiting, watching, and worrying until father returned home.

The union won a collective bargaining agreement with Hart,
Schaffner and Marx in 1913 and, after a series of additional strikes,
the balance of the Chicago market caved in and signed up with the
Amalgamated in 1919. Father was the representative of the employers' association in negotiating and administering its collective bargaining agreements, having accepted the inevitability of trade
unions. He and Hillman eventually established good, friendly relations that turned out to be neither difficult nor surprising for, despite
the militant preamble of its constitution, the union never pursued a
policy of class struggle.

* * *

Whatever turmoil engulfed father's work, our family life was
one of calm and comfort. Mother always sustained Marion and me
with her love, quiet strength, and complete understanding. Our sense
of security was troubled only by the search for an outlet that might
give some larger meaning to our lives. Mother and father were wholly lacking in competitiveness. Father often expounded on the differences between vanity and "self-appreciation" for the edification of his
children; vanity was self-promotion. We must learn, father argued, to
objectively (and quietly) appraise our self-worth, to develop our potential. "Self-appreciation," father said, "is not conceit." People who
truly appreciate themselves have no need to seek from others reassurance that they are what they are—or flattery to beguile them into
believing they are something better. In father's philosophy, self-appreciation implied a constant struggle for self-improvement, the only
competition worth entering into was with one's self.

Father loved to season a homily with a quotation: the precepts
of Polonius, coming from his smiling lips, lost their schoolroom
stuffiness:

This above all: to thine own self be true,
And it must follow, as the night the day,
Thou canst not then be false to any man.

Politics were rarely discussed at home. Like most middle-class Chicago Jews, father voted Republican as a matter of habit, I believe, rather than of conviction. Father was a pragmatist, a follower of William James, which in those days was considered quite an advanced philosophical position.

We weren't a religious family in any sense. My grandparents attended synagogue, and father tried to persuade me to go to Sunday school, but without success. My guess is that his attempts were half-hearted, for they were soon abandoned. He also gave me a copy of the Old Testament to read but he took care beforehand to blue-pencil all sexual and "scatological" passages. Jewish holidays were mainly observed as opportunities to stay home from school.

There were special country clubs for wealthy German Jews, which included most of our family friends, although we also had non-German Jewish friends. The struggles that were carried out "at the point of production" in the clothing market were in no small part between German Jewish manufacturers and working-class eastern European Jewish workers. Housing patterns also of course developed along class lines. I can't say that we, Marion and I, were ever inculcated with a sense of superiority, but there were obviously biases. I remember that the family, as a matter of course, referred to non-German Jews as "kikes." Their inferiority lay in the fact—as a common expression had it—that they were born *"drei Stunde über der Grenze,"* three hours on the wrong side of the border.

Father took a dim view of Zionism, a subject of much debate at the time. This was about 1917, the time of the Balfour Declaration when Britain announced its intention to set up a Jewish state in Palestine. Father saw assimilation as the solution to "the Jewish question," and I recall his having long arguments with Horace Kellen, a professor of philosophy and a leading Zionist. Father insisted that the creation of a new Jewish state in a land that was then less than 10 percent Jewish was a dangerous business, which would provoke the enmity of the Arab majority.

I recognize that my life might have been quite different had I not been a Jew. But I have never suffered from being one and can recall only two early instances when I personally experienced anti-Semitism. During my junior year at the University High School, the private school affiliated with the University of Chicago, I was nominated to be class treasurer as part of a slate. Normally, such nominations were unopposed. But this time a non-Jewish candidate was placed on the ballot to oppose me because of the feeling that there were "too many Jews" on the regular slate. I was soundly defeated and, in my pique, spent that summer earning enough credits to enter the University of Chicago in the fall of 1920 at the age of sixteen. The second instance occurred that same autumn when I was rushed by the Delta Kappa Epsilon fraternity for several days until they learned I was Jewish, at which point I was suddenly dropped. I reported the episode to father, who cajoled me by saying that the only Greek letter society worth joining was Phi Beta Kappa. Many years later, Marion, reflecting on our childhood but from the perspective of the Great Depression, wrote in the July 1932 issue of the *Atlantic Monthly:*

> We had a charming house with seven rooms, two baths and a garden. We had a car. We employed a maid, a laundress, a janitor and a college boy who acted as tutor to John. John went to an excellent private school of the modern, experimental type. We did not, like so many of our friends, belong to expensive clubs, keep our own horses, or entertain lavishly. Our bill at the bootlegger's was modest. But we had a delightful social life, extended an easy hospitality, went to the theatre when we chose, hailed taxis when it rained, took vacations when we were too hot, too cold, or too tired to stay at home, and usually counted our pennies after we had spent them. It was very nice—so long as we had a income of $15,000.

I count on Marion's recollection since, at the time she writes about, I was still a child and she on the verge of womanhood.

Summers, while father worked in the city, mother, Marion, and I spent three months as paying guests on a family-sized dairy farm about thirty miles north of Chicago. The farm, once called Rockefeller but in our time called Mundelein, was run by German immigrants named Schneider. They had a horse and buggy, which we loved to ride. It was there that Marion and I learned how the barn swallow flies and where the hangbird builds its nest; and we learned how to coax a steady stream of milk from a cow's udder. Father would visit us on weekends, and sometimes some of my cousins or one of my aunts would join us for our summer idyll.

From an early age I was a reader, but spending a year in bed with TB accelerated my development in this direction. Perhaps it was because my social life revolved around and within our family, but I was a very shy child and reading provided easy and satisfactory company. Mother was concerned about my shyness and pushed me into a small theater company she managed as a way of overcoming this "affliction." Mother had considerable literary skill and wrote occasional plays for various organizations in the city. She was the beneficent spirit behind the Coach-House Players, a community theater under the direction of Marion Maximilianovitch Gering, a Soviet emigre who had worked with Vsveyold Meyerhold, the great constructivist director-producer. Gering was a handsome young man with beautifully shaped, well-manicured, and most expressive hands. I wrote a short story about him for one of my English classes, which I ended by having him marry his manicurist.

While occasionally the Coach-House Players would perform Shaw or another prominent playwright, we mainly put on the modest efforts of newcomers to the theater. Some of these newcomers, like Elmer Rice and Floyd Dell and Elisha Cook, went on to make names for themselves in theater and literature. Elisha Cook, Jr., like me a novice, became a leading Hollywood character actor. My own career on stage was mercifully—for me and the audiences—brief. Gering, the director, liked me and, no doubt, my mother well enough to ask me to perform for him in George Kaiser's *Gas* at the Goodman Theater. I played a petty bureaucratic clerk, a performance that was notable only for the fact that a still photograph of one of my scenes appears in an early edition of the *Encyclopedia Britannica* under the subject heading "Little Theatre."

I can't say whether it was my brief acting career, my awareness of Marion's flowering social life, or simply my hormones making themselves amply apparent, but if I hadn't completely conquered my shyness, I would have certainly gotten some control of the situation.

After my thespian spin at the Coach-House Players, I got my first job. This was in 1921. I was seventeen years old and had just finished my sophomore year at the University of Chicago. A family friend who was also friends with the managing editor of the *Herald-Examiner*, the local Hearst paper, arranged my employment. I can hardly claim merit got me the job, which was that of "picture chaser." In those days, to save the expense of photographers, the papers hired cub reporters to solicit people in the news to give existing photos of themselves to run alongside stories about them. It was exactly the wrong kind of job for me—running around Chicago at night, knocking on doors, trying to persuade people to give me their photos when I was just barely able to talk to strangers.

The *Herald-Examiner* was making a big deal that summer of Harold McCormick, the International Harvester heir who had a monkey-gland operation in order to have satisfactory sexual relations with his lady friend, the opera star Ganna Walska. This story was obviously beyond my meager talents, so the editors had me chasing after pictures of various picket lines and strikes. In the years immediately following World War I, there was a wave of militant strikes, and that summer there was a railroad shop strike with some serious police violence directed against the pickets. I was assigned to go get some pictures of the victims, but I resisted the idea of knocking on doors at night and asking bereaved family members for pictures of injured or dead strikers. I can't say that I sympathized with the workers at that point so much as that I didn't have the chutzpah to intrude on private grieving. I came back to the newsroom empty-handed. After several days of this lack of success, the city editor called me aside and said, "Goddamnit Abt, can't you ever get anything right?" I obviously couldn't, and that day he fired me.

I spent the remainder of the summer as a guest of my Aunt Blanche, one of mother's sisters, at Beulah, Michigan, a resort on a small lake not far from Charlevoix. At some point during weeks of golf or horseback riding in the morning and tennis, swimming, and German lessons in the afternoons, I wrote a letter home that contains the first indications of some social consciousness. I told my family about the resort's recreational activities, mostly in the company of Marjorie Mack, the only person my age "who, if nothing else, is not annoying. . . . We have a good time together" (this to satisfy their unexpressed curiosity). I then wrote about what I called a "little debating club" of two middle-aged men and myself, which met before dinner to discuss religion and kindred problems. My letter home continues:

> Last evening I attacked everything from Mr. Bachrach's religious ideals to his firm belief in the immortality of the private property system, neither of which I was able to make him abandon. In vain did I point out that the present system is but a stage in general social evolution, in vain shout that private property did not exist in feudal times (I was a little shaky about proving this statement, but it passed unchallenged), in vain insist that Soviet Russia has existed in the face of the opposition of the rest of the world for five years (is it five?).

I don't remember where I got that point of view, whether I believed it or whether I was just a teenager provoking his elders. I do know I'd never read Marx or Lenin or any socialist literature, nor even taken an economics course at the university. *The Nation* and the *New Republic* constituted the extent of my political reading. As for my family's reaction, they were more concerned with my platonic affair with Marjorie, whom Aunt Blanche called my "summer complaint."

The Christmas after the summer I met Marjorie, a Wellesley student, she invited me to her debutante party in Cincinnati. Before going, father asked me to lunch with him downtown. This was a special and rare occurrence. It was clear to me that I was to receive some paternal advice about my behavior toward this girl, perhaps at my mother's instigation. We had a very pleasant lunch but father failed to raise whatever was on his mind. (Perhaps he was inhibited about sexual matters. Marion, much bolder than I in her approach to such things, once told me that she'd learned from mother that father was a virgin in his early thirties when they married.) In any case he never did discuss sex with me, then or subsequently, although once he handed a magazine article to read—again without discussion—on the dangers of masturbation.

* * *

My own school days were more notable for what took place outside the classroom than inside. I initially had some idea of becoming a chemist, perhaps because I wanted to do something practical and, as a child, I loved to tinker. But as an upperclassman at the university, encouraged by my amateur career in theater, I became an English literature major. One of my closest classmates was Bessie Zaban; together we took a class from a young instructor named Howard Mumford Jones. Howard also knew Marion, who preceded me at the university as a literature student, but I think it was Bessie who introduced him to the Jewish community of Hyde Park. In his memoirs, Howard, who became one of the leading men of American letters and professor of English literature at Harvard, recalled: "The life of this community was a revelation of what civilized behavior could demand and be. . . . I particularly remember the warm and affectionate welcomes I used to receive in the Abt family's home. . . . Marion and John were later under attack in the gloomy years dominated by Senator McCarthy." After graduation, Bessie married Howard and the two moved to Vermont, where they lived in a shed that they fixed up on Marion's newly acquired property in Randolph.

Marion had also married during my college days after a series of romances. During World War I, Aunt Blanche, who lived in Hamilton, Ontario, invited Marion for a visit. Marion fell absolutely and deeply in love with an enlistee in the Royal Canadian Army, whom I knew only as "Soldier Cohen." When her lover was later killed in France, Marion was completely distraught. Her unfinished autobiographical novel began with the words "I am nineteen, and my life is over." Fortunately, of course, Marion's life, and love life, continued. Another of her beaux was a radical, Frederick Kuhn, who later became a well-known foreign correspondent in the Soviet Union for the Hearst papers. Once, when I was fourteen or so, father bet Frederick a carton of Camels that within six weeks—this was in January 1918, two months after the Bolsheviks seized power in Russia—a man would ride into Petrograd on horseback and triumphantly put an end to the revolution. Father was not a gambler and rarely made bets, but at the time, this one seemed to be a sure thing.

Marion married Artie Bachrach, who was fifteen years her senior, or twenty years older than me. Nearly bald before he was forty, with muscular shoulders from swimming, Artie had four brothers, who all bore a striking resemblance in looks, speech, and mannerisms. Like Artie, all his brothers were lawyers but one, and he was a swimming instructor. Actually, the entire Bachrach family resembled one another, as if they were a unique species; nearly half a century after meeting Artie, I visited an osteopath named Bachrach in New York for a recurrent back problem and knew at a glance he must be related to my brother-in-law and, sure enough, he was a distant cousin. Artie was a wonderful storyteller, a jokester, again like all the Bachrach brothers, and spoke like them with a peculiar rhythm that resembled an Irish lilt. He would regale me with hilarious tales of his criminal clientele, among them Yellow Kid Weill, Chicago's cleverest confidence man. Artie was absorbed in philosophy, particularly that of Henri Bergson, who argued against both extreme materialism and extreme idealism, holding that it is consciousness, the "elan vital," that makes human beings unique. He could wax eloquently on this for an entire evening, chain-smoking cigars, lighting one from the last, blowing smoke rings of fat, perfect circles that traveled with considerable speed toward a selected target before disintegrating. "You have to make a face like a tired fish," he instructed me, "and eject the smoke with your tongue." He was an excellent lawyer, very careful, very thoughtful, never given to less than meticulous research, and was to play a most important role in my own formation as an attorney.

In 1923, my father developed a sudden gall bladder attack. His brother Isaac, the pediatrician—"Uncle Doc" to me—was also our family doctor. An otherwise superb physician, he had a terrible aversion to surgery and delayed such a course until he deemed it absolutely the last resort. So father remained at home in bed for several weeks, with Marion and I reciting the Bab Ballads with him between bouts of pain. When Uncle Doc finally ordered him to the hospital, his weakened state made it too late for surgery, and he died the morning after the operation at the age of fifty-six. Mother was only forty-eight, and father's death was a devastating blow to her although she put on a brave front and, to all outward appearances, went about her life as usual. But her love affair with father endured until her own death some forty years later.

* * *

One Sunday afternoon in June 1924, I returned from a weekend at the Indiana Dunes, a beautiful recreation area at the southernmost end of Lake Michigan. At home, I was informed by my somewhat agitated mother that the police had found the naked and battered body of fourteen-year-old Bobby Franks in a remote wooded area on the Far South Side. I was not acquainted with Bobby or his parents but knew them to be a well-to-do Jewish family who lived in a house on Ellis Avenue, just across the street from the former stable we had converted into the Coach-House Theater. Bobby had been missing for several days, and his parents had received ransom notes from the purported kidnappers.

Mother told me that the police had discovered a pair of eyeglasses not far from the body, which an optician had identified as belonging to Nathan "Babe" Leopold, son of a wealthy box manufacturer, a neighbor of the Franks and a friend and classmate of mine. I admired Babe, a brilliant student specializing in philology and an ardent ornithologist. We lunched together frequently to discuss life philosophy, girls, and other matters of mutual interest. I assured mother that the discovery of the glasses could hardly connect Babe with the crime since he frequented the area for bird-watching and had undoubtedly dropped them from his pocket on one of these expeditions. However, the intensive investigation that followed soon unearthed unassailable evidence of the guilt of Babe and Richard Loeb, son of the vice-president of Sears, Roebuck, and Company, who resided with his parents in a magnificent home, also on Ellis Avenue.

Dicky Loeb had been a classmate and friend during my first year at University High. He used to pick me up at our apartment and drive me to school in the family Ohio Electric. (Those were the days of ~ 1915 electric automobiles, driven for the most part by ladies of advanced years for whom gasoline motors were thought too difficult and too fast for their capabilities.) At the end of that school year, the Loebs invited me to spend the summer vacation at their palatial "gentlemen's farm" on a private lake near Charlevoix, Michigan. This was

my first time away from home and family. Despite the elegant sur-
roundings and sumptuous food—I still remember the huge farm-
grown strawberries served with fresh clotted cream—I became
frightfully homesick. After the first week, I wrote a forlorn letter to
my parents begging to be allowed to come home. The Loebs, worried by my complete loss of appetite and melancholy demeanor,
agreed, and home I came. I've always wondered about the cause of
my distress. Dicky was a spoiled, conceited, and overbearing young-
ster. As I later learned, he was also a homosexual, although his sexual preferences were not manifested at the time. Perhaps it was his
domineering comportment that contributed to my reaction. I didn't
see too much of Dicky after that summer. Actually, I was more impressed with Babe Leopold, whom I considered the far superior intellectually of the two boys.

Soon after Bobby Franks's murder, Leopold and Loeb were arrested and, under interrogation, confessed to the crime they said they
had committed for "the sake of a thrill." Because Babe and Dicky
were scions of two of Chicago's wealthiest and most prestigious families, because there appeared to be no rational motive for their behavior, and because all of the principal actors were Jewish, the case
became the focus of national attention. In Chicago, it created a furor,
especially in the Jewish community. The press called it "the crime of
the century," and the trial was billed as "the trial of the century."

The families of the defendants retained Ben and Walter Bachrach,
two of Artie's brothers, to defend their sons. Ben was an experienced
trial lawyer, and Walter, a senior partner in a highly respected firm,
was, like Artie, deeply immersed in psychoanalytic theory. They, in
turn, persuaded Clarence Darrow, whom I knew only by reputation,
to join the defense team.

The lawyers had little choice but to plead their clients guilty—they
obviously were not legally insane—and did so. But they also moved
for and won a hearing in motivation of guilt, a device by which they
hoped to avoid the death sentence. The trial (more properly, the
hearing) opened that July in Chicago's Criminal Courts Building on
the Near North Side. Standing like a fortress, its massive graystone
blackened by accumulated soot and grime, the setting was just right
for this "trial of the century."

The defense put a number of leading psychiatrists on the witness
stand who testified to what they identified as the personality disor-
ders of the defendants. I was called along with a number of other lay
witnesses. I testified principally to a conversation with Babe while sitting in his car after lunch one day before driving back to school. To

my complete astonishment, he told me that he regarded Dicky as a superman whom he would follow anywhere and obey whatever he asked unless and until he made a mistake. If that occurred, Babe concluded, he would then know that Dicky was indeed not a superman and would have nothing further to do with him.

Meyer Levin, another university classmate, later wrote a reasonably accurate novel about the crime and trial, *Compulsion,* which became a Broadway play and Hollywood film. "Judd Steiner" and "Artie Strauss" are Leopold and Loeb in the book. Describing my testimony, Levin wrote, "Campus intellectuals took the stand to testify about Judd's reputation for having exaggerated ideas. Jerry Fuld, an owlish Phi Beta Kappa who oddly enough was later to become a notorious Communist writer, testified that Judd believed that 'the end justifies the means' and that gratification of personal desires was the end to which each man should aspire."

I somehow missed Darrow's summation at the conclusion of the hearing. I read it only many years later and found that he said little about the details of the crime or the expert psychiatric evidence but made an eloquent and impassioned plea against capital punishment. Swayed less by Darrow's eloquence than by the wealth and prominence of the defendants' families, the judge sentenced each defendant to ninety-nine years in prison for kidnapping and a consecutive life sentence for murder, hoping thereby to preclude the possibility of parole.

For Dicky, this was a short-lived sentence: he was killed in prison in a lover's quarrel not long after. (As an afterward to this story, forty years later, I received a letter from Elmer Gertz, a Chicago attorney whom Leopold had retained to get him paroled. Gertz urged me to write the governor and parole board on Babe's behalf. I replied that given my position then as general counsel for the Communist party, a recommendation from me might be counterproductive. He heartily agreed. Leopold was later paroled, went to Puerto Rico to live, married, and died there in his seventies.)

The Leopold and Loeb case was often cited as symptomatic of the aimlessness of the "Lost Generation," as we were known in the twenties. I can't say I was "lost," at least in the way Gertrude Stein meant, but I was trying to find myself. In those days of cynicism and disillusionment that followed World War I, at least for those of us who were financially comfortable, we took a kind of melancholy delight in thinking of ourselves in the way Hemingway viewed his characters. Mencken was a personal hero and, with Mencken, I believed that politics was a dirty kind of business best left alone. Part of this was undoubtedly a pose on my part but, also like Mencken, I was neither sure that the human race could be saved nor was worth saving. Yet I was concerned with fulfilling myself, with finding a way to function usefully.

I thought for a while that the only useful profession was in medicine, because doctors could alleviate human pain and suffering, which was about all one could expect in this vale of tears. But the example of Uncle Isaac, who was so preoccupied with his profession that he never had time beyond it, steered me away from medicine. I can't say I was interested in the law or satisfied that a lawyer could perform a useful social function, but I believed that a man ought to learn a skill, socially useful or not. At least he could realize himself through the perfection of his craftsmanship.

So I applied to law school while completing my literature studies as a senior. I developed a friendship with one of my professors, Robert Morris Lovett, who later induced me to join the Chicago Civil Liberties Union, which he headed. But I was probably more attracted to another teacher, Phillip Schyler Alden, a charming giant of a man in his late fifties, who would chain-smoke through lectures on the classics of German literature—Heine, Goethe, and such—sometimes shaking from alcoholic withdrawal, sometimes passing out from drink, successfully pursuing all of the prettiest girls in class. Marion, among the prettiest girls in *her* class, had earlier studied with him. Unlike Marion, I had had no romances of any consequence, only casual dating. Mother's parents had come to live with us after father died, and I remember Grandmother Shire cautioning mother in German, "John will fall in some filth yet."

Chicago was a top-rated law school. But, like all others in those days, it used exclusively the casebook method of teaching. Homework consisted of reading and digesting the assigned opinions in cases relevant to the subject under study, and class work in reciting and discussing these opinions. No effort was made to relate the law to current economic, social, and political problems. There was no moot court, no research project, and no other exercises in the practical work of lawyering. The student body was nearly 100 percent white males, a fact that went unnoticed by me at the time. Almost without exception, they were absorbed in grubbing for high grades in the hope of landing jobs with leading law firms.

Though mercifully brief, law school was one of the dullest periods of my life. Attending both regular classes and summer school, I was able to finish in two years and a quarter, which prevented me from making law review (reserved for third-year students). I looked elsewhere for interest and stimulation. During both of my years at law school, I took a job in the English department teaching the first-quarter freshman course called Rhetoric and English Composition. I wasn't much of a teacher. Like many novices, I was more concerned with impressing the students with my intelligence than in trying to impress some intelligence into their heads. Nevertheless, the experience helped enliven my days.

Around this same time, actually on my birthday, May 1, 1924, Marion gave birth to what was to be her only child. She and Artie named him for me, and Johnny and I became very close in his infant and toddler years.

Another diversion was provided by my friend Agnes Jaques. She was the daughter of Russian immigrants, herself fluent in Russian and interested in Russian culture, particularly in the romantic years following the October revolution. Sergei Eisenstein, the great Soviet filmmaker, spent some days in Chicago en route to Hollywood and then Mexico. Agnes served as his interpreter. She asked me to join her in showing the sights of the big city to the exuberant, lively Eisenstein. The episode was most enjoyable but had no political overtones, despite Eisenstein's stature as a major Soviet cultural figure. For me it simply provided a good time.

Howard Mumford Jones had gotten a teaching job at the University of Texas the year before but since it had abolished the English department, Howard was temporarily unemployed and came to the University of Chicago for the summer with a Texan named Eyler Simpson, with whom I became fast friends. When the University of North Carolina invited Howard to join its English faculty at Chapel Hill, Eyler and I agreed to join him on his journey. We hitched rides all the way to Norfolk, Virginia, before leaving Howard to make his own way to Chapel Hill, while Eyler and I continued up to New York. Eyler led the way of course—I hadn't completely shed my bashful ways—through taverns in Greenwich Village and theaters in midtown. On a lark of literary pretentiousness, we even went out to Coney Island one day to look up Sinclair Lewis, who of course knew nothing about us but who was gracious enough to spend the day with us talking about books.

I received my law degree cum laude in September 1925. The next state examination for entrance to the bar was not held until the following spring. Mother decided that I should fill the gap with a six-month trip to Europe that she agreed to finance. So I made the grand tour: England (mainly London), Paris, southern Germany, Vienna, Venice, Florence, Rome, and Naples. I wrote mother long letters each week, which she lovingly typed and held for me after showing them to family and friends. I kept those letters for years, taking them with me to Washington and then to New York, never looking at them but thinking that they might prove useful some day. I finally read them a few years ago when I began to entertain notions of writing these memoirs. What a shameful cache they turned out to be. They were written in 1926 and 1927, the year of the British general strike, at the time of Mussolini's ascension to power in Italy, and when the voices of the Nazis were being raised in the *rathskellers* of Germany. But there was not a word or a reflection of any of this in that batch of letters. Nothing but chitchat about museums and cathedrals and vacuous (if sometimes amusing) comments about people encountered along the way and "peculiar" foreign customs. I promptly dumped the whole pile into the garbage.

* * *

Home from my travels, I passed the bar exam, was admitted to practice in the spring of 1927, and started my career as a lawyer with the firm of Levinson, Becker, Schwartz, and Frank at the princely salary of twenty-five dollars a week, the regular starting rate at that time. This was the firm that had hired Artie shortly after his marriage as its principal trial lawyer at a salary of fifteen thousand dollars a year, considered a handsome price in those days.

The firm was a wealthy one, specializing in railroad and other large corporate reorganizations. The senior partner, Salmon O. Levinson, was a bear of a man, gruff, contentious, and short-tempered. Curiously, for a man with his temperament, he was preoccupied with a scheme, which he invented and tirelessly promoted, to outlaw war. This was to be accomplished by a treaty among the major nations in which they solemnly renounced the use of armed force as an instrument of national policy. Much to the surprise of his colleagues and friends, his zeal paid off with the signing of the Kellog-Briand Pact (named for the then U.S. secretary of state and the French foreign minister), a triumph for the author of its words, which proved however to be a futile exercise in rhetoric.

Another of the firm's partners, Jerome Frank, was a very different person and one who was to have an important influence on my future. Jerome was then in his midforties, a tall, dark-haired, good-looking man. He had a keen mind and wide-ranging interests and was an enthusiastic and animated conversationalist on almost any subject—the latest novel or drama, the comparative merits of competing schools of psychology, or recent advances in astrophysics. He had a equal appetite for legal research, which he often indulged in, despite his position in the firm, by joining us "cubs" in the library. I found it intellectually exciting to work with him, piling volume upon volume of law reports, following up clues to the answer we were seeking, debating the significance of a decision, until the answer to our question became clear or it became clear that there was no answer in the law books.

Jerome was a leading member of the Chicago Bar, friend and intimate of people like Carl Sandburg, John Gunther, Clarence Darrow, and Sherwood Anderson (who preceded me at the University by a year). Yet with all this, Jerry had great feelings of insecurity. He would worry legal questions to death. For no apparent reason, he would write long memoranda for the files defending his decisions, covering himself for each step he took in any difficult case or set of negotiations. It was this aspect of his personality that made Jerry, who eventually went on to become chairman of the Securities and Exchange Commission and a judge on the U.S. Court of Appeals, the timid liberal he became.

My first court appearance was made on behalf of my first client, an Italian hat manufacturer whom I had met aboard ship en route from Naples to New York. He had an unpaid bill from a New York retailer and retained me to defend him. I filed suit and appeared in court, with Artie at my side, to argue a motion to dismiss the case. I had barely started my argument when Artie cautioned me in a stage whisper, "Stop mumbling and speak up so the judge can hear you." His honor looked down at us and sternly rebuked Artie. "I can hear him perfectly," he said. I lost the case but won a great moral victory.

My early years in law were hardly inspiring. I've often said that the first three years of my practice were devoted to floating bond issues and, once the depression hit, the second three years to foreclosing the bond issues I'd floated. In the Levinson, Becker firm, Artie was in charge of trying big arbitration cases. But once, mysteriously and without warning, he had a trauma of some kind, an episode of blockage, in the middle of a case. And from that point on, he could never again walk into a courtroom. He developed a debilitating speech defect that prevented him from effectively arguing a case, although he continued to practice law as a negotiator and in preparing briefs and pleadings. For the rest of his life, Artie underwent psychoanalysis but without result, at least insofar as this particular problem was concerned. I mentioned that he was a cigar smoker. Marion used to tell me that he'd wake up in the middle of the night, wake her up, light a cigar, and dictate his dream while he still remembered it.

Sometime after the stock market crash of 1929 and the onset of the depression, the firm fired Artie, both because business had fallen off and because he was no longer able to litigate. I felt a moral obligation to quit and said so to Becker, a senior partner. Jerome Frank had left Chicago earlier to practice law in New York so Levinson, Becker held no remaining attraction for me. Artie and I started our own firm, Bachrach and Abt, but after a year, he went to Johns Hopkins for psychiatric treatment, while Marion and Johnny B. moved to their house in Randolph Center, Vermont, to live. I hired on to another business law firm that worked primarily in real estate, handling foreclosures. If anything, this was even more torpid and numbing than law school and I knew this was not the life for me. But I didn't yet know what *was*.

Many years later, Marion read through her correspondence of those years from her village in Vermont to mother and found not a single mention of the economic disaster that was engulfing the country. In Chicago, men and women rooted in garbage dumps for food, while the police violently attacked the unemployed who demonstrated for relief. Mother meanwhile wrote about the grief that attended our own comfortable community with fortunes being wiped out and families compelled to accommodate destitute in-laws, with even an occasional suicide to provide insurance money for surviving relatives.

Marion quotes from a letter I wrote to her:

All the old familiar signs and portents of another Chicago "season" are with us again. Last night was a party by the —— sisters. Someone produced liquor and toward the end of the evening I got heavily plastered.

The law as practiced by my firm keeps me busy and tense but not interested. I can't think of a thing to tell you that would make you regret your decision to winter in Vermont.

Later I wrote:

Life in Chicago continues dullish, particularly alongside your glowing accounts of activities at the Center. I'm beginning to get acclimated to the rhythm and routine of a law factory, but it never, I fear, will altogether fit my notion of the Good Life. I'm not at all sure that I know what the Good Life is—you always seemed to be clearer on that subject than I—but this doesn't seem to be it. However, finding out what it isn't is part of the process of discovering what it is, and from that point of view my education progresses.

The compulsive drinking and preoccupation with sex prevailing at the time were the surface symptoms of a deeper malaise. The mood was one of nihilism: in the midst of material plenty we suffered from a poverty of spirit. This was the sense of Mencken, of Fitzgerald. And while Marion and I embraced them for a period, they were irreconcilable with the profoundly humanist values imparted to us by mother and father, who had always lived in a state of grace. Boredom was a total stranger to the spirit of our childhood household—repose. Each day had provided nourishment in the form of good food, good talk, good books, good music; and these were replenished by the love my parents bore each other and the pleasure they took from giving of themselves to us. For the Judeo-Christian concept of original sin, Marion said they had instinctively substituted their own concept of original innocence: their belief in the perfectibility of humankind.

* * *

The Great Depression hadn't affected me in any financial or economic way. But it, combined with the developing ennui from the meaninglessness of my work, began to open my mind to political and social concerns. As a teenager I had been unmoved by World War I, although we had some family friends who were conscientious objectors. I was untouched by—actually ignorant of—Eugene V. Debs, the great Socialist railroad workers' organizer, who from prison, for his antiwar activities, received over a million votes for president. Of course I knew of the Russian Revolution that grew out of the wartime crisis, but I was blissfully unaware of the revolution's reverberations in our country: the formation of the Communist party from the left of the Socialist party with leaders like John Reed and "Big Bill" Haywood and the language federations of Ukrainians, Slavs, Finns, and others, class-conscious workers from eastern Europe who brought with them a socialist tradition and experience. My own family, as I've said, arrived on these shores some three-quarters of a century earlier. This, and the fact that they were well-to-do manufacturers, guaranteed that we, and I personally, would feel no effects of the terror that gripped more recent immigrant communities in the wake of the "Palmer Raids," the roundups and deportations of thousands of alleged radicals under the command of the U.S. attorney general.

Now, largely, I suppose, out of boredom with my job, I joined the Chicago Civil Liberties Union. The CCLU was then undergoing an internal debate as to whether it should take on the defense of Communists. Many in the leadership vigorously opposed representing Communists for most of the reasons that still prevail. However, the

CCLU's chair, my old literature professor Robert Morris Lovett, then also an editor of the *New Republic,* took the opposite position, arguing that the Constitution protects everybody or it protects no one. I strenuously agreed with him, although perhaps as much out of personal admiration for Lovett as out of principle.

I had not previously been active on a civil liberties issue. But I had been reading newspaper accounts of the brutality of the Chicago police. Its "Red Squad" under the leadership of Make Mills, a Russian-born former socialist who emigrated after the 1905 revolution, had been ruthlessly assaulting and dispersing demonstrations of the unemployed for jobs and relief. I knew also, of course, of the Sacco-Vanzetti case, followed its progress in the pages of *The Nation* and the *New Republic,* and was outraged by their execution in 1927. But I'd never taken part in the demonstrations for their freedom, and, unlike the experience of some of my contemporaries, the case played no part in arousing my political consciousness.

In 1931, the CCLU designated me as its legal observer at a demonstration called by the Communist party. The Japanese army had just invaded Manchuria in northern China, overthrown the Kuomintang government there, and set up a puppet state which it called Manchukuo. The demonstration to protest the invasion was to be held in front of the offices of the Japanese consulate, in the Chicago *Tribune* tower. The *Tribune* Building is located on the north side of the bridge over the Chicago River on Michigan Avenue, and the marchers were scheduled to come from the south, cross the bridge, and set up a picket line in front of the building. I vividly recall the cordons of police—many mounted on horseback, the Red Squad on foot—lined up on the *Tribune* side of the bridge to prevent the marchers from crossing. As the demonstrators began to flow onto the bridge, the police advanced on them, at first slowly, then more quickly, the horses going faster and faster, driving the marchers back over the bridge and down what is now Wacker Drive, wielding their clubs unmercifully. I found that my eyes were wet with tears and I became literally sickened by the experience.

I don't recollect my report of the episode to the committee, but I don't believe that I agitated for a public condemnation of the police. The experience remained an intensely personal one that I wasn't yet ready to translate into action. I remember writing to Closson Gilbert, one of Marion's radical Vermont friends, describing the experience and trying to say how it affected me. Being a good civil libertarian, I said at the end of the letter, "I don't know whether I would feel this way or how I would feel if the clubs were in the hands of the workers and those fleeing were the capitalists." Closson's wife told me later that on receiving my letter, he told her, "John's going to be all right."

At about that time, I attended my first Communist party rally at the Chicago Coliseum. The principal speaker was John Williamson, who later became organizational secretary of the Party and was deported to his native Scotland during the McCarthy purges. I have no memory of that meeting, which was probably an election rally to support the Party's presidential candidate, William Z. Foster. It is likely that little said made sense to me since I remained illiterate in Marxist literature and Communist party approach. In 1928, I cast my first vote for Al Smith, the Democratic candidate for president, breaking with my family's Republican tradition, to protest the anti-Catholic campaign being waged against Smith. But in 1932—as a protest against the ruling currents that seemed to offer no solutions to the crisis that gripped the country (in his campaign, Roosevelt offered little more than balancing the budget)—I cast my ballot for William Z. Foster, the Communist presidential aspirant. I still had yet to read the Communist party platform.

The only Communist I knew personally was Closson Gilbert in Vermont. Marion first met Closson and his Iowa-born wife Millie in the summer of 1927. She'd taken Johnny to summer camp and liked Vermont so much she and Artie looked around for a cottage of their own and found just what they wanted in Randolph Center next to the Gilbert farm. Closson was frail, slight, with a high-bridged Roman nose and keen blue eyes; wisps of graying hair blew in the wind as he plowed the fields his father and his father's father had plowed before him. He was too rugged an individualist to be categorized. Marion recalled that though he "trained for the ministry, he was no church-goer; in many ways a Vermont super-patriot, he took delight in satirizing the weaknesses of Vermont folk. He talked like an atheist and lived like a Christian; he was a hard-headed Yankee who dreamed the dreams of the utopian socialists."

Early in the century, Closson and Millie worked in Chicago at Hull-House, though my family didn't know them. But he wanted to return to the land, his ancestral farm, where he grew potatoes for a cash crop. Millie, a lovely woman and as socially committed as Closson, was perhaps not as organizationally minded. At elections, Closson would tell her, "Millie, somebody in this family is cheating, because there was only one vote for the Communists in Randolph Center."

Marion, as apolitical as I when she first went to Vermont in 1927, was at least aware of the case of Nicola Sacco and Bartholomeo Vanzetti. Sitting that fateful summer in the Gilberts' kitchen, she listened with wonder to the stories of the winters Closson and Millie had spent in Boston, scrupulously managing the potato money in order to give something of their small substance to the cause. It was there on that farm, whose checkered fields bordered by dark sugar woods seemed so remote from struggle, that Marion first vaguely sensed how the self can grow through social commitment. Marion returned to Chicago at the end of July and shortly after, Millie wrote to describe in poignant detail the lonely vigil she and Closson kept in the sugar woods on the night of August 22, when the good shoemaker and the honest fish-peddler were put to death.

The next summer and for several summers after, Sacco's beautiful young son Dante came to Randolph Center to spend his vacations with the Gilberts. Marion and Johnny were living there while Artie was at Johns Hopkins, and I also visited summers. Closson and Millie gave Dante the love they would have given a son. Marion recalled that "Closson battled tirelessly for the boy's mind, as some Calvinist forebear might have wrestled with the devil for his soul. In Closson's eyes, Dante was the heir to a great mission—the vindication of the dead martyrs; the completion of their work had been thrust on his young shoulders." But Dante had had enough of suffering and struggle. He wanted to do well in school, play good baseball, get a job, make life easier for his mother and sister. He loved Closson dearly and hated to disappoint him. But Dante's mind was his own and he yielded not an inch. So the battle went on and Marion listened. "And who knows," wrote Marion, "maybe Closson did 'convert' me a little while he worked so hard to win Dante." In turn, I too was undoubtedly affected.

* * *

After Roosevelt was elected, it became clear that the new administration was going to go well beyond his campaign platitudes and significantly change the direction of the country. Secretary of Agriculture Henry Wallace set up the Agricultural Adjustment Administration, and Jerome Frank was appointed solicitor of the AAA. Jerome in turn brought in Artie Bachrach with the title of legal advisor for litigation. This was by no means an act of charity on Jerome's part; while Artie could no longer argue in court, his other capacities, which Jerome well knew were considerable, were in no way diminished. With Jerome, Marion, and Artie in Washington and with the excitement of FDR's first one hundred days, I longed for the opportunity to join the New Deal. But nobody offered me a job.

Then—for reasons still unknown to me—I received a telegram from Harold Ickes, the Chicagoan who was named secretary of the interior and administrator of the Public Works Administration, offering a job in the PWA. I had by then completely exhausted the possibilities in my present job and sent a letter to the senior partners announcing my resignation. Ed Ferguson, a member of the firm and a former Communist who had served time in prison in one of the anticommunist purges following World War I, came to try to persuade me to stay. But my mind and heart were already in Washington, and a few weeks later my body was as well.

The days that followed were occupied with unloading my batch of foreclosures onto the junior partner who was taking them over, parting from my current girlfriend, and dreaming of life and work in Washington. My forthcoming departure must have been a hard blow to mother. Her parents had come to live with us shortly after father's death, and Grandpa Shire had died soon after. So I would be leaving her alone with her eighty-year-old mother. But she knew of my eagerness to go and said not a word to discourage me or of pity for herself. She had often told Marion and me that, in her view, children owe nothing to their parents but that it was the latter who owe the indebtedness. Now she was practicing this principle, and I am ashamed to say that, in my self-absorption, I gave no thought to what she must have been feeling.

The great day finally came. I lunched with mother at the restaurant in the LaSalle Street Station, kissed her a loving good-bye, waved to her from the gate, and boarded the Capitol Limited. On arriving in the nation's capital, however, before I could even report to the Public Works Administration, Jerry Frank and Artie Bachrach brought me in to work as chief of the litigation section in the AAA. This was October 1933.

2

In the New Deal Maelstrom

My first impressions of Washington were kaleidoscopic. In her uncompleted memoir, Marion wrote, "The memories that surface first are sensory rather than political: the city itself was sheer enchantment." Big changes had taken place in the nation's capital since Henry Adams returned there to learn what he could from the administration of President Ulysses S. Grant. The village of the nineteenth century had become a modern metropolis of broad avenues thronged with government workers in speeding automobiles. Yet, in 1933 as in 1868, the Potomac and its tributaries "squandered beauty." Just as they appeared to Henry Adams, the wooded banks and rolling valley of Rock Creek seemed still "as wild as the Rocky Mountains." History was palpable in Washington and its environs. At Mount Vernon and other colonial estates, the cabins that once housed slaves still stood as museum pieces. Chattel slavery had of course long since been abolished, but in the Washington suburbs, signs designating "white" and "colored" made clear that old times here were not forgotten.

A Chicago nose, educated to expect a shift in the wind to bring the stench of the stockyards, sniffed with pleasure a wind that smelled of saltwater fish. Maryland crabs, clams, and oysters bought by the peck from boats tied to wharves at the foot of Seventh Street brought unanticipated sensual delights to a palate used to more conventional midwestern fare.

But these sights and sounds and smells were the least of what was new and exciting. The advent of the New Deal fissured the normal stratification of Washington society. "Except for Cabinet and diplomatic circles," Marion remembered, "life had the fluidity of a maelstrom. Hundreds of newcomers surged and swirled around the new emergency agencies. Any nobody could meet any somebody—and frequently did. The shy young man, brought to dinner by someone whose name you didn't catch, turned up in next week's headlines as one of Professor Felix Frankfurter's 'hot dogs,' assigned to help Harry Hopkins spend a half-billion dollars."

The town was full to the last rooming house with young men—I had the advantage of a hospitable sister who took me in until I found a place of my own—some not yet married, others with young wives waiting at home in other cities "to see if this is really going to last a while." Artie and I, with unlimited confidence in the elasticity of the Bachrach table, brought our colleagues home with us to dinner. Intoxicating talk took the place of bathtub gin and was more heady. One topic dominated conversation: how to put 12 or 15 or 17 million people back to work, fast. Writing of those early days in her memoir, *The Roosevelt I Knew,* Labor Secretary Frances Perkins recalled that when she took office there were two thousand different plans for "putting people back to work" on her desk and another two thousand on the president's. Several hundred of these were debated around our table and other tables throughout Washington.

Everybody I met claimed to be a New Dealer, but what this meant nobody quite knew. Such an assortment of people, from every walk of life and every region of the country, thrown together like a crowd watching the rescue of inhabitants of a burning tenement, shared a common purpose for the moment but, uncertain how to achieve it, often worked at cross purposes. Some were impractical idealists, others showed an astonishing flair for getting things done. Some of my young colleagues in the legal profession had sought in vain for promising careers in private practice; others of us had gladly given up positions in corporate law for the lower pay and uncertain future of government service. Sometimes we lawyers talked like economists, while professors of economics sought us out to learn how to change the laws to remedy an economy in poor health.

Overall, the mood was one of urgency combined with unbounded enthusiasm and even optimism. Roosevelt "brain truster" Rexford Guy Tugwell had written in college, "I shall roll up my sleeves, and make America over!" Anti–New Dealers poked fun at this Whitmanesque sentiment, but many of us, in those humid Washington evenings, sat with our sleeves rolled up in earnest. The desire to participate in so great an undertaking as making America over was the magnet that drew most of my generation to Washington. Of course the many frailties of human nature made themselves known—per-

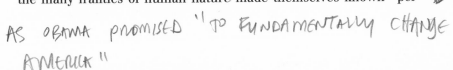

AS OBAMA PROMISED "TO FUNDAMENTALLY CHANGE AMERICA"

sonal ambition, rivalries, bootlicking. Some sought power to advance the interests of the very corporate interests that had so abused their power but were fighting to retain it. A few—remarkably, a very few—entered this government in search of self-enrichment. Nevertheless, it is quite possible that never in all its history, before or since, has Washington seen so little venality.

The peculiar nature of the nation's crisis made it so puzzling: people were hungry because there was too much food; banks were failing because those with the greatest fortunes had more capital than they could profitably invest; millions were jobless because they had produced more than they could afford to buy. The richest country in the world was choking to death on its wealth. This was simply irrational; like millions of others, we were asking, why? Washington was a vast Reflecting Pool mirroring the life of our entire country. In Washington I was to discover America at a time when the country was discovering itself.

I'd long understood that not all families in this country were as financially secure as my own, as I'd known that ours was a modest existence in comparison with the truly rich. But the Reflecting Pool shattered many of my preconceptions. I saw millions who literally had nothing more to lose. Marion remembers: "Bank savings were gone, insurance savings were gone, the 'easy payments' on installment purchases were gone—and with them went the little home, the farm, the shiny new car, the jalopy and the radio . . . the money put in a sock to see the kids through school, to take care of ma and pa in their old age. The engagement ring, grandfather's watch, the parlor set—everything of value was gone, sold, hauled away, or in hock."

There was nothing to lose but one's place in the breadline and the feeling of emptiness in your hands, so long accustomed to the feel of a machine, a plow, a tool. Time stands still when there is no time clock to punch. There was nothing left to lose but the ache in your heart when the children fell sick for want of food, and you wonder what fault of yours had made you no longer worthy of hiring. Half the industrial work force no longer had work, hadn't for months now, even years. Factory chimneys stood smokeless. Armed guards patrolled factory gates holding signs reading "No Help Wanted." A bitter joke making the rounds in Chicago told of the jobless man who recognized an employed friend drowning in the Calumet River and rushed to his place of work, asking for the job only to be told, "Sorry, we gave it to the guy who pushed him in."

Perhaps only a Dante could adequately portray the desperation to those who never experienced it: the wrecked homes; families living in alleyways; grandmas in their rockers, sitting, evicted on the side-walk; children in tears; hollow-eyed mothers staring in anguish; bro-ken, shamed fathers, living in Hoovervilles; a country in starvation— 17 million jobless, human refuse tossed on the dump like so much waste. Meanwhile orange crops were burned, pigs were slaughtered, milk dumped into rivers, a grotesque obscenity. Near the railroad tracks and the garbage dumps and the riverbanks of every city—in fact, in the very shadow of Capitol Hill in Washington—sprawled the crazy-quilt communities of tin and cardboard shacks known as Hoovervilles, in grim tribute to the former President who had prom-ised two cars in every garage and a chicken in every pot.

By the time I arrived in Washington, many of the jobless were seeking and finding friends and allies in each other: neighbors gath-ered to carry the furniture of an evicted family back into its apart-ment, defying the local sheriff; thousands in homeless shelters joined together to demand modest improvements in living conditions; the first stirring of Unemployed Councils, under Communist leadership, were already being felt. As one of Roosevelt's first acts, the Federal Emergency Relief Administration provided $500 million, giving the unemployed heart to keep struggling. FERA Administrator Harry Hopkins noted that that $500 million bought "more courage than goods."

Unemployed workers and their leaders filed into Washington to buttonhole members of Congress, testify before committees, meet with the alphabet soup of emergency agencies. New Dealers often gave them the VIP treatment, these plenipotentiaries from the hin-terland determined to obtain the New Deal it had voted for.

They came from Detroit, representing the hundreds of hunger marchers who, the year before—again under Communist leader-ship—marched on Dearborn, the Ford Motor Company's private pre-serve, demanding jobs, only to run into, a mile from the massive Riv-er Rouge plant, a column of police who first pumped tear gas shells into their ranks and then played icy streams of water from fire hoses into the shivering crowd. And after the fire hoses, they opened up with machine guns. A funeral cortege, with ten thousand marchers to mourn the four young workers killed by police gunfire, proceeded down Woodward Avenue; by the time they arrived at the cemetery, in full view of the Ford smokestacks, their numbers had grown to thirty thousand. The dead—Joe York, George Bussell, Coleman Leny, Joe DeBlasio—were lowered to their graves, their caskets draped in red, the band playing "The Internationale." In their memory, Detroiters came to Washington to lobby.

Arkansas farmers also came. One cold winter day in the tiny village of England, Arkansas, an anguished mother came to the door of a quiet, law-abiding, God-fearing farmer named Coney. "My God," she appealed, "the kids ain't et for two days—what'll I do." Coney had been wondering how to feed *his* kids. His neighbor's question gave his personal problems a new dimension. In a few hours, Coney and the distraught mother had rounded up fifty other desperate farmers, some of them white, others Black, bound together for the first time by hunger. They walked into town to call on the mayor and the chief of police. Receiving no help, they walked to the general store, their numbers swelling to three hundred. His store surrounded by hungry farmers, the storekeeper phoned the Red Cross in St. Louis to authorize a handout, the first relief of any kind to reach the starving tenant farmers of Arkansas. This first concerted action was frightening enough to move Arkansas's two senators to demand farm relief from Congress.

Battle lines were constantly shifting on top, while larger struggles loomed in the streets and at the shop gates where the victims of the crisis sought to intervene to determine their own destiny. From the silk mills in Paterson, New Jersey, to the turpentine camps in rural Georgia to the San Francisco waterfront, enormous battles for the future of the New Deal were shaping up. When I arrived in Washington, I was virtually a political illiterate; I'd heard and been moved by FDR's inaugural address with its concern for human need and promise of bold action. Stimulated by the open exchange of new ideas and fired by the spirit of high purpose that charged the atmosphere in Washington, I committed myself to the New Deal. It wasn't long, perhaps a year, before the worm of doubt began gnawing at my new faith; soon the careless rapture was supplanted by disillusion.

* * *

The Great Depression ravaged agriculture, if anything, harder than industry. The boom of the twenties had passed the farmer by, while industrial prices rose. Most farmers were squeezed between having to pay higher prices for equipment while selling their crops for less. With the collapse of the economy and the resulting drop in industrial production, farm prices hit bottom. While not as widely known as the banking crisis, the farm crisis was at least as devastating. Farmers, like their industrial brethren, were on the move—organizing to prevent foreclosures, publicly dumping milk, pressuring local judges and county sheriffs to back off.

The New Deal's answer to the farm crisis was to raise prices. Just as nationalization was rejected as a solution to the banking crisis, more profound remedies to rural social and economic injustices were eschewed by the administration. Export markets could not absorb U.S. surpluses, so the only way the authorities saw to raise prices was to cut production, paying cash benefits to farmers who reduced their output. In a 1932 campaign speech in Kansas, FDR outlined such a program. After his election and the appointment of Henry A. Wallace as secretary of agriculture, they codified this program in the Agricultural Adjustment Act of 1933. The goal was "parity" between farm prices and manufactured goods.

Wallace, a farm editor from Iowa, was new to politics. Modest, decent, combining knowledge of agriculture and scientific training with good intentions, he was a novice to the pressures of Congress and the conflicting interests at work in the administration. These pressures and conflicts would make themselves quickly felt. The Agricultural Adjustment Administration (AAA) was created by the legislation as the agency to implement the farm program. And, while the AAA made good the promise to raise farm income, how it was distributed left much to be desired. In fact it worsened the distress of the southern sharecroppers who were not parties to AAA contracts between the Department of Agriculture and the landlords, which allowed the latter to drive the sharecroppers and wage hands from the land.

The old-line farm leaders, the so-called four-hundred-acre farmers, the landed ruling class as it were, had traditionally dominated the Department of Agriculture. They were represented by the Farm Bureau Federation and were backed by the food processors—meatpackers, canners, milk distributors. George Peek, a farm businessman, was appointed the first head of the AAA to protect these interests. Going unrepresented were the 3 million sharecroppers, 13 million tenant farmers, and 8 million farm workers who had an average family annual income of six hundred dollars.

FDR signed the Agricultural Adjustment Act into law on May 12, 1933, after several weeks of congressional debate. The delay left Henry Wallace in a dilemma. Sows had already farrowed and cotton had been planted. Huge surpluses abounded. In this country where millions were going hungry, the concern in Washington was that another bumper year would undermine prices still further, leaving the AAA with an impossible task. Wallace ordered the destruction of 6 million pigs and 200,000 sows and the plowing over of 10 million acres of cotton.

The National Farmers' Union and National Farmers' Holiday Association accused Wallace of ignoring the small farmer. In the South, more than seven hundred thousand farms were operated by tenants and sharecroppers. When the landlords signed acreage reduction programs, tens of thousands of these poor farmers were thrown off their land, significantly increasing the already scandalous numbers of jobless and homeless. The Southern Tenant Farmers' Union, with an important helping hand from organizers of the Socialist and Communist parties, began to organize to enter into collective bargaining agreements with the landlords. In the view of George Peek, however, "the sole aim" of the AAA was "to raise prices." As for the plight of the poor rural population, Peek responded to critics, "This is the Department of Agriculture, not the Department of Everything."

For better or worse, it fell to the lot of the AAA general counsel's office to give voice to the millions of sharecroppers, tenant farmers, and farm workers. As it developed, the internal struggles between Peek (and later Chester Davis) on the one hand and Jerome Frank and his minions on the other were taking place on an uneven playing field. We young lawyers, on arriving in Washington in those early days of the New Deal, felt that we had the levers of power in our hands, that we could really be a factor for change. Roosevelt had promised to drive the money changers from the temple, but we quickly discovered that the money changers still had a lock on the key jobs in the administration, including the AAA.

Paying farmers to destroy their crops and to murder little piggies made no sense to us. But there was no way we could fight this business of artificially creating scarcity while millions were starving. That was the law. The real fight became over who was to reap the benefits of these increased prices—whether the poor rural workers would get any equitable share or whether it would all go to the big farmers, the food processors, the plantation owners.

* * *

The AAA had several divisions, but the dominant division was the one that was responsible for commodities. This was staffed by the big producers and the big processors and was the essential force in the administration. A consumers' council division, presumably to keep its eye out for the interest of consumers, carried a great deal less weight. The legal division was organized into a number of sections to correspond to the administrative divisions of the AAA as a whole. When Jerome was asked to head up the legal division, he brought in Artie Bachrach as a special advisor to put together the litigation section.

The marketing agreements and licensing section handled fruits, vegetables, and milk and established market shares limiting the amount each producer would sell, thereby raising prices. Lee Pressman, a young bright lawyer from Brooklyn by way of Harvard Law School and Jerry Frank's New York firm, headed up this section. I had first met Lee when I was still in Chicago and he came through representing the New York firm. I quite envied Lee at the time inasmuch as New York represented a certain attractive glamour to a young midwesterner. As it developed, Lee's career and mine closely intertwined, and we became close friends for nearly twenty years.

The benefits payments section of the legal division dealt with grains and cotton, arranging payments to producers who entered agreements to cut planned acreage, taking land out of production. This section was placed under the direction of Alger Hiss, also a Harvard Law graduate, who came to the AAA after a stint as law clerk to Oliver Wendell Holmes. Alger was quite bright and charming but liked to project an aura of great distinction. Lee once said of Alger, "If he were standing at the bar with the British ambassador and you were told to give a package to the ambassador's valet, you would give it to the ambassador before you gave it to Alger."

Another section of the legal division—for briefs and opinions, defining what the law permitted—came under Francis Shea, a lawyer from Buffalo, New York. Frank, raised as a conservative Catholic and who came to regard me as his mentor in social matters such as how to make a good martini and move among sophisticated partygoers, would one day become dean of law at the University of Buffalo. Finally, the litigation section, in charge of enforcement and defending the Agricultural Adjustment Act, was headed up first by Artie Bachrach and then myself.

In this early period of the New Deal, the courts were, nearly without exception, against us. Judges were mostly Republicans, appointees of the Hoover and previous Republican administrations, and fervently anti-Roosevelt. Also the law, established by consecutive, Republican-dominated Congresses, granted quite limited powers to the federal government over the processes of production. This was a jurisdiction reserved for the states, in which the federal government couldn't interfere. And, in addition to judicial and congressional resistance to the New Deal, there were bureaucratic tugs-of-war with the Justice Department under Attorney General Homer Cummings, which wanted to handle all litigation, while we AAA lawyers were convinced we were better placed to defend our actions. Throughout was a struggle for the soul of the administration.

In the South, for example, the Southern Tenant Farmers' Union was organizing sharecroppers whose average *family* income was $262 a year and who were actually losing out under AAA agreements that withdrew from production some of the lands that they worked. But southern Democratic members of Congress, who represented the big growers and plantation owners, were essential to Roosevelt's rule. FDR had to *appear* to be sufficiently satisfying—even if he did not satisfy—the growing mass demand for jobs and food if he was to stem the demand for more radical solutions. The hunger marches and unemployed demonstrations were asking for more than he was ready to offer. So the administration created the Public Works Administration to create jobs and the Federal Emergency Relief Administration to provide welfare. The National Recovery Act (NRA), with its codes of so-called fair competition, became the centerpiece of the early New Deal program to revive industry. And the Agricultural Adjustment Act was the agricultural version of the NRA.

George Peek had little use for Frank or for the legal division and described those who were referred by Jerome's friend, Harvard law professor Felix Frankfurter, as "the Happy Hot Dogs." In addition to Pressman and Hiss, other Harvard-trained lawyers in the division included Telford Taylor, who worked under Frank Shea and went on to become chief prosecutor at the Nuremburg war crimes trials, and Nat Witt, who became one of my closest lifelong friends. In his oral history years later, Peek said, "A plague of young lawyers descended on Washington. They all claimed to be friends of somebody or other, and mostly of Jerome Frank and Felix Frankfurter. They floated airily into offices, took desks, asked for papers and found no end of things to be busy about. I never found out why they came, what they did or why they left." This was perhaps less than forthcoming of Peek, since we in the legal division were soon labeled as less than reliable by the cotton growers, milk processors, and big farmers for whom he did their bidding.

Eventually our division grew to about sixty lawyers, mainly young, urban, with heavy Ivy League representation, civil service ideals, and a confidence bordering on cockiness. There was also an inordinately large Jewish composition to the staff. Jerry Frank later recalled Frank Shea coming to him with the names of some lawyers he wanted to hire. "One day he had three names—Schachner, Muravchik and someone else I can't remember," Jerome told an interviewer. "I said, 'Goddamnit, Frank, I've got to be careful. You've got too many Jews in here now. The people will begin to say that I'm just selecting Jews.' Shea said, 'You're a damned anti-Semite.'" This coming from a Catholic to a Jew. In his book *The Age of Roosevelt* Arthur Schlesinger, Jr., writes, "Knowledge of farming was from Frank's point of view, the least of requirements. He had a lawyer's confidence that men trained in law could master anything. 'What we need,' he told Peek, 'are brilliant young men with keen legal minds and imaginations.'" Among the others that came to the legal division were Leon Keyserling from Columbia University, who became President Truman's top economic advisor; Bruno Schachner, also from Columbia University by way of Vienna, who became a U.S. attorney in New York; Abe Fortas, Thurmond Arnold, and Paul Porter from Yale, who later became partners in perhaps the most powerful law firm in Washington (Fortas of course also went on to the Supreme Court and Arnold to the U.S. Court of Appeals); and Adlai Stevenson from Illinois, who became a U.S. senator and twice the Democratic candidate for president. In addition to the lawyers, the division also hired investigators, particularly for the consumers' protection section. Chief investigator was Gardner "Pat" Jackson, a protege of Alexander Meiklejohn at Amherst College, who became a *Boston Globe* reporter before chucking journalism to run the staff of the Sacco and Vanzetti defense committee. Pressman and Nat Witt, who knew Pat from that campaign, brought him into the AAA. Another investigator was Charles Kramer, a big, tall redhead with a penchant for careful research who would become a colleague of mine through a host of labor, political, and legal projects for the next quarter century. Peek and Schesinger were correct: we knew next to nothing about farming. (Lee Pressman once asked at a meeting of macaroni producers, "I want to know what this code will do for macaroni growers.") My childhood summers were the extent of my own knowledge of farms. But, in the end, Jerome Frank was more correct in judging the needs of the AAA legal division and in selection of staff.

The legal staff of the AAA also had a sense of community, of common purpose. The crisis gripping the country and the gathering storm of organized protest found voice among those New Dealers, like us, who came to Washington to make the government over into a government for the people. Of course this was decades before there was a Washington Beltway, but the New Deal represented an opportunity to eliminate the barriers between a government of wheeler-dealers, power brokers, and inside traders—what is today called the inside-the-Beltway mentality—and the governed. At least so we thought. Television was also a creation of the future, but everyone gathered around the radio in the evening and FDR, through his "fireside chats," mastered the medium and enhanced the sense of national purpose and commonality. The intimacy of communication and the

- THATS from your point of view of course; The US Supreme court had a majority which viewed The US constitution from a constructionis ViK Poin

developing relationship between the protests in the streets and the response in the nation's capital made remote the political alienation felt so strongly in the late twentieth century.

Hiss, in his memoir, *Recollections of a Life*, remembering the esprit de corps of the AAA lawyers, wrote: "We were few enough in number and similar enough in backgrounds and beliefs to feel common bonds. We were a band of brothers—members of a citizen's militia in mufti, mustered to fight the ills of the Depression." The AAA attorneys were, for the most part, recently out of law school, fresh from years of rigorous research, essential to an advanced analysis of constitutional theory and precedent necessary to drafting legislation with one eye on the Supreme Court's obstructionist bent.

Our work was never ending or, rather, we never ended our work. Evenings we would gather at a restaurant or someone's home—Jerome's was a favorite place, as was Artie's and Marion's apartment—to discuss strategy, chew over the latest policy announcement, exchange the newest gossip and rumors. Prohibition was still in effect, and in retrospect it might sound peculiar, but at the time it went unnoticed that we government attorneys, like virtually every other Washingtonian of age, were fueling our evening discussions with "Maryland Rye." Our debates and arguments and charting the next day's work carried over into late-night poker games, tennis matches, and horseback riding at a convenient Virginia stable.

Artie's work in the government was impeccable—he developed the strategy and arguments for Solicitor General Charles Fahey's successful defense of the Wagner Act before the Supreme Court—but his psychological problems had become chronic. He became attached to his psychologist, Franz Alexander, whom he had followed from Chicago to Boston (while Marion was in Vermont) and then to Johns Hopkins in Baltimore, an easy commute from Washington. Charlie Kramer's wife, Mildred, it turns out, was surreptitiously transporting Artie to Baltimore without Marion's (or my) knowledge. Charlie later told a story of Artie's developing claustrophobia (he would only sit on a rear aisle seat in a theater). Once the two of them were sitting in Charlie's office when a colleague came in to discuss a problem. As he entered, the man closed the office door behind him. Artie got up and reopened the door. The other fellow then rose and closed the door again. When Artie opened it, the other man closed it. This happened three times before they each recognized the other one's problem. Fortunately, Marion was extremely competent and graceful, with a facility of handling any situation, no matter how difficult. But friends wondered how she was able to sustain their relationship as long as she did.

As many young men and women find their lifelong friends and comrades in the course of school or college life, because of the intensity and sense of community of those days, I met in the AAA a number of colleagues whom I would come to count among my closest friends for life. I mentioned that Lee Pressman and I would be quite intimate for a score of years; I was probably as close a friend as Lee would allow himself, given his competitive and domineering streaks. One of my dearest friends, Nat Witt, came to the AAA legal staff a month before me. Warm, sensitive, highly outgoing, and emotionally charged but with keen intelligence and a lively sense of humor, we instantly struck up an enduring friendship. The son of an immigrant tailor, Nat grew up on Manhattan's Lower East Side and, unlike me, came by his education the hard way. He had to interrupt high school for three years and take a job to help support his family. Winning a scholarship at NYU, he still had to work nights throughout college. Upon graduation in 1927, he became emotionally caught up in the Sacco and Vanzetti case, participated in the Boston vigil on the night of their execution, and decided to study law. He chose Harvard Law School and drove a taxi full-time for two years to see him through. It was his early experience as a worker that gave Nat his working-class point of view and imbued him with a mighty sense of outrage at every manifestation of injustice. After an unrewarding year at a Wall Street law firm, Nat, like me, was attracted to the Roosevelt administration by its promise to allow us lawyers to perform socially meaningful work.

Another AAA attorney, Mattie Silverman, and his wife, Phyllis, also came from New York to Washington, where they spent a year before Mattie was sent to Puerto Rico to work on the AAA's sugar program. One of this charming and handsome couple's many attractive characteristics was a lively capacity for indignation. They would burn with the failure of government to curb runaway profits while millions were reduced to misery or with the irrationality of slaughtering suckling pigs while hunger gripped the country. Nor were all of my friends, with whom I would work, struggle, and play to our final days, gathered alone from the ranks of the legal staff.

In October 1933, just after my arrival in Washington, Jerome asked me to lunch. We stopped by the secretary of agriculture's anteroom, which housed the offices of Calvin B. Baldwin, Wallace's administrative assistant. Among Baldwin's responsibilities—he was referred to always as "Beanie" Baldwin—was the clearance of all departmental appointments. When we entered, he looked up from his desk and said to Jerome, "You sure pick lawyers with strange names. First you send me papers for Timberg and Muravchik. And now there is someone who calls himself A-B-T." His words only deepened the suspicions I, and the other young militants in the legal division, entertained of this soft-spoken, seemingly uncombative southerner who had been a household appliance dealer in Radford, Virginia. But we soon discovered that he was our staunchest ally in what proved to be a losing fight to hold down food processors' profits and to force the plantation owners to pay their sharecroppers a portion of the government's largesse for not planting cotton. And Beanie, like Nat and Mattie, would be among my dearest companions and co-workers to their last days.

In the top circles of the administration, major battles were being waged for power, authority, and policy. This was clearly true in the Department of Agriculture. Tommy Corcoran, one of FDR's top troubleshooters and power brokers, was quarreling with Jerome. The Farm Bureau and the southern Democrats were wary of the AAA general counsel's office. Jerome was in no position to appeal our case to the ultimate arbiter, FDR, and Henry Wallace fell incommunicative and, it was rumored, literally sick amidst intense quarreling and bureaucratic warfare. It became "common knowledge"—whether true or not, I never learned—that Wallace was consulting some guru in Mexico to see him through the difficulties.

There had been rumors in the legal division that Chester Davis, who came to the AAA from California agribusiness to replace a frustrated George Peek, would be ordering a purge. But there had always been rumors, the favored currency of the Washington coffee klatch. On February 5, 1935, I went to lunch with Lee Pressman and Frank Shea, and we kidded each other, speculating whose neck would be placed under the axe. When we returned to the office, we had our answer. On their desks were letters from Henry Wallace to Lee, Frank, Pat Jackson, and Jerome, demanding their resignations. The next day the *New York Times* quoted "Department officials" who predicted an end to "'business-baiting' and sharp criticism of middleman practices which Mr. Davis had always regarded as unwarranted." Unidentified "spokesmen for Secretary Wallace and Mr. Davis" charged that "those who resigned were troublemakers who let their social theories stand in the way of restoring farm prosperity."

Within weeks of the purge, its effects on AAA policy became apparent. The AAA consumers' council was reduced to a research agency—investigations were eliminated—thereby removing an irritant to the canners and packers. Meantime, the Southern Tenant Farmers' Union was complaining that hundreds of its members were being evicted despite section 7 of the AAA cotton contract, which provided

that the landlords "shall permit all tenants to continue in the occu-
pancy of their houses on this farm, rent free, for the years 1934 and
1935." Jerome Frank had been an advocate of section 7, but Chester
Davis, under pressure particularly from Arkansas Senator Joe Robinson, was prepared to abandon the tenant farmers. After the purge,
and without opposition from Wallace and Davis, the Arkansas Supreme Court upheld some five hundred eviction cases. There ensued
a reign of terror in the countryside in which Southern Tenant Farmers' Union families were forcibly evicted, their houses shot up, and
some members beaten and killed by vigilantes.

At the time, the purge was confusing to me. Why Jerome, when to
me he was anything but a militant, when he waffled more often than
not? I could maybe understand why Lee, who had a reputation as a
radical, but then why Frank Shea, who was essentially apolitical, and
not me, who was closest to Lee in viewpoint and affinity? Why Pat
Jackson, who was outspoken in his antileftist sentiments, and not
Charlie Kramer, who was a leftist? Perhaps the growers simply had
faulty intelligence or more likely were simply demanding heads, any
heads, to roll and the heads were chosen randomly. In any case, I recall meeting with Chester Davis in his office some weeks later and
his assuring me that the purge was not aimed at me, that the department didn't want my resignation and actually wanted me to stay on.
I mused that perhaps my behavior was somehow defective that it
should appear so unthreatening to those I heartily opposed.

Shortly after the purge, the Supreme Court decided the *Schecter*
case, which involved the poultry code. What the *Schecter* case did was
declare the NRA unconstitutional on the grounds that it represented
a delegation of power by Congress to the executive to issue and ad-
minister codes without specifying in any way what the codes should
contain or what the executive should do in administering them. One
of the justices called the law "delegation run riot." The Constitution
of course divides power between the three branches of government.
Congress cannot delegate its legislative power to any other branch;
the executive must be provided sufficient minimum standards so that
it knows what Congress wants done, a constitutional provision honored more in the breach than in the observance after the *Schecter*
case.

Schecter clearly affected the AAA statute as much as it did the NRA,
since it gave nearly unlimited power to write any terms AAA wanted
to write into the marketing agreements and licenses. To protect the
AAA against being ruled unconstitutional, we immediately set to
work amending it. The assignment to rewrite the act fell to me. By

then we had enough experience with these agreements and licenses to know what they should contain. So the task of amending the act was relatively without complications. For the first time I was working directly with Wallace. I can't say I was bored with the work but neither was the fascination and excitement present any longer to keep me interested.

By the time our amendments passed the Congress, the composition of the federal courts had changed with nearly three years' worth of Roosevelt appointees. AAA litigation, my department, had come to a virtual halt. The work had become routinized and no longer held its original attraction. Most of my friends had left the Department of Agriculture, voluntarily or otherwise. Pressman was general counsel of the Works Progress Administration. Nat Witt had gone to work for the National Labor Relations Board. Beanie Baldwin, about that time, became administrator of the Resettlement Administration, soon to be renamed the Farm Security Administration. And Beanie would name Artie Bachrach as his inspector general because, Beanie said, Artie was simply incorruptible. I also decided to look elsewhere.

* * *

Early in my tenure at the AAA, the limitations of the New Deal, particularly in the face of the enormity of the crisis, made themselves readily apparent. Moreover, the rapid growth of Unemployed Councils in cities and rural radicalism, particularly in the South in the form of sharecropper and tenant farmer unions, brought out the shortcomings of the New Deal in bold relief. Not only millions in the streets and on the farms were investigating more radical solutions; in Washington, talk of fundamental social change was commonplace. In his oral history, Jerome Frank, a jurist of real integrity but politically at best a vacillating liberal, recalled:

> The fellows on Wall Street, including my former partners, were in a panic. The whole damn capitalist system was on the skids. They were talking some kind of dictatorship. Tom Chadborne said, 'Well, maybe we've got to try the Russian scheme.' . . . I think American policy was a reflection of what was going on in Russia. I think it was America's way of answering the Russian technique. . . . Here we are working like crazy men trying to save the capitalist system and the big capitalists are denouncing us as Communists.

Within the AAA legal division, I noticed that, from time to time, some of my closest colleagues would get together but neglect to invite me. One day, Pressman asked me to write a critique of the milk program as a tool of the dairy interests. Lee kept pressing. "Take an afternoon off, just do it," he implored me. Obviously my critique was urgently needed. However, when I did take time off to work up my critique and hand it in, I never heard another word about it. I was a bit perturbed about these strange occurrences, and more than a bit curious.

Then one day in June 1934, less than a year after I'd arrived in Washington, a man came to my apartment—by then I'd moved out of Marion's and Artie's and taken a place of my own in the same building—and introduced himself as Hal Ware. Tall and lean, in his early forties, Ware appeared professorial, down to his wearing of pince-nez. As it turned out, Hal was a Pennsylvania mushroom farmer and the leading agricultural expert for the Communist Party USA. Himself a charter member from its founding in 1919, he was the son of Ella Reeve "Mother" Bloor, the "grand old lady" of the Party. Mother Bloor was legendary in the Communist movement, very small with snapping, dark brown eyes, enormously energetic—at the age of seventy-five she undertook a cross-country automobile trip to sell *Daily Workers*—and she was a powerful agitational speaker, on a par with Emma Goldman or Elizabeth Gurley Flynn. In 1932, she presided over a meeting of fifty farm leaders in Sioux City, Iowa, to coincide with a gathering of midwest governors. Mother Bloor called for a Farmers National Relief Conference that December in Washington, D.C., and then toured the farm belt, addressing thousands of farmers in hundreds of local meetings to build the conference.

Hal told me something about his own life. After graduating from the Pennsylvania State College School of Forestry, he settled in for a life of farming. But after a few years, with a yen to travel and a restless curiosity, he joined the harvest hands, hoboing his way on freights, following the grain harvests in the Dakotas and the Great Plains.

When the Bolsheviks came to power in Russia, Hal began to raise money for the purchase of farm implements and tractors and organized teams of farmers to bring to Russia to demonstrate the use of mechanization in agriculture. For the better part of nine years, he helped bring modern methods to Soviet farms and taught the peasants how to use them. Lenin later acknowledged that his work "was more helpful than that of any other American." Between trips to Russia, Hal served as a consultant to both the Coolidge and Hoover administrations at the behest of his friend M. L. Wilson, who became an assistant secretary of agriculture under Hoover. Still the romantic with a lust to wander, Hal told me that what he really longed to do was go to China to help the Chinese in the cotton fields as he'd helped the Russians with grain.

I was to learn that Hal was shy and retiring before large audiences, but most effective and persuasive in small committees and living rooms with a flow of colorful talk and stories. Then he was in my living room, telling me that he was the leader of the Communist party in Washington, D.C. He told me that he was impressed with my work, which he had learned about from Party members in the AAA. He said they had recommended me for membership. He told me their names and invited me to join.

I took several days to consider Hal's proposition. I'd been in the government for nine months but already had misgivings about the administration. It was becoming clear that FDR would, as its leading representative, do whatever he felt was necessary to preserve the social system but would certainly not dismantle it. While he liked to boast of driving the money changers from the temple, they may have been pushed out the front door but soon reentered through the rear and remained the most powerful force in the government. In the AAA, the big growers, big processors, big dairies were really in command. The tenant farmers, the sharecroppers, the small farmers received the short end of the stick, if they received anything at all.

I'd learned enough about the Party's views on these matters to know that they largely coincided with my own. To my knowledge, no other party was organizing others around these positions. The Communist party's leadership of the hunger marchers, its initiation of the Unemployed Councils for jobs and relief, its leading role in the organization of the sharecroppers' union in the South—together with the fact that my closest friends and co-workers in the AAA had already joined the Party—quickly convinced me to apply for membership. I had few trepidations. From my Civil Liberties Union days in Chicago, I'd known enough about the nefarious work of anticommunism; now, of course, the Liberty Lobby and other right-wing opponents of the New Deal sought to tarnish FDR with the same brush. I understood that my Party membership could not be public.

A few weeks after joining, I had one of the most delightful experiences of my life. One day, Hal told me that without my knowledge he had also met and recruited Marion into the Party. He gave me the task of telling her of her assignment to a Party club and collecting her initiation fee. Although we had long discussions about the failures and shortcomings of the administration, I had said nothing to Marion about my newfound association. It was astonishing that, given our common background, we both came to the same "bad end" and quite independently of one another. We were the closest of friends, neighbors in the same building, yet neither of us discussed the Party or the possibility of joining it with the other.

As per Hal's request, I invited her to have lunch with me in one of the capital's swankiest restaurants, without telling her why. It was a rare and beautiful occasion for both of us as we learned of each other's Party membership. Marion was then unemployed, so devoted herself to writing for the Party. Her first piece, I believe, was a pamphlet on the severe drought inflicting the Great Plains, its consequences for the farm area, and a program to meet the problem.

During our childhood summers at Schneider's Farm, Marion would always find a sick chicken or a cat with a broken leg and would spend her time nursing the animals back to life and strength. She had the same characteristic with respect to people. I suppose she felt that she had the strength to carry herself and her many men— and she had quite a number—all of whom had afflictions of some kind, as Artie did. Marion was an incurable optimist. Everything was going to turn out beautifully; she relished telling friends about her wonderful experiences, which were usually better in the telling than the reality. All of which contributed to her facility for prose. She wrote like a dream. This combination of inner strength, compassion, and optimism would make Marion a true Communist activist and leader.

My Party unit met weekly. We read and discussed articles from Marxist journals, or various works by Marx, Engels, and Lenin. We mainly talked about our work in the various agencies where we were employed, what this indicated about the drift and policies of the Roosevelt administration. If there were developments we thought were particularly interesting or important, someone would be asked to draft a report to be given to Hal, who presumably passed it on to the national leadership in New York for its consideration in estimating the direction of the New Deal and what might be done to influence it. This was the extent of my Party involvement in this period.

When, in 1948, the existence of the "Ware Group" was first exposed in the national media, we were pictured as having been engaged in espionage. That we met privately and that we did not openly reveal our membership was used to portray us as a conspiratorial group engaged in disreputable and treacherous practices. Actually, the Ware Group was a name invented by Whittaker Chambers and a freshman Congressman named Richard Nixon to make headlines and advance their own careers, which were replete with disreputable practices of their own. In fact, our Party unit had no name; because

see HAL WARE P. 39

we AAA lawyers in the group had recently concluded a marketing agreement for cling peaches, we jokingly referred to our comrades as "the cling peaches." In any case, we were hardly in a position to commit espionage or any other crime against the country, had we had a mind to do so. We had no access to military or defense information. In those days there was no such thing as classified information. And had there been classification legislation in effect, the information we dealt with would not have been so categorized. We were simply providing political analyses of New Deal policy, based on our positions as insiders in various government agencies. Our purpose was not to help foreign governments but to help our own, to defeat those who wanted to obstruct the progressive tendencies within the administration, and strengthen those New Dealers who would respond to the growing popular movements for real relief.

On reflection, I would say it is conceivable that the commentary and analyses we provided to the national Party leadership may have reached the Soviets—there were regular exchanges of information with all the fraternal parties through the Communist International— but I can't imagine they would have been interested in what we had to say; nor, had they been interested, that it could have been of any use. The fact of the matter is that although the so-called Ware Group would be the subject of countless investigations and reinvestigations by grand juries, congressional committees, and the FBI for several years beginning in 1947, there would never be a single indictment for espionage against any of its members. In later years, I've asked myself whether the whole project of the Party to recruit employees of agencies in the Roosevelt administration, and then to organize them into groups like ours, was a useful effort when you compare the minimal value of the information we provided with the impetus it gave to anticommunist repression. It probably wasn't worth it, although, for myself, I haven't a single regret regarding my own participation. Of course hindsight has its limitations, and no one in 1934 could foretell what would unfold in 1948. (I don't want to leave the impression that our group, and others like it, were the primary aspect of Party activity in Washington. Actually, the bulk of the Party membership in the city was in the various unions of government workers.)

For Americans, as a nation, theory has never been a strong suit. We are a practical people, used to getting things done. Claims to the contrary notwithstanding, the same could be said for the Communist party. This was a strength, but also a weakness. The failure to articulate a theory of, say, the state and the New Deal, in part accounts for

relying instead on a "line," a stated policy, which was always changing as circumstances changed.

In the early years of the New Deal, the Party was in opposition to
FDR. It—I should say, we—viewed the NRA, for example, in its essence as an effort by the administration to relieve the big industrial
corporations from the threat of antitrust legislation, allowing them to
enter into price-fixing and other intraindustrial agreements. Some
Party documents warned, it is now embarrassing to recount, of "New
Deal fascism." The NRA, we argued, would lead to a growth of monopolization in industry; similarly, the AAA would allow agribusiness
to flourish at the expense of the working farmer.

Eventually, we came to understand the Roosevelt administration
represented a cleavage in the methods of the governing class. At issue
was how to deal with the mass movements growing in reaction to the
policies inherited from Hoover, how to resolve the systemic crisis and
resultant social misery, and how to view the assault of the far Right in
Europe. From onetime opposition, the Communists gradually began to
move the government, as friends of the administration. Previous crises had resulted in serious third-party challenges to the ruling order.
The 1912–16 crisis brought the presidential candidacy of the Socialist
leader Eugene V. Debs, who, campaigning from a prison cell, received
nearly two million votes. The crisis of 1924 encouraged the independent candidacy of the Progressive party and Sen. Robert LaFollette of
Wisconsin. Now we were in the midst of the most serious, and long-
est-lasting, crisis, but there was no third-party challenge because FDR
proved to be different from the Republicans and not a goat of a different color. He showed himself capable of responding to the rapidly
growing labor movement and the Left. The New Deal would eventually lead to a major shift in the allegiance of Black Americans, who had
previously been tied to "the party of Lincoln"; the budding labor movement would eventually be allied with the Democratic party on a national scale. While the two major parties were both parties of monop-
olized big business, the class base of each was quite different. Since
Roosevelt's time, it has become clear, great social advances come only
when there are schisms in the ruling order.

The Party's endorsement of FDR was a process, one that was not
complete until the 1944 election. I vividly recall, in 1935, just before
his death, Hal Ware bringing us word of the proceedings of the Seventh World Congress of the Communist International. This gathering of Communists from all over the world, under the leadership of
the Bulgarian Georgi Dmitroff, called sharp attention to the growing
fascist danger in Germany, Spain, and Italy and urged unity of Com-

munists, Socialists, and all democrats in governments (popular fronts) and in mass movements (united fronts). Dmitroff warned that in the United States the main danger emanated from the "finance capitalist forces" that were attacking Roosevelt and that failure to understand this would be "tantamount to misleading the working class." (Clearly, the Comintern was not basing its conclusions on the narrow and wrong-headed assumptions we "cling peaches" were sending to the Party leadership in New York.) The implications for us were obvious.

The Seventh World Congress, largely influenced by Dmitroff and his experience in the fight against fascism—after the mysterious fire in the Reichstag, the German parliament building, which Hitler used to consolidate his power, Dmitroff was arrested and successfully used the occasion of his trial to accuse his accusers from the dock—was meant to send a signal not only to the CPUSA but to Communists the world over. In the early thirties, the German Communists were attacking the Social Democrats but were now working to build a united front. In Spain, Communists would now enter and defend with their lives the Socialist-led Republican government. American Communists who had once referred to their Socialist brethren as "social fascists" (socialist by pretension, fascist at heart), would now put together electoral coalitions like the American Labor party in New York and collaborate in the labor movement against right-wing forces.

The Communist party has always been accused, with much justice, of making zigs and zags in policy that the membership then followed unquestioningly. In this particular case, it has always seemed to me that the Party was correct in changing direction. In practice, the change actually preceded the Seventh World Congress. In 1934, in California, the socialist writer Upton Sinclair ran for governor in the Democratic primary on the End Poverty in California (EPIC) designation and won several hundred thousand votes. In New York, Vito Marcantonio, the left-wing populist from East Harlem, was sent to Congress for his first term. Communists were not ignorant of the importance of such campaigns and could draw the proper lessons. We could bring something to the table, so to speak, in contributing to making Comintern policy, as well as simply receiving it for implementation in local conditions. The Young Communist League helped establish the mass-based American Youth Congress and was credited by Dmitroff at the Seventh World Congress as having pioneered in action the concept of the united front. American Communists of course were among the delegates to the Comintern Congress; and Gil Green, the YCL chair, was a member of the Comintern Executive.

Moreover, the change of the Communist International's positions coincided with the mass struggles here to organize unions along industrial lines, building the constituency that would be essential for passage of the Wagner Act. The Roosevelt administration was not always moving as far or as quickly as we wanted, but it was responding to mass pressure for social security, unemployment insurance, jobs programs like the WPA. The decisions of the Seventh World Congress were not in conflict with or superimposed on the struggles of the American working class; to the contrary, they contributed to consolidating and accelerating those struggles at a particular moment in history. And as the Party threw itself into these struggles and achieved successes, it validated the leadership in the eyes of the membership. The structure of the Party resembled that of a revolutionary army, with commands from on high dutifully followed; but like an army, the submission to discipline was one of willingness because of overriding faith in the cause and the leadership.

Not that all Party decisions followed a fine logic. In 1936, for example, the leadership decided that Earl Browder, the general secretary, should run against Roosevelt, although the Party's clarion call was to "defeat Alf Landon (the Republican presidential candidate) at all costs." At the base, in their places of work and in their communities, Communists were encouraged to campaign for Roosevelt but to personally vote for Browder. Looking back fifty years later, I have no doubt that I voted for Browder, but clearly then—as later when Gus Hall, in the first of his several presidential campaigns, ran against Nixon and McGovern—the circuitous logic behind the position was much too clever for me (and most Communists) to grasp. Fortunately I was a government lawyer and never had to give much thought to these weighty matters. I was not a Party militant in the classic sense of one involved in base-building, agitation, and organization among fellow workers. I was certainly as devoted but not nearly as involved.

On August 13, 1935, Hal Ware was on yet another of his innumerable excursions, driving one night through the mountains of Pennsylvania, when he collided with a coal truck. He died the next morning in a Harrisburg hospital at the age of forty-five.

With Hal's death, responsibility for our group fell to J. Peters, who came from the Party national organization department in New York to meet with us once a month or so. Pete, as he was called by all, had participated in the ill-fated Hungarian revolution and brief socialist government of Bela Kun after World War I. He abandoned his family name of Goldfarb when the counterrevolution overthrew the Kun regime and he was deported. Built like a fire hydrant, with a shock of blond hair, a pronounced Hungarian accent, and a grand sense of humor, Pete was a most attractive personality. He and his wife, Anne, became lifelong friends. He had recently written a manual on Party organization, perhaps the most hidebound, imperious piece of Communist dogma we ever produced. Marion offered and actually tried to edit the manual, but Pete would allow no changes. (Years later, during the Smith Act trials and McCarran Act hearings to repress the Party, *Peters' Manual on Organization* was invariably the government's exhibit A, and rightfully deserved this place. Ironically, in the seventies, in one of the myriad attempts to "correct" or supplant the CPUSA, a small "new communist" group reissued Pete's manual as its own new testament.)

Marion's skills were put to far better use when, in November 1936, John Bernard was elected to Congress from the Messaba iron range in northern Minnesota. A Corsican by birth and a fireman by profession, Johnny was a rare and lovely character. Elected on the Farmer-Labor ticket, he enjoyed walking to the top of the Capitol steps and, in fine and boisterous voice, belting out "The Internationale." In January 1937, upon being sworn in and facing his first vote in the House—at issue was the Neutrality Act, which would deny arms to the Spanish republic under siege from fascist troops armed and supplemented by troops from Nazi Germany and fascist Italy—John Bernard cast the single negative vote against the Act. When he first arrived in Washington, Johnny hired Marion as his administrative secretary. She did all his research and wrote his speeches. He liked to brag about her, telling how, if there was a conference taking place in his office, with a lot of back-and-forth arguments, Marion would sit in a corner, completely oblivious to what was going on, cigarette hanging from the corner of her mouth, writing out his next speech on the typewriter. She was enormously facile in writing, and he trusted her implicitly. Although I recall one time Johnny rose to make a speech to the House, was well into the written remarks and, after reading off a particular passage, stopped in midspeech to declare, "Hey, I don't agree with that."

* * *

Lee Pressman, now Harry Hopkins's general counsel at the WPA, proposed that I come there as his assistant general counsel. The WPA was the successor agency to the Federal Emergency Relief Administration (FERA), with the notion that the government would provide jobs in lieu of welfare. Opponents of the New Deal called the WPA pay for raking leaves, but in fact the parks, public buildings, works of art, and theater produced under WPA have left a legacy that to this day continues to enrich the country.

If there was one area of the WPA, however, that could be fairly accused of improvising work where none existed, it was the post of assistant general counsel. There simply wasn't much legal work to be done and no court challenges to be made. The work of the general counsel consisted almost entirely of winning approval for funding various WPA projects from Comptroller General McTarrel. The comptroller general is appointed by Congress to head the General Accounting Office for fifteen years. McTarrel, a Republican appointee with a profound distaste for the New Deal in general, and the WPA in particular, had the authority to approve or disapprove projects, exercising Congress's power of the purse. WPA procedure called for administrative personnel to first conceive of a project, then to formulate and budget it, and then for the general counsel, after consulting with the administrator, Harry Hopkins, to go to the comptroller general to argue for approval.

Pressman was very smart and a clever operator, made for this kind of work, which was essentially political persuasion. Though he was one of my closest friends, he was also a man of great ambition and sense of competition, always protective of position and prerogative. As a result, I had a job but no work. Lee never introduced me to Hopkins, and I don't recall ever seeing the man in the whole time I worked at WPA. Pressman never took me with him when he met with McTarrel and never sent me as his proxy.

My only contribution to the agency came in September 1935 as the result of a natural disaster, a hurricane, hitting Florida. In 1932, after the Great Crash and the ensuing human catastrophe, thousands of veterans of World War I gathered in an encampment on Washington's Anacostia flats along the Potomac. They intended to march on the Capitol, demanding that the Hoover administration and Congress make good on promises of veterans' bonuses. Hoover ordered the army, under a couple of junior officers named Douglas MacArthur and Dwight Eisenhower, to line up machine-gun emplacements to stop what became known as "the bonus army marchers." In the ensuing violent dispersal of the marchers, over one hundred veterans were injured and two infants were killed. The bonus army, not unlike hundreds of thousands of Vietnam veterans a half century later, were driven to the margins of society, without benefits, without attention. When Roosevelt came to power, the newly formed FERA dispersed the bonus marchers to different centers along the East Coast to prevent another march on Washington; the largest group was dis-

NOT ACCURATE MR. APT. The BONUSES WERE PROMISED TO BE PAID TO THE WWI VETS FROM govt BONDS which WOULD NOT MATURE UNTIL THE MID 1940's. The BONUS MARCHERS WANTED FULL PAYMENT BEFORE BOND MATURITY. FDR FINALY gave in.

patched to the Florida Keys, about as far away from Washington as
you could put them without dumping them in the ocean. In those pre-
condo, pre-tourist days, this was akin to banishment to a Devil's Island or a Siberia. It was the Keys, and the veterans, that the hurricane attacked in that autumn of 1935.

The veterans were "housed" in tents and shacks in several camps.
Altogether they numbered several thousand. The hurricane hit with
savage force and utterly devastated the encampments. The front page
of the *New York Times* of September 4, 1935, was dominated by a story of 351 socialites stranded on the luxury cruise ship *Dixie*, with accompanying photos of some of the partygoers in their cotillion gowns.
At the bottom of the page was a smaller story reporting the destruction of Veterans Camp Number 1, in which all but two shacks and the
hospital that usually housed sixty patients were all swept away; the
destruction of railway and highway bridges leading to Plantation Key
on which sat Veterans Camps Numbers 3 and 5 by wind and raging
torrents of water, wiping out any access to the Key; the first rescue of
a camp victim, Dorothy Van Ness, age six, whose father, two brothers, and a sister lost their lives; and the initial estimate of seventy-
five lives lost in the veterans camps.

On September 5, after the top story in the *Times*—"Passengers Tell
Thrilling Stories" was the headline—came the report from Florida. It
told of one veteran who saw his wife, two children, and two grandchildren killed before his eyes; of 11 survivors out of 192 reported in
one camp; of the WPA estimated fatalities reaching 300 veterans, with
200 more unaccounted for. The September 6 *Times* (banner headline:
"Dixie Passengers All Safe Ashore") reported that Harry Hopkins said
the failure to evacuate the vets was not traceable to negligence by
the government and announced he was sending Aubrey Williams, his
top deputy, to Florida to investigate.

Williams, a strapping, handsome Alabaman, like Beanie Baldwin
one of those progressives who defied the stereotype of the racist
southern retrograde, had previously headed up the National Youth
Administration and was deputy administrator of WPA. He brought me
to Florida as his assistant. We were on a political mission to defend
the administration against charges of negligence. There had been
some advanced notice of the hurricane. At question was whether the
government had heeded the warning by dispatching a train from
Jacksonville in time to pick up the vets and their families. The "investigation" took all of a day. A letter I wrote to my mother from Miami reflected my mood and tells the story:

I suppose, if you tried to imagine the situation in advance, you could supply most of the actual details: Governor Paul Shulz, surrounded by his bodyguard of pug-uglies, eager to ingratiate himself with Washington and impress it with a proper sense of appreciation for his cooperation in keeping any unpleasant facts from being revealed, before he dashed off to Hyde Park to attempt to nick the President for ten million to build a new road over the Keys. Colonel Lajuies of the Veterans' Administration, vastly concerned over the details of the burial of the mangled bodies that were pulled out of the Keys before cremation becomes imperative—there was a mad scramble for flags on Friday night so that no box (there was no time or money for coffins) might be lowered without a stars-and-stripes covering—although the colonel was finally forced to compromise (due to a shortage of bunting) into using a single flag with which, momentarily, to drape each box before it was lowered. More bickering about identifying the dead in order to guard against false war risk insurance claims, accompanied by gruesome details. Heated arguments between the Red Cross, the VA, FERA, the governor, the city administration, the sheriff, etc. about who was in charge of what and how it should be done. More arguments between the American Legion and the VFW about who should have the honor of first honoring the fallen heroes, who the day before were regarded as drunken bums.

The climax came last night with a memorial service in the park across the street, presided over by the governor (all washed up and trying hard to look suitably solemn) and more bemedalled generals, admirals, legionnaires, boy scouts and other uniforms than were ever assembled on a battlefield.

P.S. Two survivors tried to get in to hear the services for their fellow veterans, but having first drowned the memory of the disaster in liquor, were thrown out by the police.

Obviously, with only a day of looking around, talking to weather bureau people, camp administrators, and a few veterans, we hadn't gathered much evidence and couldn't say we'd conducted a serious investigation. But political pressures being as they are, Aubrey asked me to draw up a preliminary report of what we'd found so that he could call the president at Hyde Park and tell him what was going on. I sat down and drafted a necessarily brief report that tended to exonerate the WPA. The report, I had been given to understand, was only for FDR's information. I well remember Aubrey sitting on the bed in our room at Miami's McAllister Hotel, calling Roosevelt and reading him my report over the phone, then reading it again to a stenographer. Much to my amazement and chagrin, this became the official public report of the government as to what happened in the Keys.

The Veterans Administration was full of Republicans, who sought to discredit the report and thereby embarrass the administration. A VA investigator was appointed to investigate our "investigation," to hang the responsibility on the Roosevelt administration for not evacuating the vets. I was assigned by WPA to defend the initial report. So I returned to Florida, this time for several weeks, most of which I spent in Jacksonville hospitals interviewing injured veterans. When I came back to Washington I wrote a lengthy report in preparation for hearings before the House Committee on Military Affairs. The VA was of course pressing its point of view. The House Committee was chaired by John Rankin of Mississippi, whose antebellum mentality made him one of Congress's worst reactionaries. But he was a Democrat with a political stake in the administration, so he and I teamed up as allies to exonerate the government, in an episode of my life I look back on without pride.

As it turned out, it fell to Ernest Hemingway on September 17, 1935, to file the best report on the hurricane, in his capacity as sometime-reporter for the *New Masses:*

> Whom did they annoy and to whom was their possible presence a political danger? Who sent them down to the Florida Keys and left them there in hurricane months? Who is responsible for their deaths?
>
> The writer . . . would not know the answers. . . . But he does know that wealthy people, yachtsmen, fisherman such as President Hoover and President Roosevelt, do not come to the Florida Keys in hurricane months. . . . You do not see them because yacht owners know there would be great danger, unescapable danger, to their property if a storm should come. . . . But veterans, especially the bonus-marching variety of veterans, are not property. They are only human beings, unsuccessful human beings, and all they have to lose is their lives. They are doing coolie labor for a top wage of $45 a month and they have been put down on the Florida Keys where they can't make trouble. . . .
>
> As this is written five days after the storm, nobody knows how many are dead. The Red Cross, which has steadily played down

the number, announcing first 46 then 150, finally saying the dead would not pass 300, today lists the dead and missing as 446, but the total of veterans dead and missing alone numbers 442 and there have been 70 bodies of civilians recovered. The total may well pass a thousand as many bodies were washed out to sea and will never be found. . . .

I knew a lot of them and some of them were punch drunk and some of them were smart; some had been on the bum since the Argonne almost and some had lost their jobs the year before last Christmas . . . they were all what you get after a war. But who sent them there to die? . . . I would like to make whoever sent them there carry just one out through the mangroves, or turn one over that lay in the sun along the fill, or tie five together so they won't float out, or smell that smell you thought you'd never smell again, with luck when rich bastards make a war. . . . Who left you there? And what's the punishment for manslaughter now?

* * *

When I was still with the AAA, I made acquaintances with Tom Corcoran and Ben Cohen, who would occasionally visit Jerome Frank. Tommy and Ben were two more Harvard proteges who had come to FDR's attention through Felix Frankfurter. It wasn't long before the two of them rose to become among the more powerful personalities in the New Deal. Ben was soft-spoken, gentle, and an excellent attorney, a true craftsman at developing legislation and author of some of the best bills to come out of the New Deal. Tommy, while a lawyer, was essentially the classic Irish clubhouse politician, a powerful political operator who did the president's bidding. Though he was on the payroll of the Reconstruction Finance Committee, Tommy rarely put in an appearance there; rather, he roamed the corridors of all the government agencies, the ultimate power broker with a host of administration officials obligated to him for their jobs.

Ben had drafted the Public Utility Holding Company Act and, when the act came under challenge, he and Tommy came to the WPA to tap me to work on the case. I assume Jerome recommended me but I never found out for sure. A peculiar situation prevailed in Washington in those early years of the New Deal. Staff members, particularly lawyers, were borrowed from one agency and lent to another as a matter of course, doing work for the borrowing agency while remaining on the lender's payroll. The work I was asked to do meant heading up a team of lawyers to prepare the case for the Securities and

Exchange Commission against the Electric Bond and Share Company, the biggest of the public utility holding companies. But while the work would be for the SEC, I would continue to be paid by the WPA.

While I was to operate with a good deal of autonomy and authority, the lead lawyer—the one who would actually argue the case after my team prepared it—was Robert Jackson, then the general counsel of the Internal Revenue Service. Later he would of course become an assistant attorney general, then solicitor general, attorney general, Supreme Court justice, and chief prosecutor in Nuremburg at the Nazi war crimes tribunal. From Jamestown in western New York State, Jackson was short in stature, nondescript physically. But he was a brilliant lawyer then in his prime, an ardent New Dealer, at the time on the left in the administration, an outspoken defender of Roosevelt's plan to increase the Supreme Court from nine to fifteen members to get around the court's adverse decisions. I recall several conversations with Bob around this time—there was an impending strike in the coalfields—and he would argue that the only real solution for the mines was nationalization, which was quite an advanced position for a New Deal official. I discovered that Bob was quite easy to work for; it would be some time before I also discovered the reach of his ambitions.

Before I came into the case, Electric Bond and the government had come to an accord that rather than enter into a protracted trial with a lengthy period to gather voluminous evidence, an effort would be made to reach an agreement on the facts, in legal terms a "stipulation" of the facts, to submit to the court as the basis on which to argue the constitutionality of the act. I was to be in charge for the government in preparing the stipulation. Tommy Corcoran and Ben Cohen had assembled a staff of seven other attorneys to work under me. Before going to New York, I spent several weeks in preparation by studying the Federal Trade Commission investigation of and report on Electric Bond and Share.

The lawyers for Electric Bond were Simpson, Thatcher, and Bartlett, a big Wall Street firm that still exists today, with offices in the Equitable Building on lower Broadway in the heart of the financial district. We also took an office in the Equitable Building, a few floors below their firm. This allowed me to walk to work from the Brevoort Hotel, on lower Fifth Avenue in Greenwich Village, a third-rate hotel but with—most important—a first-rate restaurant.

While I was working on the *Electric Bond and Share* case, Marion called me from Washington to tell me that Jessica Smith, Hal Ware's widow, was working in New York. She and Jessica had become quite friendly, and Marion suggested that I look her up. I first met Jessica at a New Year's Eve party at Pat Jackson's house in December 1934. For obvious reasons, Hal would never attend a social affair of AAA or other administration personnel. Jessica was then employed at the Soviet embassy—FDR had finally granted U.S. recognition to the Soviet government in 1933—putting out an information bulletin. She and Hal invited me to their home in Sandy Spring, Maryland, where I also first met their seven-year-old son, David. What still today stands out for me from that lunch was Jessica's roast lamb with inserted slices of garlic, the first of countless meals of this magnificent cook that I would come to enjoy.

Three years later, my hotel in the Village was not far from Jessica's apartment on Nineteenth Street, so we met occasionally for dinner or for the theater, which was one of her great passions. She loved to tell of her many adventures, which happily coincided with my enjoyment at hearing of them. But I was not romantically inclined: though quite beautiful with a shock of honey-colored hair and blue eyes one could drown in, Jessica was then forty years old, eight years my senior. I became quite fond of her but romance was not on the horizon.

Her father, Walter Granville Smith, had been a successful commercial artist, regularly commissioned by magazines such as *Scribner's, Harper's,* and *Atlantic* to do their frontispieces. Once Jessica discovered an old Hart, Schaffner and Marx catalog with illustrations of men's clothing done by her dad. But around the turn of the century— she was just a small child then—he decided that he would no longer allow himself to be "reduced" to commercial art, and from then on devoted his life to painting, mainly seascapes and landscapes, and some portraits. He became a national academician, and his paintings still hang in many museums around the country, but he also went broke. Jessica's mother, Jessie May Stout, herself an accomplished pianist, was embittered that because of her family responsibilities and their impoverished existence, she was never able to fulfill her talent. Her relationship with Walter was rather unhappy, and she ended her own life some years before I knew Jessica.

Jessica had a Quaker education, first at Friends' Seminary in New York City and later at Swarthmore College, though she never was a Quaker nor had religious leanings of any sort. After graduating college at the age of nineteen, she became the movie critic of the *Philadelphia North-American,* predecessor to the *Inquirer.* But these were the days of World War I, and above all, Jessica was against war. The peace movement of the time was highlighted by Eugene V. Debs's presidential campaign. Jessica joined Debs's Socialist party and, simultaneously, became an organizer and speaker for the women's suffrage movement. She traveled to Nevada for a period to campaign for Anne Martin, the first woman to run for U.S. Senate, campaigning on the People's party ticket.

Jessica used to attribute her political development to her childhood although, like mine, her family was not in the least political. Growing up on elegant Stuyvesant Square in New York, she lived only a block or two away from the squalor of the First and Second Avenue tenements, and she could never reconcile the disparity. She ran with Max Eastman and the Greenwich Village Socialists of that day, and later, as executive secretary of the Intercollegiate Socialist Society— predecessor to the League for Industrial Democracy—she helped organize meetings for Albert Rhys Williams and John Reed and others who had been in Soviet Russia during, and in the early days of, the Revolution. (Her association with John Reed was later captured on thirty seconds of celluloid as one of Warren Beatty's "witnesses" in *Reds*, his romantic epic about Reed that captured the 1982 Academy Award.)

Jessica went to Russia in 1922 to do famine relief work in the Volga region on behalf of the American Friends Service Committee. She stayed for two years, falling in love with the Russian people, the Revolution, and Hal Ware, whom she met on a farm where they both worked. Soon after they returned to the United States, they were married in a ceremony performed by Norman Thomas, the Socialist leader. Together, they organized and raised money for Hal's projects in agricultural development, and together they returned to Russia, working for two more years in Maslov Kut in the North Caucasus as part of a Russian-American experimental model in state farming.

When they came back home this time, Jessica threw herself into Friends of the Soviet Union, the organization coordinating the campaign for U.S. recognition of the USSR. For four years she was employed by the Soviet Information Bureau in Washington and worked alongside Maxim Litvinov, Moscow's foreign minister, during his missions to lay the basis for diplomatic relations. When I met Hal, Jessica was setting up an information department for the newly established Soviet embassy, under Ambassador Alexander Troyanovsky. A few years earlier, the Friends of the Soviet Union had begun publishing *Soviet Russia Today* as a primary means of promoting U.S.-USSR diplomatic relations. That goal having been accomplished, the Friends of the Soviet Union soon dissolved but the magazine continued as an independent entity. After Hal's death, Jessica came to New

York to take over the editorship. It was between deadlines that Jessica's and my theater dates were squeezed in.

My friend from the AAA, Mattie Silverman, was living in New York and working as counsel for the city's Home Relief Administration under its quixotic director, Charlotte Carr. He was working closely with the Communist-led Unemployed Councils, doing battle to win relief for New York's poor. He and his wife, Phyllis, became frequent companions when Jessica and I went out, and Jessica teased me that I brought the Silvermans along "for protection." When she moved the remainder of her belongings from Washington into her new apartment—her distaste for moving was as passionate as her taste for theater—she asked me to help. Naturally, I mobilized the Silvermans to join me.

Once Jessica called to invite me over for dinner—she was preparing oyster stew, I recall—but I begged off. (I would later discover that she made a truly magnificent oyster stew.) My evasive maneuvers—I see them as such only in retrospect—continued. We went to a movie in Times Square one night. Coming home, the bus stopped first at the Brevoort and would later pass her apartment. When we came to my stop, instead of escorting her home, I rose, said good-bye, and departed the bus.

A few nights later, we had a date to see *Bury the Dead* on Broadway, featuring Hetta Ware, a niece of Hal's and Jessica's. I returned from my labors on the *Electric Bond and Share* case to freshen up before picking up Jessica. A letter from her was waiting for me at the Brevoort. She wrote that she could no longer refrain from telling me that she had fallen in love with me, a confession that knocked me for the proverbial loop. The fact is that I was starting to worry about myself. I was thirty-two years old, and though I'd been with many women, both as friends and intimates, I had never been in love. I wondered if perhaps something was wrong with me. It had always been my practice with all my girlfriends not to lie, so I had never declared my love to any woman. My first girlfriend—Marjorie Mack at Camp Beulah in my teenage years—continued a correspondence with me after that summer, when I returned to Chicago and she to Wellesley. I remember, after tiring of our letters, writing to tell her I wasn't in love. I still remember my pontifical first line: "Sincerity has always been the guidepost of my life."

When I picked up Jessica that night for the theater, I told her I'd received her letter, but I didn't want to abuse her confidence. I felt I must explain that I wasn't in love, never had been, and that this was simply my nature. This didn't seem to disturb her in the least. We went to dinner—I remember sauntering down Broadway with her hand-in-hand—then to the theater. That night we slept together for the first time.

Jessica had a friend, Helen Black, who was the U.S. agent for Sovfoto, the USSR agency that bought and sold U.S. and Soviet photos for newspapers and magazines. Helen was about to leave for Moscow for an extended trip and offered to lend us her apartment during her absence. The flat was also in the Village, on Eighth Street just off Fifth Avenue. It was only a one-room affair with a makeshift kitchen, not much more than a hot plate, but I moved out of the Brevoort for the remainder of my time on the *Electric Bond and Share* case. And it was there that I discovered, among her many other virtues, that Jessica was a splendid cook. We were quite happy together but I still cannot say that I was in love.

I had to travel to Washington one day to interview for my next job—chief counsel to the LaFollette civil liberties committee. This was before the days of commercial airlines, so if you worked for the government and traveled, you went by rail. Government attorneys rode first class, which meant parlor cars. On the way back to New York, I had settled back in my luxury seat, my mind wandering, thinking about Jessica and me and our life together. It suddenly hit me what a lovely person she was and that I was truly, absolutely in love. I became terribly impatient to get back home and tell her of this wonderful news. I arrived back at the apartment before Jessica came home from the office. When she came in the door, I immediately took her in my arms to tell her of my terrific discovery, that I was in love with her. She hardly registered excitement, let alone astonishment or surprise. Later, I chided her about this. "Here I finally get around to declaring my love for you," I told her, "and, moreover, for the first time in my life, and you didn't even react." She said, "Well, I've been so in love with you that I was sure you couldn't help but return my love." And we lived happily ever after, for forty-six years.

* * *

I accepted the job with the LaFollette civil liberties committee—formally the Sub-committee to Investigate Violations of Free Speech and the Rights of Labor of the Senate Committee on Education and Labor. Aubrey Williams first approached me about the job; as with the *Electric Bond and Share* case, I would be on loan from and remain on the payroll of the WPA. Jerome Frank, Lee Pressman, and Pat Jackson have each been credited or taken credit for pushing my appointment with Bob LaFollette, but I never actually found out how he came to approach Aubrey about me.

Young Bob, as he was called, was a political maverick like his father, Senator Robert LaFollette of Wisconsin. Elected as a Farmer-Labor candidate to the Senate, the elder LaFollette had been nearly alone in the Congress in opposing Woodrow Wilson's declaration of war in 1916. Six years later, he helped initiate, with the support of the American Federation of Labor, Sidney Hillman's Amalgamated Clothing Workers' Union, and the railroad brotherhoods, the Conference for Progressive Political Action in Chicago. The conference led to the calling of the Progressive party convention in Cleveland in 1924, which nominated Senator LaFollette and Senator Burton Wheeler of Montana to run for president and vice-president against Calvin Coolidge and the Democrat, John W. Davis. The Progressives, with LaFollette as their standard-bearer and the backing of a section of organized labor, received 4.8 million votes—the United States then was less than half its current size—at that time the largest vote ever for an independent ticket. Unfortunately, the Progessives were just that, a ticket, without a grass-roots organization, and failed to contest for Congress or for state and local government.

The following year, the senator died and Young Bob was elected as a Republican to fill his father's seat. In 1934, he joined the Wisconsin Progressive Republicans to form a statewide third party and was reelected to the Senate as a Progressive. Like his dad, Bob was a leading Progressive voice in the Senate and became a firm supporter of the New Deal.

The National Labor Relations Act of 1936, sponsored by New York's Senator Robert Wagner, with its establishment of the National Labor Relations Board (NLRB), became the cornerstone of FDR's collective bargaining policy. But enforcement of the act floundered because of the employers' use of labor espionage against, and violent resistance to, labor organization. The act was a response to the great upsurge of industrial unionism. The Mine Workers' John L. Lewis had put together the Committee on Industrial Organization and, inspired by passage of the Wagner Act, thousands of local organizers—many from the Communist party and Young Communist League—were laying the foundation for industry-wide unions in the rubber, steel, automobile, electric, and other mass-production industries.

My friend Nat Witt had left the AAA in 1934 for a job with the labor board that had been set up under the National Industrial Recovery Act. After passage of the Wagner Act, he was appointed to a staff job with the NLRB. The NLRB (and Nat in particular) immediately became the target of the open shop monopolies, their spokesmen in Congress, and the AFL craft unions. Heber Blankenhorn, an industrial economist with the NLRB, had taken a particular interest in la-

bor espionage and compiled enormous amounts of data about the
detective agencies employed by the corporations to undermine and
sabotage the CIO unions. One couldn't separate labor organizing
from the question of civil liberties, certainly not in that period in
which the right to freely organize was the most pressing civil liberties issue.

Bob LaFollette, since coming onto the Senate Education and Labor Committee in 1932, had been a leading voice for industrial democracy and workers' rights. Pressed by the NLRB and impressed by
Blankenhorn's information and arguments, LaFollette convinced the
Senate to establish a subcommittee to investigate "the full extent to
which the rights of labor to organize . . . [are] being denied and the
extent to which civil liberties are interfered with." Joining LaFollette
on the subcommittee was Senator Elbert D. Thomas of Utah, a
former missionary in Japan for the Church of Jesus Christ of Latter-
day Saints and a Greek and Latin scholar who liked to hold forth on
the Senate floor on the philosophical legacies of Thomas Aquinas and
Thomas Jefferson. Senator Thomas was convinced of the rectitude of
the New Deal and was himself the leading sponsor of the Civilian
Conservation Corps.

At the same time LaFollette took me on as chief counsel, he hired
Robert Wohlforth as staff secretary. Wohlforth was a young Republican from Connecticut, a West Point graduate recommended by Blankenhorn because of Wohlforth's staff work for the Nye Committee,
which was investigating the munitions industry, popularly known as
"the merchants of death," and its war profiteering. (Alger Hiss was
chief counsel for the Nye Committee, and Wohlforth would later joke
that it was his luck that the attorneys for the two committees he
worked for would be Hiss and Abt). Bob's tasks included making all
arrangements for the hearings, editing committee publications, hiring nonlegal staff, and maintaining press relations. Together the two
senators—an energetic forty-year-old Wisconsin Progressive and an
elderly Mormon intellectual—and the two senior staffers—an articulate and idealistic young Republican and myself, a rather laconic
young "closet" Communist lawyer, established a collegiality and
smooth working relationship in the midst of great turmoil in the industrial heartland and great pressures in the nation's capital.

Our investigations and hearings were to become a serious factor
in educating public opinion on the state of labor relations. In this
sense we became something of a model of how such a committee
should function. I developed a technique of holding hearings in
which we would bring all the witnesses together around a table.

LaFollette would ask questions and any of the witnesses were allowed to answer and any others could contradict them. The debate between witnesses was geared to developing the facts and letting the truth emerge. Being a committee investigating civil liberties violations, we were supremely conscious of allowing witnesses to say what they wished. Too many congressional investigations have been fatally flawed by the absence of procedural safeguards. I took the idea of such hearings, with witnesses confronting one another, from the Moscow trials then taking place. Subsequently, of course, we learned that these were grotesque persecutions Stalin used to consolidate his rule against political opponents within the Soviet Communist party. But at the time, I was blithely ignorant of this and took the example on good faith. As it developed, the structure of such hearings, properly administered, were helpful in getting at the truth.

About the same time I was hired by the subcommittee, Lee Pressman, who had ingratiated himself to John L. Lewis, left the WPA to become chief counsel to the CIO and the Steel Workers' Organizing Committee. What endeared him to Lewis was Lee's quick mind together with an almost intuitive ability to foresee the consequences of a course of action. It speaks volumes of his ambition and competitiveness (even with closest friends and comrades), that when Lee heard about the job with the LaFollette Committee, he decided he'd like to have that one in addition to the job with Lewis. Clearly this would have been a conflict of interest, in addition to a practical impossibility given the enormous workload of both jobs, but Lee nevertheless became rancorous when he didn't get the LaFollette job as well.

My job, as counsel, was to help select the targets of investigation, direct the investigation itself, and then prepare the hearings. But I didn't ask any questions of the witnesses except on the rarest of occasions. Earlier, in another set of widely publicized hearings that led to the establishment of the Securities and Exchange Commission, Ferdinand Pecora, counsel for that committee and later a New York State Supreme Court judge, did all the questioning. Consequently Pecora received all the headlines, much to the dismay of Senator Hugo Black, who headed the panel. LaFollette was determined not to have a repetition of that experience and quite properly insisted that the chairman should play the leading role in the investigation. But as a senator, and not being a lawyer with experience at examination of evidence and cross-examination of witnesses, he couldn't possibly sift through and study the available material to prepare the questioning. It was one of my roles to develop the examination in ad-

vance for the senator. Sometimes this became quite elaborate because I'd have to anticipate all possible answers to the questions. Preparing examination is like a family tree with branches sprouting
smaller branches. I'd have to not only write out the questions, but
also anticipate where to take the examination depending on each answer, indicating—all this was written out for LaFollette—what the
next question would be if the answer were "A," "B," "C," or whatever. This was a tedious process and a difficult experience but it was
also excellent training. To the extent that I was later skillful in cross-
examination as a trial attorney, it was due in no small part to my
work for the LaFollette committee. Initially, LaFollette was not much
of a cross-examiner himself—I'd sit beside him and whisper what to
do next—but he was a quick study and soon learned to handle himself well. He was anything but a figurehead, although he gave the
staff wide latitude to investigate and shape testimony. The hearings
themselves were sensational, drawing wide attention. There wasn't
a single first-rate Washington reporter who failed to attend, and some
of them, like Marquis Childs and Joe Alsop, would never write better
stories in their lives.

Wohlforth and I would make preliminary determinations regarding priorities for investigation, then present them to LaFollette, who
made the final decisions. Initially, our line of investigation was the
detective agencies and their relationships with the employers. It was
known for years that the agencies were used for strikebreaking, but
it is one thing to know this in general, quite another to compile a detailed record with all the evidence. Nobody, certainly not ourselves,
knew just how pervasive it was, to what extent the unions were infiltrated by professional informers, to what extent tear gas and Thompson submachine guns had been stockpiled by the employers. Most
trade union leaders took as a given that there were paid stool pigeons
in their ranks. But they were to learn how extensive was the practice, how high in the leadership some informers rose, and even, in
some cases, that their closest friends and co-workers were on the
employer's payroll. When word of what we were doing became
known, a host of people who had been roughed up or otherwise
abused started coming to us.

We were blessed with a team of dedicated and determined investigators. On my suggestion, Charlie Kramer, who had worked in a
similar capacity in the AAA's consumer counsel office, was hired and
immediately sent to Detroit. Luke Wilson, a Justice Department investigator, came to Bob Wohlforth to ask for a job and was told,
"There's a desk over there. Go to work." Allen Rosenberg, fresh out

of law school and full of enthusiasm—enough to work the first three months without pay—showed up and was immediately assigned to check FBI files on company use of tommy guns. We subpoenaed the industrial espionage agencies like Pinkerton's and William Burns Detective Agency and the Railway Audit and Inspection Company to appear before the committee and to bring their records with them. The night after the subpoenas were served, we subpoenaed their trash from the management of the buildings that housed their offices around the country. We came away with a mountain of torn-up papers. This was long before the days of the office shredder, so we had an infinite number of picture puzzles to put together. The entire staff—when we needed others, we'd borrow them from the NLRB— would work for days, sometimes weeks, pasting together these papers, which usually turned out to be company reports of their industrial spies, often complete with the informers' signatures.

Largely through Heber Blankenhorn, we learned about the extensive labor spy network—with an annual budget of nearly a million dollars, which was no small amount at the height of the depression— established by General Motors in the wake of the sit-down strikes at Flint and the Fisher Body plant in Kansas City. One GM employee from Saginaw later told the committee General Motors "so completely run this town and have it so well propagandized to their own good that one don't even dare talk here. You have no liberties at all. You couldn't belong to a union and breathe it to a soul. That soul would probably be a spy." The announcement by John L. Lewis that the UAW would seek a collective bargaining agreement with GM obviously spurred our work. For several weeks, Charlie Kramer and others interviewed United Automobile Workers officials, who provided evidence of spies and blacklists. We learned, during the Flint sit-down, that in addition to detective agencies hired by GM, the Flint Police Department maintained its own spy system and infiltrated the plant. At one point during his stay in Flint, Charlie Kramer learned of the possibility of the local police and sheriff's departments storming the plant on behalf of GM. Concerned about a potential bloodbath, he phoned me in Washington to ask that I get Senator LaFollette to intervene. He also called Pressman to alert the CIO. LaFollette and John L. Lewis consequently called Governor Murphy, who sent in the National Guard to prevent a massacre.

After first subpoenaing their files and spending several days examining them, we summoned the vice-presidents in charge of personnel for GM, Ford, and Chrysler to hearings in Washington. The GM hearings began on February 15, 1937, just after the end of the Flint sit-down, and lasted for seven days. We discovered that in the two previous years, fifty-two UAW members were Pinkerton spies who reported to GM headquarters. These included the president of a Chevy local in Flint and a vice-president of a Fisher Body local in Lansing. At various times, the union leadership—Homer Martin, Wyndham Mortimer, Walter Reuther, Bob Travis, among others—were kept under surveillance. Between January 1934 and July 1936, GM paid a total of $839,764.41 to detective agencies for labor espionage. The company's labor relations director, Harry Anderson, was hardly ingenuous in his explanation of these activities: "We were interested to know," he told the committee, "if there was any particular labor organization going on in town, and if so, why? The thing I was interested in was what was there about the plant operation that would give any need for an outside organization." A UAW organizer in Flint and Saginaw spoke more to the point: he informed the committee that he was trailed wherever he went in Flint; his car was sideswiped and three of his companions, also organizers, were hospitalized with injuries; hired goons forcibly detained him in a Bay City hotel room; no hall in Saginaw would allow him to rent premises for a union meeting. We also heard testimony from a Pinkerton spy who reported that through the agency's activities, one Lansing local virtually dissolved when it was discovered that it had no membership and all five officers were Pinkerton operatives.

Richard Frankensteen's story was particularly illustrative of the situation. For ten years he had worked in Detroit for the Chrysler Corporation as a trimmer in a Dodge plant. His father had also been a Dodge employee. Popular with his fellow workers, Richard rose to become chairman of what was then the company union local. When the limitations on collective bargaining became obvious, the workers formed an independent union of their own, the Automotive Industrial Workers' Association. Fourteen AIWA locals were organized in Frankensteen's Dodge plant, and he was elected president. This required a lot of energy for it meant speaking to and working with all fourteen locals. One night after meeting with the paint local, the local's vice-president, John Andrews, gave Frankensteen a ride home. This was the beginning of a close working relationship and an even better friendship between the two men. Their families lived only a few blocks from one another and they became frequent visitors in each others' homes. Their wives shopped together and their children were constant playmates. Five nights a week and all day Sundays the two men spent together in union work. Saturday nights the Frankensteens and the Andrewses got together for dinner and the movies. When vacation came around, the families would join together for a lakeside holiday, sharing a cabin and expenses. Their friendship lasted for a year before it was discovered that, since the evening they first met, John Andrews had been submitting detailed *daily* reports on Richard Frankensteen to the Corporations Auxiliary Company, a spy agency contracted to Chrysler.

For his services, Andrews was paid $40 a month; Corporations Auxiliary billed Chrysler $9 a day for the reports. In 1935, Chrysler paid Corporations Auxiliary the sum of $72,611.89 for all of its undercover work. The Frankensteen story was obviously only the tip of the knife. Heber Blankenhorn estimated that in 1936, some 236 detective agencies were involved in industrial spying, with the number of operatives totaling at least 40,000 and perhaps as many as triple that amount, for our records were far from complete. The William Burns Detective Agency operated in at least forty-three cities and Pinkerton's in thirty-five. A partial list of their clients included corporations, railroads, employers' associations, mine owners, and department stores. Besides Chrysler, Corporations Auxiliary's clients included the Aluminum Company of America, Dixie Greyhound Lines, Firestone Tire and Rubber, Quaker Oats, Radio Corporation of America, Standard Oil, Kellogg, Kelvinator, and the Statler Hotels. Pinkerton's serviced, among others, Bethlehem Steel, Campbell Soup, Continental Can, Montgomery Ward and Co., National Cash Register, Pennsylvania Railroad, and Shell Petroleum. Railway Audit's clients included Borden Milk, H. C. Frick Coal and Coke, Frigidaire, Brooklyn Jewish Hospital, Western Union, and Westinghouse.

I wrote the LaFollette committee's report on industrial espionage to the Senate Committee on Education and Labor. We found that the rationales offered by the employers for the use of labor spies included: protecting industry against communism; preventing sabotage, closely linked to the first rationale; detecting theft; improving efficiency of production; and improving relations between employers and employees, or "human engineering." Never advanced was the obvious goal of breaking the unions.

In our report, we noted that Pinkerton's had 309 industrial clients in the years 1933 to 1936; Corporations Auxiliary, 499; Burns, 440. Our fragmentary records of Railway Audit listed 165. The list read like a blue book of American industry. "The committee," I wrote, "was impressed with the overwhelming power inherent in the size and wealth of these corporations opposed to the individual worker who is spied on. Thus, Pinkerton's largest single industrial client was the General Motors Corporation, a billion-dollar corporation with a gross income in 1936 of almost a billion and a half dollars. In that same year, General Motors employed 230,572 workers, not one of whom, it was evident from the records, was exempt from espionage."

We found spies in every union, including AFL unions and even company unions. They were in rubber plants and textile mills, printing plants and saw mills, warehouses and glass factories. In a typical city like, say, Indianapolis, Pinkerton's alone had operatives in the Amalgamated Clothing Workers' Union, the Street Railways Union, the American Federation of Hosiery Workers, the Brotherhood of Railway Shop Crafts, the Brewery Workers' Union, the Gas Station Attendant Union, the Pulp and Paper Mill Workers' Union, the Teamsters' Union, the United Auto Workers, the Electrical and Radio Workers' Union, the Wire and Cable Workers' Federal Union, and local unions of clerical workers, glass blowers, grocers, warehouse workers, molders, and stereotypers. The same story repeated itself in scores of industrial cities across the land. Our evidence, we reported to the Senate, "provides a most convincing demonstration that no occupation group is free from the spy's constant surveillance—not miners deep in the earth, nor sailors at sea; neither cannery workers, skilled engineers or nurses in hospitals."

The spy system placed the employers at the very heart of the unions from the inception of organizing drives. News of organizers traveling through town, contacts among the employers, names of those workers who showed an interest, names of those who joined, all plans and activities of the union—all were as available to employers as if they were running the unions themselves. The corporations had advance notice of all union presentations of grievances and demands, strike plans, strengths and weaknesses, and ability to sustain a strike action. "To take a comparable situation," we wrote, "if detective agencies had sent a number of operatives into business houses and one had become vice president of a large national corporation, others had become presidents of small firms and others had worked their way into positions of confidence and power of various kinds throughout the corporate set-up of the country, their capacity for wrecking would be practically limitless."

With the espionage system shrouded in mystery and concealed in myriad ways, the craving for yet more information increased. We presented the terrifying picture of General Motors as a hopeless maze of distrust. Without exception, every GM plant manager engaged a private detective service. This was insufficient. The personnel directors of Fisher Body and Chevrolet also hired spy services, spreading a superstructure of espionage over the basic spy network of these two divisions. Yet another superstructure was erected, however, by the labor relations division of the GM executive offices, responsible directly to the president, which did not trust the plant detective service or the division detective service. A separate Pinkerton's contract was entered into, in which a weird framework of spies among spies was created. Finally, the irresistible logic of espionage reached its apex when GM used its Pinkerton's agents to spy upon its Corporations Auxiliary Co. spies. I was reminded of this in the McCarthy years when we used to sing, "Who's going to investigate the man who investigates the man who investigates the investigator?"

We summarized the report to the Senate by declaring: "Not only is the worker's freedom of association nullified by the employers' spies, but his freedom of action, of speech and of assembly is completely destroyed. Fear harries his every footstep, caution muffles his words. He is in no sense any longer a free American. In a constitutional sense his very position reflects the mockery and contempt those who demand constitutional rights for themselves deny to others. . . . The right to work means nothing if it is at the expense of more important rights."

* * *

The LaFollette committee developed a wide range of inquiries. We sent Allen Rosenberg to Harlan County, Kentucky, scene of the greatest violence in the entire coal industry. "Bloody Harlan," it was commonly called by miner and mine owner alike. The Harlan County Coal Operators' Association, the employers' group, had vowed to keep Harlan union-free and had been successful for years. But the United Mine Workers, under John L. Lewis, were organizing nevertheless, under conditions controlled by sheriff's deputies, local police, and thugs, all in the hire of the coal operators. Years earlier, a group of concerned private individuals, primarily religious workers—my latter-day friend and political comrade Arnold Johnson among them—had conducted an investigation of civil liberties in Harlan County that was abruptly terminated by the mine owners' threats of violence. In Bloody Harlan, company gunmen were as common as company spies in Detroit.

When the LaFollette committee investigators went to Harlan, they were compelled to stay in another county. Coal thugs planted bombs in a number of cars with out-of-state licenses. Allen Rosenberg remembers paying a bellhop to open the hood of his car each morning, much like the storied Mafia don's wife. When the companies ran out of gunmen, they convinced the local law authorities to release prisoners, who would then be deputized. Rosenberg interviewed the warden of the Frankfurt jail after a mysterious fire caused the deputies, in moving the prisoners elsewhere, to allow a number of "escapes."

I remember perusing a copy of the constitution and by-laws of the Harlan County Coal Operators' Association, which enumerated the duties of members and designated dues assessments. One of the purposes of the association listed in the constitution was to keep Harlan County free of trade unions. In a hearing we held on the matter, LaFollette asked the employers' representatives what percentage of the dues collected was dispersed for this purpose, for that and the other purpose, and it turned out that the entire budget of the association was for antiunion activities. Our investigation of Harlan was a significant factor in allowing the United Mine Workers to finally organize in the county.

In March 1937, Lewis's Steel Workers' Organizing Committee was rebuffed in its request for signed contracts by Youngstown Sheet and Tube, Republic Steel, and Inland Steel—the giants of "Little Steel." This followed on the heels of successful organizing drives ending in contracts with U.S. Steel and Bethlehem. On May 26, the Little Steel Strike pitted the companies against two hundred thousand striking workers in a dozen communities in what would become one of the bloodiest and costliest labor conflicts in American history. Armed attacks by company police, supplemented by American Legionnaires, were launched against striking workers in Masillon, Ohio; Monroe, Michigan; and Johnstown, Pennsylvania. Company unions organized back-to-work campaigns, while the steel companies flooded the air waves and print media with talk of "outside agitators" and "mob rule."

On May 30, Memorial Day, two thousand union supporters, including large numbers of steelworkers' wives, mothers, and children, gathered at union headquarters in Chicago, several blocks away from the Republic Steel plant. Four days earlier, the first day of the strike, twenty-three persons were arrested on charges of unlawful assembly, but in the next days the police commissioner assured the union that peaceful picketing would be allowed. After a brief rally, the demonstrators marched peaceably—unarmed—across a huge empty field toward the plant. The Chicago police, armed with guns and tear gas to "protect company property," spread out across the field, although it did not belong to Republic Steel. They opened fire with guns and tear gas, killing nine demonstrators and injuring one hundred, including forty who were wounded by gunfire.

Predictably, the major newspapers displayed hostility to the victims rather than the police. The *Chicago Tribune* described the demonstration as an "attack" by "a trained military unit of a revolutionary body." The *New York Times*'s headline announced, "Steel Mob Halted." We learned that Paramount News, a motion picture news agency, had a photographer at the scene who had filmed the entire incident. Paramount told us that it would not exhibit the film publicly because its graphic depiction of the event could incite riots throughout the country. We subpoenaed the film and showed it, in great secrecy, to an audience consisting only of Senators LaFollette and Thomas, Bob Wohlforth, and myself. We examined it over and over, in slow motion, duplicating each frame.

What we saw were scenes of peaceful demonstrators, some of them children, with placards reading "CIO" and "Republic vs. the People," confronted by dozens of uniformed policemen firing point blank into the crowd and then moving in to club the survivors as they tried frantically to escape. The sound system recorded the roar of police fire and the wails of the victims. Subsequent scenes showed the ground strewn with dead and wounded, while other demonstrators were isolated alone, surrounded by two or three policemen clubbing them to the ground. One cop would strike a demonstrator across the back, another on top of the head, while a third policeman would smash in the person's face as if wielding a baseball bat. One man was shown with his hands in the air, surrendering, when the police closed in with their nightsticks, beat him from all directions, until he fell to the ground, then beat him some more. (One of the dead was delivered to the undertaker with his brains literally beaten out of his skull.) Another scene showed a man shot through the back and paralyzed from the waist. Two policemen tried to make him stand to get into a paddy wagon, but on releasing his arms, he crumbled face first to the ground. Only two words on the sound track were clearly audible: "God Almighty."

Wohlforth, myself, and three other committee staff members flew to Chicago to conduct a ten-day investigation into the massacre. The day we arrived the ninth victim died, a seventeen-year-old boy who had joined the pickets in hopes of getting a job at the plant after the strike was settled. When we later held hearings, LaFollette questioned some of the police who had been present. A Sergeant Lyons testified that the demonstrators were marching "as if under command." When asked if they resembled any military formation he'd ever seen, Lyons said they looked like "the army of the 'Reds'" or maybe "the Mexican army." A patrolman testified that he thought the demonstrators "were under the influence of marijuana cigarettes" because of their "monotonous chant, 'CIO, CIO.'"

A crucial witness was Dr. Lawrence Jacques, a childhood friend of mine. (His sister, Alice, was the one who asked me to accompany her in hosting Sergei Eisenstein in Chicago.) Larry was a pathologist who was present on the day of the massacre because the union anticipated trouble. As a witness before our committee, Larry brought along a rubber doll and a sharp steel pick. He had performed autopsies on some of the victims and had seen all of the corpses at the mortuary. He demonstrated the entry and exit wounds of each victim, using his doll and pick. Each one of them was shot in the back or the side, none in front. Of those wounded by gunshot, twenty-seven were hit from behind, nine from the side, and only four from the front. Clearly the police claims of having "fired only in the air" or in self-defense could not be reconciled with the medical evidence.

Our hearings received front-page publicity across the country. If they were not decisive, they were certainly helpful in settling the Little Steel Strike and winning union recognition. I wrote the LaFollette committee's report of those hearings, which would be my last job with the committee. LaFollette raised the question of ending the committee's work; he was tired and he had no assurance of further funding from Congress. (Although, as it turned out, the committee's mandate was renewed and it went on, without me, to conduct an important investigation and a memorable set of hearings into the near-feudal working conditions in the agricultural fields of California.)

The LaFollette civil liberties committee hearings never resulted in any legislation. LaFollette himself never proposed any, although we had many discussions about restricting corporations from using espionage against workers, prohibiting the importation of scab labor under interstate commerce statutes, and other possibilities. But the work of the committee was a powerful aid to the CIO organizing drives, and it put the private detective agencies out of the labor spy business. Not that it ended corporate espionage against labor radicals. That business was socialized when J. Edgar Hoover took it over. I suppose there was a certain ironic continuity to my life: in my days as counsel for the LaFollette committee, I cross-examined stool pigeons as a government lawyer. In the cold war years, I cross-examined stool pigeons employed by the government. There was also a continuity in the nature of the stool pigeons. Then, they insisted they were not interested in harming unions, only "Communists." Later, they were still concerned only about "Communists," never the peace movement, the labor movement, or the civil rights movement.

* * *

While I was still with LaFollette, the National Lawyers' Guild held its founding convention in Washington, D.C. The guild was established by a broad range of lawyers grouped in support of the New Deal, including from the labor movement and from within in government itself. The guild was a reaction to the American Bar Association's establishmentarian positions, which defended the Republican-dominated Supreme Court against FDR's court-packing plan, and to the ABA's refusal to admit Black lawyers to its ranks. A leading Washington radio station offered the guild thirty minutes of air time to broadcast to the nation, and the convention organizers wanted LaFollette and Robert Jackson to speak on their behalf. Then working for LaFollette and previously for Jackson, I was asked to extend the invitations. Both accepted, but LaFollette—who was not a lawyer—only on condition that I write his speech. I can't recall the content of his remarks but I do remember the opening line: "As a senator, I have learned to live with lawyers, but not to love them." The words were written for LaFollette, but the sentiment—or lack of it—was strictly my own.

About the time I left the LaFollette committee, Rep. Martin Dies of Texas convened the first public hearing of the Special Committee on Un-American Activities. The Dies Committee, as it became known, assuming the more famous mantle of HUAC (House Un-American Activities Committee) only with the onset of the cold war, quickly became a counterweight to the LaFollette committee. Because the latter enjoyed the support of the CIO, the civil liberties community, and New Deal partisans, the right-wing was unceasingly hostile. In the Dies Committee, the anti–New Deal forces found a rallying point. Besides the manufacturers who were thrown on the defensive by the CIO, some of the more conservative AFL leaders volunteered to testify before Dies as to the nefarious conspiracy that was the Congress of Industrial Organizations.

The infant National Lawyers' Guild also became an early target of the consolidated right wing. Besides the CIO, the LaFollette committee, unemployment compensation, social security, and other threats at home, the right found in the guild and other creatures of the New Deal era homegrown reflections of the Spanish republic fighting for its existence against European fascism. The Liberty League, Henry Ford, Father Coughlin, Gerald L. K. Smith, the German-American Bund, and other apologists for the Third Reich organized a mass base for the falsehoods and slanders of the Dies Committee. The National Lawyers' Guild also had right-wing detractors—albeit with civil libertarian rhetoric—within its own ranks. Morris Ernst, a leader of the American Civil Liberties Union—who, years later, it was discovered, was reporting on the ACLU to his close friend, J. Edgar Hoover—led a campaign to dissolve the guild only a few months after it was organized. Even such New Deal liberals as Jerome Frank, a founding member of the guild, wilted under the pressure and left the organization within a year.

A decade later, of course, HUAC was in full bloom and the Time of the Toad—in Dalton Trumbo's memorable phrase—had taken hold in the country. In this atmosphere, when I was beginning to come under public exposure and attack, Bob LaFollette—who had just been defeated in his reelection bid by a freshman senator named Joseph McCarthy—contributed an article to *Collier's* (February 8, 1947) in which he wrote: "When I was chairman of the Senate Civil Liberties Committee, I was forced to take measures in an effort to stamp out [Communist] influences within my own committee staff." As his father had opposed U.S. entry into World War I, Young Bob opposed U.S. entry into the war against fascism. During the course of the war, he abandoned much of his Progressive heritage, leading to the tragic deterioration—and eventual suicide—of one of the country's most outstanding public figures. LaFollette's assertion in *Collier's* was pure fantasy: there had been no purge of any kind—let alone against Communists—in the Senate Civil Liberties Committee. Pat Jackson, a LaFollette confidant and himself a resolute anticommunist, reflected on recommending me to LaFollette in his oral history many years later: "John Abt . . . was an unpretentious, reserved mild-spoken fellow, with terrific precision in his utterance and in his cutting aside all superfluous matters, getting at the heart of any problem. . . . Because of his obvious, fine intellect, plus his apparent lack of any self-aggrandizement, he would be ideal for the job. In subsequent conversations with Bob [LaFollette], he, on numerous occasions, said to me that we couldn't have had a better choice than John Abt."

About the same time, Bob Wohlforth was compiling his own oral history. He remembered: "I wouldn't say that any of Abt's work was tinged by a communist slant while he was on the Committee, whatever his allegiance might have been. On the other hand, what the hell was communism? LaFollette and I went to the reception at the Soviet Embassy for those Russian flyers, you know the 37 who flew over the Pole. We had been working late and he had an invite and we wanted something to eat and drink, so we went there. And who did we run into? The Chicago *Tribune* reporter. The next morning on the front page was a big story—LaFollette and chief investigator at Soviet Embassy getting instructions on what to do next."

For the record, I don't recall having a single meeting with a Party functionary during my tenure with LaFollette. Of course I met with CIO organizers all the time, many of whom I knew to be Communists. Wyndham Mortimer and Bob Travis were top leaders of the UAW, for example. Lee Pressman was chief counsel for the CIO. I met with Jim Matles, then an organizer for the metalworkers' industrial unions, to discuss an investigation of the detective agencies infiltrating their shops. It is to their credit and honor that the Communists were to be found in the midst, and usually at the head, of every great labor struggle of the period. It was precisely because of their dedication, selflessness, and class-consciousness that John L. Lewis—no more a Communist than FDR or Martin Dies, for that matter—tapped the Communists to head up hundreds of organizing drives. Lewis knew that after the slaughter at Republic Steel on Memorial Day, it was Communist party workers that laid out the dead bodies and that two hundred Republic strikers joined the Party that day because they knew that the Communists were willing to die for them.

* * *

Had I been "purged" from the LaFollette committee, it is hardly likely I'd have then been hired by the Justice Department, which is, in fact, where I next landed. When I had made up my mind to leave LaFollette, I visited Bob Jackson, who was now assistant attorney general in charge of the antitrust division, to inquire about a job in his "shop." Jackson greeted me warmly and on the spot offered me the position of chief of the trial section of his division, with the title of special assistant to the attorney general. The title was lofty but the fact is that all attorneys in the department had the same title. Although I hardly went there for mercenary reasons, the job paid $7,500 a year, quite an exorbitant sum, the maximum for a government lawyer at the time.

Jackson left the department just a few months after I came on, when FDR named him solicitor general. The solicitor general, in essence the government's attorney, is responsible for selecting, organizing, and preparing all government cases that reach the Supreme Court. The position is often a stepping stone to the Court itself, as it would prove to be for Jackson and as it had been for his predecessor, Stanley Reed, whom the president had just nominated. Bob's place in the Justice Department was taken by Thurmond Arnold, whom I'd known slightly in the AAA. A Rocky Mountain native, Thurmond was a Yale Law professor before coming to the AAA and government service. Extremely energetic and a persuasive talker, full of a variety of novel ideas about the law—many of them sound, some of them half-baked—I always thought of Arnold as a wild man from the Wild West.

The work at the department turned out to be rather dull, particularly in comparison with the LaFollette committee job. The Anti-trust Division was and remains today responsible for enforcement of the anti-trust acts passed by Congress. When I took the job, I was under few illusions about the social usefulness and validity of the present laws to be a real brake on the growth of monopoly and the concentration of wealth in the United States. The principal anti-trust law, the Sherman Anti-trust Act, predated the New Deal by two decades and was enacted under the administration of FDR's uncle Teddy, giving the latter the unearned reputation as a "Trust Buster." Understanding the ineffectiveness of the antitrust laws, I came to the Justice Department without confidence that we could accomplish any serious social innovations or establish a more just and equitable economic system. Nothing I did or saw at the Department of Justice did anything but bolster that skepticism.

My responsibility as head of the trial section was to supervise the work of some fifty lawyers who would investigate reports as we received them of violations of the antitrust laws, then decide whether they were meritorious and either settle the matter with the offending companies or institute lawsuits to enforce the antitrust statutes.

While I was working at the Justice Department in 1938, FDR sent a message to Congress—to my mind, among his strongest and most perceptive—calling attention to the danger of monopoly. He talked about the growth of "private power" in this country, which was threatening to become stronger than the public power of the government itself. FDR warned that such private power was at the essence of fascism. He concluded with a proposal to establish the Temporary National Economic Commission (TNEC) to investigate the growth and role of monopoly power in the United States. The TNEC would include representatives from the various cabinet departments and federal agencies dealing with monopoly—Treasury, Justice, Securities and Exchange Commission, Federal Trade Commission, etc.—as well as representatives of the House and Senate. The TNEC would hold public hearings on the danger of monopolization of the economy, and each member agency and department would present examples of monopoly practices within their respective jurisdictions. Because of my experience with LaFollette, Arnold asked me to prepare the Justice Department's presentation to the TNEC.

I was intent on leaving government service, however. I'd long since concluded that the antitrust approach was no answer to U.S. monopoly, that nothing short of a fundamental restructuring of the economy would suffice. I could propose no reformist remedy. The TNEC would eventually hold its hearings and make its report, and that would more or less conclude the government's concern with the matter, thereby implicitly underlining FDR's initial alarm. In 1938, World War II was becoming imminent and simply took precedence as the New Deal ground to a halt. The war would of course greatly secure the grip of U.S. monopoly and would create the military-industrial complex. FDR's warning of monopoly's dangers and the ineffectiveness of the government's response would, a generation later, reverberate in President Eisenhower's warning of the dangers of the military-industrial complex.

When I left the Justice Department, Bob Jackson wrote me a very warm and fulsome letter, telling me how much I would be missed in the government. Some time after his appointment as solicitor general, he had called me to his office to ask me to take on a case about which, he told me, the president was greatly concerned. The case concerned the removal of the director of the Tennessee Valley Authority and involved the undecided question of presidential power to remove a high-ranking administrative officer whose appointment required Senate confirmation. The case was disposed of without my intervention, but I felt complimented that Jackson would ask me to handle it. A couple of years later, I went to see Bob to congratulate him on his appointment as attorney general. This was during the difficult period of the Finnish-Soviet war. The Dies Committee's activities were being stepped up and, in general, a more intense period of anticommunism was underway. Hitler's invasion of the USSR was imminent. After congratulating Jackson, he told me, "Well, John, while I'm attorney general at least, the Roosevelt years won't end like the second Wilson administration with the Palmer Raids," referring to the Justice Department's postwar roundup of thousands of radicals and the deportation of those who had immigrated from other lands. Of course with the death of Roosevelt and the end of the war, the cold war brought a series of repressive legislation that would chill every aspect of American political and cultural life. In the end, if there weren't Palmer Raids, there was McCarthyism; and on the Supreme Court, no justice was more Draconian than the Court's ideological leader, Robert Jackson.

After I left the department, Thurmond Arnold was appointed to the U.S. Court of Appeals in Washington, D.C. Not much later, he left the court to become founding partner of Arnold, Fortas, and Porter—Abe Fortas and Paul Porter had also been with us in the AAA—which he built into one of Washington's largest and most lucrative law firms. The firm also acquired a reputation—quite unjustified by my standards—for progressivism. In the fifties, when the first McCarran Act challenge cases reached the Supreme Court, I called Thurmond to ask if he would represent the Communist party before the Court. We had a very warm conversation, basking in friendly nostalgia. He said he would have to "consult his partners," an old and familiar dodge. Two days later he called to say, with of course his "deepest personal regrets," that his "partners" had decided against taking the case. That was the last I ever heard from him.

* * *

When I returned to Washington in 1936 to take the job with the LaFollette committee, Jessica remained in New York. We commuted on weekends, she to Washington one week, me to New York the next. David, her son, was eight years old and boarding at a progressive school in Washington while Jessica completed her months-long move to New York. Once the move was complete, David lived with Jessica and, on those weekends she visited me, he was always in tow. David was quite a bright boy, with a quick wit and real intelligence, but he was also a difficult child, given to uncontrollable rages, although it was some time before his illness was diagnosed. Judy, David's teenaged stepsister—Hal Ware married Jessica after Judy's mother had died—had been orphaned by Hal's death. At the age of fifteen she decided that, of the available adult candidates, she wanted Jessica to adopt her. Their love was mutual and Judy became Jessica's daughter.

When I told Marion about my relationship with Jessica, she was quite pleased and liked to think that she had initiated our love affair, a typical indulgence of Marion's imagination. In early 1935, my Grandmother Shire died, and mother moved to Washington to live with me. We found an elegant apartment for the two of us on northwest Fifteenth Street, across from Meridian Park. The flat included a two-story living room, with a fireplace at one end; a second-floor master bedroom (this was mother's) with a balcony overlooking the living room; and a top floor with three tiny rooms, one of which was my bedroom. When I brought Jessica home to meet mother for the first time, mother was quite taken with her. But like mothers everywhere, she firmly believed that no woman was quite good enough for her son. She indicated nothing to me, but confided in Marion: "Why does John have to pick a wife older than himself?" That Jessica beat me into the world by eight years was the only "flaw" mother could find. But Marion had decided that she wanted Jessica for a sister well before I had made up my mind about marriage. My tendency to dawdle in those days was noted by all who were close to me. "Don't worry, my dear," Marion comforted mother, "Jessica is one of those durable blonds. She'll outlast him."

By the time I took the job at the Justice Department, we'd been exchanging weekend commutes for over a year. The situation had become intolerable; I would go mad waiting for each weekend. We finally decided to marry, and one weekend I came to New York with the intention of making good on my honorable intentions. But I learned that New York required a Wasserman blood test for a marriage license. Friends told us, however, that Connecticut had no such requirement, so early that Saturday morning we set out for Greenwich. At the town's city hall, we discovered that our information was false. A Wasserman was required there as well, and we could no more arrange a blood test on the spot in Greenwich than we could in New York. Meantime, we had confided our plans to Mattie and Phyllis Silverman and Pete and Ann Peters, who waited in our Village apartment with a friend from the Soviet embassy who was providing champagne for our triumphant return. Jessica and I spent the day in the small towns of western Connecticut and Westchester County trying to find some place that didn't require a Wasserman. Finally we located a justice of the peace in Pound Ridge, N.Y., who performed the ceremony. It was evening by then and Jessica slept during the drive home. The Silvermans and the embassy fellow had long since departed but Pete and Ann had stayed on to toast our marriage.

Jessica constantly put me to shame by the amount of work she assumed and by the quality of her product—be it literary, political, or culinary. A dear Soviet friend christened her the "Sweet Horse" because no matter how heavy the load on her back, she never balked. Work for her, in Marx's phrase, was not a means of existence but a vital necessity of life. In her personal relations with her family and co-workers; with her readers with whom she conducted a voluminous correspondence as a daughter of the American revolution who was an accomplished interpreter of the Russian revolution; with scores of students, scholars, and writers who came to her for assistance and whose requests she unfailingly honored, Jessica gave something of a preview of what human relations might be like if the social transformation to which she devoted her life was ever able to mature and prosper. It was always a point of some pride with me to be introduced, as I was frequently was, as Mr. Smith.

Jessica's workaholic tendencies were balanced by an equally powerful side of her personality: she was an incurable romantic. I quickly lost count of the number of times I sat beside her at a performance of Romeo and Juliet in one version or another—play, ballet, opera, movie—and handed her a clean, dry handkerchief when, early on, hers became sodden and useless. A sentimentalist of monumental proportions, she read *War and Peace* perhaps a dozen times through.

And while, unlike me, she never indulged in frivolous reading, she avidly followed the adventures of Mary Worth and couldn't bear to miss an installment.

During the summer of my year with LaFollette, we decided to rent a house on Long Island, where the Silvermans would live and Jessica and I would join them on weekends. We had the good fortune to meet up with John Howard Lawson, the playwright and teacher, who was then in Hollywood writing screenplays. One of Pete Peters's Party responsibilities was the Hollywood crowd, and through him, we befriended Jack Lawson. Jack had a house out on the island, in Mastic, an early American house dating from the seventeenth century, complete with seven fireplaces, which he gave to us for the summer. It was here that Jessica and I examined every aspect of the question of children and collectively decided with Mattie and Phyllis that they should have a child. Besides the Silvermans and the Peterses, Nat and Anna Witt and Harry Freeman, the American director of the TASS news agency in New York, and his wife, Vera, were frequent guests. One weekend we entertained twelve people, and Phyllis, then young and inexperienced as a hostess, had prepared enough provisions to allow for exactly one drink and one peanut-butter sandwich per guest.

Besides inheriting David and Judy from Jessica, my new family included her fabled mother-in-law, Ella Reeve Bloor. We became quite fond of each other and she was also quite close to Marion. My mother would say of this energetic old lady with the flashing eyes and the warm handclasp, "She is a natural phenomenon, like Niagara Falls." For two years after our marriage, Jessica "ghosted" *We Are Many*, Mother Bloor's autobiography. In her introduction to the book, Elizabeth Gurley Flynn quotes from the Irish play *Cathleen-ni-Houlihan*, in which a young man is asked as he enters the house, "Did you see a little old lady going down the road?" He answers in surprise, having seen Ireland itself in the form of a woman, "No, but I saw a young girl, and she had the walk of a queen."

The Party urged us—Communists working in the government—to expand our contacts and associations, to influence others. Happily, this meant a good deal of socializing, something at which we had accumulated a large body of experience, dating to my AAA days. One evening, when I was still at the Justice Department, I organized a cocktail party at mother's and my apartment. It was considered a great and notable success, with the attendance of Bob LaFollette, Bob Jackson, every member of the National Labor Relations Board, and most of my co-workers. But Jessica, who was also in Washington—this was her weekend to visit—was hidden away in Marion's apartment. Like our Party membership, our marriage remained in the closet. It wouldn't do in official Washington to have a special assistant to the attorney general married to the editor of *Soviet Russia Today* at a time when the administration was still torn in debate over whether Moscow was to be an ally or enemy.

Our situation was untenable and clearly couldn't continue in that manner much longer. The question of our jobs arose. Should Jessica give up the magazine to move to Washington or should I leave the government for New York? If we moved to New York, what would I do for a job? In my own mind, I was prepared to be a Party section organizer, coordinating and helping the work of a collection of local clubs. This was of course a terrible idea, one for which my particular skills and abilities were uniquely ill-suited.

Jessica and I decided to ask for an appointment with Earl Browder, the leader of the Party, and he invited us to his home in Yonkers. I'd never met Browder before. I told him a little bit about myself, my background, my father, his relations with Sidney Hillman. Browder stopped me right there and said, "That's what you should do. You ought to be Hillman's attorney. Sidney would be delighted to have a 'Pressman' of his own." (Lee Pressman was now Philip Murray's lawyer in the CIO.) Browder was convinced that Hillman "would love" to have me, with my background and his relationship with my father.

I called Hillman, told him who I was, and made a date to meet him in Washington on July 5, 1938. I told Sidney I was leaving the government, that I'd married Jessica—Hillman knew her from the mid-twenties when she had helped him and the Amalgamated set up a clothing factory in the Soviet Union—and that I was looking for work and was interested in labor law. He offered me a job, duties unspecified, at five thousand dollars a year, considerably less than my Justice Department job paid. Later that afternoon, I wrote to Hillman:

> I fully recognize and indeed anticipated what you said about the limitation on monetary reward to be found in labor work. That question, however, I regard as entirely secondary, if I can be assured of an opportunity for plenty of useful work. . . . [Thurmond] Arnold places a rather inflated value on my usefulness to him—particularly in connection with the monopoly investigation which lies very close to his heart. I have therefore given him no hint of my present state of mind. . . . It will be helpful to me if an

early decision can be made so that I can beat my retreat before I get too heavily involved in the monopoly investigation."

Two weeks later Sidney Hillman hired me. I was to be chief counsel of the Amalgamated Clothing Workers' Union, and would remain so for the next decade.

3

At Hillman's Side

Beginning with the campaigns in Chicago when I was a child, the Amalgamated succeeded by the midtwenties in organizing more than 90 percent of the men's clothing industry nationwide. Hillman proudly boasted that the union had, after being organized, never called a single strike. This record continued throughout my tenure, which lasted until December 1947. Consequently, despite its almost 100 percent rate of organization, the wage rates in men's clothing remained among the lowest of all industries in the country.

The Left in the labor movement had always considered the Amalgamated a "class collaborationist" rather than a "class struggle" union. Its "perfect" no-strike record gave credence to the charge. Whatever leftist opposition to the leadership policies that may have existed had been crushed in the twenties, long before I became associated with the union. Those partisans of social democracy who had long criticized—with much justice—the discipline and top-down leadership structure of the Communist party never took a very careful glance at the practices of Sidney Hillman and other adherents of their own ideology. But the union was not without its own contradictions. The entire leadership, not only Hillman, emerged from the socialist traditions of the Jewish working class that emigrated from eastern Europe. They were fiercely independent, and the Amalgamated never affiliated with the AFL. Its origins were as a breakaway competitor—at the time of the strikes at Hart, Shaffner and Marx during my boyhood—of the AFL-affiliated United Garment Workers.

The Amalgamated had always exhibited a bit of independence in electoral politics. In 1924, it was a strong supporter of the presiden-

tial candidacy of Robert LaFollette, Sr., as a Progressive. When the
union organized a clothing factory in the Soviet Union in the infancy
of the revolution, it was alone among U.S. labor in such efforts; my
guess is that the factory was, in part, a maneuver by Hillman to still
the voices of the leftist forces in its ranks. Len DeCaux, my friend and
colleague as editor of *CIO News,* wrote in his memoirs: "The Communists brought misery out of hiding in the workers' neighborhoods.
They paraded it with angry demands through the main streets to the
public square, and on to City Hall. They raised particular hell." Sidney respected this role of the Communist party and was at times prepared to enter into a partnership with it. But such hell-raising would
never be allowed within the ranks of the Amalgamated Clothing
Workers' Union.

Sidney was a superb operator, an opportunist par excellence with
a long nose for where the opportunities lay. He was physically unprepossessing—heavyset, medium height, in general nondescript—
and spoke with a heavy Jewish accent. But he had enormous drive
and was the unchallenged boss of the union. His temper was explosive; he would fly into incredible rages, particularly against his immediate associates, men with whom he had grown up and with
whom he had fought for decades to build the union. If difficulties
arose, he of course was never at fault, it was invariably someone else,
and Sidney would raise hell. Alone among his close co-workers, I was
seemingly immune from his verbal abuse. Ours was always a pleasant, warm relationship. He always extolled my father and told me
that had he not died so young, father would have certainly become a
big shot in the National Recovery Administration. This, from Sidney,
was indeed high praise. I assumed that it was because he always saw
me as my father's son and deferred to my class roots that he exempt-
ed me from the rage he exhausted on others.

Characteristically, in terms of his position in the union, none of his
associates ever called him Sidney. He was always Hillman, distinguished from all others; although when he wasn't present everyone
called him Sidney. I had to conform and called him Hillman to his
face, never addressing him as Sidney. In CIO circles, on the other
hand, he was known only as Sidney. It took a while to master the
proper etiquette, depending on the setting.

In 1938, Sidney was also chair of the Textile Workers' Organizing
Committee (TWOC), established by the CIO to organize the completely unorganized textile industry located primarily in the South—
just as Phil Murray was named by John L. Lewis to head up the Steel
Workers' Organizing Committee. Being Sidney's man, I was also the

attorney for the TWOC. My initial work in the union was the normal
fare for a labor lawyer—helping negotiate and then drafting collective bargaining agreements, appearing before the NLRB in election
and complaint cases, drafting legal documents and convention reso-
lutions. Early on, Sidney had me redraft the union constitution to
omit the original preamble, which used language about "class struggle." Because of the nature of the Amalgamated and the absence of
any real strike struggles or militant organizing drives, none of these
jobs was too rigorous.

I had been a member of the Illinois Bar, and as a government lawyer in Washington, I didn't need to belong to the District of Columbia
Bar. But at this time I was living and working in New York and membership in the state bar was a necessity. Ordinarily, if an attorney is
of "good moral character" and has practiced for five years or more,
this is a pro forma procedure. One is admitted "on motion" to a new
state bar. I had letters in hand, testifying to my good moral character, from Jerome Frank, Robert Jackson, and Thurmond Arnold, as
prestigious a legal trio as one could imagine. Living in Jackson
Heights, Queens, I applied to the Second Judicial Department (Brook-
lyn-Queens) of the New York State Bar and was asked to appear before its character committee. Only later did I learn that the Second
Judicial Department had the reputation of being exceedingly reactionary and anti–New Deal. The first question put to me by the character committee was, "Does the fact that you have been in all of these
New Deal jobs mean that you are a member of the Communist Party?" I answered, truthfully if not entirely forthcoming, "No, it does not
mean that." I was next asked, "Are you raising your son with a religious education?" I again said no. The committee members said they
would have to consult with others to see if my failure in this area was
grounds for disqualification. At the end of the interview, I was told
that it was obvious that I was a good lawyer but that, in several
weeks, I would have to take the bar exam. I asked why, if they
thought I was such a fine lawyer, and was told, "Oh, if you're as good
as you say you are, you shouldn't have any trouble passing." I didn't,
but it was an annoyance nevertheless and a sign of the changing
times.

My first job for both the Amalgamated and the textile workers was
to handle negotiations in setting minimum wage standards under the
Wage and Hour Act of 1938. For this task, the Amalgamated set up a
small, one-room office for me next to those of Labor's Non-partisan
League in Washington. The law set a maximum work week of forty
hours, a twenty-five-cents-an-hour minimum wage with time and a

half for overtime, and prohibited homework, a provision particularly important for the clothing industry. Various industry-wide committees, which included the interested unions, could recommend a higher minimum wage for their particular industries to the government's wage-and-hour commission. The Wage and Hour Act, as it developed, was the final piece of New Deal legislation—FDR was to declare that after Doctor New Deal retired, Doctor Win the War became the national physician—and was passed over bitter opposition in Congress and from Roosevelt's own vice-president, John Nance Garner. I was with Hillman and John L. Lewis at one hearing being conducted on the law by the House Committee on Education and Labor. The two men differed as to which one was going to speak, but it quickly became obvious that Lewis had long since decided to testify and what he would say. Referring to Garner's opposition to the law, Lewis, with a rhetorical flourish typical of him, characterized the vice-president as a "poker-playing, whiskey-drinking, evil old man."

I went to Atlanta for hearings on our proposal to raise the statutory hourly minimum wage in the textile and clothing industries to 32.5 cents. The manufacturers were bitterly opposed to this increase. The industry's primary witness was a southern professor of economics who testified that 25 cents was a perfectly adequate hourly wage with which one could enjoy a nutritious, healthy diet. On cross-examination I asked what such a diet would consist of—fatback? Greens? Chitterlings? The professor said yes, that was a nutritious diet. I asked if it was as adequate as, say, tenderloin and mushrooms, and harassed him along these lines throughout the morning. Afterwards, the manufacturers agreed among themselves that none of them should take the stand and subject themselves to similar treatment.

A few months later, the TWOC was transformed into the Textile Workers' Union of America (TWUA), with Emil Rieve, head of the hosiery workers' union, becoming president. The TWUA would make little headway in organizing the southern textile mills, the heart of the industry, until forty years later when it again merged with the Amalgamated to become the Amalgamated Clothing and Textile Workers of America. This was of course someone else's history: Hillman, and therefore I, left when the TWOC dissolved.

Only a couple of weeks after I started working for the union, Sidney was to make a speech on "the Jewish question" before some clothing manufacturers' association. Sidney was no orator and rarely spoke extemporaneously, preferring to read prepared speeches. He asked me to draft some remarks for him but I had next to no knowledge of the issues confronting the Jewish community except for, of course, anti-Semitism and the catastrophe facing European Jews. But I did some basic research and prepared a draft. Sidney was astounded by the information I provided and from that day to the end of his life, he had me pegged not only as the one to write all of his speeches but also all of the testimony for his not infrequent appearances before several congressional committees.

He took me everywhere, which made my life interesting. The existence of an Amalgamated lawyer was fairly mundane since the union was not part of the great industrial union organizing drives of the period. But Sidney was a leader of the CIO as well, and I accompanied him to all CIO conventions, all CIO leadership meetings in Washington, many of his private conferences and lunches with John L. Lewis or Philip Murray, and conventions of the other CIO unions to which he spoke and at which he maneuvered. We traveled together to Pittsburgh in 1938 for the pivotal United Automobile Workers' convention. Homer Martin, the UAW president, was in complete decline and could claim no real following within the union. His natural heir was Wyndham Mortimer, who had led the successful drive to organize General Motors, the giant of the industry. Mortimer, however, was a man of the Left; his militancy—including the sit-down strikes—was no small factor in the success of the drive. Nevertheless, Mortimer's politics drew the opposition of the union's Right—left and right, in political terms, is always variable given the context—led by Walter Reuther. It became clear that to avoid a nasty schism while the union was still in its infancy, there would need to be a compromise over the question of leadership. R. J. Thomas was the compromise candidate whom the Communists in the union found acceptable. Hillman, in his address to the convention, threw his support behind Thomas, giving the candidacy the imprimatur of CIO backing.

The Amalgamated was in large part Sidney's creation. But with the development of the CIO, the union became primarily a platform from which he could step onto the national and international political stage. As vice-president of the CIO, he could speak not only to the pedestrian concerns of the mens' clothing industry but on behalf of millions of newly organized workers. Only Lewis and Murray had more power and influence. The three were mutually respectful of one another. Lewis was clearly the dominant figure in the labor movement and with the other two, a fact that was understood by both Murray and Hillman, which allowed them to function easily with one another. At my first CIO convention, in November 1938, Sidney made a much acclaimed "unity" speech, which I had a hand in preparing, criticizing AFL divisiveness. "It was not the act of those who orga-

nized the CIO which had brought division in the labor movement,"
Hillman declared. "We made every effort . . . to organize the unorganized workers within the fold of the AFL. Our only guilt was that we
were not satisfied to sit back with folded hands while the labor movement remained weak, ineffective, and in the process of disintegration. Instead, we insisted that the unorganized workers of this country must be organized. For that crime we were expelled from the
AFL." Then, to AFL proposals that the CIO "return to the fold" but in
a subservient position, accepting the AFL's posture of self-satisfaction
and abandoning organizing drives, Hillman told the convention: "Yes,
I want . . . a unified labor movement. But we also agree that two organizations are certainly better than no organization at all." Lewis,
speaking to the same issues of labor "unity" on another occasion, said
in his inimitable style: "I have been asked to explore the mind of [AFL
president] William Green. I can tell you that I have explored the mind
of William Green. And I can assure you that there is nothing there."

Sidney was not a particularly stimulating personality. His intellectual reach was limited. But he was very clever and extremely knowledgeable about anything that concerned the Amalgamated and the
CIO. Although he never once asked me, even obliquely, about what
my political affiliations might be, I have no doubt he knew I was a
Communist. Sidney and Jacob Potofsky, who would eventually succeed him as Amalgamated president, both knew Jessica from the
twenties, were always quite fond of her, welcomed her at all union
social activities, and couldn't have helped but know where her sympathies lay. I learned some time after coming to work for the union
that he had inquired around Washington, particularly through Ben
Cohen and Tommy Corcoran, to find out if I was a Party member. Bob
Jackson, in his oral history, reported that Hillman asked him. (Some
years later, in 1943, I would convey a message to Sidney from Earl
Browder, which confirmed for Sidney his understanding of where I
stood.)

As a matter of fact, one of the key reasons Hillman found me to be
useful was because I was a Communist. Lee Pressman's relationship
with Phil Murray was much the same as mine with Sidney. Murray
knew Lee's politics, which was precisely what made Lee valuable.
The fact that Lee and I had the confidence of the Left leadership in
the CIO, which was largely though not exclusively Communist, made
it worthwhile for our bosses to have us, our professional skills and
talents aside. Ironically, Lee's considerable ego blinded him to this
fact of our lives. When, in 1950, he cooperated with HUAC in his testimony, he was seeking to cleanse himself in order to return to Mur-

ray's good graces, failing to realize that it was his Party ties that kept him in Murray's employ in the first place. That Murray and Hillman never confronted Lee and me directly with what we Communists came to call "the $64,000 dollar question"—i.e. "Are you now a member, etc."—had nothing to do with good manners or bashfulness. These men were hardly shrinking violets. Rather, their reticence in asking us directly had everything to do with what later became known in government circles as "deniability." If they didn't ask us, they didn't "know." For our part all that was asked, in addition to our professional help, was that we not embarrass them. None of this was ever spoken but all of it was always understood.

Within the Party, Lee and I—and others—were "on ice." We were never integrated into the Party rank and file, belonged to no Party unit, were largely unknown within the Party, even within the leadership. I met Browder only rarely, more often with Roy Hudson, the Party leader responsible for union work, or Gene Dennis, in charge of legislative and electoral matters. Frankly, a good number of our ideas of what the CIO should be doing came from the Party. And I can't remember any time when we disagreed with the Party, although in retrospect I can see moments when perhaps we should have. But in life, there seemed to be no difference between the best interests of the CIO and the best interests of the Communist party. Certainly it was my experience that the Party had the best interests of the CIO in mind and in heart.

* * *

The period of 1939–40 was less than happy for the labor movement in general, and for me personally. The fascist defeat of the Spanish republic, with the tacit support of England and France and in the face of official U.S. "neutrality," signaled to Hitler that his aggression would be rewarded. This was confirmed with the Western powers' acceptance of the Munich agreement and rejection of Stalin's entreaties for a collective security alliance. I believed that the Soviets had made every effort to build a multinational alliance against the advances of Nazi Germany, that the British and French had made it blatantly obvious that their interest was not in an alliance but in persuading Hitler to march east rather than west. Everyone knew that war in Europe was imminent; what remained unclear was exactly when it would come and with whom we would side. It was in this context that Stalin sent Molotov to negotiate the famous nonaggression pact with von Ribbentrop.

I had no difficulty in understanding and defending the treaty as an essential move by the Soviets to buy time while they prepared for war. The secret protocols between the Soviets and Germans, essentially ceding the Baltic states to the USSR, which have come to light in recent years, are more questionable in retrospect. Of course here was a contradiction between the right of small nations to self-determination and the right of the USSR to self-preservation. I was convinced that the defeat of fascism—my paramount concern—tipped the balance toward the Soviet position. I believed that only the USSR would be able to stop Hitler, and events proved this to be so.

At the same time it must be acknowledged that the Soviets, having signed the pact, and the Communist Party USA, having fully supported it, went terribly and tragically overboard in assessing the nature of the war. Molotov at one point made the atrocious statement that "fascism is a matter of taste." We U.S. Communists were unable to differentiate between England and France, on one side, and Nazi Germany, on the other. After the Seventh World Congress of the Comintern in 1935, we made much of the distinction between fascism and "bourgeois democracy" and called for unity with the latter in a no-holds-barred effort to defeat the former. Now, with the Soviet-Nazi pact, we again obliterated the distinction between the two. Frankly, I can't say I recognized this at the time, in part because the opposition from the Right to the nonaggression pact was so intense. We so often exaggerated our positions when we came into sharp collision with our opponents. Our political "line" sometimes mocked our pretensions to being masters of dialectics, understanding the "interpenetration of opposites." Not that we were alone in our one-sidedness and extremities of position. Opponents of the pact then, and hindsight critics today, virtually dismissed any consideration of Soviet concerns or even of subsequent history. Still, it was we Communists and not our detractors that claimed our position was based on "scientific" socialism. Obviously we found it far easier, particularly in urgent circumstances, to mobilize support around an agitational line, rather than a serious analysis.

The events half a world away also caused great division within the U.S. labor movement. Of all the CIO leaders, Hillman enjoyed the closest relationship with FDR; it was generally considered that Sidney was the president's man. And during this period prior to U.S. entry into the war, Sidney was the one who carried Roosevelt's line into the labor movement. Nor can it be said that only the Communists were opposed to what we then referred to as "the phony war." Actually, John L. Lewis was the most outspoken critic of FDR, arguing that the struggles of organized labor could not be put on hold while the administration prepared for war. To no one's surprise, the president named Sidney to help run the Office of Production Management, later the War Production Board, to supervise the unfettered production in preparing for, and then in conducting, the war.

This meant, in actuality, that Sidney's role was to prevent and, if necessary, to break strikes, particularly in war production industries. He was largely responsible for breaking an important 1940 strike, called under Communist leadership, at North American Aviation in California. Because of political differences over the interpretation of the prewar period, but also because Communists and others were still involved in militant strike struggles, the Party and other labor militants came into collision with Hillman.

As further indication that Sidney knew where I stood politically, without even asking, he screened me out of his activities during this period. My views were neither offered nor solicited. He was quite pleased with my work but certainly didn't want me on display and understood that I would not be in accord with him in his work in Washington. Instead he brought as his counsel in the capital Maxwell Brandwen, the attorney for the Amalgamated Bank, the lone remaining union-run bank in the United States, and an old personal friend of Sidney's.

With Hillman working in Washington, I had little useful work to do. This was a rather dull period in my life, since I was still "on ice" and unknown to the Left in the New York labor movement, which in any case was quite opposed to Sidney at that point. Hillman's earlier anti-communist biases again emerged. He got the Amalgamated executive board to pass a resolution for submission to the 1940 CIO convention—a resolution that was dead on arrival—declaring that "no person shall be eligible to hold any paid office or employment in the CIO who is a member of the Communist Party, any nazi or fascist group or organization, or any other subversive group or organization."

I had a very uncomfortable time of it at the convention that November. Sidney came to Atlantic City from Washington to speak and I came down from New York to listen. John L. Lewis made his dramatic break with FDR there, declaring his support for Wendell Wilkie, the Republican presidential candidate that year. Then Lewis resigned the presidency of the CIO, turned it over to Phil Murray, and took the mine workers out of the CIO. Sidney's speech was a vicious attack on the Communist party as outsiders who had infiltrated the labor movement rather than militants who had given their lives and blood to build it. Camouflaged with rhetoric like "Whether their orders come from Rome, Berlin, or Moscow, it is the same thing"—no one had ever accused the Nazis or fascists of being union organizers, so his target was clear—Hillman went on to accuse those who built the "united front" of being "scoundrels" who should be excluded from the CIO. This was not my happiest moment but fortunately, none of this washed off on me. Our relationship was a sound one and Sidney was too much the politician to burn all his bridges. Shortly after the Atlantic City convention, he suffered a severe heart attack and went to Florida for several months of recuperation.

Sidney was hardly alone among FDR's inner circle in attacking the labor Left. In February 1941, my old friend the attorney general, Robert Jackson—he who personally pledged to me that his Justice Department would not behave in the manner of Woodrow Wilson's and its Palmer Raids—ordered the deportation to Australia of Harry Bridges, the left-wing leader of the West Coast longshoremen's union and hero of the 1934 San Francisco general strike.

Hillman returned from Florida in June 1941, fully recovered from his heart attack. On June 22 the long-awaited German invasion was launched against the USSR. And with the invasion there came a new realignment of forces within the labor movement. John L. Lewis remained adamantly opposed to Roosevelt; but the Left, which had opposed the "phony war," characterized the new circumstances as an antifascist war and threw its full support behind the military mobilization. Hillman and the Left were again in partnership.

With the new political situation, and Hillman back in New York, I was once again fully employed and enjoyed the complete confidence of the Amalgamated leadership. Sidney took me to lunch every day, sometimes bringing along Potofsky, Frank Rosenblum, Hy Blumberg, or another of the union officers. They insisted that Jessica be present at all union social affairs and banquets. I remember one Amalgamated dinner at the Commodore Hotel, atop Grand Central Station, when Jessica and I were getting ready to go home. A long marble stairway led from the second-floor ballroom to the ground-floor lobby, and at the bottom of the stairs was a floor-to-ceiling mirror. As we descended the stairs, Jessica said, looking at the mirror, "There's one more big, fat Amalgamated wife," momentarily blinded to the fact that she was watching herself. The next day, she began a most rigorous diet.

For the next two years, Hillman devoted much of his enormous store of energy to campaigning against the Axis, taking to the air waves, speaking at labor rallies, Labor Day parades, union meetings. Whenever the occasion called for a written speech, Sidney asked me to supply it. If the Communist party and the Left zigged depending on the circumstances, Hillman zagged. He again abandoned his anti-

Soviet posture to embrace the Red Army. In an address on November 9, 1941—Pearl Harbor and U.S. entrance into the war were still a month away—he declared:

> The forces of Hitlerism are determined to tear down all that we have built with such care and sacrifice. We all know that their way is in direct and irreconcilable conflict with our own.... Ours is the conference table; theirs the concentration camp. Ours the dignity and development of the individual human being; theirs the debasement and degradation of all who are not members of their self-appointed master race.... And this we know too—that if Russia should be defeated ... for our lack of aid—quantity enough and in time enough—we might be compelled to turn back the Nazi invaders at our own doors."

The Party's unqualified support of the war effort was unquestionably, then and in retrospect, the correct policy. Thousands of individual Communists joined the armed forces and many became heroes under fire. Collectively the Party played an honorable role in mobilizing public support for the antifascist cause and in defeating detractors from the Right. However, it must also be acknowledged that we were not without blinders in our enthusiasm. In 1941, the federal government launched a prosecution of a group of Trotskyists who were active in the Teamsters' union in Minneapolis. They were charged with violating the Smith Act, a little-known and heretofore unused law, which forbade "conspiracy to teach or to advocate the overthrow" of the U.S. government by force and violence. Behind the charges was the fact that the Socialist Workers' Party (SWP), the primary U.S. Trotskyist grouping, was counseling draft resistance and thereby interfering with the war effort. The Communists in Minnesota, bitter foes of the SWP, nevertheless opposed the prosecution. But on a national level, the Party remained silent, while individual leaders spoke of a "fifth column" at work in the Twin Cities. At the time, I accepted the Party estimate of the case, but paid little attention to it and did not read the legal documents, briefs, opinions, and appeals. Little did we know that in the postwar period the Smith Act would become the primary legal weapon to attack our Party and imprison its leaders. It wasn't until 1949, with the first Smith Act indictments of the Communist party, that I read the documents against the Minnesota Trotskyists and saw that the cases against the two organizations were virtually identical. The Communists had made a terrible mistake in not defending the SWP. (Many years later, in the eighties, I was in a meeting with the CPUSA national board; under discussion was an SWP appeal for support in its lawsuit against the government for political harassment. I referred to the Party's mistake in the 1941 case and said that those who now opposed supporting the SWP lawsuit were repeating the same error. A longtime Party leader from Michigan replied, "Ah, that was entirely different. They were interfering with the war effort." Dogma reigned and the Party again refused to defend the SWP against government persecution. The Party has never engaged in any self-criticism—presumably the Leninist corrective—of that episode or other unworthy policies that we advocated, e.g., support for the relocation camps for Japanese-Americans, in our ardor for the anti-fascist war effort.)

* * *

The new alliance between Hillman and the labor movement Left in New York was directed in the first place against David Dubinsky and his followers. Hillman and Dubinsky, the president of the International Ladies Garment Workers' Union, had sustained a merciless mutual antagonism for years. Dubinsky's driving force was his anticommunism; even with the changed character of the war and the grand alliance it had brought about, he could in no way adjust his opposition to the Communist party and his embitterment toward the USSR. The blood feud between Hillman and Dubinsky took personal as well as political forms. I'd guess that Hillman's respectful relations with the Left were in no small measure because of his animosity toward Dubinsky, who represented the Right in the New York labor movement. Their rivalry earlier led Dubinsky to pull his union out of the CIO to remain in the AFL. (John L. Lewis remarked that Dubinsky "swore by his beard and by his bowels" to be faithful to industrial unionism, only to become scared and leave.) An alliance between them was an impossibility; Hillman was compelled to look to his left to find friendly faces.

The Hillman-Dubinsky rivalry manifested itself within the American Labor party (ALP), organized in July 1936 by the two men and Alex Rose, leader of the New York hosiery workers; all three headed up unions of Jewish garment workers with a strong socialist tradition, for whom a labor party was welcome. The initial idea was to guarantee the support of these socialist-oriented workers for Roosevelt and to overcome their reluctance to vote for the two old parties. Hillman, a pragmatist above all—he used to say, "leaders must not be hampered by any political or social theories"—was the primary mover and shaker. The ALP was organized as the New York branch of John L. Lewis's Labor's Non-partisan League, a coalition of AFL unions brought together to support FDR's reelection. Lewis launched the league at the same time he began the CIO, the idea being to accompany the new labor militancy with political militancy. For Hillman, the goal of the ALP was nothing less than the realignment of the two major parties, bringing the organized working class into the Democratic party behind Roosevelt, using ballots to improve labor's economic position.

At its founding convention, on August 13, 1936, the ALP brought together 427 delegates from 18 international unions, 298 locals, eight joint boards, seven district councils, 18 government employees' locals, and the Social Democratic Federation, a breakaway from Norman Thomas's Socialist party. The next year, Fiorello LaGuardia, a Republican, saw the ALP as his future home. In his mayoral election, he received 673,000 Republican votes. The ALP delivered 482,000 votes, more than his plurality of 454,000.

With the growth of the CIO, the influence of the industrial unions quickly overwhelmed that of the AFL unions, and the first Hillman-Dubinsky split in the ALP took place along CIO-AFL lines, with Hillman the dominant figure. In 1938, Harold Lehman was the Democratic candidate for governor, Thomas Dewey the Republican. Dewey received 2.3 million Republican votes; Lehman got 1.97 million Democratic votes. But again the ALP was the balance of power, giving Lehman 408,000 votes and a 70,000-vote plurality. At this point the ALP, with clubs in every assembly district in New York City as well as a firm base in Rochester, Buffalo, and Syracuse, had virtually absorbed the remnants of the Socialist party in the state. The Communists, who had thrown all their energies behind the ALP, began to win the leadership of many of its clubs. In the 1938 election, the Communists ran only one candidate, Israel Amter, who received 100,000 votes for representative-at-large; the Party supported the ALP in every other race.

Vito Marcantonio, elected as a Republican congressman from East Harlem—like his mentor LaGuardia, he was a Republican out of defiance of the Tammany Hall machine that ran the New York City Democratic party—lost his reelection bid in the 1936 Roosevelt landslide. Then Marc, as he was known to all New Yorkers, joined the ALP and won back his old congressional seat in 1938. LaGuardia first discovered Marc as an eighteen-year-old tenant strike leader, groomed him as a lieutenant, made him head of his own political organization, and helped elect him to Congress. But Marc, who shared Fiorello's temperament and popular touch, was also a socialist by belief and thus to the left of LaGuardia. Fiorello would say of his protege, "Vito my good son, Vito my erring son."

Now Marc became leader of the ALP Left, Hillman of the Center, and Dubinsky the Right. Marc's main aide-de-camp in the ALP leadership was Mike Quill, head of the Transport Workers' Union and of the ALP organization in the Bronx. After June 22, 1941, the Party agreed that I could let myself be known to the comrades in the CIO. Almost immediately I went to see Saul Mills, secretary of the New York City CIO Council, who was also a Communist. Without saying in so many words, I let him know my politics and told him I wanted to be helpful. At the same time, Sidney had essentially anointed me as his political lieutenant, a role that, far more than as a legal advisor, I would fulfill for the duration of our relationship. This was the beginning of my real involvement in ALP and CIO politics.

Two years later, the Hillman-Dubinsky split led to an alliance of Hillman with the Left to defeat Dubinsky in the ALP. The ALP Left included Saul Mills, Mike Quill, and Ben Gold and Irving Potash of the Furriers—under Marcantonio's leadership. Dubinsky despised the Furriers because their leaders, Ben and Irving, were open Communists. Sidney, on the other hand, had enormous respect for them because they did such a good job inside their union, and, even more than the Amalgamated, had fought off gangster encroachment and won. And unlike Dubinsky, the Communists were not competitors with Hillman in the sense of self-promotion and seeking prestige. Sidney rejected out of hand Dubinsky's demand for the exclusion of the Left from the ALP.

Phil Murray weighed in with national CIO support for Sidney. On March 25, three days before the primary, Hillman sent out a personal letter to 180,000 enrolled ALP voters, urging support for the Center-Left coalition's Committee for a United Labor Party. Counterattacking the Right and its supporters in Congress and the press, Hillman wrote:

> The venom and the vigor with which they have gone to work on the CIO-PAC, the Committee for a United Labor Party, the Amalgamated, and on me personally is the best proof that we are on the right track. But I didn't expect to find the leadership of the State ALP hunting with this pack and leading the hue and cry. I thought it possible that Messrs. Rose, Dubinsky, Alfange and the rest might disagree with my proposal. . . . I didn't think they would sink to the level of Martin Dies and compete with him for first honors as America's number one Smear Master. When they did that, they forfeited the respect, the confidence, and the support of every honest progressive.

In the week before the primary, both Hillman and Dubinsky brought delegations to Fiorello LaGuardia to solicit the mayor's intervention on their respective sides. LaGuardia issued a public appeal for unity, but much along the lines urged by Hillman and opposed by Dubinsky. When the votes were finally tallied, our Committee for a Unity Labor Party won 620 of the 750 seats on the ALP state committee. At which point Dubinsky and Rose left the party and announced the formation of the Liberal party, which has led an undistinguished life up to the present.

The 1943 primary election featured Hillman and Marc and their common slate against one led by Dubinsky and Alex Rose. Hillman was terrified that Mike Quill would demand a position on the ALP executive in the event that the Center-Left won the election. "Red Mike," as Quill was known, was not only Transport Workers' Union president but also president of the New York City CIO Council and an ALP member of the city council. He was militant, with a dramatic flair and a beautiful Irish lilt to his speech that made him a popular figure among New York workers. Mike never, to my knowledge, publicly admitted his membership in the Communist party, but always supported the Party's positions (as did his union), and on the city council worked in tandem with Ben Davis and Pete Cacchione, who were elected as Communist candidates. Mike was a favorite target of Dubinsky, who missed no opportunity to denounce him, and Hillman worried that the possibility of Mike on the ALP executive might be just the weapon Dubinsky needed to win the primary and thus control of the ALP.

About this time, Lee Pressman and I went to see Earl Browder on quite a different matter, and when we had finished our business I told Browder of Sidney's concern. Browder said, "Tell Sidney that he needn't worry. Mike will not ask to be on the ALP executive if the primary is won." Of course I reported this to Hillman. I visited him at his apartment, and when I told him that I had a message from Browder, he brought me into his bedroom closet to communicate it. Sidney considered the assurance quite authoritative, given its source. He expressed great relief and felt that he could go all out for the coalition to take control of the ALP.

That Browder could speak so confidently of what Mike Quill might do spoke not only to the Party's important relations to mass movements but also to its methods of work. "Communism is twentieth-century Americanism" may have been Browder's favorite credo, but he was not one to shirk from centralist methods of rule. Mike was, after all, the leader of an independent union, the elected head of the main New York labor body, and an elected public official; and yet Browder could speak with assurance as to what he would do within the ALP.

On union matters, I'd often meet with Roy Hudson, the Party's labor secretary and a familiar figure at CIO conventions. Hudson was a prototype proletarian character out of a socialist realist painting, who came off of the waterfront to work for the Party. He had married an upper-class Hungarian woman whom many Party workers, out of their class biases, always viewed with suspicion. Jessica and I occasionally would have them up to our weekend retreat, where they were invariably out of sorts with country life and with each other. I never felt Roy's leadership qualities although he always exhibited sound working-class instincts. When Browder was eventually removed from the Party leadership at the war's end, Hudson was his lone supporter in the political executive. He soon left the Party entirely and went back to work on the San Francisco waterfront.

For Party guidance in my work in the ALP and other CIO-connected politics, I met with Eugene Dennis, the Party secretary for electoral and legislative matters. The first time I ever saw Gene was in early 1937, when I was in New York on the *Electric Bond and Share* case. The Party was holding its national convention and I dropped by to hear Gene deliver his report. He was a big, strapping, handsome figure and I recall feeling a trace of envy for his attractiveness. He impressed me with his great political sense. Gene's near-fatal flaw—in this respect he somewhat resembled my brother-in-law Artie Bachrach—was that every time he had to speak publicly, even to a living-room gathering, he went through the tortures of the damned. Part of his inhibition could be attributed to the fact that, by his nature, Gene was a compromiser. He would walk a block out of his way to avoid a confrontation. When, after Browder's demise, Gene was tapped by William Z. Foster, the Party's venerable chair, to become general secretary, his leadership was characterized by alternating concessions to the Right one time, to the Left the next. Conciliation can often be an important gift, but those stormy days demanded more strength.

* * *

Back in 1940, in the midst of the prewar anticommunist atmosphere, the Party anticipated the possibility of a serious repression when the war actually came—again it was by no means certain under which circumstances and in alliance with whom the U.S. would enter the war—and feared the elimination of all Communist and Socialist publications. Doris Berger, who ran Cuneo Press, which published *Vanity Fair* and a host of other magazines, was a Party supporter. She agreed that Cuneo Press would launch a new enterprise, its only publication in newsprint, to be called *U.S. Week.* The new paper would be inexpensive, its content factual and informational rather than opinionated and agitational, to allow its survival when the other Left journals failed. Of course, the very idea in retrospect was thoroughly unrealistic, but clairvoyance was never a strong suit of the Party.

Doris lived in Milwaukee, so it was agreed that the new publication would be based there. Vita Friend and Dick Boyer were sent out from New York to serve as business manager and managing editor. The premiere issue began with twenty-five thousand subscriptions, underwritten with a grant from the William E. Dodd Foundation. Young Bill Dodd—Ella Winter's husband—unsurprisingly was given a regular column.

Right after *U.S. Week* started, my sister, Marion, went out to Milwaukee for a visit with the staff. They were impressed with her capacity for political analysis and her bright sense of humor and asked her to stay on to help run the paper. Her marriage to Artie had recently ended, the gap between them no longer bridgeable, so she agreed. The paper moved to Chicago, and with it went Marion, Vita, and Dick. Johnny, Marion's son and my namesake, was just finishing high school and went to Chicago as well.

Jessica and I were living in a rented house in Jackson Heights, Queens. Saturday nights were invariably spent in the company of the Peterses and the Silvermans, and often included the Witts and Freemans, for roast beef, drinks, and poker. One night Pete, knowing the pressures of Jessica's and my work and the pleasure we had taken in our Long Island retreat the summer before, told me that we should find a place of our own, "where no one can see your belly." For the next several weeks, he and Anne and Jessica and I would peruse the Sunday *Times* real estate ads, looking for country places. We'd circle attractive candidates, then drive out of the city to take a look.

One Sunday in April 1940, Pete and I drove up to Kent, at the southern tip of the Connecticut Berkshires, to investigate yet another possibility. We found a local realtor in town, got directions, and headed for Skiff Mountain (actually a foothill), where we found dirt roads that we followed for little more than a mile. At the road's end, hidden in the woods, we found a lovely chestnut log cabin. Nobody appeared to be home, but we peeked through the windows to discover an absolutely beautiful fieldstone living room. We drove back to New York and the next day returned with Jessica and Anne. Again, nobody was home, but we daringly entered the house. The living room was perhaps twenty by forty feet, with a fireplace at one end, and was furnished, as were the five bedrooms, with handmade country furniture. The kitchen was also fully furnished, from gas stove (also a woodburning stove) to crafted crockery. At the very top of Skiff Mountain, deep in the woods, nobody here would be able "to see our belly."

Of course Jessica immediately fell in love with the place. The owner was a Dr. Dowdorf, who lived across the state line in New York's Westchester County. We drove to his home to talk price and conditions of purchase. Dowdorf was a biologist who specialized in cancer research. He owned a considerable amount of acreage around the Kent house and offered to sell us the house, fully equipped and furnished, and twenty acres of land for the grand sum of $5,500. The house had no electricity—the power lines did not extend up Skiff Mountain—and only a hand-dug well for water. A deep well had been drilled but not connected. And of course there was no phone, which is a blessing for a country retreat. The doctor explained that he was forced to sell the place because his asthmatic daughter was severely affected by the wood mold. We didn't hesitate to accept his offer. The next week, we drove back to the house and paced off twenty acres of property for description in the deed. I still had some money saved from my Chicago days, and we bought the house outright.

Within a week of the purchase, I received a letter from Dr. Dowdorf: "Dear Mr. Abt: If you look on the fireplace, you will find a package of white powder. This is potassium cyanide. You cannot burn it; you cannot throw it away or otherwise dispose of it. I suggest that you take it to town and offer it to the pharmacist." The only druggist in Kent was open only occasionally and it took several trips into town with my package before I finally found him in. I showed Dr. Dowdorf's letter and offered him the white powder. He looked up into my eyes and said, "Mr. Abt, I am not a murderer." Again I returned to the house with the package. Two weeks later, Dowdorf and his wife were in the area and came by to check on us. Mrs. Dowdorf was distraught and wouldn't come onto the property. It contained too many fond memories for her. I told the doctor about my experience with the pharmacist. He offered to take the cyanide off of my hands and use it to kill the cellar rats in his Westchester home unless, he said with a grin, "you want to use it on weekend guests."

For the next thirty-five years, the Kent house was to provide Jessica and me (and our many friends) with many of our best times and warmest memories. When power lines were finally built up Skiff

Mountain in 1950, we were able to replace the kerosene and Aladdin lamps and our secondhand generator. And when we finally sold it in 1975, Jessica was just like Mrs. Dowdorf: her attachment to the house wouldn't allow her to come onto the property. But keeping the place by then was out of the question. My chronically bad back prevented me from driving long distances and from chopping wood and the other strenuous pleasures of life in the woods. Jessica was no longer up to cooking for weekend guests. Certainly, we couldn't have a weekend house without guests. And of course I'd long since given away the potassium cyanide.

With the Nazi invasion of the USSR on June 22, 1941, everyone's political calculus changed, and with it their lives. *U.S. Week* folded, since there was obviously no sense in continuing publication. Vita Friend and Dick Boyer came home to New York, and Marion came with them. My nephew, Johnny, like hundreds of thousands of his generation, enrolled in the service, in his particular case, the merchant marine. With Marion and I both in New York, mother also moved from Washington to live near us, in a serviceable apartment on Fifty-ninth Street at Lexington Avenue. Marion lived in the Village with Maxine Wood, a playwright with a number of off-Broadway productions and *On Whitman Avenue* on Broadway to her credit. Marion herself worked for a while for *PM* magazine before accepting Gene Dennis's invitation to serve in the national Party office as his lieutenant. Our circle remained unbroken.

After leaving Chicago nearly ten years earlier, I maintained relations with few of my old friends from school or my earlier law firms and none with my quite extensive family, save for Uncle Doc. They were, to a person, apolitical but with a strong anti-Roosevelt bent. For my part, I carried a good deal of snobbishness. I felt that I had outgrown my Chicago friends and family and couldn't be bothered with sustaining old ties. But my closest family, my "real" family—Jessica, Marion, mother—and our dearest friends and co-workers—were together constantly, in New York City during the week, in Kent on weekends. In addition, Jessica's adopted daughter, Judy, came east to stay with us during her breaks from Reed College in Oregon. A beautiful, lovely girl with a bright wit, Judy had met a boy at school, Daniel Dotson, who during their engagement had, like so many others, joined the air force to serve as a B-24 pilot during the war.

Jessica's son, David, had begun living with us in Jackson Heights. His tortured emotional state was becoming apparent. What we had at first taken to be childhood temper tantrums were becoming the norm. The public schools were no match for him. For days at a time,

David locked himself in a room, listening to the radio. We arranged for him to see what would be the first in a long line of psychologists and psychiatrists, who strongly urged his institutionalization. On the doctor's recommendation, we brought David kicking and screaming—I say this figuratively but it is not far from the literal truth—to the Anderson School in Hyde Park. He stayed there for perhaps a year, but that year included his running away and coming home to us in New York on a number of occasions. Obviously the Anderson School was not the answer to David's condition, and we brought him home. He was entering adolescence, which we were warned by all would be far more troubled than most. But he seemed momentarily calmed and did well enough to be admitted to Stuyvessant High School, New York's elite public school for mathematics and the sciences, where he would excel.

Jessica threw herself into creating Russian War Relief, which she initiated with Dr. Edward Barsky, the gifted surgeon responsible for setting up medical care for the Abraham Lincoln Battalion during the Spanish civil war. Like Jessica, Eddie was an accomplished organizer and fund-raiser. His gruff exterior belied a selflessness matched by few, and he began no public fund appeal without himself making the first, sizable donation. In starting Russian War Relief, he and Jessica gave birth to a tremendous campaign, although they were hardly alone in the effort. Vita Friend, Marion's co-worker at *U.S. Week*, was a big help in building the fund-raising apparatus. Vita and Eddie quickly became an "item" and, before the war's end, were married. And, as Vita remembered, "taking up with Russian War Relief and Eddie Barsky meant taking up with the Smith-Abts."

Russian War Relief also had a labor division, headed up with great vigor by Hillman. Sidney spoke on every possible occasion and turned down no invitation to help in the common cause. On June 27, 1943, during its Tribute to Russia Week on the second anniversary of the invasion of the USSR, Russian War Relief organized a mass rally at Madison Square Garden. President Roosevelt and General Dwight Eisenhower sent messages to the twenty-five thousand who gathered in the Garden. Vice-president Henry Wallace was the main speaker, but Hillman was also featured. Announcing the pledge by the New York City labor movement to give $250,000, a huge sum a half century ago, to help care for "the indomitable people of Stalingrad who suffered wounds, disease and shock in the historic defense of their beloved city—street by street, house by house and—when the houses were gone—stone by stone," Sidney told the crowd:

AND W. CHURCHILL correctly shared DUBINSKY'S WARINESS OF THE USSR — UNLIKE APT'S NAIVETÉ.

Labor joins today with Americans in every walk of life in expressing our gratitude to and admiration of our Soviet ally and our deep affection for its people. . . . We believe that one of the important tasks before us is to promote closer understanding between the Soviet people and ourselves, to clear away all misconceptions and suspicions which have divided us in the past, and by every means to deepen and extend the collaboration between our governments and our peoples. . . .

We must recognize that grim, hard days lie ahead. We Americans have only made a beginning toward committing our full strength in men and munitions. The Soviet Union still bears the brunt of battle. Our losses will be great. But, thanks to Russia's unremitting struggle, we will not have to bear as much as her people have suffered. Every Nazi killed by a Red Army man in defense of his Soviet land has saved the lives of American boys. Let us remember that in assessing our debt to our Soviet ally.

While I may have drafted his speech, these were the heartfelt sentiments of Sidney Hillman, at least for the moment. Perhaps because of his place of birth and upbringing, certainly in spite of his anticommunism, Sidney had an emotional attachment to the Soviet Union. Often in bad times—as in the period before the Nazi invasion and later—his feelings for the USSR were not strong enough to overcome his opportunism, the "what" in "what makes Sidney run." But he was a man of some complexity, in contrast with, say, a David Dubinsky, who could never reconcile himself to the fact that the USSR was our wartime ally.

* * *

In 1943, Gene Dennis came to me and Lee Pressman to first raise the idea of a political action committee to organize labor support for Roosevelt in the approaching 1944 election. Pressman approached Murray with the idea, as I did with Hillman. Both men seized upon the proposal with great enthusiasm.

On July 7, the CIO Executive Council officially formed CIO-PAC to organize labor's political activities. It was to function as a full partner in coalition with FDR Democrats, but also to lend help to progressive Republicans. A couple of weeks later, on July 26 in Philadelphia, CIO delegates from Pennsylvania, New York, New England, New Jersey, Delaware, and Maryland, representing some 2.5 million trade unionists, met in the first CIO-PAC organizing conference. A million

CIO members were overseas in the armed forces, and Hillman warned of reactionary forces in Congress who would "subordinate the war against the Axis to an offensive against the Roosevelt Administration, organized labor and our national unity."

In setting up CIO-PAC, we first had to contend with the Smith-Connolly Act, passed by Congress several months earlier. For twenty years, the Corrupt Practices Act had prohibited corporations from making contributions to a political party or a candidate. Now, with the rising power of the CIO, there was lots of talk of labor's ability to exert political muscle, talk that didn't sit well with the reactionary forces in Congress. The Smith-Connolly bill—Smith was the Virginia representative who also gave us the Smith Act—extended the Corrupt Practices Act to include trade unions, making it a crime for a labor organization to contribute to a political party or to the election or defeat of a candidate for public office.

My first task was to erect a series of stratagems to circumvent Smith-Connolly. From the outset, we articulated the distinction between "contributions to" a candidate or political party and "expenditures in support of" the campaign of a candidate or political party. The law didn't, and constitutionally couldn't, prohibit expenditures— phone banks, printing literature, rallies, etc.—as long as they were not made by prearrangement with the candidate. Such expenditures were well within an organization's First Amendment rights to free political speech. So the CIO and its constituent bodies could, even under Smith-Connolly, issue leaflets or hold meetings supporting presidential or congressional candidates. Still this wasn't quite sufficient, because candidates wanted money paid directly to them out of which they could run their campaigns. So we adopted a second device: voluntary gifts from CIO members to the CIO-PAC, which could then contribute money to the candidates. These weren't contributions by the unions themselves or compulsory contributions by individuals, both of which were forbidden by Smith-Connolly. The CIO carried out a major campaign for "a dollar a member" among its 7.8 million members. Phil Murray named Hillman as chairman of CIO-PAC, most likely to give him a place where he would want to operate— Murray knew that Sidney enjoyed his role in Washington as a friend of the president and co-head of the War Production Board and would want to enlarge his sovereignty—and at the same time keep him out of Murray's way in actually running the CIO. Hillman naturally told me that I would be the counsel for CIO-PAC. I say "naturally" because I was already his counsel in the Amalgamated, his chief political aide, and had crafted the legal tactics that allowed the CIO-PAC to operate. One day, Sidney came back from a visit to the CIO offices in Washington and stopped by my office. He told me, "Your imperialist friend, Lee Pressman, wants to be co-counsel with you." Hillman was always a quick study in sizing up ambition. By "imperialist," Sidney was referring of course not to Lee's politics but to his penchant for overreaching. This was characteristic of Lee. We were always good and warm friends, unless there was the possibility of competition, anything he felt threatened his own position—which of course this didn't—to which he was inordinately sensitive. In such cases, one was no longer considered his friend, but a rival. In this case, Lee's concern made no difference to me. So, on the CIO-PAC letterhead, we were thereafter listed as co-counsel, though I continued to act as such while Lee had more than enough to keep him busy in the CIO.

Our ability to get around Smith-Connolly excited much interest but also much hostility in the Congress. Hillman was called before the House and Senate labor committees to testify about the work and the financing of the CIO-PAC. As always, I accompanied him to the hearings and explained the legal basis under which we operated. Sidney's testimony before the House committee was given a good deal of press coverage. We understood that his testimony before the Senate committee, saying substantially the same things he told the House, would not get much attention. But the next day, Louis Stark, the labor writer for the *New York Times* arranged for the paper to run the entire testimony. There was obviously considerable interest and controversy in the entry of organized labor into political campaigns.

Sidney and I undertook a national tour, putting together the PAC as a separate entity, apart from the CIO itself, in each place we visited. For some time, Sidney had made a practice of taking me wherever he went, making no attempt to keep me in the background. On the contrary, he seemed to want me to participate in his every activity. Dick Roman, Hillman's public relations guy, accompanied us on the CIO-PAC organizing tour, writing press releases en route and arranging news conferences at each stop. Sidney made at least one major public address in each city, and we generated a good deal of publicity. The real purpose of the tour was to allow Sidney to survey the field in order to select staff. Although he was again working closely with the CIO Left, primarily the Communists, he remained quite suspicious and fearful that it might take over CIO-PAC. We traveled to California, Oregon, Washington, Colorado, Michigan, Ohio, Pennsylvania—virtually everywhere the CIO was a major political force. And of course, in a number of cities, like New York, Los Angeles, and San Francisco, Communists and other Left trade unionists were in the leadership of the

local CIO Councils; in some cases, they also became the regional or
state directors of the CIO-PAC despite Sidney's worries. In this respect,
Hillman was not paranoid in the manner of Dubinsky. When we visited Minneapolis, one of the candidates for the job of Minnesota regional director was Hubert H. Humphrey, then a local school teacher. Neither Sidney nor I could bear the man—he simply talked endlessly and
heard no one else—and together we vetoed his job application. Not
long afterward, he ran for and was elected mayor of Minneapolis and
of course continued onward and upward.

Some anticommunist historians have accused Pressman and me of
maintaining a kind of placement bureau for Communists and leftists
in the CIO and, upon its creation, the CIO-PAC. To this, I confess that
it is true. When I had a say in selecting staff, I looked for the best,
most selfless and militant organizers who, invariably, were of the
Left. I recommended them to Sidney and he accepted the recommen-
dations for precisely the same reasons. When Hal Ware recruited me
into the Party, he warned me early on against any Pollyannish notions
of Communists. "Don't think just because someone is a Communist,"
Hal told me, "that he is a good person or a nice guy. Communists can
also be selfish, opportunists, careerists, bureaucrats, and even bru-
tal." I've never forgotten Hal's admonition, but of course the other
side of Hal's coin was that many Communists were also quite beautiful human beings, with the most wonderful qualities of self-sacrifice,
commitment to the general welfare, and unqualified dedication to
making the world a sweeter place in which to live. In recommending
staff to Sidney, I saw political affiliation as incidental to the question
of whether or not one could perform in the job at hand.

When Hillman needed a national director for CIO-PAC, I recommended Beanie Baldwin, Henry Wallace's administrative secretary
when I was in the AAA. Beanie was remarkable, a white Virginian
who grew up in a small town enveloped in Jim Crow culture and became a staunch antiracist and progressive. He was never a Party
member, and the likelihood is that he never read a page of Marx or
Engels, but he had a great feel for and attachment to the labor movement and the working class. While I was working for the Amalgamated, Beanie had been administrator of the Farm Security Administration, which organized communities of small farmers and financed
projects that combined farming with industry. One of his projects in
Pennsylvania included a shop that manufactured men's work pants.
The Amalgamated was then organizing cotton garments in Pennsylvania, and this shop came to the union's attention. Knowing my
friendship with Beanie, Hillman asked if I would visit him and try to
secure a contract. To my surprise, I never had such an easy negotia-

tion in my life. Actually Beanie berated me and the union for taking so long in getting around to organizing the shop. When I proposed the terms that the union suggested for wages and conditions, he again criticized us for not asking enough. The contract was concluded and signed on the spot.

Beanie had served in one or another post in the administration since FDR first came into office in 1933. He next was tapped to head up the civilian occupation government in Italy, where the U.S. forces had just driven out the fascists, but he gave up the appointment to become CIO-PAC director. At first, Sidney remained suspicious of Beanie. He may have figured that I was trying to foist another Communist on him. Beanie's appointment was delayed while, I assume, Sidney made judicious inquiries among his friends in Washington about him. Nothing of this was said to me, however. Beanie's expertise, his knowledge of the Washington government bureaucracy, his contacts in Congress, his ability to maneuver through the conflicting interests that defined the Roosevelt administration all served to quickly overcome Hillman's initial reluctance.

While the officers of CIO-PAC were all leaders of important industrial unions—R. J. Thomas of the auto workers, Emil Rieve of the textile workers, Albert Fitzgerald of electric, Sherman Dalrymple of rubber, David MacDonald from steel, etc.—and together conducted official executive meetings, this was clearly Sidney's show and they deferred to him. Beanie ran CIO-PAC out of its New York office. I still worked at the Amalgamated office but was in constant contact with Beanie. My official duty was to give legal advice but there was no political question or problem about which we didn't consult and agree. We had, as they say in diplomatic communiques, a complete identity of views.

Beanie of course knew of my Party affiliation; from our Washington days, he was a personal friend of mine and of Marion's as well. He had a great deal of respect for the Party, for its ideals of course, but mainly for its ability to produce. He was not reluctant to consult with the Communist leadership; actually, he considered it an imperative since the Party was an essential ally in building the CIO and CIO-PAC. When Gene Dennis was unavailable, we generally met with Al Blumberg, his deputy in electoral-legislative matters. Blumberg was known as "Doc," a reference to his previous career as a professor of philosophy. Doc's Party responsibilities included being the organization's contact with the CIO-PAC and the American Labor party and, later, with the Independent Progressive party. He was understood by one and all to be Gene's "messenger boy"

More specifically, he was responsible for the Party's support of Vito

Marcantonio's congressional campaigns and building Marc's base within the ALP. Usually Marc was dissatisfied with what he considered insufficient Party sustenance. Blumberg was the precise opposite kind of personality from Marc, and they constantly quarreled. Doc had a full head of hair, which he groomed with a well-defined part straight down the middle. I remember, after one of their many arguments, Marc announced that, "One day, I will place a meat cleaver right down that part." From then on, Blumberg was generally referred to as "Meat Cleaver." (His lovely wife, Dorothy Rose, was later imprisoned as one of the Baltimore group of Smith Act defendants. My attitude toward the two of them was identical to the famous Dorothy Parker one-line movie review: "Loved her; hated him." In the midfifties, when the Party was embroiled in a destructive internal fight, Jessica and I were invited to their house for dinner. Dorothy Rose adored Al but I abhorred him. I remained as silent as the tablecloth throughout dinner, for which rudeness I was later severely scolded by Jessica. Not long after, Blumberg left the Communist party and later went on to occupy several leadership posts in the New York State Democratic party.)

Looking back on CIO-PAC today, I feel not unlike Dr. Frankenstein, having created an untamed monster. For while CIO-PAC was the very first PAC in American political history, it was unfortunately not the last one. After the nomination of George McGovern as the Democratic presidential candidate in 1972 and the reelection of Richard Nixon that year—this was the Watergate election—Congress passed the Federal Election Campaign Act limiting to one thousand dollars the contributions that any individual or organization could make to a candidate. This led to a proliferation of corporate PACs, all modeled after CIO-PAC. But these "voluntary" contributions by the employees and stockholders of corporations to a special fund to finance candidates were a terrible perversion of our original idea. The device that I invented to benefit working people in their political action has come back to haunt us in the service of labor's antagonist.

In 1976, when the Federal Election Campaign Act was challenged before the U.S. Supreme Court, the justices upheld my original rationale for CIO-PAC, that the Constitution did not limit the right of either individuals or organizations to make expenditures on behalf of a candidate, so long as it wasn't by prearrangement with the candidate. It might seem unbecoming for me to say so a half century after developing the idea in the first place, but the best thing Congress could do to cleanse the present political system would be to abolish

PACs altogether. Not that the senators and representatives are the least bit anxious to bite the corporate hand from which they feed.

* * *

Hillman developed the idea of a second PAC, the National Citizen's Political Action Committee (NCPAC), composed of liberal and progressive individuals who wished to be associated with the labor movement and its politics. These were mainly middle-class artists and intellectuals but Sidney also included a number of clothing manufacturers with whom he dealt and who supported FDR. As long as labor set the agenda, we were hardly adverse to wealthy supporters. The CIO-PAC had a women's division headed up by the likes of Mrs. Marshall Field, wife of the *Chicago Sun-Times* publisher, and Eleanor Gimbel of the department store chain, whose primary activity was the raising (and giving) of funds. The NCPAC was not really a PAC in today's sense. Its real purpose was to round up some wealthy people to contribute to campaigns we supported. The CIO-PAC never collected or distributed the money raised through NCPAC; we simply told them to whom it should go.

Sidney was NCPAC's honorary chair, Beanie one of several vice-chairs but, in effect, its executive vice-chair, and I was general counsel, as always. Other vice-chairs included Robert Kenney, the California attorney general; Freda Kirchwey, publisher of *The Nation*, Dorothy Parker, and Orson Welles. Other prominent individuals associated with NCPAC were the magnificent actor and concert artist Paul Robeson, the writers and poets Louis Adamic and William Rose Benet; my old boss from the WPA, Aubrey Williams, at the time with the National Farmers' Union; and Clark Foreman of the Southern Conference on Human Welfare.

Most important—in terms of the actual functioning of the NCPAC—was Elmer Benson, its chair. (Earlier, Sidney and I visited Eleanor Roosevelt in her New York apartment to ask her to accept the post; though she respectfully declined, she was always ready to receive us for consultations, and we took her up on her invitation several times.) Elmer was a former governor of Minnesota, as well as a former senator, which he was when we first became friends in Washington. He came to the Senate at the same time that Johnny Bernard came to the House, so Minnesota undoubtedly had the most progressive congressional delegation of its time. A farmer with a good bit of acreage, Elmer was the first, perhaps the only, governor in history to call out the National Guard *in support of* a labor strike, in this case of meatpackers. He was simply too outspoken and direct to be a clever politician, and, unsurprisingly, he was only a one-term governor.

While CIO-PAC and NCPAC were first organized to build labor and leftist support for Roosevelt's reelection campaign of 1944, the two PACs went far beyond where the Democratic party was prepared to lead. For example, we campaigned to eliminate the poll tax, the "white primaries," and the entire Jim Crow structure erected to legally bar and terrorize the southern Black population from voting. The great majority of Black Americans then lived in the South and constituted a majority in a large number of congressional districts. With the massive influx of Black workers from the South into the mass-production defense industries in the North and West, we also helped initiate the campaign for a national Fair Employment Practices Commission to ban racist hiring, promotion, and pay practices of the corporations. The CIO itself was hardly organized in the South. Antiunion terrorism was of a piece with racist violence and stemmed from the same source.

In perhaps Hillman's most ringing address on the question—delivered to New York's St. James Forum on October 15, 1944, and to which I acknowledge my own modest contribution—Sidney declared, speaking on behalf of CIO-PAC:

> We are fighting a war against the Nazi doctrine that one race is superior to other races. Yet 13,000,000 Americans, who are fighting this war side by side with their white brothers against the Nazi "Herrenvolk," are still denied full equality by the doctrine of white supremacy. . . .
>
> Our failure to abolish the ancient fears and prejudices has kept not only the Negro population but most of the white population of the Deep South in poverty and ignorance. . . . The war has brought the Negro much nearer to economic equality. . . . Many doors hitherto closed to the Negro have now been opened, but there are still many which remain firmly shut in his face, and once the manpower shortage is over there will be a tendency again to exclude Negroes from opportunities now open to them. . . . To a very large extent, the problem of the Negro is identical with the problem of all workers. One might say the same thing about the problem of women in industry. We have learned that we either believe in democracy and practice it . . . or else we do not believe in democracy, in which case not only the minorities but all the people are threatened with the loss of their freedom.

To its great credit, the Communist party set the tone for the CIO-PAC, NCPAC, and the CIO itself in assaulting the racist political and legal structure of the South and therefore of the entire two-party political system. On the other hand, our record was not spotless. Because of our—not only the CIO's but the Communist party's—unyielding support of the no-strike pledge, we failed to understand the significance of, and to support, the March on Washington for equality organized by A. Philip Randolph. Although some Communists, such as those working in the leadership of the Southern Negro Youth Congress, conveniently (in this case) located in Birmingham, Alabama, a thousand miles from Party headquarters, on their own went ahead in mobilizing for the march.

In a completely different arena, when John L. Lewis pressed a strike of the United Mine Workers in 1943, Earl Browder led the attack on Lewis for being anti-FDR and harming the war effort. I certainly had no quarrel with Browder's (and Hillman's and Phil Murray's) position at the time. But in hindsight, perhaps the Party went too far in its no-strike pledge support. I would say now that the Party viewed the war effort and the no-strike pledge in something of the same light as Mikhail Gorbachev a generation later argued that there are times when common issues of all humanity supersede narrow class issues.

A national smear campaign against the CIO-PAC was launched with the Republican party leading the charge. Some of the propaganda was simply crude filth along the lines of the "Protocols of the Elders of Zion." A GOP leaflet in Philadelphia featured a cartoon of a hook-nosed Jewish caricature labeled "Hillman" with a book, covered with hammers and sickles and a Star of David, under one arm, his other arm raised with a dagger in hand about to plunge it into the chest of a slumbering Uncle Sam, with the caption, "Will Uncle Sam Wake Up in Time?"

Similar anti-Semitic attacks on Hillman and the non-Jewish Earl Browder in Delaware brought severe criticism by the Democratic U.S. senator from that state, James Tunnell. Delaware's attorney general, Clair Killoran, rose to the defense of his Republican party:

Sidney Hillman, Earl Browder and, as a matter of fact, all Communists and others of un-American principles are being attacked by the Republican Party because we do not desire to have such ideologies imbedded in our government. Their racial beliefs and background have nothing to do with these attacks. The Republican Party does not and will not countenance racial attacks on anyone. Sidney Hillman comes of a race which can be proud of its part in our American history. . . . A man's race, however, regardless of what it may be, cannot immunize him from attack on

other grounds. We believe the attack against Hillman, Browder
and all others attempting to place European principles of government into our national administration, is warranted.

A national leaflet for Thomas Dewey, the Republican nominee for
president, attacked FDR under the heading "A Man Is Known by the
Company He Keeps" and reminded the reader that FDR commuted
an earlier Earl Browder prison sentence, that Browder was supporting Roosevelt's reelection, that Hillman had been a Roosevelt appointee to several posts since 1933, and that Hillman had been born in
Russia.

Nor were all the attacks from the far Right. Louis Waldman, a
former Socialist party candidate for governor of New York, wrote an
article for the *Saturday Evening Post* entitled, "Will the CIO Capture
the Democratic Party?" *Reader's Digest* weighed in with the suggestion that if Dewey won in 1944, labor would and should be punished.
When red-baiting, anti-Semitism, and undisguised threats weren't
employed, those who feared organized labor in political action fell
back on the old saw "Big Labor," conjuring up the image of a well-
bankrolled Iron Heel bringing the corporations asunder. But while
the Republicans had put together a treasury of some $50 million to
defeat Roosevelt that year, CIO-PAC had raised all of $671,000 for its
political activity, the bulk of which had already been spent in primary campaigns.

FDR's renomination was never in question. At issue in 1944 was
who would be his vice-presidential running mate. The CIO and CIO-
PAC made its views known at its national congress: all-out support
for the most liberal of the potential nominees, the vice-president,
Henry A. Wallace. On the eve of the Democratic convention, a Gallup
Poll indicated that Wallace was the overwhelming choice of registered Democrats, with 65 percent in his favor. Fourteen percent
wanted Sen. Alben Barkley of Kentucky, 6 percent supported Sen.
Harry Byrd of Virginia, and the remaining 16 percent scattered
among such possibilities as James Byrnes, Sam Rayburn, Paul Douglas, Edward Stettinius, and Harry Truman.

Actually, Wallace only needed one vote, Roosevelt's, and that was
by no means assured. Wallace's backing from the CIO; his unqualified support for the grand alliance with Britain and the Soviet Union;
his discomfort with machine politics; his disdain for Jim Crow rule,
the basis of Democratic party control of the South—all served to create a powerful stop-Wallace alliance within the party's leadership.
Led by California oil millionaire Edwin Pauley, the party's national

treasurer, the cabal included big-city machine bosses like Mayor Edward Kelly of Chicago and Edwin Flynn of the Bronx; Postmaster General Frank Walker; FDR's press secretary, Stephen Early; and perhaps most important, Robert Hannegan, chair of the Democratic National Committee.

Roosevelt was perhaps the cleverest politician not only of his time—this is a certainty—but in all of U.S. history. He knew, we all did, that Dewey was going to be the Republican candidate and was clearly fearful that a liberal like Wallace might be too heavy a load for him to carry. (As it turned out, Dewey's chances were close to nil, but a good politician always runs scared.) In response to the anti-Wallace pressure, he wrote, in a letter to the convention delegates: "I personally would vote for [Wallace's] nomination if I were a delegate to the Convention. At the same time I do not wish to appear in any way as dictating to the Convention. Obviously the Convention must do the deciding." This was hardly an unqualified endorsement of his sitting vice-president and signaled the delegates to open fire.

A great deal of maneuvering on the convention floor and in the legendary "smoke-filled rooms" occurred around the naming of the vice-presidential candidate. The CIO had a significant number of delegates from its constituent unions marshalled behind Wallace. Beanie Baldwin, Wallace's main aide in the Department of Agriculture a decade earlier, was his floor manager in Chicago. I was present throughout the convention, primarily as a watchful observer, as the CIO and its allies organized big pro-Wallace rallies on the floor when his name was placed in nomination, when he addressed the convention, whenever we felt it propitious to do so.

The anti-Wallace forces, fearful of a stampede of votes, forced an overnight postponement. Bob Hannegan went to work. He had his own candidate in mind, Harry Truman, a veteran of the Pendergast machine in Kansas City. After buttonholing the various state chairs and big-city bosses, Hannegan got FDR's agreement on Truman as the candidate. But Roosevelt also told Hannegan, "Clear it with Sidney." Hillman had a breakfast date with Truman the next morning and, while I wasn't present, I have no doubt that this is when the "clearing" took place and Sidney, ever the operator, ever the Roosevelt loyalist, gave his consent to change the CIO position. Undoubtedly, Phil Murray did the same. When the story got out about the "Clear it with Sidney" incident, the Republicans had grist for their propaganda mill. Hence the campaign to smear FDR with Hillman and the CIO.

The choice of Truman over Wallace was a fateful one. FDR would not live another year; with victory in Europe, the decision was made to drop the atomic bombs on Japan; the projections at Teheran of a postwar entente and a United Nations at peace were abandoned; and Winston Churchill would come to Truman's home in Missouri to officially declare the cold war. One can't say with any assurance that given the powerful forces at work, Wallace would have rejected this new direction, or even that Roosevelt would have, had he lived. But it certainly is pretty to think so.

* * *

Just after the November elections, the CIO received an invitation to London from Sir Walter Citrine, the head of the British Trade Union Council (TUC). In December, the British labor movement would host a consultative conference on the possibility of launching a new international trade union federation. Murray appointed Hillman to chair the CIO delegation, which also included R. J. Thomas and Emil Rieve. Sidney, as a matter of course, asked me as his political eyes and ears to accompany him.

Besides the TUC and CIO, the All-Union Central Council of Trade Unions (AUCCTU) of the USSR was also invited. Present as something of a gray eminence was Walter Scevenels, the venerable Belgian president of the International Federation of Trade Unions. The IFTU was a creature of the Second International, the confederation of Socialists and Social Democrats, as opposed to the Third International, its Communist breakaway.

In those days, most transatlantic passages were made by ship. Flying required several fueling stops. Sidney, R. J. Thomas, Emil Rieve, and I flew first to Bermuda, then to the Azores, and finally to Prestwick, Scotland. At each stop, I shared a room with Thomas, a heavyset man who was more rough-and-tumble than parry-and-thrust. R. J. was easy-going and eager to please, being, as he was, in Hillman's and Murray's debt for his elevation to the UAW presidency. My only serious problem with him was that he was adenoidal in the extreme; nobody could snore like R. J. Thomas, and I was exhausted upon arrival. Even this late in the war, German buzz bombs were hitting London, so we finished our journey from Prestwick by train. We were put up at Claridge's, London's finest hotel, but this being wartime, our daily breakfast consisted entirely of powdered eggs. British powdered eggs were simply vile; it wasn't until I went to Paris that I learned that powdered eggs could be made edible, not to mention delicious. Hillman's connections in London allowed us some reprieve from Claridge's wartime cuisine. We spent an evening at the home of Harold Lasky, the socialist historian; and one day we dined at the U.S. embassy, where we were served white bait, a dish of tiny minnows, fried crisply, which the Italians use as a Christmas delicacy.

Citrine's appearance was more that of an Oxford don than a hard-bitten labor leader. Tall, thin, bland, he was rather stiff and unbending with only an occasional glimmer of humor buried under several layers of decorum. It was amusing that the head of the British trade union movement should be knighted, but years later, after serving as director of the nationalized coal industry, Sir Walter eventually became Lord Walter. I recalled the old British Communist joke that the road to socialism would only come under the slogan "Save the Crown from the bloody bourgeoisie," so steeped in royal tradition was the country.

In any case, Citrine's enthusiasm for the proposed new international federation fell short of overwhelming. He was being pushed by the British labor Left and Center forces. This period of glowing cooperation with the Soviets and the impending defeat of Hitlerism produced in Great Britain optimism about the possibility of building a postwar all-inclusive labor unity to match the alliances built in wartime. The Soviets strongly favored the proposed federation, as did Hillman. I believe Sidney felt that here was a mechanism through which labor—and he—could really exert its power. His residual warm feelings for the Russians were reinforced by the fact that, for the moment at least, this meant being on the winning side, which appealed to Sidney's omnipresent opportunism. He took the lead in pressing for a conference to lay the foundation for what would become the World Federation of Trade Unions (WFTU).

After several days of meetings in London, we finally agreed that a preliminary conference should be convened in February 1945, with Sir Walter, for the host country, serving as the prime organizer. Besides being headquarters of the TUC, London was the wartime center for the IFTU. When the IFTU was first founded ten years earlier, the AFL was the U.S. constituent organization. With the formation of the CIO, however, the international labor movement found a far more willing collaborator. The Soviet AUCCTU, like the CIO, was not affiliated with the IFTU, but also, like the CIO, the Soviets were supportive of the proposed world federation, and the AFL was not. Invited to every meeting, including all the preliminary consultations, the AFL never came to one.

After returning to the United States for a couple of months, we reconvened in London from February 6 to 17. Altogether we were 135 delegates and 30 observers representing forty national trade union centers from the allied powers, 17 delegates from international bodies, and 9 observers from neutral countries. Every IFTU affiliate, except for the AFL, attended; in its absence, the CIO, AUCCTU, and TUC were the main national labor centers in the conference. Altogether the combined membership represented in London was 60 million, half of whom were from the vast AUCCTU. Never before in history was there so representative, so all-inclusive a gathering of the leaders of organized labor around the world. The eleven-person CIO delegation headed by Hillman included R. J. Thomas; Jim Carey, the CIO secretary-treasurer; Joe Curran, president of the National Maritime Union; Albert Fitzgerald, president of United Electrical Workers; and Reid Robinson, president of the Mine, Mill, and Smelter Workers. Lee Pressman, as CIO general counsel, and I were also there as official delegates. For myself, the London conference and the ones to follow were some of the most exhilarating experiences of my entire life. Many of the delegates were Resistance leaders in Europe or partisan fighters from Asia, some were fighting under colonial or semicolonial rule, and some had just emerged from fascism. At that time we came together in a marvelous spirit of determination to unite in a postwar world in which tens of millions of workers would have a say about their own conditions and their own destiny.

Sidney was assigned the responsibility of delivering the most important report, on organization, which I wrote for him. The report called for the establishment of a preparatory committee for a founding conference (eventually Philip Murray, R. J. Thomas, and Sidney would be named the CIO representatives on the committee, with Hillman the operative member and I his proxy).

From London, Sidney, Martin Kyne of the Department Store Workers, and I left for Paris to confer with the Confederation General du Travail (CGT), the French trade union center, which was to organize and host the founding conference. Although the war was still on and, with the Nazis still occupying parts of France, the fighting still fierce, Paris had been liberated after the Normandy invasion the previous June. This was my first visit since my mother gave me passage to Europe as a graduation present twenty years earlier. We stayed at the Ritz, which had shortly before been Nazi occupation headquarters but was then serving as offices for the U.S. Army.

Louis Saillant, a Socialist, was general secretary of the CGT, but it was his marvelous first secretary, Benoit Fraichon, who in actuality organized the conference. Benoit had been a top leader of the Resistance, carrying out his activities disguised as a tomato farmer. He looked the part, with a huge, bushy moustache and a pipe invariably clenched in his teeth; moreover, he was an acclaimed gardener and wine connoisseur. With a single taste, he could name the vintage and grower of whatever wine was being served. Benoit was also a leader of the French Communist party and quickly recognized in me a fellow "Red," which allowed us to consult one another on a close and confidential basis. I should say that at this point I hadn't really met the Soviets except on a formal level, and they had no idea of my politics.

Back home in New York, Hillman went on a speaking tour to report on the London conference and the meetings in Paris. To an American Labor party dinner at the Commodore, he said (and I wrote):

> I saw the tea room of the Ritz at tea time. I noted the costly furs, inhaled the expensive perfume and heard the cultivated chit-chat of France's privileged few. But . . . I was able to get something more than a Ritz-eye-view of liberated Paris. I spent many hours with the leaders and active workers of the French trade unions. I heard the story of the Resistance movement from the heroic men and women who . . . lived to participate so magnificently in the liberation of their country from the invader. I heard from the lips of our own military leaders how the exploits of the maquis and French Forces of the Interior disorganized and destroyed the German rear. . . .
>
> Today the progressive forces of France of every political coloration have forged a coalition that transcends all ideological differences and unites them for the performance of their common tasks and the effectuation of their common program. In this gathering together of the forces of progress, the French labor movement occupies an outstanding place. Today, only six months after the liberation, the membership of the trade unions already number over five million. I have seen them in action. Here is real power. But here is also discipline and restraint."

Sidney didn't say so but he knew that here too, as with the Resistance, was the French Communist party. He was exhilarated, as we all were, by the results of the Yalta meeting—which occurred while we were in London—of Roosevelt, Churchill, and Stalin. A new world was aborning, he and we thought, and the upcoming founding conference of the United Nations was its surest indication. At a Madison Square Garden labor rally, he felt it necessary to issue a cautionary note, however: "We [the CIO] must intensify our efforts in support of the Yalta decisions and for the effectuation of President Roosevelt's program of international cooperation. The realization of that pro-

WHAT DO you THINK THE SOVIETS were DREAMING of AT THAT TIME you IDIOT; BUT WORLD DOMINATION

PATRIOTIC

gram has by no means been assured. Powerful and unscrupulous forces are at work in an effort to sabotage and defeat it. . . . They do not want peaceful economic collaboration among nations. Instead they seek domination of world markets and dream of an 'American Century.'"

* * *

I was in Washington when President Roosevelt died. His death was sudden and it was a terrible blow, a loss personally felt by tens of millions of Americans. One could easily see that FDR was not well upon his return from Yalta. His face was drawn, his wonderful voice terribly strained. For his report on Yalta to a joint session of Congress, he asked, for the first time, to be allowed to speak while sitting. Anyone who knew him well must have understood that his remaining time was limited.

Pressman and I were in Washington for a CIO meeting to plan a joint AFL and CIO conference with the National Association of Manufacturers at year's end. The subject was to be postwar labor relations. Pressman and I, influenced by the optimism that emerged from Yalta—and the Communist party's assessment, which bordered on euphoria with its projection of postwar class peace—told each other how fortunate we were that this conference would take place in the wake of FDR's death.

Meantime, the WFTU leadership assigned Lee and I the task of drafting the new organization's constitution, implicit in which was winning the agreement of the Soviets. Again, here it was clear that Hillman and Murray knew our politics and found them useful to their own purposes. The Soviets were quite leery of Citrine, a skepticism dating back several years. On the other hand, they vastly overestimated the political reliability of the CIO, misreading its wartime support for the Grand Alliance and inflating the Left's influence within it. Of course the same mistake could also be attributed to some in the Communist party leadership who tended to exaggerate their own importance.

The WFTU executive met in the San Francisco Bay Area to coincide with the founding conference of the United Nations. Here I made the acquaintance and the beginnings of lifelong friendships with the two leading Soviet representatives to the WFTU. I'd first met Vassili Vassilovich Kuznetsov at the second London conference that February. He introduced himself and indicated he knew of me and of my Communist affiliation. Kuznetsov was then the head of the AUCCTU but for several years in the late twenties and early thirties, he worked

YOU FOOL, The COMMIES were euphoric BECAUSE They would BE ABLE TO EXERT STRONG POLITICAL CONTROL OVER EASTERN EUROPE AND DENY STALI PROMISED DEMOCRATIC ELECTIONS IN THOSE COUNTRIES.—

at the Carnegie Steel works in Pittsburgh. He was the stereotypical steelworker—husky, heavyset, with large calloused hands. His English was excellent, though spoken with a pronounced accent, and he never used an interpreter. When he arrived for the Oakland meeting, we were already in session discussing the proposed constitution and sitting around a table at the end of an elongated hall. I still remember Vassili walking down that hall, his shoes squeaking with every step. Dressed in a three-piece suit befitting an international labor diplomat, he wore poorly constructed Russian shoes. The squeaks were a bit of an embarrassment for the elegant Sir Walter Citrine and the other Western trade union big shots. In later years, Vassili became the Soviet ambassador to China and a deputy foreign minister and was vice-president of the USSR when he died in the late eighties. We always met whenever his diplomatic schedule brought him to the United Nations in New York or when I was in Moscow, and he never failed to talk about how much he preferred trade union work to diplomacy.

The AUCCTU first secretary and Kuznetsov's colleague in the WFTU was Mikhail Petrovich Terasov, a former railroad worker and one of the loveliest human beings I have ever known. Warm, with a particularly open sense of humor, he knew no English but was always able to convey his ideas. For the next thirty years we met when there was an opportunity and came to understand one another well. Terasov was a devoted Communist, and this meeting in Oakland was his first visit to the capitalist United States. One evening over drinks he said, "You know, John, your country has all the physical plant and infrastructure that is required to make a successful socialism. But I'm afraid that you will remain an island of capitalism in a socialist sea." His was an optimism—grossly misplaced as it has developed—that I shared. But in fact his assertion about the possibilities of an American socialism, given our advanced economic development, was one that Marx—who considered such development the necessary and natural precondition to socialism—would have appreciated.

In Oakland I was also to meet for the first time Vincente Lombardo Toledano, the militant and dramatic general secretary of the Confederation of Latin American Workers. Lombardo had an immense following not only in his native Mexico but throughout Latin America. He had a silver tongue that gave voice to millions of workers from the Rio Grande to Punto del Este. In Latin America, where most of the workers were illiterate, it was this verbal communication that served him so well; within the WFTU leadership, these communications skills were much less valued. Though Lombardo was never af-

[handwritten:]) AND USE ALL NECESSARY MILITARY FORCE AGAINST THOSE COUNTRIES [eg. HUNGARY] TO CONTROL THEM. STALIN COULD HAVE CARED LESS ABOUT "CLASS PEACE".

filiated with any of the Mexican leftist parties, he and my sister, Marion, became quite close through her work as secretary of our Party's Committee on Latin American Affairs, which organized our solidarity work in the hemisphere.

Hillman was impressed with the company we kept. He wrote, in a lengthy testimonial to the WFTU, "Once Voice for Sixty Million" in the *Collier's* issue of September 29, 1945:

> Here sat men of every school of training, of every tradition and temperament. They had come from great industrial nations, from undeveloped semicolonial lands. Here were leaders of old and well-disciplined organizations fraternizing with representatives of new, militant labor unions. Here were men who knew that the answers being sought across the bay in San Francisco cannot be left to governments alone.
>
> They knew, too, that the answers cannot be left to men who control monopolies and international cartels, men who share the responsibility for the rise of Fascism, for the outbreak of war, who are already beginning to jockey for positions from which to launch a new imperialistic scramble for power. The answers that San Francisco was seeking would come rather from the earth's common people. And here in Oakland sat the representatives of sixty million such people.

* * *

Back in November 1943, while Sidney was basking in our victory within the ALP in New York and the CIO-PAC was building up a head of steam heading into the 1944 election campaign, events half a world away were validating our positions. Roosevelt, Churchill, and Stalin met in Teheran to project a postwar world of peace, cooperation, and friendship between the Big Three and, consequently, among all of the United Nations in formation.

A few months earlier, the Communist International, the Comintern, had been dissolved on the basis that it could no longer determine policy and tactics for the scores of Communist parties that operated under such diverse circumstances and that had sprung from such disparate cultures and stages of historical development. Of course this had always been the case. More likely the dissolution of the Comintern was a wartime gesture to Roosevelt, Churchill, and their ideological brethren that, for the USSR and the Communists, victory in the war was paramount. The decision to dissolve was essentially an international equivalent of our domestic no-strike pledge.

These two events—the Teheran summit and the termination of the Comintern—had an enormous impact on the Communist Party USA. Browder more or less argued that Teheran represented not so much a series of tactical agreements by three major powers who shared an alliance in wartime as it was the architecture for a new world order. The Big Three would work together to guarantee the peace; our job, as Communists, was to do everything to make this possible and to do nothing to alter it. The postwar world would produce new markets for U.S. capitalism which in turn would serve the anticolonial cause of economic development. Moreover, the U.S. ruling class would profit from a hugely expanded trade with the USSR. The long period of international peace to come would be accompanied at home by increasing class harmony. In essence, Browder (and the Party) advocated a rejection of the principle of a revolutionary working-class party working exclusively in the interests of the workers and Lenin's theory of the expansive and exploitative nature of imperialism *as a system.*

Under Roosevelt, the Democratic party had distinguished itself from the Republicans both in terms of policy and in the realignment of its class base. From that point on the two-party system would remain dominant in the United States. The CPUSA could not, in the American sense of politics, be a party that contended for power through the ballot. Rather we were to be a loyal opposition whose role was to push the Democrats to the left. While we had elected Ben Davis and Pete Cacchione, both public Communists, to the New York City Council, all other Communist officeholders were elected under different banners. The two Communists who were elected to Congress—Johnny Bernard from Minnesota and Hugh DeLacy from Washington State—were elected as Democrats. Marcantonio, who was a friend of the Party but never a member, was elected as a Republican, a Democrat, and as the ALP candidate. (Although it was also true that in each of these successful political campaigns coalitions were built on the basis of an alliance between advanced working-class forces and middle-class liberals and civil reformers. Never was there a coalition with even a section of the ruling class—which Browder was advocating—for not even Roosevelt would welcome a Ben Davis or a Vito Marcantonio as a preferred candidate.) If there was to be a third party, a party of the Left that could contend for power, it would not be the CPUSA but some united front like the ALP. Consequently the Party, *as a party,* should dissolve itself and become the Communist Political Association (CPA), in which we would carry on as before—working in mass movements, most important the trade

unions; critiquing capitalism from a Marxist standpoint; building coalitions—but no longer running candidates for public office. The proposal for an association rather than a party was the culmination of a
process—the uncritical support of FDR's domestic and international
programs, the no-strike pledge, the blindness toward the Japanese-
American relocation camps, the subjugation of the fight for African-
American equality to the antifascist war mobilization, etc.

This was the proposition Browder placed before the Party, and one
that enjoyed the support of the entire leadership except for William
Z. Foster and one or two others. There had always been an atmosphere of tension between Browder and Foster. Bill was one of the
great labor leaders of the twentieth century, one of heroic proportions, but his orientation nearly approached syndicalism. The
founder of the Trade Union Unity League, he not only approached
things from a thoroughly working-class prism but saw organized labor per se as potentially revolutionary. The differences between
Browder and Foster were symptomatic of a problem in any revolutionary organization that works in a nonrevolutionary situation. If
you are, and enjoy being, a sect, no temptation will attract you; but
once you are immersed in mass struggles, leading and influencing
hundreds of thousands and millions outside of your membership,
there will be pressures to surrender some of your purity. Our main
goals of the previous ten years had been consolidating the CIO's unity and defeating fascism. In the interests of these goals we developed
uncritical attitudes toward people like FDR and Phil Murray and, yes,
Sidney Hillman. In the interests of unity, we surrendered our independence and critical judgment.

Perhaps Browder also suffered from illusions as to the Party's real
strength. He believed that through certain intermediaries he not only
communicated with, but influenced, President Roosevelt. The fact
that Communists were in the leadership of some eleven CIO unions
undoubtedly gave us a position of some real influence in the labor
movement and, consequently, in the Democratic party. But this influence could also be easily inflated and was, both by the Party leadership and by our enemies, who saw us lurking behind every bedpost.
The fact is that the Left was never the dominant force in the CIO, let
alone the AFL, the railway brotherhoods, and other independent
unions.

To the overwhelming majority of the Party leadership, there was
an unacknowledged understanding that no major change of direction
would be made without the consent of the international movement.
While the Comintern was dead, old habits and beliefs were not. If

there were misgivings about the CPA, besides Foster's, they went un-
declared with the assumption that Browder must be speaking for the
world movement in his analysis. That Foster chose not to take his differences to the membership indicated that he too may have felt that,
at least while the war was still raging, it made no sense to carry on
an internal Party fight about what the postwar world might look like.

I got my first inkling of how the international movement viewed
our developments when I met privately with Benoit Fraichon in Paris. "What do you people think?" he asked me. "You're going to have
class peace with J. P. Morgan?" I made what I'm sure was a poor defense of the Party's position, which didn't impress him in the least.
(Benoit later invited Pressman and I to his apartment where we met
with Jacques Duclos, one of the French Communist party's top leaders and a deputy in the National Assembly. It was a social evening
and we didn't discuss the situation of the CPUSA or CPA, as it were.
But Duclos was soon to have more than a fleeting influence over our
situation.) When I returned home, I mentioned to Gene Dennis the
initial exchange with Fraichon. Gene didn't respond—that wasn't his
way—but he absorbed the information and passed it on to Browder.
(In his oral history, Browder said he first learned of international dissatisfaction with his position from me. Since I never reported directly to Earl, I assume he was referring to my meeting with Gene.)

In the April 1945 issue of *Cahiers du Communisme,* the French
Communist magazine, Jacques Duclos wrote his famous article that
feigned to be an informational piece for French readers who were
uninformed about the direction the U.S. Communists were taking.
But it was clearly meant, and understood, to be a direct challenge to
the leadership of Earl Browder and the course of the CPUSA. Duclos
wrote that Browder had come to "erroneous conclusions in no wise
flowing from a Marxist analysis of the situation"; that Browder had
become "the protagonist of a false concept of social evolution in general, and in the first place the social evolution of the United States."
Duclos went further: "By transforming the Teheran declaration of the
Allied governments, which is a document of a diplomatic character,
into a political platform of class peace in the United States in the postwar period, the American Communists are deforming in a radical
way the meaning of the Teheran declaration and are sowing dangerous opportunist illusions which will exercise a negative influence on
the American labor movement if they are not met with the necessary
reply."

The Duclos article has since been almost invariably referred to by
historians as "the Duclos letter," a directive from the world move-

ment to U.S. Communists to overturn its positions of the previous fifteen months. It was the New York *World-Telegram and Sun* that first reported to U.S. readers about the article, giving the interpretation that these were instructions from Moscow. The tone of the article lent itself to this interpretation. Here was not a questioning attitude about the policies of a fraternal party, but simply *diktat*.

By the time the Duclos article actually appeared in the United States in the summer of 1945, Roosevelt was dead, the war in Europe was over, and there were already clear indications that, under Truman, the wartime alliance was insecure at best. Even as the Party leadership met to discuss the Duclos article and to reconsider our earlier analysis and decision to dissolve the Party, the atomic bombs were dropped on Hiroshima and Nagasaki. While some in the Party leadership hailed the bombings in the belief that they would hasten the end of the war, others had misgivings about this entrance into the nuclear era. Stalin was quick to read the bombings for what they were—the opening shots of the cold war. After all, the Red Army, victorious in Europe, had entered the Asian theater and was only a couple of weeks away from Japan. The atomic bombs had followed earlier American and British carpet bombings of Dresden in Germany and the Skoda works, the main industrial center of Czechoslovakia, just as the Red Army was approaching. The countries of eastern Europe, under Soviet occupation, were in the process of erecting "new people's democracies," popular front governments led by antifascist and nonfascist parties. This concept, which eschewed the "dictatorship of the proletariat," was one initially advocated and developed by Georgi Dmitroff, the Bulgarian Communist. With the dropping of atomic bombs, the "new people's democracies" were doomed in all but name, as Stalin demanded Communist central control throughout eastern Europe, which ended only with the popular uprisings of 1989, forty-four years later.

In short order, the Party reversed its earlier decisions, repudiated Browder's theses, and reestablished the CPUSA. Gene Dennis and Gil Green, who was then the chair of the Party in New York, came to my house to "take my temperature," as we said, to find out my feelings on the matter. They were both pleased and surprised to find I was in full agreement with the reversal. It wasn't simply a thunderclap of orders from Moscow—the Duclos article—that resulted in the Party's change. The new reality, the realignment of forces, abroad and at home, was already becoming apparent.

Was the Duclos article necessary? Of course the Party was off base in its estimate and needed correction, but the facts of postwar life would have done that for us. With Browder repudiated, Bill Foster became Party chair and Gene Dennis our general secretary. And with "instructions" from Duclos, we swerved in the completely opposite direction, which tends to happen when one isn't thinking for oneself. The elimination of "Browderism" opened the door to the emergence of "Fosterism," which was characterized by dogmatism. Without the Duclos letter, had the changes in Party policy come naturally through our own analysis of the changing times, we might not have lost a number of good people, as we did in that period. Prior to 1945 there had been plenty of room in the Party for supporters of both Browder and Foster. Why shouldn't this have been the case after 1945? Ever since that time, the Party has denigrated Browder and "Browderism," without a serious assessment of its history or acknowledgment of its errors. (Although this weakness is not confined to the Browder years.) Yet it was under Browder that the Party saw its greatest growth and widest influence.

* * *

The CIO delegation to the formal founding congress of the WFTU in Paris in September 1945 was led, as usual, by Hillman. The congress itself was mainly a ratification of all of the preparatory meetings we had held over the past ten months—in London, Paris, Washington, and Oakland. Sidney was called upon to give the report of the administrative committee, including the presentation of the constitution, which was adopted in full.

Hillman concluded his report, which as always I had prepared, with the following words: "We must recognize that there are those—and not in Germany alone—who do not want to see Germany's war potential utterly destroyed and the roots of fascism relentlessly eradicated. We of world labor must firmly and effectively express our will that these forces, who bear primary responsibility for plunging the world into war, shall not again prevail. . . . We will have to look to German labor if that country is ever to join and participate in the family of democratic nations."

He moved that the congress agree to appoint a commission for the purpose of visiting Germany, making a full examination and investigation in all zones of the occupation, and report on the status of the execution of the Potsdam decisions of the Big Three to decartelize and denazify Germany, included in which was the reestablishment of a free, democratic trade union movement. The motion was unanimously adopted.

From Paris, most of the CIO delegation went on to Moscow. This was the first—and as it turns out even now, nearly half a century later, the only—official CIO (or AFL-CIO) delegation to ever visit the Soviet Union. Hillman was compelled for business reasons to return to New York from Paris, so the delegation was headed by Jimmy Carey, the CIO secretary-treasurer. In the context of the CIO, Carey was on the Right. He had been president of the United Electrical Workers but was defeated in an election for that position by Albert Fitzgerald, who was on the Left. Fitzie, as a CIO vice-president, was also on the delegation to Moscow. He had little regard for Carey, who though he was CIO secretary-treasurer represented no union, and considered him an officer without troops. I can't really say anything outstanding about Carey; he wasn't an outstanding person. But in the worst years of McCarthyism, when others would literally cross the street rather than encounter me, Jimmy was always friendly. I suppose that as a good Catholic and ardent churchgoer, he felt he was above suspicion and had no fears of being branded.

Len DeCaux, editor of *CIO News,* wrote the report of the delegation, which was signed by Jimmy Carey and distributed in the hundreds of thousands. A nearly lyrical tribute to the accomplishments of the Soviet working class, the report told of our visits to factory floors and our formal and informal meetings with farmers, craftspeople, and antifascist Resistance fighters, at workers' clubs and cultural centers, in Moscow and Leningrad. At an exhibition on the Nazis' nine-hundred-day siege of Leningrad, the unswervingly anticommunist Carey wrote in the visitor's record: "We hail your great feats that have surpassed anything in history. What you have accomplished to defend the freedom of the people of your land and the civilization of the world, will remain in the memory of the workers forever. On to victory together, with peace and prosperity."

The CIO delegation left after eight days but I stayed on for a few weeks to be with Jessica, who was in Moscow on business. My friends Kuznetsov and Terasov arranged tickets for us to the ballet and theater each night, and afterward we met them at the AUCCTU headquarters. The all-union office was open throughout the night because Stalin frequently worked at the Kremlin until 4 A.M. and would call for information or to give instructions. At some point we would go out for dinner and to talk. Often the talk turned to public and union elections, of how you could not have any kind of real democracy when there was no choice of candidates. The Soviets defended this practice on the grounds that their nomination process was so extensive: potential candidates had to meet with their constituencies, which would then arrive at the best possible nominee. They

— But the USSR wasn't classless, and had an opulent ruling bureaucracy — which Leon Trotsky pointed out and was murdered for his exposure of this + other commie lies

pointed out that in our country, we had the appearance of competition but no substantive differences between the two major parties. I would have to concede their point in most cases. They also offered the "scientific" explanation of why pluralism was unnecessary, i.e., that parties are representatives of various classes and, since the Soviet Union was a classless society, there was no point to competing parties. I recognized back then, but far more forcibly later, that this "scientific" analysis did not hold, most certainly not for the United States. True, competing parties can and do represent competing classes in struggle; but there can also be competing interests, different answers and responses to some problems that transcend narrow class interests. Anyway, the debates would rage on each night.

I also recall our discussing the issue of the union dues checkoff. This is the process by which, in most U.S. union-management contracts, union dues assessments are deducted from the workers' paychecks and given to the union by management. The Soviets were adamantly opposed to the system of checkoffs, for what I considered valid reasons. Terasov would argue, "Between the time the worker puts his hand in his pocket and the time he comes up with his dues money, he thinks about all his grievances—on the job and in the union. If the union doesn't take care of his grievances, it won't get his dues money." In a whole number of countries with powerful union movements—France, Italy, and the USSR among them—checkoffs were rejected on the basis that it would encourage laziness and corruption.

I came home to New York in 1945 with the approach of Christmas. Jessica wouldn't return until January. By the time she got back, the WFTU delegation to occupied Germany had been selected and Hillman was the CIO's representative. He insisted I accompany him to Germany and I had little choice but to agree. The WFTU commission consisted of delegates of the CIO, the AUCCTU, the British TUC, and the French CGT, that is, the trade union centers of the four occupying powers. Sir Walter was the British delegate, Terasov the Soviet, and Leon Jouhaux, a French Social Democrat, came for the CGT. Sidney and I represented the CIO. Of the four chief members, only Terasov could be considered on the Left.

Because of the large Jewish membership in the Amalgamated and because of his own identification as a Jew, Sidney was particularly concerned with the status of the few remaining Jews—primarily displaced persons—in Germany. But the overall goal of the delegation was to determine the extent of denazification under occupation—in general, in the schools, the press, etc.—and specifically in the newly emerging trade unions. To this end, the commission spent a week in each zone of occupation. We visited mines and steel plants, apprentice training centers and union headquarters; we met with shop workers and floor stewards, leaders of the new unions and military authorities of the four powers. (When we were in Nuremberg, the war crimes tribunals were in progress and Sidney and I had lunch one day with Bob Jackson, then on leave from the Supreme Court to serve as chief Allied prosecutor. While we were primarily interested in denazification, Jackson, ever the politician, was more interested in discussing the possibilities of a run at the New York governorship. Had he thought there was a real possibility for his candidacy, he would have given up his position on the court. As governor of New York he would have been within reach of his real ambition—the presidency.)

In the French Zone, we discovered that as many as 80 percent of the French occupation military officers had also been officers in the Vichy government, that is, they had served as collaborators with the Nazi occupation of France. It was difficult to see how they would supervise the denazification programs in Germany, particularly in the new trade unions. These former Vichy officers who a year earlier, on behalf of the Nazis, were hunting down and imprisoning French Communist and Socialist Resistance fighters, could hardly be expected to allow German Communist and Socialist trade unionists to displace former Nazi party members.

Prior to Hitler's seizure of power in 1933, the German Communists and Social Democrats were the two most powerful political organizations in the country and together dominated the German trade union movement. Yet their combined strength—understanding that they tragically never combined their strength but directed their energies against one another—was not enough to either prevent Hitler's rise or to undermine his power. Hence, the Allies at Potsdam had agreed that Germany must be deprived of the economic means to disturb world peace, i.e., the former monopolies that financed Hitler and greatly profited from his war machine needed to be decartelized and the new German economy had to be based upon agriculture and peaceful domestic industries. The production of arms, munitions, and implements of war should be prohibited.

It is striking, in retrospect, that the four leading members of the commission—a benighted British Labourite, a French Socialist, a U.S. liberal Democrat, and a Soviet Communist—were virtually unanimous in their findings and conclusions. Outside of the Soviet Zone, denazification was a secondary consideration. In Frankfurt, the largest city in the American Zone, for example, we found that over 50 percent of the eight thousand plus city government workers had been Nazi party members. Communists and Social Democrats—granted hundreds of thousands, even millions, had perished in the Nazi genocide—were nearly nonexistent. We found that in the British, French, and American Zones, denazification was implemented without vigor. When Nazis were discovered and dismissed from a post, they would simply get jobs in another of the Western zones. Agriculture remained in the hands of the Junker class, the wealthy, ultrareactionary, landed aristocracy, except in the Soviet Zone, where the landed estates had been broken up and distributed to the farmers. The Junker class had been among Hitler's primary supporters and were kindred spirits of our own southern plantation owners.

We returned to Paris to prepare a report. I was asked to draft the preliminary report that—like the one I wrote on the Florida hurricane for the WPA—became both the preliminary and the final report. That such a diverse delegation could arrive at a virtual unanimity of views augured well for the future of the WFTU.

* * *

Two months later, the CIO-PAC adopted its political action program for 1946, reflecting the optimism from our international contacts. The program called for the "destruction of the economic and social roots of fascism in Germany and Japan through the full implementation of the Potsdam decisions." It declared, "The war-born unity of Great Britain, the Soviet Union and the United States was the key to victory over the enemy. Their unity is no less essential if the United Nations is to be the sure guardian of the peace. . . . We reject proposals for American participation in any bloc or alliance which is inimical to their unity."

The CIO-PAC program also called for United Nations control over "all phases of atomic energy"; UN action to restore democracy and eliminate fascism from Spain and Argentina; full independence for the colonial peoples of Africa and Asia; statehood for Hawaii; a progressive income tax directed in particular at the corporations who made enormous war profits; full farm production; elimination of the poll tax and other Jim Crow voting practices in the South; destruction of the Ku Klux Klan and other "fascist, subversive movements"; curbing of illegal injunctions and police violence against striking workers and minorities; national health insurance; an enlarged GI Bill of Rights; enactment of minimum wage laws that allowed for a living wage; social security benefits to be extended to white-collar and professional workers; guaranteed affordable housing for all; and, not least of all, substantial wage increases—wages had been frozen throughout the war—to be agreed upon through collective bargaining. We declared that "Now the fight shifts from the picket line to Capitol Hill and to the ballot box, our victories on the economic front will be swept away if the people meet defeat on the political front." In short, the CIO-PAC of 1946 would carry into the postwar period the progressive and militant traditions it inherited from the New Deal and antifascist years.

But things would soon change. And Hillman, his nose ever to the winds, could smell the changes. The previous fall, President Truman had invited Sidney to the White House. When he returned to the Amalgamated offices the next day, Sidney was quite pleased if not exuberant. "I can work with him," was Hillman's pronouncement to me on his pleasure in being in the president's company. Truman received Sidney respectfully without regard to his politics, and for Sidney this was what mattered most. His loyalty to FDR was placed primarily because the president received him and confided in him, thereby allowing Hillman's influence to grow.

After Roosevelt's death, the CIO-PAC and NCPAC supported Truman for the first few months, taking issue with him first in October 1945, six months after FDR's death, in opposing the new president's support of universal military training. With Truman in office, however, Hillman modified his views to coincide with those of the White House. He became far more skittish in his relations with the Left, although this did not include our personal relationship. He began to put a tighter rein on Beanie Baldwin and had strenuous arguments with Beanie and others in NCPAC over their criticisms of Truman.

Some critics of the Communist party have made a career of pointing out its swift changes of positions over the years, but Hillman was a virtual weather vane with the added feature that he was able to turn in advance of a change in the weather. Had he lived, he would likely have reverted to the role he played in the 1940 CIO convention when he sought the ouster of the Communists from the labor movement, which itself was a reprise of his internal struggle with the Left rank and file in the Amalgamated during the twenties.

In July 1946, Sidney suffered a massive heart attack and died at home on Long Island. The Amalgamated General Executive Board held a lengthy meeting to choose his successor. I was not invited, the first meeting from which I was excluded since Hillman hired me nine years earlier. There were some efforts to elect Frank Rosenblum to the post but Jacob Potofsky, for years the secretary-treasurer, was elected the new president. I had no doubts that I would be retained

as general counsel, but I questioned my usefulness to the Party—my
first concern—to stay on without Hillman. Gene Dennis persuaded
me to remain. None of the other Amalgamated officers would play
Hillman's role in the CIO or in the political life of the country. They
would simply try to hang on to what they had; they would pioneer in
no direction and lead to no great accomplishment. Frank Rosenblum
was designated by Phil Murray to be Sidney's successor in the international field and would continue to take me to WFTU meetings.
Jack Kroll, the Amalgamated's Cincinnati director, would take over
the CIO-PAC and continue to retain me as counsel. I remained friendly with Jacob, Frank, and Jack on both a professional and personal
level, but none of them had Sidney's reach or grasp. The world was
turning, quickly.

4

Progressives

I was completely unprepared for the terror that was to face the labor movement and, most particularly, the Communist party in the coming years. I can't speak for others but I know of no one who was any more clairvoyant than I was on this score. Of course we knew things would be different. The parochial Truman was clearly no Roosevelt. With Europe destroyed and the USSR nearly prostrate, an unscathed United States, its infrastructure and industry not only intact but greatly expanded by the war, would become the dominant world power.

The brilliant Italian Communist Antonio Gramsci once wrote that the revolutionary must have "pessimism of the intellect, optimism of the will." Too often we Communists suffered from an "optimism" of the intellect, but rarely from a "pessimism" of the will. In 1946, our optimism of the will was unimpaired. The same enthusiasm with which we greeted the early New Deal period—that sense that we could actually be a factor in determining the course of things, which first attracted me to the Party—and which carried us throughout the Roosevelt years and the world war was not lessened by the new situation.

Major strikes were called in the auto, mining, steel, and electrical industries to win wage hikes and benefits that had been postponed through four years of war and labor's no-strike pledge. While the monopolies made enormous profits in wartime, workers' income had been essentially frozen. Real income was actually reduced during the war and, in the postwar inflation, reduced still further. In some instances the strikes were met with police violence, but in each case the union actions were successful. The companies were not out to break the unions; on the contrary, they were anxious for a labor peace in the coming years, the better to secure their enhanced power at home and abroad.

The strikes were also necessitated by the loss of the Office of Price Administration (OPA), another wartime innovation cherished by Hillman and Murray, which limited price increases and thereby maintained workers' (and consumers') purchasing power. The loss of the OPA demonstrated to labor that it could not count on majority support in Congress, and the strikes were launched to redress the imbalances the government would otherwise allow. Then in September, right after the loss of OPA, Truman dismissed Henry Wallace from his cabinet. Wallace, the remaining "unreconstructed" New Dealer who, as Truman's secretary of commerce, continued to give voice to Roosevelt's projection of a U.S.-Soviet-British alliance in the aftermath of the war, could not be silenced by Truman. But he could be fired. By the time of the November congressional elections, the CIO was already on the defensive—Murray was being harassed by the news media about "Communist domination" of the CIO—and the voters gave the Republicans a rare majority of both houses of Congress. This was a major defeat for the CIO-PAC and gave the labor leadership further argument to abandon an independent electoral stance and subordinate CIO-PAC to the Democratic party.

Two weeks after the elections, the CIO held its convention in Atlantic City. Murray and the leadership tried to go in two directions simultaneously. On the one hand, they moved to attack the price increases, to launch a southern organizing drive, to continue their cooperation with the WFTU, and even to reaffirm their opposition to Truman's foreign policy. Shortly before his death, Hillman told the convention of the Amalgamated that the people of the United States would not support an anti-Soviet foreign policy and rejected Churchill's attempt to build an Anglo-American alliance to the exclusion of the USSR. In what was to be his last speech, Sidney said, "In Russia, it is their business to build the kind of government they feel they want. We expect them to have the same respect for us. That is the understanding, and it stands up." Several months later, the CIO as a whole essentially echoed Hillman's position.

On the other hand, Murray sought to deflect the anticommunist attacks on the CIO by himself attacking the Left. To prevent a floor fight, Murray raised the question of the CIO's relations with the Communist party in an executive board meeting held on the eve of the convention. After two days of argument and division, the Left in the executive board compromised and agreed to a statement condemning all outside interference in the CIO. Murray's formulation was to "resent and reject" interference by the Communist party or any other "outside" party. To avoid a divided convention, Murray decided that rather than presenting such a resolution to the floor, he would incorporate its essence in his speech. Calling for limitations—passed as constitutional amendments—on the political independence of local and state CIO councils, where the Left had its greatest strength, Murray said: "This movement of ours . . . does not care to be bothered with, it will not tolerate, interference from not only the Communist Party . . . but all other political parties. . . . The Congress of Industrial Organizations is an American institution dedicated to the attainment of its well defined social and economic objectives within the framework of American political democracy." By singling out the Communist party, he left no doubt as to his intended target. On the other hand, it was understood that there would be no purge—at least not yet—as the Right had been urging.

Nevertheless, this departure from several years of Left-Center unity marked the beginning of a process that would culminate in the expulsion of the Left and Communists, including eleven of its constituent international unions, from the CIO four years later. The concession by the Communists and their allies to allow this position to be projected, in exchange for agreement that there wouldn't be a purge, has been much debated in subsequent years. Len DeCaux wrote in his "personal history," *Labor Radical,* "There was some method in the meekness of the lefts. They had to retreat under conditions that threatened a rout. To preserve the unity of a still relatively progressive CIO, they continued to make concessions as they had done since the CIO began. . . . All aggression came from the right. The lefts conceded, compromised, even turned around. To break up unity, the right had to do it." In arguments with friends, I have often been considered "sectarian," and I acknowledge the merit in the accusation. Nevertheless, I believe that it was a mistake back then for the Left to support unity at all costs. The Party and its followers thought that they could buy peace with Phil Murray. By going along with him, we would save our own skins, it was argued. We erred in not understanding that we couldn't save ourselves by giving on principle. The really serious red-baiting attacks hadn't even begun yet, but we were already retreating as if they had. We could at least have preserved our principles instead of opening the way for our own destruction. Admittedly this was a minority position back then, and remains so today. One problem Communists have always had, and not alone in the United States, is in not recognizing the distinction between the Party and the movements and organizations within which it works. Trade unions are reformist by their nature and it is an error for revolutionaries to demand that they be more. How to be a revolutionary in a reformist movement—leading in struggles, dispelling illusions, etc.—is a Communist's key task and not an easy one to master. It is crucial to understand that one cannot impose a revolutionary line on a reformist movement, but it is also essential that the revolutionary fight for the right to be active—including the right to hold elected leadership positions—in such movements. That Communists often fail in these matters is no crime; this is not an exact science and nobody can claim proficiency. But it is a severe deficiency, one impossible to overcome, not to learn from one's errors.

In the interests of the war effort, the Party overemphasized support for and reliance upon Murray, Hillman, and the centrist leadership of the CIO and underplayed such essential principles as rank-and-file democracy. When the leadership later turned on the Party, we were disarmed. Moreover, the extended period of class peace throughout the war years strengthened the position of those, like Walter Reuther, who were then on the Right in labor's ranks and who argued for policies of "class collaboration." On the other hand, one couldn't argue with the wartime no-strike pledge. The overriding goal of winning the war against fascism dictated this; and it was accepted with near unanimity by the working class. Further, it must be admitted that the Left, while an influence throughout organized labor and the leader of several important national unions and many local and state federations, was at no time the dominant or majority force in the trade union movement. In her memoir on life in the Party, Dorothy Healey, the leader of the Southern California district in those years, argues that the single most important event in the postwar labor movement was the victory of Reuther over R. J. Thomas for the presidency of the UAW, the CIO's biggest union. This, she says, set the tone for the swing to the Right. Unquestionably Reuther's victory was a defeat for the Left, but I would say, from my knowledge of the man, that R. J. Thomas would not have constituted a hindrance or a block to the elimination of the Left in the CIO. The powerful forces at work—with the United States as the commanding world power, the huge corporations as the dominant influence in the international economy, and the readiness of the Center and Right of labor to enter into a modus vivendi with them—were simply too strong to overcome. Certainly R. J. was not the man to challenge them, even had he defeated Reuther within the UAW.

In January and February 1947, in its first six weeks, the new, Republican-dominated Congress introduced more than sixty bills and amendments directed at "curbing labor's abuses." In May, it passed the Taft-Hartley Act, the cornerstone of all subsequent anti-labor legislation, aimed at neutralizing if not eliminating the Wagner Act of the New Deal. As Amalgamated's general counsel, I wrote the memoranda to the union's locals, joint boards, and national officers, analyzing the bill and suggesting a strategy for action. For the CIO-PAC, I drafted a campaign to reverse Taft-Hartley. The legislation's purpose was nothing less than to stop organized labor dead in its tracks.

It gave the courts the right to issue injunctions to stop strikes, a right they were prone to exercise at the request of any major corporation. It outlawed secondary boycotts, an essential weapon in labor's arsenal, thereby isolating a striking union from the solidarity of sister unions, making impossible the ultimate weapon of the general strike. Banning secondary boycotts also gave back employers the power they had in the pre–Wagner Act days, with unfettered access to suppliers and distributors and thereby unimpeded marketing. It changed the nature of the National Labor Relations Board from a partisan of labor's right to organize to an arbiter of allowable conditions. It placed severe restrictions on unions in organizing, strikes, political action, and plant elections.

Under Taft-Hartley's article 14(b), perversely named the "right-to-work" section of the law—perverse because it gives no one the right to work—employers were encouraged to move out of states with a strong organized labor base to those with a "union-free environment." Taft-Hartley 14(b) was thus a throwback to the days of "states rights" and, not by coincidence, the primary open-shop states were those of the Deep South. The law also required all union representatives to sign noncommunist affidavits, thereby denying workers the right to choose their own leaders. The bill was not only anti-labor, it was, in my opinion, unconstitutional. Some academicians claim that the intent of Taft-Hartley was to provide a balance in labor-management relations after a presumed "tilt" toward labor with the Wagner Act a decade before. This is patent nonsense of course. The nature of labor-management relations is inherently unbalanced. The employer always has the power to hire and fire because the employer has the jobs, so the employee is always in a defensive and weakened position.

Heber Blankenhorn, whose pioneering studies led to the formation of the LaFollette committee, quit the NLRB in protest. One Taft-Hartley proponent said the bill would "instill in American unions the spirit of fidelity to America." In response, Blankenhorn said it was not the spirit of fidelity that the act would bring but the "spirit of Fido, who must learn to lie down, roll over, and play dead, at the snap of a finger." John L. Lewis, who was anything but a Communist, proposed to the AFL board that the unions refuse en masse to sign the noncommunist affidavits, rendering the Taft-Hartley Act unworkable. The AFL leaders, however, had been instilled with "the spirit of Fido" and accepted the essence of Taft-Hartley. Lewis pulled the United Mine Workers out of the AFL, and it remained independent for the next four decades. Within the CIO, there was less acquiescence; after all a number of CIO unions and local CIO councils were led by Communists. The newly constituted National Labor Relations Board sweetened the pot for the Reuthers and Careys by ruling that any contract an employer signed with a union advocating noncompliance with Taft-Hartley could be upset if another qualified union sought an election to determine bargaining rights.

It may appear strange coming from me, but in retrospect, the trade union movement might have been better off without the Wagner Act in the first place. Of course, at the time, the Wagner Act seemed to be a great stimulus to the growth of organized labor. The problem is that labor became completely dependent on the Wagner Act and, with the passage of Taft-Hartley, the NLRB became a hindrance rather than an aid. The subsequent dependence of organized labor on the apparatus of the state has been a brake on its militancy and its ability to organize and grow.

* * *

In the early autumn of 1947 I was visited at the Amalgamated offices by a special agent of the FBI. He informed me that he was investigating charges of an alleged Communist espionage ring in Washington in the thirties. Following my own advice to my clients, I refused to answer the agent's questions. The FBI was hardly a disinterested party or seeker of justice when it came to the labor movement or the Communist party. It had, on behalf of the state, essentially replaced the professional spy organizations we had exposed during the LaFollette committee hearings. A few weeks after this visit, I was subpoenaed to appear before a federal grand jury that had been secretly sitting in New York for several months. This same grand jury, after nearly eighteen months of hearings, ended not with any indictments for espionage but—as something of a concession prize to the government—with the Smith Act indictments of Gene Dennis, Bill Foster, and ten other top Communist party leaders.

My appearance before the grand jury was something less than dramatic. Altogether I was there for perhaps forty-five minutes, refusing to answer any questions—including some with a none-too-subtle anti-Semitic slant about my religious upbringing—based on my First and Fifth Amendment rights under the Constitution. There was no immunity statute in those days, so the use of the Fifth Amendment essentially blocked the prosecutor's line of questioning. It became clear from his questions that my telephone was tapped: an intimate party for Jessica and me in Kent prompted questions from the federal attorney.

After my appearance, I told Jake Potofsky, Frank Rosenblum, and Hy Blumberg, the top officers at the Amalgamated, of my experience before the grand jury. They expressed no surprise or shock and even found it a bit amusing, except for the anti-Semitic episode. Looking back, it is difficult to understand their lackadaisical attitude, but this was still some months before the anticommunist hysteria hit full force. The idea that I should be investigated for being a spy struck them as simply ludicrous, something not to be taken seriously, perhaps a good story to tell over cocktails. I attached no more importance to the episode.

That fall, Pressman and I attended the annual CIO convention in Boston. It quickly became clear that the shift to the right in the CIO had greatly accelerated since the previous year. By its "Truman Doctrine," the administration had announced its intention to replace British colonialism as the dominant power in the Mediterranean through massive intervention on behalf of the rightist forces in the Greek civil war and underwriting the military dictatorship in Turkey. In June, the Marshall Plan had been proposed to rebuild Europe, including Germany, under U.S. hegemony. Rather than loan the USSR, our wartime ally and the greatest victim of Hitler's destruction, $2 or $3 billion for reconstruction, Truman asked Stalin to participate in the Marshall Plan, an invitation promptly declined by the Soviet premier. I suppose that it was the idea of rebuilding Germany without first exacting reparations that most repelled Stalin. In Boston, Murray announced that support for the Truman Doctrine and the Marshall Plan was "CIO policy" and that he would allow no detractors.

Moreover, Murray invited General George Marshall, then the secretary of state, as the featured speaker at the convention, the only time, to my knowledge, that a secretary of state ever addressed a national trade union convention. Marshall appealed for support on familiar jingoistic grounds. Supreme Court Justice William O. Douglas, wearing his liberal credentials on his sleeve, was more to the point in asking what the administration wanted from its friends in labor. Particularly concerned about winning over European social democracy to the Marshall Plan, Douglas appealed for labor's help: "They [European trade unions] fear the threat so frequently voiced in Soviet propaganda, that an American imperialism may be extending its power in to Europe. . . . Out of this arises the importance of the fact that American labor carries good credentials to Western Europe. Doors tightly closed to all others may open at its knock. Words from American labor promise to find quick acceptance." (While this appeal was being made to the CIO, the CIA was working with the AFL to set up pro-U.S. opposition unions in France, Italy, Greece, and other centers of leftist-led labor movements.) Of course the Left voted against CIO support of the Marshall Plan, but opposition became synonymous with disloyalty to the CIO and to the country. On first glance it appeared that the CIO was inconsistent in its foreign policy stance, shifting from "right" (prewar) to "left" (wartime) and back to "right" (postwar). But the constant thread throughout its history was fidelity to the foreign policy of successive administrations. If there were shifts, they were in the pattern of U.S. foreign policy, and the top leadership of the CIO clung to each successive change as if it were its very own.

This loyalty to government policy—and the CIO was not alone in this respect—would eventually split not only the CIO but the World Federation of Trade Unions as well. Shortly after the CIO convention in Boston, I went to Prague with Frank Rosenblum who, as I indicated, had succeeded Hillman as the CIO's international relations director. We were attending what was to be the last WFTU meeting in which I would ever participate. Jim Carey headed the CIO delegation, although he had heretofore played no role in the WFTU. His purpose at this point was to make a vigorous effort to persuade the WFTU to support the Marshall Plan. Given the composition of the WFTU, this was, of course, a futile endeavor.

From Prague, Carey went to Moscow to meet with Kuznetsov, then the chair of the AUCCTU. Carey carried with him an ultimatum—on behalf of both Murray and the CIO and Citrine and the British TUC—that either the Soviet trade unions support the Marshall Plan or the CIO and TUC would withdraw from the WFTU. The response was preordained. Of course the Soviet trade unions would not defy the Soviet government over the Marshall Plan, so the ultimatum was rejected. Shortly afterward, the CIO and TUC made good on their threat and left the WFTU. The unity of the world organization was broken, its effectiveness thereby materially diminished, and our aspirations for international trade union cooperation in the interests of peace and labor solidarity effectively destroyed.

There had always been differences within the WFTU between Left and Right. But with victory over Hitler and the beginning of the cold war, the unity expressed within the WFTU came under new pressures and began to disintegrate. Each of the major component parts—the CIO, the TUC, and the AUCCTU—adopted the positions of their governments, right or wrong, and these positions simply came into collision at the 1947 WFTU meeting in Prague.

In the field of foreign policy, this was the first but by no means the last time the U.S. labor leadership carried water abroad for the government. With the postwar national security state established, the Central Intelligence Agency replaced the wartime Office of Strategic Services. It wasn't long before the agency, in cooperation with the AFL, began to organize counterunions in Italy and France to oppose the massive labor federations headed up by former Resistance fighters and Communists. With the anticolonial revolutions in Africa, Asia, and Latin America, the AFL, after coalescing with the CIO in the fifties, used these European experiences to spearhead anticommunist union efforts in the Third World, again in cooperation with the CIA. What had once been an honorable CIO role in developing international labor unity had been turned on its head in a campaign to split workers' organizations abroad. The case can easily be made that the Soviet unions were never independent of the control of the Soviet state, but it is also true that for thirty years of cold war history, the AFL-CIO's and state department's policies were indistinguishable. To this day, that remains largely the case with the federation as a whole. However, during the Vietnam War, fissures began, and by the time of the Reagan arms buildup, some national unions declared their independence in foreign policy from both the AFL-CIO and the state department.

* * *

One thing that greatly impressed me in the WFTU was that there were Communists working in labor movements the world over, many under the most severe circumstances, as in those countries still under colonial domination or fascist control. Most impressive was that these women and men were all working as Communists, not concealing their affiliations. It occurred to me, and I've often thought about it since, that perhaps one of the errors made by the Communist Party USA was in keeping secret the affiliation of the comrades in the labor movement. The Fur and Leather Workers' Union, led by Ben Gold and Irving Potash, was the only one in the CIO whose officers were public Communists.

Of course there were good reasons for our not doing so. Len De-

Caux wrote in his memoir that "a rule of the game was that the Communist player should not proclaim his communism. That way the respectable, if caught at it, could say with shocked innocence, 'Good gracious, we never knew he was a Communist.'" Certainly there were "legal and extra-legal penalties on Communists," as Len wrote, but also "such camouflage . . . was expected, if not demanded, by the allies that [we] battled alongside." This was definitely true of Hillman in my case and of Murray in Pressman's.

Still, by not acknowledging our party affiliation, the Communists in the labor leadership never received credit as Communists for their many accomplishments in organizing and struggling for better conditions. Moreover, when the cold war came and these most dedicated unionists were denounced as Communists, the fact that they had kept their political relationships secret fed the conspiracy stereotype of "infiltrators" with which our opponents painted the Party. Finally, by burying their Party membership, some Communists in the leadership of unions were encouraged to be opportunistic, to change spots, so to speak, as the times dictated. Which is not to argue that there wouldn't have been serious problems if the Communists had been open in their membership. They might well have been ousted from the CIO in the cold war anyway, although the fight to remain would have been waged on a different set of principles.

Faced with the mounting political terror of the McCarthy years and the generally aggressive posture of a relatively united ruling class at the peak of its powers, I'm not sure that expulsion of the Left from the CIO could have been averted. Anticommunism had become the litmus test for "Americanism." Short of abandoning all political principle, the Left had no means of tactical retreat. It was left to Arthur Goldberg, a fellow Chicagoan and my successor as general counsel of the Amalgamated, to conduct the purge. I'd known Arthur in the union—he'd gotten his start in the Chicago local—and always detested him for his long-standing red-baiting. When I left the Amalgamated in 1947, he took my place; and when Pressman left the CIO a year later, Arthur took his place as general counsel.

These ironies would pile upon new ironies in the next years: Goldberg conducted the expulsion proceedings against the leftist-led unions, adopting techniques that would prove identical to those used by the government under the McCarran Act to outlaw the Communist party. The CIO hearings were based on the concept of "an identity of views" of the Communist party, the Left unions, and the USSR on a series of international questions—the Marshall Plan, the Truman Doctrine, etc., going back to the demand to open the second front

during World War II. Estimating one's orthodoxy for CIO membership based on whether one shares a commonality of views with the
USSR was on the face of it absurd—should membership today be
based on a commonality of views with, say, Israel?—but these were
not normal times.

The fact is that for an important period of time, the Communists
did set the tone for the CIO, playing an ideological role in formulat-
ing the concept of industrial unionism and organizing a number of
the most important CIO member unions. It is arguable that the main
 legacy of the Communist party of the United States is not the CPUSA,
but the CIO. In later years, even some of the anticommunist labor
leadership bemoaned the damage to the CIO—the loss of its militancy, class consciousness, energy, and many of its best organizers and
cadres—caused by the purge of the Left. But it must also be acknowledged that the Party's influence was great when the times allowed it
to be; when the times changed, its influence declined. The loss of
Communist influence and presence in CIO inner councils also meant
a loss of CIO influence and presence in the inner councils of government, although this was quite contrary to the intentions of the purge.
Murray, Reuther, and the others who, in the name of blocking the
imposition of an ideology on the CIO, themselves established political criteria for membership and leadership—i.e., support for the Truman Doctrine and the Marshall Plan, nonmembership in the Communist party, etc.—sought to place the CIO squarely inside the
two-party system in support of "the American Century." The decline
of the labor movement from that period to the present has been so
well charted as to be axiomatic. Suffice it to point out that the CIO
drive to organize the South, launched at the 1946 convention, was
abandoned by 1949. In three years of cold war, the priorities had
changed from organizing southern labor to driving out the Reds, including eleven international unions. In those same years the CIO-
PAC, industrial labor's political arm, became completely subordinat-
ed to the Democratic party and the Truman administration, leaving
the CIO with no independence and thus no real influence.

　　　* * *

Before the split in the CIO, when the outlines of Truman's policies and their break with those of FDR were first becoming apparent, the CIO-PAC organized a conference in Chicago of all the organizations of the progressive Left. The Chicago Conference of
Progressives, as it was known, met in September 1946 to develop a
common program and to coordinate activities in this new period. In

addition to the CIO-PAC (Phil Murray himself came, together with Jack Kroll of the Amalgamated, Lee Pressman, and myself), our ranks included the National Citizens PAC, of which I was still general counsel; the Independent Citizens' Committee of Arts, Sciences, and Professions (ICCASP), chaired by the sculptor Jo Davidson (ICCASP's executive chair was FDR's secretary of the interior Harold Ickes, and its board ranged from Leonard Bernstein, Duke Ellington, and John Hersey to Linus Pauling, Gene Kelly, and Eddie Cantor); the NAACP, represented by Walter White; the railroad brotherhoods, represented by A. F. Whitney; the National Farmers' Union; and the Southern Conference for Human Welfare. Instrumental in conceptualizing and organizing the conference were Beanie Baldwin and Hannah Dorner, ICCASP's executive director, with whom Beanie and I frequently met.

The program that emerged from the Chicago Conference perfectly befit a coalition that saw itself as the rightful heir to the progressive New Deal alliance. Combining postwar concerns like GI rights and veterans' benefits with a increased emphasis on civil rights and eradicating Jim Crow, the conference broke with the Truman administration and the Congress on foreign policy concerns. We demanded the complete demolition of German economic royalism and Japanese militarism; advocated unilateral disarmament initiatives to eliminate the military budget of $13 million—pocket change by today's standards—and foreign military bases; and called for cessation of atomic bomb production, destruction of atomic stockpiles, and an international agreement to outlaw atomic weapons. The demands paralleled positions put forth around the same time by Henry Wallace, named by Roosevelt (and later dismissed by Truman) as secretary of commerce as something of a concession prize following the 1944 Democratic Convention. Although the Chicago Conference emerged with a unity program, it was clear that the unity was fragile. Phil Murray was particularly apprehensive about the foreign policy critique and clashed at the conference with Elmer Benson of NCPAC over presumed "Communist influence." But NCPAC was, like CIO-PAC, a creature of the CIO, and in the end Murray held all the cards. It was only with the CIO's financial and human resources that the program of the conference could be implemented. And although Murray appeared to bless the conference by his participation through to its conclusion, this was the last unity conference he attended. The first meeting of the conference continuations committee met in a three-hour closed session to assess the political moment. Besides myself, others in attendance included Beanie, Walter White, Jake Potofsky, Bob Kenney, and Elmer Benson. Harold Ickes announced his resig-

The USSR sure would have loved this. They could then extend their totalitarian ways over more countries s U.S. Interference.

nation as chair of ICCASP because the Chicago Conference reaffirmed its opposition to a U.S. atomic monopoly. Phil Murray let it be known that, as far as the CIO was concerned, this would be both the first and only meeting of the continuations committee.

Beanie Baldwin, however, was not easily deterred. He was of that generation of southerners who came of political age in the depression and had been educated by it. His work as head of the Farm Security Administration shocked him: rural poverty in the South was so glaring and the efforts to ameliorate it so abysmally meager. With a great deal of physical and moral courage, he grew in each job he held. Had he chosen to do so, he could easily have had a "good" career, perhaps as a cabinet secretary, with his grasp of political tactics and his set of acquaintances in Washington. He was gracious and exceedingly polite in dealing with people.

Beanie let it be known what he had in mind after the disastrous congressional elections that November gave the Republicans control of both the House and the Senate for the first time in more than a generation. At an NCPAC luncheon the day after the elections, Beanie warned the Democratic party that it could not claim in perpetuity to being on the side of the angels:

> Unless the Administration changes its course, swings back onto the road of progress and stops dallying at the crossroads, unless the Democratic leadership stops coyly holding hands with spokesmen of privilege and bigotry, unless it ends this clandestine honeymoon with reaction and takes a firm, aggressive fighting role in the struggle for a liberal America, then we will challenge that claim. We have no place in a party controlled by the [southern racist senators] Bilbos and Byrds. . . . We are going to build a powerful instrument of the people so that there will be no politically displaced persons in '48. We will attempt no compromise.

Beanie was never less than sincere but, in part, the warning was little more than old-fashioned southern political hyperbole. I emphasize this because a historian, looking back at how things developed—with Henry Wallace heading up an independent challenge to Truman in 1948 in a campaign chaired by Beanie Baldwin (who had been Wallace's chief of staff in the Department of Agriculture and who had stage-managed his bid for the vice-presidential nomination at the 1944 Democratic Convention) might see some grand design in what we said and did in 1946. In fact, the unity of the movements that gathered in the Chicago Conference was based entirely on the twin premises of preserving the heritage of the New Deal and the grand alliance and of antipathy to the Republicans. None of us were consciously laying the base for a third-party effort. At the time of the Chicago Conference, Wallace was still in Truman's cabinet. As independent political organizations, all were distressed that, except for Wallace, the Truman administration had dismissed the surviving members of FDR's progressive political family—Frances Perkins, Harold Ickes, Henry Morganthau. And Beanie knew better than most that only Roosevelt had the capacity to keep the New Deal coalition of opposing forces together while still going in a progressive direction.

Not long after the Chicago Conference, Wallace was the featured speaker at a Madison Square Garden rally called to build public support for the program of the conference. As a matter of policy, speeches of cabinet officers on subjects not under their jurisdiction were supposed to be cleared by the White House staff. In this case, Wallace, who would speak in favor of sustaining the U.S.-Soviet alliance in peacetime, short-circuited the bureaucratic process and brought his speech directly to the president, who gave him clearance. The speech was a rousing success, containing as it did the foreign policy agenda of the Chicago Conference. The White House, however, was less than thrilled, and in late October, Truman fired Wallace, leading to speculation that the secretary of commerce, never especially prescient as a politician, was set up by the president to take a fall.

With the Republican victory in November and the sacking of Wallace (who then became editor of the *New Republic*), we felt that unity of the progressive forces was imperative. Beanie and I and Hannah Dorner met and agreed to work toward the merger of NCPAC and ICCASP, which were already working in such close synchronization as to nearly duplicate one another. On December 29, 1946, a merger conference was held at the Hotel Commodore in New York, giving birth to the Progressive Citizens of America (PCA). It surprised no one that Wallace was the keynote speaker. His speech was quintessential Wallace—idealistic, even naive, stubborn in the face of the present reactionary drift:

More and more the American people will question a program of imperialism and heavy armament as the true road to peace, prosperity and freedom. Your job as a progressive organization is to reach that majority of the population which is potentially progressive. . . .

We have less use for a conservative high-tariff Democratic Party than we have for a reactionary high-tariff Republican Party. If need be, we shall fight one and then the other. At the moment our objective is to make the Democratic Party out and out progressive. If the new [Progressive Citizens of America] is to be effective as an organization, its members will move into every precinct in the country to educate the people and control the political machinery. . . .

We shall never be against anything simply because Russia is for it. Neither shall we ever be for anything simply because Russia is for it. . . . If it is traitorous to believe in peace—we are traitors. If it is communistic to believe in prosperity for all—we are Communists. If it is Red-baiting to fight for free speech and for freedom of the press—we are Red-baiters. If it is un-American to believe in freedom from monopolistic dictates—we are un-American. I say that we are more American than the neo-fascists who attack us. The more we are attacked, the more likely we are to succeed, provided we are ready and willing to counter-attack. On with the fight!"

The PCA constituted the remnants of the progressive united front, but the rise of the "American Century" abroad in the wake of the war gave rise to a liberal support system as well as one from the Right. In response to the PCA, a group of prominent liberals—among them Reinhold Niebuhr, Chester Bowles, Hubert Humphrey, and Arthur Schlesinger, Jr.—convened a few weeks later to form what became the Americans for Democratic Action (ADA). Hailed by Schlesinger as "the vital center," ADA's immediate priorities were support for the Marshall Plan in Europe and for the reelection of Truman at home. By then it was clear, in the labor movement and among its supporters in the middle class, that the New Deal alliance was fractured beyond repair. PCA's lineal parent, CIO-PAC, would disown the child in its infancy. Without the backing of the CIO—even though we could still count on the support of many of its constituent unions and even more local and state bodies—our possibilities were limited.

At that point, the Communist party, still somewhat reeling from the split over and shift away from "Browderism," faced a repression of potential gale force. Most important, this would mean exclusion from the CIO, which, in no small part, it had built through great sacrifice, courage, and tenacity. Meantime, we watched the Truman administration, with an atomic monopoly, begin to cultivate the remnants of Nazi Germany as the centerpiece of a policy to "contain" our former ally, the USSR, which had suffered the greatest losses of the war to

YOU ASSHOLE, WE BUILT WAR TORN GERMANY [+ JAPAN]
INTO VIBRANT, PROSPEROUS DEMOCRACIES

defeat Hitler. The newly established CIA would absorb the Nazi intelligence apparatus and bring thousands of Nazi scientists and bureaucrats to the United States, while the Marshall Plan rebuilt the German cartels that underwrote and constructed Hitler's war machine. While the CIO top leadership and the liberals polished Truman's image as labor's champion in the face of the Republican-dominated Congress—aided by a period of economic expansion and political hegemony in Europe—the Communists and its allies in the CIO and progressive movements began to consider an electoral challenge to Truman.

Under PCA auspices, Wallace spoke to huge rallies around the country, challenging Truman's foreign policy and the unfolding anticommunist purges. On March 13, Wallace used a radio address to challenge the Truman Doctrine of intervention on behalf of the rightists and royalists in Greece and Turkey, announced by the president the day before. "It is not a Greek crisis we face," Wallace said, "it is an American crisis. It is a crisis of the American spirit." Wallace feared that Truman's goal was to police every Soviet border, that no nation was too reactionary for us, as long as it was near the USSR: "There is no country too remote to serve as the scene of a contest which may widen until it becomes a world war." Wallace chided Truman's assumption that without U.S. aid, the 130,000 men of King Paul's army, backed by 10,000 British troops, were somehow helpless against the 13,000 Greek leftist guerrillas fighting a civil war. Wallace similarly criticized our intervention on the side of Turkey's military, wondering aloud what the U.S. reaction might be had the Soviets poured tens of millions of dollars into Canada to support a leftist political opposition. He criticized the Marshall Plan for its unilateralism, pointing out that tens of millions of people in India were starving and there was no plan to aid them. He argued that the Marshall Plan was a plan for U.S. hegemony in Europe and that aid should be coordinated through the newly created United Nations, that by bypassing the UN we were helping to create opposing political blocs.

Huge crowds gathered everywhere for Wallace. In Los Angeles, 32,000 packed Gilmore Stadium not once, but three times to hear him. Another rally on that city's east side was attended by 10,000 Chicano supporters calling themselves Amigos de Wallace. On the South Side in what is now known as Watts, Wallace spoke to a packed hall of 2,500 Black supporters. Beanie, as leader of the PCA, was effectively leading a movement to persuade Wallace to run for president. In addition to the rallies, Beanie arranged to have a series of delegations

OUR INCREASED INFLUENCE IN EUROPE WAS CERTAINLY RECEIVED MORE FAVORABLY THAN BY THE PEOPLE WHO BECAME RULED BEHIND THE IRON CURTAIN DUE TO RUSSIA'S HEGEMONY from Left-led trade unions, African-American organizations, women's and veterans' groups meet with the former vice-president to urge him to run. Wallace decided to at least explore an electoral challenge. And nobody understood the challenge better than Truman. In November 1947, Clark Clifford, the president's chief political advisor, urged Truman to call upon his liberal supporters—in particular, the ADA—to renounce Wallace for the backing he received from Communists and others on the Left.

On December 16, the PCA leadership met in New York and urged Wallace to run. The next day, I was part of a small delegation, led by Beanie, to meet with Wallace in his quarters at the Hotel McAlpin and deliver the PCA resolution on his candidacy. At that point, Wallace made his first declaration to run. His break with the Democratic party was complete. Next the PCA initiated a new party to be called, for the time being, the New party. It was not until the nominating convention the following summer that it officially adopted the name Independent Progressive party. Beanie very much wanted me to be general counsel for the new formation—I was still working for the Amalgamated—and approached the Communist party leadership for its concurrence. The Party wanted me to take the job but I had my doubts. I told Beanie that I thought it imperative I meet with Wallace to explain to this self-described "progressive capitalist" the political hazards of my taking the job. Even though he was head of the Department of Agriculture when I was at the AAA, I didn't know him well. More important, however, was that he didn't know me. When Beanie and I met with him, I told him that I'd recently been subpoenaed before the federal grand jury; that I was married to Jessica, the editor of *Soviet Russia Today;* and that my sister, Marion, was public relations director for the Communist party. Wallace was no more alarmed than he would have been had I informed him of my admittance to the Illinois Bar. He brushed aside my concerns and said, "Well, let them shell that position if they want to." Then he urged me to become general counsel for the New party.

My last public function with the Amalgamated was attending a meeting of the American Labor party executive board, which had decided to endorse the Wallace candidacy. Hy Blumberg, the Amalgamated's vice-president and representative on the ALP executive, announced the union's withdrawal from the party. He made no fight to persuade the ALP not to support Wallace, knowing that he would lose such a struggle. But my departure from the Amalgamated was most cordial. The union leaders probably thought I was being foolish in taking the position with Wallace, but they were quite friendly and there was nothing in the way of recriminations.

* * *

Despite the absence of support from the official CIO, we were optimistic at the beginning of the campaign. The mass rallies from coast to coast, together with the outspoken support of leaders of several trade unions and the secondary leadership of non-Left unions, were bolstered by Truman's lack of popularity among workers after he broke a major strike of the nation's railroads. Our optimism was confirmed when Leo Isaacson, an ALP candidate from the Bronx and a Wallace supporter, easily won election to Congress in a special election in February 1948.

In the beginning, my primary function was to secure ballot access for the New party in as many states as possible, to comply with all the legal requirements of the then forty-eight states. Each state has its own election laws governing such things as the required numbers of signatures on nominating petitions, but at that time with the exception of New York, which had the ALP, every state had laws skewed so as to guarantee the primacy of the Democrats and Republicans. The two parties not only control Congress and the White House, in what more closely approximates a governing coalition than a party in power and a loyal opposition, but also the state legislatures and governor's mansions that determine the election laws. While many may hail multiparty democracies abroad, the two-party system at home is exactly that—a system to perpetuate the two parties in power. (One of Wallace's active supporters was the lyricist E. Y. "Yip" Harburg who wrote, among other musicals, *Finian's Rainbow*. Yip composed a song for our campaign called "It's the Same Old Merry-go-round, the Elephants and Donkeys Bounce Up and Down.")

Most states required exorbitant numbers of nominating petitions. The more experienced campaigners in the New party hoped we could obtain ballot status in as many as twenty-five to thirty states. Not even the most sanguine of us thought more was possible. In 1944, Wendell Willkie had investigated the state laws and concluded that a third-party effort would be futile. I cannot attribute the successes we did achieve solely to my legal skills. In the South, then the "solid South" firmly under Democratic party control, we were fortunate in finding help from an unexpected source. Some months into our campaign, and with Truman under constant pressure from Wallace, who was hammering away at Jim Crow laws and voting procedures,

Strom Thurmond announced his candidacy. Thurmond, a Democratic senator from South Carolina (who remains in the Senate today as a Republican, having found the Democrats in the sixties too liberal on race), ran for president in 1948 as a Dixiecrat. Of course he faced the same problems we did in getting on the ballot. But he pulled a lot of weight in the South, and his counterparts throughout the old Confederacy let down the barriers to allow him to qualify as a candidate. The Progressive party took advantage of the momentary change of procedures to also achieve ballot status in the South.

As it happened, the party got on the ballot in forty-five of the forty-eight states, a not inconsiderable achievement. We failed in Oklahoma and Nebraska, but neither state had a sizable body of voters so we were not terribly hurt. However, we also lost out in Illinois, and this would cost us considerably, given the large labor base, Black population, and the country's third largest number of voters. Illinois required the New party to file petitions signed by twenty thousand registered voters in the state, a standard we easily met. But the state law also required that of those twenty thousand voters, no fewer than one hundred signatories come from each of at least half of the state's counties. There were one hundred counties in Illinois, so we needed at least one hundred signatures from each of fifty counties. Our potential base was clearly in and around Chicago and its industrial areas, which was also the center of Democratic party strength in Illinois. The law meant we had to find signatures in the traditionally conservative and Republican downstate counties.

Our legal position was that this requirement was a violation of the equal protection clause of the Fourteenth Amendment to the Constitution, because relatively few voters in several downstate counties could essentially exercise veto power over millions of residents of Chicago when it came to placing a candidate on the ballot. Even though the voters of Cook County, embracing Chicago, far outnumbered those of the other ninety-nine counties, we lost the argument in the state courts. I appealed to the Supreme Court. This was my first argument ever before the Court, then headed by Chief Justice Fred Vinson, whose perceptions of the law would have appealed to a legal scholar with the vision of, say, Ronald Reagan. Felix Frankfurter contended that I was arguing a political, not a legal, question and that the Court had previously ruled in another Illinois case that the whole question of apportionment was not a legal question. My old friend and former boss, Bob Jackson, was sitting on the bench but, given the political time of day and my own newfound notoriety, he was far from friendly. After making my arguments, Jackson responded that the ALP had obtained ballot status in New York despite legal provisions much the same as those in Illinois. I granted him the point, but also said that of course the ALP had the backing of FDR and the Democratic party, who understood that the ALP would act in support of the New Deal and therefore wanted it on the ballot. The Supreme Court turned down our appeal by a six to three vote, with Jackson voting against us. This was the first time I'd seen Bob since Hillman and I dined with him in Nuremburg, and it was also the last time we met. And it wasn't until 1963 that the Court would enunciate the "one person, one vote" doctrine and declare the Illinois election law unconstitutional.

Though in the beginning my principal function as general counsel was to secure ballot access for the New party, I participated in and worked on all policy and political decisions. Occasionally I wrote speeches, and I played a primary role in organizing the July 1948 nominating convention in Philadelphia. Wallace—former vice-president, former secretary of agriculture, former secretary of commerce—was of course our strength. The self-styled "prairie idealist" was well placed to denounce Truman's betrayal of the FDR legacy. But Wallace did not come without his own problems. He was, quite literally, a mystic, and it was often impossible to appeal to his practical political sense. Charlie Kramer, a good friend who had been my chief investigator on the LaFollette committee, was on the campaign staff. He recalled conversations with Wallace when the candidate would interrupt himself to talk about the emanations he was receiving from the sky. Later, Charlie approached Beanie to inform him of this development. Beanie looked at Charlie, as if at an innocent, and said, "Of course. Didn't you know that about Wallace?"

Wallace's vice-presidential running mate was Senator Glen Taylor of Idaho, who cut a sort of Wild West figure by way of central casting. He campaigned throughout Idaho on horseback. In Progressive party campaign swings, he was rarely without his guitar to warm up the audience and was often joined by his wife for duets. Glen was quite tall but his most imposing physical feature was his absolutely bald pate, which modesty decreed would always be covered by a hairpiece. (After defeat in his 1950 bid for reelection to the Senate, Glen set up his own business manufacturing wigs, called Taylor Toppers. He offered to hire me to incorporate him but I respectfully declined.) For all of his eccentricity, Senator Taylor was a man of great principle who put his entire, successful career on the line to run alongside Wallace. While he proved to be quite courageous in challenging Jim Crow in the Deep South, his great passion, like Wallace's, was foreign policy. An early critic of the Truman Doctrine, Taylor told the Senate in 1947: "The gallant warriors of the State Department, with their well-polished attache cases, bravely borne by well-manicured fingers, came riding down the caucus room like the gallant 300 who held the pass at Thermopylae. But the anti-Communist guise hardly fits either, for the Greek government bears no relationship to democracy and it is not combatting communism but defending right-wing monarchy."

Shortly before the Philadelphia convention, Lee Pressman resigned as CIO general counsel. After submitting his resignation to Phil Murray, Lee received a check for $20,000, an enormous sum in those days, as a most generous severance payment. I was taken aback. I knew Lee would never achieve a position of greater influence. But we all had grandiose ideas of the possibilities of the Wallace campaign. Ever ambitious, Lee ran for Congress from Brooklyn on the Progressive party ticket, convinced of his chances for victory. At the convention, Lee served as secretary of the platform committee, at the request of Rex Tugwell, FDR's brain truster who chaired the committee. I more or less scripted the convention after intense discussions with the candidates and the Progressive party leadership. I directed the staff to prepare an outline for the platform and then Lee prepared three separate drafts of the platform itself. This was soft work for Lee, who for years had mastered the craft of writing resolutions for CIO conventions.

A major portion of the platform was devoted to bringing the South into the twentieth century—eradicating Jim Crow laws, eliminating the poll tax, abolishing chain gangs, calling attention to and attacking the wave of lynching that was aimed at terrorizing southern Blacks. The Progressive party could arguably claim to have helped lay the base for the civil rights revolution that followed a decade later. And of course the platform challenged the Truman arms buildup: "Peace cannot be won," the platform stated, "but profits can, by spending ever-increasing billions of the people's money on war preparations."

During the convention, I served as secretary of the rules committee, chaired by Vito Marcantonio. A dispute broke out over the rules governing the composition of the national committee for the New party. It had been agreed that each state would have two or three members of the new national committee, with an additional undesignated number of "constituency" representatives, for a total membership of 180 persons, with 50 percent constituting a quorum. Hugh Bryson, head of the Marine Cooks and Stewards' Union, argued that of the 180 national committee members, 60 should come from constituencies—

youth, women, labor, veterans, nationalities, etc. Beanie Baldwin persuaded the rules committee to reduce the number to 40. The *New York Times* and much of the daily press, reinforced later by anticommunist historians like William Shannon, portrayed the move as a grab by the Communist party for additional influence because the Communists were leading activists at the constituency level. That the rules committee was chaired by Marc, whom they considered to be a Communist, reinforced them in this view. The facts, however, are that the Communist party was active at every level of the Progressive party, most important in the state and local organizations, and that Marc, in particular (with my support), *opposed* the constituency representation because it would weaken the influence of the ALP within the Progressive party. If there was one group that particularly favored increasing the constituency representation so as to build up its own power, it was the trade union leadership within the new party.

Another dispute arose around what became known as "the Vermont resolution." Offered by members of the Vermont delegation, the resolution read: "Although we are critical of the present foreign policy of the United States, it is not our intention to give blanket endorsement to the foreign policy of any nation." In retrospect, this was clearly a sensible position—declaring that we were a party concerned about the interests of the American people—to stem the red-baiting directed at the Progressive party. Incredibly, the Vermont resolution was soundly defeated. The Communist party opposed it, and Lee Pressman led the public opposition in the platform debate, on the grounds that it was "unprincipled" and engaged in "self-red-baiting." I was as sectarian and arrogant as the rest of the Party comrades— perhaps this was another example of the "swing of the pendulum" after Browder—and also opposed the Vermont resolution. But it should be said that opposition to the resolution was carried out with the full knowledge and blessing of Henry Wallace—who opposed it on precisely the same grounds as the Communists. In fact, given Wallace's pivotal position, the Vermont resolution could have been defeated only with his approval.

In his accepting the nomination, Wallace established the tone of his election drive, warning of the emergence of the military-industrial complex in the same ringing terms president Dwight Eisenhower would enunciate on his retirement from office twelve years later: "In one fleet of heavy bombers lies the wealth and skill . . . that could have taken a million veterans out of trailer camps and chicken coops. We can build new schools to rescue our children from the firetraps where they now crowd. . . . We can end the murderous tyranny of

You FOOL, YOU STILL DIDN'T REALIZE THAT THE COMMIES WANTED US IN A MILITARILY WEAKENED STATE which WOULD ENABLE THEM TO PURSUE THEIR COMMUNIST REVOLUTION WORLD WIDE, TRUMAN UNDERSTOOD THIS.

sickness and disease. . . . The facts are that we spend $20 billion dollars a year for cold war."

However, in the end, it was neither Henry Wallace nor the newfound Independent Progressive party that set the tone for the campaign, but the federal government. The day before the convention opened in Philadelphia, the Justice Department announced the conclusions of the grand jury before which I had appeared the year before: the twelve members of the national board of the Communist party, including its chair, William Z. Foster, and general secretary, Eugene Dennis, were indicted under the Smith Act for conspiracy to advocate the overthrow of the U.S. government by force and violence.

* * *

Two weeks after the Philadelphia convention, the House Un-American Activities Committee went after the Progressive party. Fresh from its triumphs in ridding Hollywood of the likes of Dalton Trumbo, Jack Lawson, Bertolt Brecht, and Charlie Chaplin, the committee subpoenaed me to appear in closed session, together with Charlie Kramer, Lee Pressman, and Nat Witt. Nat was then in law partnership with one of his old Harvard classmates, Hal Cammer, and on moving back to New York, Pressman also joined the firm. Nat and Lee remained old friends from the New Deal and still had summer cottages together in the same Vermont community of Randolph Corner, where my sister, Marion, spent vacations. When Lee, as CIO counsel, needed legal work done in New York, he had passed it on to Nat and Hal. So Hal agreed to represent each of us before HUAC.

We had been named by Whittaker Chambers in his testimony against Alger Hiss as members of "the Ware Group" of Communists "infiltrating" the Roosevelt administration. I had met Chambers a couple of times in my Washington days and found him somewhat odd. He spoke cryptically, affecting an air of mystery with a simulated central European accent. I imagined him to be German, perhaps a representative of the Communist International, and was surprised to learn later that he had become a staff writer for *Time*.

Rep. John Rankin of Mississippi, with whom I'd crossed swords during my AAA and WPA days, was still hoisting the burning cross of white supremacy in the halls of Congress. A dominant member of HUAC, he pointed out that Pressman and I were on the Progressive party staff and urged the committee to subpoena Henry Wallace as well, for whom Alger Hiss had also worked in the Agriculture Department. (Shortly after our appearance, Marion was also brought before HUAC on the basis of her friendship with Alger during our Washington days;

her husband, Artie, of course was yet another of our colleagues and social partners in the AAA. At that hearing, Karl Mundt, the undistinguished chair of the committee, announced: "The Chairman would like to state that the crime involved here is very definitely a capital crime. It is either treason in wartime or treason in peacetime.")

It was clear that these were not regular, garden variety hearings. Implicit was a threat of great danger. We had engaged in no illegal activities but we were radicals, with unacceptable politics, and thereby suspected of high crimes against the state. The drive for cold war victory abroad would be matched at home by a cold war not only against those upholding the legacy of the New Deal, but against the New Deal itself. Hence, Richard Nixon's memorable phrase "twenty years of treason."

Backing up Whittaker Chambers's accusations of a Communist "espionage ring" inside the New Deal was Elizabeth Bentley, who made a career for herself throughout the McCarthy years as a professional government witness. I met Bentley once: she worked for Intourist, the Soviet tourist organization, and during my years with the Amalgamated, she came to a meeting at Jessica's and my apartment on Central Park West. The little I knew about Bentley came from an unusual source—a farm woman who lived about a mile from our cottage in Kent. We bought our butter, corn, and vegetables from Mabel Richards, who also passed on local gossip. A Seventh-Day Adventist, with no formal education, Mabel liked to keep up with world events and was well informed. Bentley, it seems, came from New Milford, a neighboring Connecticut town and was somewhat known in the community. It became apparent that the FBI had been around Kent, asking the local merchants and farmers about me. Mabel and I generally confined our conversations to the weather and other matters of little moment. Certainly she never asked about my politics. But one day I stopped by the Richards farm to pick up some milk and Mabel, ever the antipapalist, remarked: "Well, what do you know, Mr. Abt? Did you see that Elizabeth Bentley has turned Catholic?" (About this same time, Mabel was in a squabble over some land with the adjacent Kenney farm, and someone asked her, "How can you spend so much time with that Communist, John Abt." To which she replied, "I'd rather spend days with John Abt than one minute with Celia Kenney.")

Richard Nixon, then a freshman member of Congress, asked most of the questions during my appearance before the committee. My main impressions of my inquisitor were of a callow young man, somewhat seedy, uncertain of himself. I recall his turning to another of the representatives as I took the stand and saying in a stage whisper, "Watch your step with this one. He's a smart cookie." What prompted him to say that, I cannot say. My performance was not particularly brilliant, consisting almost entirely of refusals to answer the questions about whether I was a Communist and whether I knew others who were Communists, citing my Fifth Amendment protections under the Constitution. As soon as the executive session ended, Nixon rushed out to the corridor—the original spin doctor—to challenge us before the press, which he seemed incapable of doing while facing us in the closed hearing room.

The use of the Fifth Amendment before congressional committees, in particular HUAC and its counterpart, the Senate Internal Security Committee, became a matter of considerable debate among liberal and left-wing lawyers during that period. Of course Nixon, Rankin, Senator McCarthy, and their minions did whatever they could to discredit the Fifth Amendment. But the Fifth, like the other nine amendments in the Bill of Rights, was added to the Constitution by the Founding Fathers not out of some caprice but as a fundamental protection of civil liberties. The concept of refusing to answer potentially self-incriminating questions arose in response to the practices of the star chamber proceedings, which demanded that people accused of being political or religious dissenters accuse themselves and confess. For centuries, from the Inquisition to the Salem witch trials, coerced testimony was a favored device by oppressors to condemn their opponents. So the Fifth Amendment's origins were not as protection for criminals accused of illegal acts but for precisely the sort of proceedings in which the House and Senate inquisitors were engaged. Taking the Fifth to defend against the McCarthyite inquisition was to honor our own political traditions.

The Fifth was an essential measure for self-preservation in the days of the cold war, because if you testified and acknowledged, say, membership in the Communist party, you would be obliged to identify all of your co-workers and friends as fellow members; or you could risk perjury by denying your membership. The Supreme Court had debased the Fifth Amendment by ruling that it could not be used to decline to answer some questions while answering others. Witnesses were required to use the Amendment to decline to answer all questions, whether they could possibly lead to self-incrimination or not. The remaining alternative was to refuse to answer on the grounds of First Amendment protections of free speech and association, but you would then risk a citation for contempt of Congress and subsequent imprisonment, as happened to the Hollywood Ten.

In those days, using this essential piece of the Bill of Rights to defend oneself was tantamount, in the eyes of the investigators and

LIKE YOUR HERO STALIN'S PURGE OF THE
"12 TROTSKYITES"

their supporters in the media, to an admission of guilt. Senator Joseph McCarthy, no less, coined the phrase "Fifth Amendment Communists" to describe anybody who dared protect themselves. Editorial writers, who in a few years sought to put distance between themselves and McCarthy, weren't the least bit hesitant to appropriate the senator's slander. "In the eyes of hearing-room habitues," Russell Baker later recalled of his days as a reporter covering such hearings, "claiming the Amendment's privilege is lower than the foul play the witness may hope to conceal. Washington is always willing to pump the hand of the rogue who winks openly about his misdeeds, but 'taking the Fifth' is looked upon as an odious breach of good form, like bringing the town madam to the Sunday school picnic." But it seemed to me at the time, and it still does, that Leftists had to engage in whatever maneuvers the law allowed in order to preserve our liberty. The Fifth Amendment was designed expressly for this purpose and was the only instrument at hand that could be so used. So I never felt a need to apologize for using the Fifth Amendment, and I advised all my clients to do the same.

Our appearance before HUAC received some negative publicity. This was to be expected; after all, that was the primary purpose of the hearings. A few days later, I was in San Francisco for a Progressive party regional conference and told the gathering about my appearance. I reported that all of Chambers's accusations had been heard a year earlier by a federal grand jury, which found no evidence on which to return a single indictment; indeed none of us called before the committee were ever charged in the courts with even a misdemeanor. Nevertheless, when I returned to New York, I went to Henry Wallace and offered to resign to protect the campaign. He would hear nothing of it, however, and dismissed the hearings with barely a shrug of his shoulders. I was happily relieved by his reaction but, looking back, it seems one further illustration of Wallace's impracticality as a politician. The transparent "coincidence" of Smith Act indictments on the eve of our nominating convention, the HUAC hearings in Hollywood and Washington, the accusations against Alger Hiss, the developing split in the CIO, the loyalty oaths, the blacklists in show business and the teaching profession—all were ample evidence of the domestic cold war being launched. A retrograde Republican party and a desperate Democratic president, on the defensive, had opened up another front against an independent, progressive candidacy that challenged their primacy. Clark Clifford's memorandum to Truman urging the president to pin the "red" label on the Wallace candidacy reinforced the obvious dangers.

I've said that Wallace was an unorthodox politician. In the orga-

nized sense, he was hardly a politician at all. He didn't like the practice of politics, and he counted no politicians among his intimates.
The building of a political organization on a ward or precinct level
simply held no interest for him as it did for, say, FDR, who was the
supreme politician, or for Truman, who grew up in the Pendergast
machine in Kansas City. But it would be selling Wallace short to attribute his disdain for the anticommunist campaign simply to his un-
conventional manner. He was obviously a man of courage, as he
showed by breaking with his party to run against a sitting president,
and as he would show throughout the campaign, braving physical
threats and, in the Deep South, actual assaults on his person.

Still, Wallace's reaction to the red-baiting attacks was the more
surprising because Ilo, Mrs. Wallace, had always been, in Henry's
words, "violently anticommunist." Her group of personal women
friends, he recalled in his oral history, used to sit around gossiping
about the Progressive party. Ilo Wallace refused to play a role in the
campaign, although she did accompany her husband to a luncheon
given in his honor at the luxurious Marin County home of Vincent
and Vivian Hallinan, who helped lead the Independent Progressive
party in Northern California. Afterward she complained to her husband, "Why can't we have more respectable people like the Hallin-
ans on our side?" Mrs. Wallace could not have known that Vin would
soon go to jail for contempt of court while defending longshore union
leader Harry Bridges from deportation or would be the Progressive
party presidential candidate in 1952 while imprisoned on income tax
charges.

We had an extremely vigorous Women for Wallace organization,
under the leadership of Eleanor Gimbel, but Mrs. Wallace would
have nothing to do with it. Eleanor, the widow of the department
store scion, used to joke that she was "a traitor to her class," a self-
deprecation that Ilo obviously didn't share. Mrs. Wallace was particularly suspicious of Beanie Baldwin and myself. The Wallaces had a
farm in South Salem, New York, just across the state line from our
Kent place. During the campaign, we—Beanie and I and sometimes
a couple of others—would frequently meet there for business "lunches." I bracket *lunches* in quotes because, except for once making us
poached eggs, Mrs. Wallace never served a meal.

* * *

It is perhaps unfair to attribute such parsimony to Mrs. Wallace
alone. Wallace himself was notoriously tight. He and Beanie and I
would often go out to lunch together. Invariably, Wallace would reach

for the check, make a calculation, put down some money on the table, always an insufficient amount, and announce, "That's my share." One summer day, the Progressive party staff and leadership met at the Yorktown Heights home of Sam and Helen Rosen. A buffet was served, and when the meeting ended, a collection was taken up to pay for the meal. Everyone was asked to chip in a dollar. Sitting next to me, Wallace leaned over to ask, "John, can you lend me a dollar?" It was one dollar I'd never again see. The only person toward whom I ever saw Wallace show a glimmer of generosity was Lillian Hellman, a sometimes member of the Progressive party brain trust. Wallace's South Salem farm was quite near Lillian's, and at one of the meetings held in her home, Wallace brought her a present—a huge sack of cow dung for her garden.

Lillian saw her role as being a political advisor. I don't recall her ever volunteering her considerable writing talents to the campaign. Not that we were bereft of such skills. Charlie Kramer had been put to work on what he considered the disagreeable task of coordinating volunteer writers. He and I first discussed the themes, then Charlie would develop them, collate the research, and superintend the speech writers. Among our crew, we could count on regular contributions from Norman Mailer, Howard Fast, Clifford Odets, and Walter Bernstein. Howard wrote quickly, but his talent did not lie in writing speeches. For a while, Walter Bernstein and Arnold Perle traveled with Wallace as a team, but in the middle of the campaign, Wallace called us together to declare his dissatisfaction with the speeches. He wanted to only stress the peace issue to the exclusion of all others. To mollify him, we assigned Robert Shaw, then head of the Screenwriters' Guild, to be his chief speech writer. Wallace's determination to run only as a peace candidate presented us with an unending headache for the duration of the campaign. We argued strenuously that he must broaden his appeal by addressing other real concerns— Truman's wage freeze, the housing shortage, Jim Crow, etc. Although his best-known book was titled *The Century of the Common Man*, Wallace's understanding of the "common man" was negligible.

The campaign had a decidedly southern influence. Its prime mover of course was its director, Beanie Baldwin, from Virginia. Beanie brought on another Virginian, Palmer Webber, who had also worked for us in the CIO-PAC as a lobbyist, as southern co-director of the campaign. He had earlier served as executive secretary to the Truman-Kilgore committee in the Senate, working out of Truman's office. He had intimate knowledge of members of Congress, the health situation of their family members, what the price of each vote was worth, who owed on a mortgage, and such. Many of my good friends were fond of Palmer and regarded him as a brilliant economist. Personally, he was too much of an operator to suit me, and I didn't trust his flamboyance. He probably didn't care for me either, and I admit to possible fallibility in judging Palmer. After the Wallace campaign, he went into the securities business as an investment counselor. In short order, he accumulated a small fortune and, during the Smith Act trials, was generous in his contributions to the defense fund.

Not all of our white southerners were equally enlightened. Lillian Hellman, who always hearkened back to her New Orleans roots, brought some excess baggage when she came north. Extremely self-centered, she was never at peace, forever worried about exhausting her creativity and finding herself unable to write her next piece. One day in the Progressive party office, she and I got into quite a tough argument over some matter. After pausing some moments, she looked at me and said, "Oh John, and I always regarded you as such a gentle person." I was a grave disappointment to her throughout the campaign. On occasion, Lillian's famed temper turned ugly. She lost it one day in a dispute with Louis Burnham, the Black co-director of the southern campaign and one of the top leaders of the Independent Progressive party (IPP). Exasperated with Louis's reasoned calm, Lillian let her southern slip show, calling him "boy."

Until the Progressive party, my own life's experience was almost totally devoid of Black acquaintances, not to mention friends. My German Jewish childhood, followed by a University of Chicago education, several years of corporate practice, several more years in government, left me—I say this without irony—culturally deprived. The Amalgamated leadership was all white as was the CIO leadership. Despite the large numbers of African-American industrial workers, especially with the outbreak of war, I operated only in the labor stratosphere. Of Black co-workers among my labor associates, I can recall only Ferdinand Smith, the secretary-treasurer of the National Maritime Union. In the Communist party, I only functioned in a semi-clandestine capacity, meeting with this or that Party official responsible for my area of work. So, while the Party had such important African-American leaders as James Ford, Ben Davis, Henry Winston, and Pettis Perry, I had no contact with them until I went to work as the Party's general counsel in 1951.

In the wake of Wallace's devastating defeat, there was much debate over the wisdom of the decision to form a third party. I never thought it was a mistake, but part of my reasoning is subjective. Overall, the campaign was an exciting and stimulating experience.

But if I were to identify the single most positive result for me personally, it was the enrichment my life acquired with the friendship bestowed upon and infinite patience shown me by Louis and Dottie Burnham, George Murphy, Paul Robeson, Thelma Dale, Ruth Jett, and other African-American activists and staff members of the Progressive party. In my study of Marxism, I had developed some theoretical or "book" knowledge of the question of Black liberation. But the Progressive party gave me my first opportunity to work alongside Blacks, become friends, and, most important, to learn from them. The above-mentioned friends were my teachers in what I consider a major part of my education.

They brought to the campaign impeccable credentials. This was still a time when African-American GIs were discharged from the armed services, having played a vital role in defeating fascism abroad, to return to a wave of lynchings in a South where they were denied the vote. No voices were more unwavering or more consistent than those of people like Paul Robeson and W. E. B. Du Bois and Louis Burnham and George Murphy. Who else was capable of and willing to put together a coalition of church, labor, cultural, and political forces into a political party that made primary the fight for the eradication of all traces of Jim Crow? These were the men and women who had built the Council on African Affairs to promote U.S. support for the decolonization struggles in Africa. These were the same people—not, popular mythology to the contrary notwithstanding, Branch Rickey—who, through demonstrations and boycotts and exposure in the news media, compelled major league baseball (and consequently all sports) to truly become the national, not just the whites-only, pastime.

If the Wallace campaign could be judged a failure for the number of votes received, it was not without important successes. Foremost among these was its work in the South, under Louis Burnham's leadership. The Independent Progressive party was the first political party in the twentieth century that refused to participate in any meetings that were not desegregated. When Wallace made a southern tour, each stop resulted in a bitter struggle. He was scorned by the news media, physically attacked with tomatoes and eggs by racist mobs, and threatened with lynching. But he stuck to our position of refusing to speak unless the meeting was desegregated. In some places, we were able to break down the Jim Crow barriers; in others, we'd try to hold desegregated meetings but if they were prevented, Wallace would simply walk out.

The two major parties absolutely despised this principled stand

and never forgave us. The Republicans were the party of the big corporations and feared a militant resurgence of the labor movement in
the postwar period, which could only threaten the Pax America hegemony being sought overseas. The Democrats, for their part, were
essentially a coalition party dependent in large part on the "solid
South," which is to say, solidly white. The voting rights campaign of
the Progressive party was greeted by the southern components of the
Democratic party in much the same spirit they would greet the efforts a few years hence of Medgar Evers and Fannie Lou Hamer. The
IPP's head-on assault on segregation, particularly in the electoral arena, was, I believe, a historic example that helped lead to the civil
rights movement storming heaven, as it were.

On one occasion, Glen Taylor was invited to speak to a campaign
rally in Birmingham, Alabama. In those days, Birmingham was commonly known as "the Johannesburg of the South" because of its rigid
segregationist structure and the open terror used to enforce it by the
local authorities. The only place one might even attempt to hold a
desegregated meeting was in a Black church. Lou Burnham, having
lived for years in Birmingham, knew the community well and was
able to prevail upon one of the local ministers to open his church to
the Taylor meeting.

But, in conformity with the Birmingham segregation ordinance,
the church posted a sign at the front entrance reading "Black Entrance," and another, "White Entrance," at the back. The atmosphere
in Birmingham was, in ordinary times, tense; and these were not ordinary times. Birmingham police, under the direction of Chief "Bull"
Connors—who, fifteen years later, made headlines around the world
by sicking attack dogs on peaceful demonstrators—were stationed at
the church for the meeting. When Glen Taylor arrived at the church,
accompanied by Lou Burnham, and saw the two signs, he declared
his refusal to go through the "white" entrance and attempted to enter through the front. He and Louie were immediately arrested for
violating the local ordinance, the only time a candidate for national
office—and of course he was a U.S. senator—went to jail during an
election campaign.

(After the election, the case came to trial. I went back to Birmingham with Earl Dickerson, a Black attorney from Chicago—we'd actually been classmates in law school—who had been a Progressive
party candidate for Congress that fall. Earl was prominent in Chicago, owned an insurance company in addition to his law practice, and
had served on the federal Fair Employment Practices Commission
during the Roosevelt years. Neither of us belonged to the Alabama

Bar, so we were compelled to find a local attorney to appear with us in the case. The day before the trial, the local attorney told us, "Now when we're in court, you, Mr. Abt, will sit beside me in front of the bench, and you, Mr. Dickerson, will sit over to one side. If Mr. Dickerson has any contributions or suggestions to make while I'm trying the case, he will tell Mr. Abt, who will then tell me." We informed him that we would behave in no such way. Earl and I would sit together and try the case together. But we had no control over Jim Crow laws outside of the courtroom and were forced to stay at separate hotels. Arriving at the courthouse in the morning, Earl was required to go up the "Black" elevator—in truth, the freight elevator— and I the "white." The courtroom itself was segregated as well. Diners were also segregated of course, so we couldn't lunch together. There was virtually nowhere we could meet. I think this was my first encounter with "southern hospitality." Soon after the trial opened, Earl leaned over to me and whispered, "John, there is only one cure for all of this—Revolution!" Predictably, we lost the case, but Senator Taylor and Lou never returned to Alabama to serve out their sentences. The state supreme court affirmed the conviction and the U.S. Supreme Court refused to review the Alabama decision. Only Justices Black and Frankfurter voted to hear the case.)

The Progressive party, under Lou's direction, continued its pioneer efforts to break down the walls of segregation throughout the campaign. Lou came to the Progressive party after years of quiet but innovative leadership of the Southern Negro Youth Congress. The SNYC itself represented a brilliant chapter in southern history, one deserving of serious attention by some enterprising scholars. Founded in 1937 in Richmond, Virginia, at a conference keynoted by Mordecai Johnson, then president of Howard University, the SNYC eventually developed over 150 chapters throughout the South. Led by a collection of young Black Marxists like Ed Strong, James and Esther Jackson, and with an Adult Advisory Board chaired by F. D. Patterson, the president of Morehouse College (and whose members included the Rev. Martin Luther King, Sr.), the SNYC had a tremendous impact until its demise at the outset of the cold war. Its annual conferences drew one thousand Black delegates and several hundred white supporters together, and its leadership received a White House welcome from Eleanor Roosevelt. The SNYC organized cultural centers in Nashville and New Orleans, led petition campaigns for voting rights and support activities for sharecroppers, miners, and steel workers, and served as the shock troops against southern apartheid a generation before the Rev. Martin Luther King, Jr., became a household name. In fact, many of the people who assumed leadership of the civil rights movement in the fifties and sixties—in local NAACP chapters and in national organizations—got their grounding in the SNYC. (The organization was forced to disband when the cold war terror was accompanied by increased racist violence and a new wave of lynchings. The Communist party, already on the defensive itself, was unable to fully appreciate the need and the work of a young Black organization in the South, and there had been insufficient training of a secondary leadership to replace the founding leaders who had gone elsewhere. The Party had sent Jim and Esther Jackson to Michigan to head up its organization in that state, Ed Strong returned to New York, and Lou Burnham took charge of the Progressive party in the South.)

One of the loveliest human beings I've ever met, Louis was a tremendous influence on me. His origins were West Indian; a distant cousin, Forbes Burnham, was for several years prime minister of Guyana. He was very proud of his heritage, his "blackness," and very persuasive with whites when faced with their racism and chauvinism. A rich cultural apostle who swam in music, poetry, and literature, he read and listened out of need and habit and counted among his circle of friends and co-workers virtually the entire spectrum of Black cultural figures of the time. He was always pleasant company and had a great facility to move in all kinds of circles, for which I am forever thankful, since he became one of my closest friends. Lou was also a most eloquent public speaker and could engage an audience at will. After the Wallace campaign, he became editor of Paul Robeson's newspaper *Freedom*—assisted by a then unknown but aspiring playwright named Lorraine Hansberry—and was a founding editor of the *National Guardian.* In 1960, while in the middle of making a speech in Brooklyn on Negro History Week, he collapsed. Jim Jackson called me in the middle of the night to tell me that Louis had died from cardiac arrest. He was only forty years old but every day of his adulthood he had put his life on the line for his people and for U.S. democracy. I've always thought that his death contributed to my own heart attack shortly thereafter.

George Murphy was another remarkable personality—the polar opposite of Louis Burnham—who became a big influence on my life. George was a scion of the Baltimore Murphys who, as the owners and publishers of the *Afro-American* newspaper chain, were very important figures in Black life. After graduating college, George came under the wing of his uncle, the publisher, and went to work as manager of the Washington, D.C., edition of the *Afro.* He was never less than outspoken and would argue at length with his uncle. In the thirties, George was employed by the NAACP, working with W. E. B. Du Bois, then editor of the organization's magazine, *Crisis*. George became radicalized in this period and joined the Communist party, eventually leaving the NAACP after a political row. When the war came, he joined the army and, as always, became a militant defender in the armed forces of what was then referred to as "Negro equality." At war's end, George organized the United Negro and Allied Veterans of America, which he brought into the Progressive party. We met when he was placed in charge of the IPP's "nationalities division," which included not only Black organizations but all groups organized along ethnic lines—Poles, Ukrainians, Puerto Ricans, etc.

George was loquacious, a continuous talker, quick to scold white people—not least of all, myself—for their foibles, constantly challenging, provoking, nudging, even abusing, but forcing a response. He had known my sister for some time before we met and was quite fond of her. Whenever he detected a racial slight on my part, as he often did when we first became co-workers, George would be quick to confront me with it, complain about me to Marion, and even go to Henry Winston, a member of the Party's top leadership, who was Black. After some months of working together, we were fast and warm friends. George also grew close to Jessica and to mother, with whom he'd have long discussions on books and literature. However, his friendship with me and my family never precluded a stern lecture from him upon detection of anything he considered a racial affront. These were matters of principle, and George wasn't about to let me slide by; he was determined to help me overcome my cultural deprivation.

Because of his political convictions, George sacrificed what could easily have been a lucrative career at the *Afro* newspapers or the NAACP. After the Progressive party folded, he did go back to the *Afro* in a minor capacity. But radical politics were his great passion and compelled him to live on modest means. Still, his family background and political acumen allowed him to always be involved with the major personalities in Black cultural and community life—the leaders of the National Negro Congress, the Negro Elks, the Masons, and other fraternal orders. He was perpetually widening his circle of contacts and sought approaches within the African-American community to build all-class unity. Again, he would bring white people up short who felt that Blacks had to be down on their heels to be oppressed or in need of human solidarity.

One of the greatest pleasures and privileges I received in the Progressive party was the friendship of Paul Robeson, perhaps the towering figure of twentieth-century U.S. culture. Many books have been written—though *the* book about Paul has yet to see the light of day—songs have been sung, plays performed, tributes organized, even a mountain (in Central Asia) named for him. All-American athlete, laureate scholar, attorney, linguist, cultural anthropologist, arguably the greatest actor and concert singer of his time, Paul was also (perhaps foremost, in the years I knew him) a political activist and thinker of the broadest dimension.

The Soviet Union had his complete and unwavering support, as did the colonial and national liberation movements. An intimate of Nehru, of Nkrumah, of all the independence leaders of Africa and Asia, Paul was himself the leading figure of his time in the struggle for Black equality in this country.

As co-chair of the campaign, Paul traveled around the country with Henry Wallace and was often a larger drawing card than our presidential standard-bearer. Other performers like Zero Mostel and Canada Lee and Pete Seeger also appeared. Ben Shahn designed the posters, and Studs Terkel was often the emcee. But it was Paul whom people came to hear. Wallace had great personal respect for Paul. He liked to be with him, to hear him sing, to listen to his ideas. But Wallace disagreed with Paul's confronting head-on the forces of native fascism, as he did in Peekskill, fearing that they were too powerful. Robeson of course held that any person who really believes in the Bill of Rights has to be prepared to face hostile crowds, be willing to picket and demonstrate, because that is precisely how you defend your rights if you are in a minority.

One evening we had a Progressive party meeting in Philadelphia where Paul was to sing. He and I and Larry Brown, Paul's gifted accompanist, took the train from Penn Station and shared a drawing room. Ordinarily the easiest person in the world to be with, Paul was very unlike himself on this occasion. He sat quite silent and didn't want to talk. When we went to the dining car for lunch, he still wouldn't speak. Finally I asked Larry, "What's the matter with Paul today?" And Larry said, "Don't you know? He's going to sing. He goes through this before every performance."

But that occasion was unique in my experience. Paul was a frequent guest of ours at Kent, and once remarked, "John, I've known lots of folks who tried to get away from it all, but no one who has succeeded like you." We always enjoyed a relaxed time together. He loved to hold forth on the subject of the universality of music, on the relationships between African or Chinese music and Western classical music. He would expound at great length and, to my great plea-

sure, illustrate his points by singing. To Paul, music was a symbol of
the intimacy of the human family.

* * *

Beanie later recalled of Wallace: "He had no hopes or expecta-
tions of becoming president when he ran. He thought the issues had
to be joined, had to be presented to the American people. I've heard
him say a number of times that the Progressive party platform of 1948
was the best platform of a political party that has ever been adopted." In his oral history, Wallace confirmed Beanie's recollection. Nevertheless, all of us were far more optimistic than the election results
showed we had any right to be. We hoped for several million votes.
When we learned that we only received a million and a half, it was
devastating.

We knew beforehand and rediscovered every day of the campaign
that an independent third party is severely handicapped. As the states
reported, this was substantiated. In Ohio, nearly 150,000 Progressive
party votes were voided as a result of confusing voting procedures.
In Georgia, where we obtained 80,000 signatures on our nominating
petitions, the authorities recorded only 1,636 votes, a fraud the extent of which cannot be attributed only to Jim Crow voting laws. In
Missouri, our 5,000-plus votes were credited as 500. In Michigan, the
Democratic candidate for U.S. Senate, Frank Hook, said that he was
told by election inspectors that they hadn't counted the 36,000 Progressive party votes split in his favor. Altogether, we estimated that
as many as two million votes were stolen, and this of course doesn't
include Illinois, where we were knocked off the ballot. But, if one
adds up our most optimistic vote count, we still received a *maximum*
of only somewhat more than 3 million out of 49 million votes cast.

The results stunned Wallace, but he sounded like the victor, telling the *New York Times* of November 3: "Tonight we have had an extraordinary victory because nothing can beat a spirit of this kind. You
cannot do the impossible at once; we have done extraordinary won-
ders in the last 10 months. I am not in any way disappointed by the
results. I am truly heartened by Marcantonio's victory [in his bid to
return to Congress]. Our party has been in existence for 10 months
and we do not have, except in New York City, any organization of the
kind it takes. We didn't have a chance, but we are going to have it."

In the middle of the night, before going up to Marc's election headquarters in the Bronx, Wallace approved the telegram I wrote, con-
ceding the election to Truman. The message said that bankruptcy of
the country could not be avoided "so long as the policy of the Cold

War is continued and we spend increasing billions of American dollars to support reactionary regimes abroad, arm Western Europe and militarize America." It called for "a comprehensive program of assistance to farmers, rollback of consumer prices, public housing, social security, conservation, irrigation and public power development" which would be possible only under a foreign policy of "one world at peace, not two hostile worlds arming for war."

After showing my draft to Clark Foreman, Charles Howard, and other IPP officials, they argued that the wire offered no congratulations and was a breach of good sportsmanship. Wallace held firm, however, supporting my draft. "Under no circumstance," he announced, "will I congratulate that son of a bitch."

Wallace interpreted his defeat as I did—the result of Truman's co-opting our domestic program. We didn't reckon with his ability to maneuver, nor with the prevalence and weight of lesser-evil thinking among the voters. Early in the campaign, a significant number of Jewish community leaders and cultural figures came aboard the Progressive party, not entirely incidental to Soviet support for the newborn state of Israel. By early autumn, Truman also recognized Israel, undercutting our appeal on that issue. The Progressive party campaigns against Jim Crow laws, for Fair Employment Practices Commissions, for anti-lynching legislation—all were adopted by Truman in the course of his campaign. So too were our programs for veterans' rights, public housing, expanded social security, etc. Truman went on a whistle-stop tour, denouncing the Eightieth Congress as reactionary, calling for every measure we had enunciated. This included the establishment of a commission to end discrimination against Blacks in the armed forces. By election day, Truman was running on the Republicans' foreign policy and our domestic program. The famous day-after-election photo of Truman grinning as he holds a newspaper with the early morning premature headline declaring victory for Dewey obscured what should have been the big story. If it is true that we lost big because Truman co-opted our program, it is similarly true that he won for the same reason. The Progressive party lost the election but its issues were the difference between Truman winning and losing.

There is no denying that the Clark Clifford strategy of tying Wallace to the Communist party in the minds of the electorate had a great effect. The Smith Act indictment of Party leaders on the eve of Wallace's nomination and the HUAC subpoenas of Pressman, Kramer, and myself right after the convention were only the most obvious tactics of this strategy. Of course the Communist party supported the

[handwritten note:] ie.. Truman saying that we could have both "guns & butter" simultaneously.

IPP from the beginning, and a number of comrades—in my opinion, too many and too prominently displayed, by far—were active on every level. Acting as essentially chief deputy to Beanie Baldwin, the campaign director, I suppose that I was the Communist placed highest in the campaign organization. I can say without fear of contradiction that the Communists did not operate as an organized unit within the Progressive party. We didn't meet or caucus together at any time. For one thing, there was never a need to do so. Beanie, by no means a Communist or even a Marxist, met on his own with Gene Dennis and had no hesitation in doing so. The Communists were part of the coalition and Beanie would no more stay away from them than he would from, say, the United Electrical Workers or the Southern Conference on Human Welfare, whose leaders were also part of the coalition.

There was no secret about Communist support. Wallace and Taylor knew this, never tried to hide it and couldn't if they wanted to. This was still at the outset of McCarthyism, so the Party was still considered a legitimate political entity that had earned its stripes in building the CIO, fighting fascism, pioneering the struggles for unemployment compensation, social security, and equality for African-Americans. Why shouldn't the Communists have every right—the same as all other U.S. citizens—to participate openly in a political campaign? Communists throughout Europe and Japan and Latin America were a legitimate part of the political landscape, winning seats in parliament and holding offices in city halls around the world.

Moreover, the Communists brought important gifts to any campaign. We had a body of experience at grass-roots organizing, licking stamps, putting up posters, selling tickets to rallies, and fund-raising. It can be said that the Communists did the bulk of the nitty-gritty work in the campaign and that, without them, there would have been no campaign to speak of. We would go where liberal angels perhaps feared to tread, unafraid of bringing down the wrath and disapproval of the powers that be. We had a track record at building coalitions of diverse forces, among them the CIO, CIO-PAC, ICCASP, NCPAC, American Labor party, etc. And we had a great deal of talent—cultural, political, and tactical. Of course we also brought problems, not least among them the certainty of ruling-class attacks, and our own unfailing support of all things Soviet. Nor were we beyond mistakes— some of them whoppers. When the Party's journal, *Political Affairs,* endorsed Wallace just days after his announced declaration to run, it cast a die. Particularly with the growing Red Scare and the schism developing in the CIO, it would have been the better part of wisdom

Little did you know of Stalin's "horrors"

to abstain from a public endorsement. Those who looked to the Party for direction would have gotten the message in myriad other ways. And if the Party, as a legitimate political force, had every right to endorse whomever it chose to, it might at least have waited a couple of months to join a growing list of endorsers instead of insisting on being first in line.

Despite later attempts to characterize Party cadres as "infiltrators," conspirators operating with a hidden agenda, the main noncommunist leaders and the candidates of the Progressive party had only respect for the work of the Communists. I've noted Wallace's insistence on my own participation at the highest levels, not only after I told him of my sister's Communist party responsibilities and my appearance before the federal grand jury but also after I was subpoenaed by HUAC. Glen Taylor publicly declared at the time, and often afterward, that the Communists in the IPP were absolutely scrupulous in their behavior. Rexford Tugwell recalled in his oral history, "Of course the Communists supported Wallace. I think as a matter of fact they would have been very inconsistent if they hadn't supported him. In general, I think, the Communist Party has supported progressive candidates. I don't think there can be a successful progressive political party that doesn't accept the support, without strings, of any group that wants to support it."

When the Progressive Citizens of America was formed, a year before Wallace announced his candidacy, it was understood—certainly this was Beanie's conviction, one shared by the Communists—that if a third party was not yet in order, certainly it was important to project a third *candidacy.* This would challenge Truman's break with Roosevelt's policy vis à vis the USSR, following Winston Churchill's "iron curtain" speech at Fulton, Missouri. So it is clear that the Communist party was in on the Progressive party from the outset, at the process of conceptualization. But after the 1948 elections and in hindsight, a number of Communist leaders argued that it had been a mistake to run against Truman. Bill Foster, Will Weinstone, and, to some extent, Gil Green raised questions. Their arguments were not without merit. Will was concerned that the campaign aggravated the split in the CIO, that it gave Murray and the CIO "Right" the weapon it was looking for to club the Left. Even Mike Quill broke with the Party over the Wallace candidacy, although others—like Harry Bridges, Albert Fitzgerald and Julius Emspak of United Electrical, Ben Gold, and most of the CIO Left—stuck with the Wallace campaign. Will argued, and I'm compelled to agree, that we gravely miscalculated, that we thought we could win the CIO membership despite the opposition of

Murray and the leadership, that the vote demonstrated the weakness of the Left forces in the country. Still, I believe that Will went too far with his argument. The CIO would have split even without the Wallace candidacy. But the point about miscalculations is indisputable. I'm not a betting man—generally, outside of politics, I'm quite a conservative person—but I made the biggest bet of my life at the beginning of the campaign, based on the massive response to our rallies and petition campaigns. I bet a friend $250 that Wallace would receive at least 10 million votes.

Other Communists, in retrospect, advanced the proposition that rather than forming a third party, we should have convinced Wallace to challenge Truman within the Democratic primary process. But a challenge within the Democratic party, in those days, would have been futile. For one thing, Wallace had no base within the Democratic party. He was a creature of Roosevelt in the days when FDR was the party boss. Also, back in 1948, the Democratic party rarely conducted primary elections. Local machines and party bosses—these, remember, were the famed days of "smoked-filled rooms"—decided who would run as candidates. For the four previous national elections before 1948, Roosevelt was the candidate, and it was unthinkable that a Democrat would challenge him. So primaries had simply become irrelevant to the nominating process.

My own recollection is that the mistakes of the IPP were often encouraged in the first place by Wallace himself. He was "out in left field," as we used to say. Any politically sensitive and sensible political party wouldn't have retained me as general counsel, certainly not after my HUAC appearance. Moreover, Wallace was the first to excuse the events in Czechoslovakia that year, when a Communist-dominated government replaced what had been coalition rule that included the Communists. On his own and without consultation, Wallace called a press conference to justify it. (I myself justified it in my own mind, but wouldn't have considered doing so in such a publicly provocative manner.) Even the subsequent death by possible suicide of the popular and liberal foreign minister Jan Masaryk raised no doubt in Wallace. Never was there a shade of criticism from Wallace over the direction being taken in eastern Europe. At the nominating convention, as I've said, he was instrumental in allowing the defeat of "the Vermont resolution" staking out an independent foreign policy. (Dorothy Healey fondly recalls my sister's bright humor during a Communist party leadership meeting after the nominating convention. Gene Dennis and Fred Fine were trying to figure out a means to allow the IPP to establish some distance from the USSR, to undo

WHAT A USEFUL "NAIVE IDIOT" JOHN APT WAS FOR THE USSR. TO APPROVE OF THE MILITARY TAKEOVER OF CZECHOSLOVAKIA BY THE USSR.

[Handwritten annotations:]
EVEN A SO-CALLED SIMPLETON AS RONALD REAGAN w CALLED THE USSR AN "EVIL EMPIRE," WAS ABLE TO h BRING DOWN THE USSR AND MOVED BACK THE "DOOMSDAY CLOCK" WAS SMARTER THAN YOU IVY LEAGUE INTELLECTUALS

the defeat of the Vermont resolution. When Bill Foster and Ben Davis challenged Gene and Fred, Marion remarked, "The Soviets would be the first to understand that we need to find a broad approach. Only donkeys don't understand that.") Having said all of this, however, I remain unconvinced that had the IPP been less keyed to the Left, it would have substantially changed the election results.

Yet, despite our errors and grievous overestimations, I have never thought the Progressive party was a mistake. I believed (and still do) that it was essential to challenge—even at great risk—the reversal of Roosevelt's policy of friendship with the USSR, given the real dangers of war. With the growing repression of civil rights and civil liberties, it would have been inexcusable not to have offered the U.S. voters a progressive alternative.

[Handwritten annotations:]
REAGANS FEARLESSNESS IN CONFRON The "EVIL EMPIRE" HELPED END The COLD WAR YOU PINHEAD.

At its election postmortem, the Progressive party's executive decided to continue as an organization, issuing information and position papers, pressuring the Truman administration to the extent it could, and looking forward to the day when it might reemerge on the electoral front. Soon Wallace recognized the folly of having rejected the Vermont resolution. He began to speak publicly about his differences with the Communist party, about not allowing "anyone the slightest, legitimate reason for believing that any working member of the Progressive party puts Rome, Moscow or London ahead of the United States." He also began to enunciate a form of Christian idealism, particularly regarding the mounting nuclear stockpiles. But whereas we Communists placed the responsibility for the cold war and the arms race on the United States—the first to make the atomic bomb, the only country to ever use it, the one that sought a monopoly on atomic power—Wallace saw the United States as a potential moral leader, "an international Good Samaritan," as one scholar of the period put it.

When the Korean War broke out on June 25, 1950, the IPP was thrown into a crisis. The United States moved quickly in the United Nations to support its South Korean surrogates. Through a disastrous tactical blunder by Stalin, the Soviet delegate absented himself from the discussion, thus failing to exercise his Security Council veto of the U.S.-proposed mandate for UN troops to go to war against North Korea. The "UN" troops, in reality, were overwhelmingly made up of the U.S. armed forces and commanded only by U.S. generals. So in effect the U.S. was at war against a Communist-led North Korea, backed by the USSR and China. Only a year earlier, a Communist-led revolu-

[Handwritten annotation at bottom:]
NOTE TO YOU PINHEAD - The COMMUNIST NORTH INVADED The Free SOUTH + NOT VICE-VERSA

[Handwritten annotation left margin:]
See p. 149

tion had come to power in China, leading to frenzied recriminations within the State Department over the rather peculiar and chauvinistic question "Who lost China?" This set off a new round of anticommunist hysteria in the news media and the Congress.

The IPP executive committee met ten days after the outbreak of hostilities to establish a position on the Korean War. Marcantonio, the sole member of the House of Representatives to oppose the "police action"—the euphemism for declaring war on North Korea—distributed copies of his speech to the executive committee. Wallace soon found himself in a small minority defending the UN action. Most of the more liberal or mainstream leaders of the IPP had left the organization after the defeat of Wallace in 1948. More departed as the Red Scare gripped the country in the wake of the cold war division of Europe, the coming to power of the Chinese revolution, the conviction of the Communist party leadership under the Smith Act, the expulsion of the Left-led unions from the CIO, and the rise of Joseph McCarthy. That Henry Wallace stayed as long as he did must be considered a testament to his own courage or lack of political sagacity.

When it became clear to Henry that he would not prevail in the executive committee, he informed Beanie that he would issue his own public pronouncements. We held a series of meetings at Lillian Hellman's home in Westchester. I remember Beanie, Louis Burnham, Bob Lovett, my old professor from Chicago, the sculptor Jo Davidson, and others participating. It fell to me to draft the IPP's formal position. I tried to finesse the matter—primarily to permit Wallace to remain in the party—by stating that "the continuance of hostilities is not in the interest of the American people. It is not in the interest of world peace," by calling for a unified and independent Korea with the "inalienable right to self-determination," by condemning the repressive Rhee regime in South Korea as a U.S. proxy, and arguing that the UN "cannot fulfill the high purpose of its charter and serve the people of the world so long as the 450 million people who compose the Chinese nation are excluded." Tom Emerson, a member of the IPP executive and a distinguished Yale Law School professor, supported my contention that the UN decision to go to war was improper and illegal under its charter because it was taken in the Security Council in the absence of the Soviet representative.

The statement was issued on July 15, 1950. Two days later, Julius Rosenberg was arrested on charges of conspiring to pass atomic secrets to the Soviets. Ethel Rosenberg would be arrested on the same charges three weeks later. Opposition to the Korean War was being portrayed as no less than treasonous. I remember Wallace saying at one of our last meetings, "I'm a man of the West, and when the question becomes one between the East and the West, I take my stand with the West." On August 4, he formally withdrew from the Independent Progressive party. There followed a round of vituperation directed against Wallace, accusing him of cowardice and treason, by Communists and others remaining in the IPP that is embarrassing to recall.

Until Wallace made his position clear on the Korean War, I personally had not recognized how deep the crisis in the Progressive party had become. But shortly after Wallace's defection, most of the remaining noncommunists in the leadership—people like Tom Emerson, Lillian Hellman, Jo Davidson—also left, not so much out of opposition as because they understood the future effectiveness of the IPP would be nonexistent. The war would last for three years, while at home the federal government indicted the secondary, then the tertiary, and finally the local leadership of the Communist party throughout the country. The Rosenbergs would be tried, convicted, and sentenced to their unquiet deaths. Loyalty oaths, blacklists, and purges were imposed on every significant institution in the life of the country. And Senator McCarthy, mad hatter though he obviously was, became the dominant personality in the Congress of the United States. The McCarran Act passed in both houses, establishing the Subversive Activities Control Board and authorizing the FBI to arrest and confine all "suspected" security risks. Detention camps were prepared to receive them.

In Korea, after the initial push into the South by North Korea, General Douglas MacArthur's troops landed in Inchon, in effect surrounding the North Koreans and driving them to the Yalu River, which divides Korea from China. This brought the Chinese Red Army en masse into the war. The Chinese drove the U.S. forces back, inflicting and receiving huge numbers of casualties. It looked like the war would drag on interminably. MacArthur, featured in *Time* and *Life* as the country's greatest hero, called for Truman to use the atomic bomb against China. I can still recall photos of John Foster Dulles—Wall Street mogul, *eminence gris* of the intelligence community, and soon to be secretary of state—sitting in a trench at the Thirty-eighth Parallel, sighting a rifle in the direction of the Communist enemy.

Such were the circumstances that the remnants of the Progressive party faced in early 1952. The Republicans were about to nominate Eisenhower and the Democrats Adlai Stevenson as their respective candidates for president. Both publicly supported pursuit of the war;

neither was questioning, let alone opposing, the growing repression in the country. The Communist party view was that, immense as the difficulties might seem, it would be irresponsible to allow a presidential election campaign without a single voice heard in opposition to the war and McCarthyite repression.

After Wallace's departure from the IPP in 1950, the Communist party leadership held intense discussions about the future of the Progressive party. Gene Dennis was serving a jail sentence at the time for contempt of Congress for refusing to testify before HUAC but declining to take the Fifth Amendment. Gus Hall, a member of the political bureau, was sitting in for Gene in his absence. The first time I ever met Gus was when I went to discuss my views of the Progressive party. I strongly felt that the IPP should fold, that it had no future. Gus agreed with me, in fact told me in unmistakable terms that the IPP should fold. Later, however, I learned that in a subsequent political bureau meeting, Gus argued precisely the opposite, that the IPP must continue by all means, and this decision set into motion the ill-fated 1952 campaign. Fred Fine, Gene's (and the Communist party's) official spokesperson within the IPP, later sympathized with me about Gus's proclivity to go overboard in two directions simultaneously, a tendency I came to experience more or less regularly for the next forty years.

In any case, our difficulty in 1952 was the selection of viable candidates. The IPP was stripped of liberals within its ranks. We no longer had people of the public stature of a Henry Wallace, a former vice-president, or a Glen Taylor, a member of the Senate. The growing antiwar sentiment in the country was without organized expression and therefore without prominent spokespersons. Marcantonio, who was defeated in the 1950 elections when the Republican, Democratic, and Liberal party machines coalesced against him, was uninterested in running for president. The House of Representatives was his passion, and his only ambition as a politician was to return to Capitol Hill. His own political sense told him that this would not be feasible before 1954. But he was among the most insistent on the IPP running a presidential candidate in 1952, precisely to maintain the organization for his own race two years later. There was never a serious debate on the question of whether to run, only on who should do so.

We continued to cast about for candidates. Vincent Hallinan, the famed San Francisco criminal lawyer who, with his wife, Vivian, became spark plugs of the IPP in Northern California, allowed as how he would be available if no one else was. Charlotta Bass, the publisher of the *California Eagle* newspaper serving the Black community of Los Angeles, was projected for vice-president, the first African-American woman ever to be nominated for that office. Their nominations came on July 4, 1952, before eighteen hundred delegates to the Third Convention of the IPP. Actually, Vin was still in a Puget Sound federal penitentiary on income tax charges brought by a vindictive Justice Department for his foiling four attempts to deport Harry Bridges. Vin would be unavailable to campaign until the fall, so Vivian and their sons, Patrick and Terence, became proxies at public appearances. We could still mount impressive public rallies, as we did in May when we put sixteen thousand people into Madison Square Garden.

At the peak of the 1952 campaign, the Communist party developed second thoughts about the effort. The Party's top leaders were in prison. (A Party decision on the eve of their imprisonment sent Gil Green, Gus Hall, Bob Thompson, and Henry Winston underground to run the Party while the others served their terms. Hall and Thompson were captured by the FBI, but the G-Men never did find Gil and Winnie, who turned themselves in several years later.) The remaining leaders, who were presumably in contact with Gil and Winnie, presided over yet another swing of the pendulum. A draft resolution for the Party's convention that year called for abandoning "sectarian politics," i.e., the IPP, and "rejoining the mainstream." I was infuriated, having been recalled by the Progressive party, at the urging of the Communist leadership, to serve as director of the Hallinan-Bass campaign. I wrote a long memo criticizing the Party's new line, considering it to be a retreat. The lack of enthusiasm by the Communists was duly noted by Vin Hallinan, who was understandably upset. Marcantonio, whose temper was legendary and who was not imprisoned as Vin was, let his displeasure be known in no uncertain terms.

The 1952 campaign was at best a rear-guard action, albeit a valiant one. The platform was almost entirely geared to demanding a cease-fire in Korea and ending the war. I cannot claim that our campaign was even a factor in compelling Eisenhower to pledge, late in the campaign, to bring an end to the war as he eventually did with the 1953 armistice. The IPP was effectively finished before the war ended.

* * *

For radicals and progressives, surviving these most difficult years summoned up a great deal of courage, grit, forbearance, patience, humor, and perspicacity. Tens of thousands of comrades and friends—a few in the spotlight, many more in anonymity—prevailed over McCarthyism in maintaining their integrity. Yevgeny Yevtushenko, in one of his anti-Stalinist poems, wrote about the "strange, bizarre time / when a simple flash of honesty / had 'courage' as its name." He might well have been writing about McCarthyism. Unfortunately, not all were endowed with sufficient "courage," and a great human and personal toll was exacted.

After Wallace's defection in 1950, HUAC again called Pressman, Nat Witt, Charlie Kramer, and me to testify. The four of us had been best friends and the closest of co-workers for thirty years, since we came together in the AAA. In the case of Lee and Nat, their friendship preceded the New Deal, going back to their Harvard days when they were active in the campaign to save Sacco and Vanzetti. They bought cottages in Vermont (with my sister, Marion) and vacationed together each summer. Next they were united in the same law firm with another Harvard classmate, Harold Cammer. Lee and I had worked together in the WPA, Charlie and I at the LaFollette Committee, while Nat was at the NLRB. When Lee was counsel to the CIO, I was counsel to the Amalgamated and the CIO-PAC. The four of us again came together during the Wallace campaign.

In 1950, Nat and Charlie and I asked Hal Cammer to again represent us before HUAC, as he had in 1948. Lee broke: on the day of the hearings, he was the first one called and, pronouncing himself anguished but relieved, decided to cooperate with the committee by identifying his three best friends, perhaps his only three friends, as Communists. He said that he was breaking with the Communist party over its opposition to the Korean War. Having admitted to neither private nor public reservations about opposition to the war any time previously, Lee simply found in the war a convenient rationalization for betraying his closest co-workers and his own life's work.

We later learned that he had been interviewed in his law offices a few weeks before by William Sullivan, one of J. Edgar Hoover's most influential lieutenants, in an attempt to exculpate himself. Hal Cammer recalled, after the arrests of the Rosenbergs and during the ensuing spate of public anti-Semitism, Lee discussing the possibility of converting to Catholicism and even considering a visit to the television priest Bishop Fulton J. Sheen for this purpose. Lee's flirtation with the bishop brought to mind Ring Lardner, Jr.'s, brilliant satire *The Ecstasy of Owen Muir*, about a man who, under McCarthyite pressure, converts to Catholicism and becomes a monk. Hal didn't take Lee seriously, but then Lee approached Hal about evicting Nat from their firm as a "danger" to their practice. Hal, whose partnership with Nat preceded by ten years Lee's joining the firm, of course rejected the idea. Lee left the firm just before his HUAC appearance. His interest in Catholicism was short-lived; instead, he became a religious Jew.

Lee always had a great deal of talent. But he was a far better negotiator and political operator than he was a lawyer. He didn't have the necessary patience to do the thorough analysis required in tackling a difficult legal case. Similarly, he was an excellent draftsman, a quick study when it came to drawing up contracts and agreements. But putting together a brief requires lots of careful, and often dull, research, which was beyond Lee's tolerance. His obvious intelligence and great charm were exceeded only by his ambition and self-centeredness. He was intrigued by power and liked to exercise it. Lee was attracted to those on the other side of the table: he developed a series of warm relationships with the cotton brokers during the AAA days and with industrialists like Henry Kaiser and Cyrus Eaton during his CIO years. It seemed a bit of a contradiction that this idealist who hungered for a better world could always seem to be reaching for power, manipulating those around him without relent. I suppose that for the better part of his life, Lee's politics—in which he truly believed—didn't interfere with what he wanted out of life. On the contrary, his politics were helpful in achieving the status he sought. But when the conflict between his politics and ambition came into collision, ambition proved the stronger.

Lee's callousness was a constant source of pain for Nat, who was an extremely sensitive, sentimental man. One day, soon after our appearance before the committee, Nat told me that he was walking along lower Broadway and saw Lee coming his way. I asked Nat what he did. He replied, "I turned my head away." I said to Nat, "You jerk, why did you turn your head? Lee should have turned his head away." Not long after that, as it happens, I was walking down Broadway and saw Lee coming. I stared right at him, saying nothing. He turned his head away.

Lee could not have been a happy man at the end. The Luce publications and other journals of the conservative establishment placed his appearance before HUAC in the too-little-too-late category. He had to have been gravely disappointed in his personal miscalculations. He had left the CIO for the Wallace movement and figured that by making his peace with HUAC, he would be welcomed back by Phil Murray. Murray of course rejected Lee's attempt to restore himself. For Lee's usefulness to Murray was only in part based on his considerable talents; it was in Lee's ties to the Party and the broader Left that he brought something to Murray's table, so to speak. Lee also tried to reach Jerome Frank, our old boss and friend at the AAA, who was then a U.S. Appellate Court judge in New York, hoping to return to Jerry's good graces. But Jerry also refused to see him, explaining to others that he couldn't trust a man who had betrayed his three best friends, and besides, Lee had never told Jerry that he had been a Party member.

Pressman cut quite a figure, but it was my delicious pleasure to note that it was Nat's testimony before the committee, not Lee's, that Russell Baker chose to remember more than thirty years later. Writing in one of his pungent columns about the "velvet-glove treatment" accorded Col. Oliver North and Admiral John Poindexter after they pleaded the Fifth Amendment before the congressional committee investigating the Iran-Contra scandal, Baker recalled (in the *New York Times,* December 13, 1986) with great amusement Nat's manner before the committee:

> The investigators would read doggedly through their piles of questions, and Witt would work them up to a deep red flush around the cheekbones by pretending to be elsewhere. After an involved question, he might let his attention flicker momentarily over the interrogator, as though trying to recall where he had seen the fellow before. Then, returning his gaze to the window or studying his hands with the abstracted air of a man musing on a manicure, he would sigh: "Repeat the question please." And the investigator would go through it again.
>
> If the interrogator's face was a particularly deep crimson, Witt might mutter in a barely audible register: "I decline to answer," knowing the interrogator would take the bait. And the interrogator, taking it, would demand: "On what ground?" And Witt, still playing him, would murmur: "Fifth Amendment." And the interrogator, suppressing a scream, would admonish him: "Mr. Witt, you know you must give the complete statement on each response!" Then, like a schoolboy showing up a doltish teacher before the class, Witt would recite in sing-song, "I must decline to answer that question on grounds that it might tend to incriminate me."

Commented Russell Baker, regarding the Iran-Contra hearings: "Those politicians this week talking about their respect for the Fifth Amendment—that was rich."

5

The Case of a Lifetime

The pressures of the cold war—those that drove a man like Lee Pressman to flail around, looking for God in a television priest or a neighborhood rabbi, desperately longing to restore long-broken ties, trying anything to salvage a career after betraying those closest to him—affected all of us in different ways. In my case, I was drawn even closer to my family and friends. The house in Kent became ever more a retreat for us from the corruption gripping the country's political culture.

Even—perhaps especially—the Party comrades were no longer as kind, as gracious, as forgiving of error as in the halcyon days of our not so distant past. But for the Abts and our closest friends, we became an extended family. At Kent, Jessica more or less presided. The original workaholic, Jessica never came for a weekend of presumed rest without having in tow a pile of papers and articles to peruse, collate, and work into pieces for the magazine. A gifted raconteur, she could entertain the weekend guests with stories piled onto stories while putting together the next issue of *New World Review* (changed from *Soviet Russia Today* after the Chinese revolution), meantime producing gourmet quality meals for ten or twelve persons. Only Marion was Jessica's equal at being able to cook exquisitely for a large dinner party while, say, typing a manuscript. But Marion far more resembled me when it came to an ability, even an affinity, for simple loafing.

She often spent weekends with us, as did mother, who had undergone a series of heart and angina attacks, which she handled with the superb grace that was her overriding characteristic. Aside from

the unqualified ease we all felt with one another, it was an additional pleasure that our friends felt equally comfortable spending time
with mother or Marion as with Jessica and me. Mother Bloor also
joined us from time to time when she could travel from her home in
Allentown, Pennsylvania. Small in stature, with lively blue eyes which
seemed to read any situation, then "retired" from decades of love affairs and marriages beyond enumeration, politically active to the end
of her life, Mother Bloor was particularly close to Jessica and Marion, whom she saw perhaps as younger sisters more than daughters.

Ours was hardly a conventional family, even in terms of blood
lines. Mother Bloor's granddaughter and Jessica's stepdaughter, Judy,
considered me, Marion, and mother her family. When Judy's daughters, Dorian and Elizabeth, came along, I was their adopted grandfather. Together with Judy's husband, Daniel, a Columbia University
literature professor (and their three dogs), they frequently helped fill
up the house in Kent. We of course loved Judy and the kids and always had a good time with Daniel in Kent. He was devoted to making his way up the academic ladder, and our family connection was
obviously not something one would brag about in a curriculum vi-
tae. After coming back from the war as a B-24 pilot, he tried to work
for the State Department but was firmly turned down after an FBI
family check.

Jessica was not one to restrain herself when she felt strongly about
something, and in Judy's younger days, it was sometimes my place
to intervene when she and Jessica seemed on a collision course. Happily, those days were long passed by the time Judy had her own family. She was particularly concerned, given the fear abroad in the land,
that her children be given as secure a sense of family as possible, and
she was able to do this to a remarkable degree despite the many obstacles. Jessica's son (and Judy's brother) David was diagnosed as
manic-depressive, but it did not mean that he functioned irrationally
at all times. Often, particularly at Kent, he was amusing and interesting, enjoyable company when he chose not to keep to himself. It was
not uncommon to organize poker games for three generations of
family. Jessica, who approached the game as if she were seeing playing cards for the first time, usually wound up with most of the chips.
Our ten acres of grounds, huge living room, large kitchen, and six
bedrooms made accommodating a dozen weekend guests quite comfortable. Although having only one bathroom sometimes presented
problems.

Regrettably, Marion's son, Johnny B., as we called my namesake,
never joined us. He was the youngest commander of the nation's

merchant marine fleet during the war and fancied himself a prototype rugged individualist and hard-drinking seaman. Then, with Senator McCarthy and HUAC on the rampage, Johnny lost his commission because of his mother's politics, which the national security state
looked upon as a terrible threat. Unfortunately, in his pain for having
lost his chosen way of life, Johnny blamed Marion rather than those
who were responsible. From that day until her death, Johnny dis-
owned his mother. Marion, in all other instances ever the cockeyed
optimist, was in this hurt beyond description.

If our family was neither conventional nor casual, neither were
our friends. Pete and Ann Peters, perhaps our most frequent guests
at Kent, had just been deported. It was the Peterses who helped name
our Kent place "October Hill"—by which it was thereafter known—
both because of the stunning autumn foliage and so that we could
say, as we left New York for the weekend, we were "taking the road
to October." Pete was born in Hungary, joined the Communist party
there as a teenager, studied law as a youth, and became active in the
short-lived revolution that took power in 1919 under Bela Kun. When
the revolution was overthrown, he emigrated to the United States but
never applied for citizenship. In the Party, Pete was usually active in
the organization's security apparatus, although I met him when he
took over responsibility for our group in Washington after Hal Ware
was killed. Pete was also responsible for our members in Hollywood
and became close to many of the movie people. When the blacklisted
Joseph Losey left the States to live and make movies in England, he
and his wife, the fashion designer Elizabeth Hawes, maintained their
relationship to the Peterses and visited them in Budapest when Joe
was planning a movie—which never was made—about Leon Trotsky.
Another of Pete's cronies—and a sometimes poker player at Kent—
was Gerhardt Eisler, brother of Hans, Berthold Brecht's frequent collaborator. Gerhardt, who, with his wife, Hilda, accompanied Brecht
to Hollywood to escape certain death under Hitler, had been the Comintern operative responsible for relations with the CPUSA. One time
in Kent, he was stricken with an excruciating gall bladder attack and
I remember him lying in bed singing revolutionary songs to take his
mind off the pain that seized him.

Ann Peters was born in Paterson, New Jersey, to a family of silk
mill workers and spent part of her childhood in a mill. When I first
met her, she was working on the Lower East Side as a Party section
organizer. (A section, in the Party structure, is a collection of clubs
organized in a particular community or industry.) She was a dedicated worker and wonderful organizer, but this was the depression and,

even in the best of times, a Party functionary could expect scarcely more than a monk. She and Pete lived on the edge of starvation as long as I knew them. When Pete was ordered deported in 1948, of course Ann joined him. They arrived in Budapest in 1949, during the regime of Rakocsi, the Stalinist party leader. They had left the American "Red Scare" for the Hungarian "White Scare," during which anybody from the West, including the Peterses, were under suspicion. Pete and Ann had no employment for several years, until Rakocsi died and was replaced by Imre Nagy. Pete was rehabilitated and became editor of the Party magazine devoted to international affairs, while Ann was assigned work in shortwave radio broadcasts to English-speaking countries.

The Kent house was constructed on the edge of a steep, rocky hill, and a few years earlier, Pete and I built quite a large platform abutting out from the rocks to serve as a deck. Of course, construction of the deck could commence only after lengthy days of theoretical discussions, over bourbon, about the design. We finally decided to cantilever the platform out from the rocks. A chestnut blight some years before had killed all the trees in that particular glade, leaving us an abundant supply of magnificent wood for chairs, beds, and for support of our platform that, because of its dimensions, we called the "bandstand." Needless to say, the bandstand never served as a dance floor. But as a setting for predinner drinks, it was incomparable. When Jessica and I visited the Peterses' home in Budapest in 1961, Pete's first question to me as I came off the plane was "Is the bandstand still standing?" It was, and continued to stand for a considerable number of years later.

The first weekend after we bought the Kent place in 1938, we hosted seventeen friends for a housewarming. One of our guests that first weekend was Kastia Dunansky, the Soviet diplomat who was killed soon afterward in an airplane crash in Mexico on his way to assuming the ambassadorship to that country. Rarely were we without weekend guests thereafter, and often our company included friends from the Soviet diplomatic community. The Soviets were particularly enthusiastic about picking wild mushrooms, which inundated the woods on our property. Their zeal for mushroom hunting was contagious, and we gorged ourselves with some regularity until I read one day about an entire family that was wiped out by poisonous mushrooms in an adjacent county.

Thanksgivings in Kent were especially festive. Jessica outdid herself with a culinary display. A neighboring farm raised wild ducks, pheasants, and wild turkeys, so we had our pick of holiday bird. Besides Marion, mother, David, Judy and Daniel and the kids, and the Peterses before their deportation, we'd import our Jackson Heights poker regulars—the Silvermans, the Kramers, the Witts, Gerhardt Eisler if he was available—for the occasion. Poker rules were invariably dealer's choice. Pete was always the liveliest member of the party—he loved the chancy game of "baseball"—but Gerhardt was the craftiest, his skills honed from playing regularly with Eddie Barsky, our good friend and family doctor. I was never much of a player but enjoyed sitting in for the bourbon and conversation. Marion always played but not well. Her game was Scrabble, at which she excelled, although you had to keep a close eye on her or she'd cheat. Her favorite ploy was to take out the dictionary, thumb through the pages until she found what she was looking for, nod sagely, close the book, and put down a nonexistent word.

My immersion in the Progressive party significantly widened our social circle and brought an ever larger crowd to Kent. Beanie and his wife, Lillian, were frequent visitors. Lillian had been raised a conservative Republican and trained as a chemical engineer, but the ravages of the depression caused her, like many others, to revolt against her upbringing. I first met her in Paris in 1945 during one of my trips to help put together the WFTU. She was winding up her wartime stint for the Office of Strategic Services, and I suggested that she look me up about job possibilities when she returned to the states. Two months later, she showed up in my office. I told her, "Why don't you go over to see Beanie Baldwin at NCPAC. I think he needs someone with just your talents." She did—and he did. This began a thirty-year romance and working partnership. Lillian joined the NCPAC staff, became field director of the Progressive Citizens of America in 1947, and shortly before the Progressive party founding convention, she and Beanie were married. In forgoing what might have been a lucrative career in the top apparatus of the Democratic party, the Baldwins accepted a life of austerity and scrimping for economic survival. Jessica and I turned to them for counsel and companionship for so many years that when they finally retired in 1968, it was natural that we provide them with a piece of our lovely Kent woodland on which to build their home. Even in retirement, however, their political genes continued to function. Beanie was elected to the Kent Board of Tax Assessors and Lillian as chair of the Town Democratic Committee.

Lou and Dottie Burnham also became regulars at Kent. Sometimes they came just with their kids, other times with George Murphy and with Thelma Dale, another Progressive party activist. I'd take the Burnhams' boy, Charles, fishing on the Housatonic. The river flowed just past the town of Kent at the foot of Skiff Mountain, five miles from our house. I had enjoyed deep-sea fishing off of Long Island when we spent summer vacations there in the thirties. In our first years at Kent, however, I spent the bulk of my time outdoors either chopping down trees or hiking. Then I had the pleasure of making acquaintances with Arnold and Aurelia Johnson. Arnold was a lapsed Christian minister. Through the ministry he became the U.S. equivalent of what is known in Latin America as a "worker priest," carrying his teachings into the mine communities of eastern Kentucky and the rubber plants of southern Ohio during some of the fiercest and most militant organizing struggles our country has ever seen. When we became friends during the McCarthy period, Arnold had already been a Communist party member for nearly twenty years.

Arnold came up to Kent with some regularity to teach me to fish. A man of unparalleled patience—with fish and with people—he'd never tire of fishing, whether he caught anything or not. I first learned to fish for smallmouth black bass, which grew to no more than twelve or fourteen inches long. These were too elementary for a man of Arnold's experience, but he joined me when I graduated to fly-fishing for trout. It was great fun to wade into the river in waist-high boots, and succeeding generations of our friends' children thrilled to the experience. Charles Burnham was the first, then his sisters and Thelma Dale's kids, finally my granddaughters Dorian and Elizabeth, a.k.a Bouj. Bouj was, even as a small child, ecologically minded—this was nearly forty years ago, decades before the fragility of the planet was commonly understood—and remains so to this day. It pained her to see any living thing harmed, so it must have been quite a sacrifice on her part to find frogs in our pond to use as trout bait.

With the Baldwins, Burnhams, George Murphy, Thelma Dale, and whatever Abt, Smith, and Ware offspring were resident, we'd play outdoors by day—"play" for us might be hours clearing brush—and talk politics into the night. We rehashed the successes and the foibles of the IPP and worry over the friends and comrades of the Party who were underground. Jessica and Louis talked about the exasperation of putting out their respective publications—*New World Review* and *Freedom*—at a time when not only were finances precarious (this was true in the best of periods) but when they might be arrested at any moment. Marion had already been indicted under the Smith Act, and any one of us might be next.

Thelma was another veteran of the Southern Negro Youth Congress who came into the leadership of the Progressive party, eventually becoming Beanie's deputy campaign manager for the Hallinan-Bass ticket in 1952. A native of Washington, D.C., her upper middle-class upbringing—an uncle directed the Phelps Stokes Fund—gave her a social ease and exuberance that was enchanting. I believe George Murphy first introduced us to Thelma, although she and Dottie Burnham were extremely close, so it might have been Dottie. Thelma was always amused by George's combativeness and enjoyment in provoking fierce arguments, as when he named one of his kids George Josef Tito, after himself, Stalin, and Stalin's Yugoslav nemesis. Thelma also found in Kent an oasis from the worrisome existence of Progressive party activism in the heyday of McCarthyism. She and her family, like the Burnhams, used October Hill as their vacation retreat. We also gave her, like the Baldwins, a piece of our property but, to our embarrassment, we discovered that the land we gave Thelma didn't belong to us. After a lifetime in Black schools and colleges and organizational experience in SNYC and the National Negro Congress Thelma found the IPP something of a change with its largely white leadership. She was entranced by Beanie's soft Virginia accent and liked to repeat the story of George's visiting the Baldwins for drinks at their apartment on Central Park West, only to be stopped by the doorman. Upon being buzzed, Beanie came down to the lobby and raised a ruckus. Thereafter, whenever George visited, he was always addressed by the doorman as "Mr. Murphy."

Another Kent regular was Ruth Jett, who came to the IPP through the office workers' union. Ruth became my personal secretary during the Wallace campaign and, as it turned out, she was the last one I ever had. One time, while Ruth was swimming in the Housatonic, the dam locks broke and she almost drowned. She credits me with saving her life but I think this is historical charity on her part. Looking back through the cultural fix of the 1990s, it might seem a bit of an anomaly that a twenty-four-year-old Black woman and her forty-four-year-old Jewish boss would find a sense of not only collegiality but friendship, that they and their families would be part of the same weekend social circle. I think that speaks to the comradeship that the Progressive party engendered and what makes those days, arguably the most repressive of our lifetime, so warmly remembered and treasured.

The year 1951 brought a significant change to October Hill: the power lines arrived. Until then, our source of water was a deep well, pumped by a crank and belt attached to an old-fashioned gasoline engine. I may have been an Illinois lawyer like Old Abe Lincoln, but a rail-splitter of legend I was not. Although I must say that chopping logs and kindling was my major form of exercise and source of satisfaction. One day I cranked up the motor, which spun as usual, but unfortunately the belt was loose. I unthinkingly touched the belt, thereby activating it. The belt pulled my hand over the motor wheel, which took off half of my forefinger. This was during one of those infrequent weekends when Jessica and I had the place to ourselves, free of guests. Luckily, I had an old jeep that I'd unloaded from my stepdaughter, Judy's, husband for $150, and we drove into town to have my bloodied hand attended to. Jessica always detested driving, so the brief drive to town was doubly distressful for her. In our panic, I left the severed finger behind at the house; the best the doctor could manage was to place a pressure tap on the damaged finger. Two days later, back in New York, I brought the truncated finger to our doctor, Eddie Barsky, whose bedside manners were legendary. "What have you been doing," Eddie asked, "rubbing this in cow shit?" He sent me to his brother, Arthur, a plastic surgeon of some genius. But Arthur could only remove the exposed bone, leaving me fingerless but with a good yarn to spin to friends and children who visited Kent in succeeding years.

* * *

After Henry Wallace left the Progressive party in 1950, there was little work for me to do even though I was still employed by the IPP as chief counsel. That November, Marcantonio was defeated in his race for reelection by a coalition of the Bronx Republican, Democratic, and Liberal parties. Soon afterward, Marc and I were asked by the Communist party to represent it in challenging the McCarran Act, which had been passed a few months earlier. The law, popularly known by the name of its sponsor, Senator Patrick McCarran of Nevada, was enacted—over Harry Truman's veto—as the Subversive Activities Control Act, Title 1 of the Internal Security Act. (Title 2 was the so-called concentration camp act, which authorized the attorney general to order the FBI to apprehend persons suspected of disloyalty in time of national emergency and to hold them in detainment camps which were constructed for the purpose. Title 2 was never used but remained on the statute books until its repeal in the seventies.)

Title 1 was first introduced in the Eightieth Congress in 1948 as the Mundt-Nixon bill (formulated by Rep. Karl Mundt in the House and, in the Senate, Richard Nixon). In their initial effort, the bill simply outlawed the Communist party, making membership illegal. Truman's conservative attorney general, Tom Clark, reviewing the bill, noted the obvious: Mundt-Nixon was on its face unconstitutional as a bill of attainder, a law that imposed criminal penalties on an identifiable person or organization by name. When first introduced, Mundt-Nixon inspired a broad and vociferous opposition. Virtually the entire labor movement, scores of religious denominations, women's groups, and African-American organizations all moved to prevent its passage in both the Eightieth and Eighty-first Congresses. But with the Korean War, the anticommunist fever reached proportions of hysteria. Three months after the war began, the McCarran Act was passed. In Truman's veto message—a splendid piece of work and, to my mind, the best thing he ever did—he denounced the act as a fascist enactment, "a clear and present danger" not only to Communists and their supporters but to the entire country.

I came to understand the law as nothing less than a blueprint for American fascism. I say this without hyperbole. Nixon later acknowledged that the McCarran Act would accomplish the purposes of the Mundt-Nixon Act, but by "constitutional" means. The complicated legislation began with congressional "findings of fact," a recital of what Congress found to be fact. In this case, Congress found that there was a worldwide Communist conspiratorial movement, under the control of an unnamed foreign power. The objective of this movement was the overthrow of the world's capitalist governments, using as its methods sabotage, espionage, terror, deceit, and all possible criminal means, to establish in their place what the act called "Communist totalitarian dictatorships."

The act's first section found that the world communist movement organized, in each country where it operated, "Communist action organizations" to implement its designs. Further, in the United States, the Communist movement was a clear and present danger to the national security. The act set up a Subversive Activities Control Board (SACB), consisting of five persons appointed by the president, to conduct hearings to determine whether an organization accused by the attorney general of being a Communist action organization was one in fact. Other hearings were held to determine if groups charged as "Communist front organizations" were so. Communist action organizations were defined as those having the objectives the act attributed to the world Communist movement and that were dominated by the world movement. Communist front organizations were those having the aims of, and being dominated by, Communist action organizations.

If the SACB determined that a group was a Communist action organization, it had to order the group to register as such with the attorney general. The registration requirements were extraordinary: the organization had to give the justice department a list of its entire membership; give an accounting of all of its finances, presenting sources of all of its receipts, and listing all of its expenses; give a full inventory of all of its office and printing machinery—mimeograph machines, multigraph machines, typesetting equipment (the fifties were of course prehistoric by today's electronic standards). The authors of the act obviously viewed a printing apparatus as more dangerous than firearms. Finally, the registration provisions required that the organization acknowledge that it was a Communist action organization, i.e. that it engaged in a list of criminal activities for the purpose of establishing a totalitarian dictatorship in the United States.

Once the registration order became final—after the organization exhausted its right of appeal to the courts—it was subject to a penalty of $10,000 for each day it refused to register. Thus, after one week, it would be penalized $70,000; after two weeks, $140,000, etc. Moreover, its principal officers were also required to register and were subject to sentences of five years in prison for each day they refused to register. Thus the officers faced thirty-five years' imprisonment for the first week of refusing to register, seventy for two weeks, and, well, it hardly mattered beyond that.

Should neither the organization as such, nor the officers, choose to register, any person whom the SACB found to be a member of a Communist action organization would be required to register. If the individual or individuals refused the order to register, they also faced penalties of five years' imprisonment and a $10,000 fine for each day of their refusal. Moreover, if the courts upheld an SACB order of an organization to register, and even if it did register, its members were subject to penalties. They could not apply for a passport; application for a passport incurred a penalty of five years' incarceration. Members were forbidden to apply for or hold employment in the federal government—this was not limited to intelligence agencies like the FBI but included any job, be it park ranger, mail handler, or grain inspector. Similarly, members could not apply for or hold employment in any labor organization or any enterprise designated as a "defense facility" by the secretary of defense. As wartime bombing patterns indicate, the secretary of defense has the widest latitude in designating what constitutes a defense facility.

Obviously, the only "Communist action organization" the government had in mind was the Communist party, which is all but described as such at the beginning of the act. But such a finding against the Communist party would soon be followed by similar registration orders against "Communist front organizations," those that might—as, for example, the American Labor party in New York—have an open working relationship with the Communist party. Communist front organizations were subject to substantially the same penalties as the Communist action organization.

The act listed eight criteria from which the attorney general could select "proof" that a group was a Communist action organization. Significantly, the attorney general was not required to offer proof of sabotage, violence, espionage, and the other designated means by which a Communist action organization was said to operate. The most important "proof" was the extent to which the political positions of the organization coincided with those of the unnamed foreign government that ran the international Communist conspiracy. Others included the extent to which members of the organization, by their act of membership, disavowed their allegiance to the United States and the extent to which the organization was financed from the unnamed foreign power.

By the time the Communist party asked Marcantonio and I to represent it, the attorney general—then J. Howard McGrath, successor to Tom Clark, who had been appointed by Truman to the Supreme Court—had already announced that he was about to file a petition with the SACB to begin hearings to determine if the Party was a Communist action organization. The timing was hardly propitious. The war was on. The Rosenbergs were under arrest. Truman's loyalty order had gone into effect with a vengeance, and thousands of government employees facing dismissal were being brought before "loyalty boards" to be examined. Gene Dennis and the other members of the national board of the Party had already been tried, convicted, and sentenced to five years in prison under the Smith Act for "conspiracy to teach and advocate the overthrow of the U.S. government by force and violence." Their appeal was pending before the Supreme Court.

I found that the Party leadership was debating tactics in the face of the McCarran Act. Some felt that it would be a mistake to appear before the SACB, to cross-examine witnesses, offer testimony, etc; that we should boycott the hearings; that otherwise we would create an illusion that a fair hearing was possible. But the terms of the act prohibited a fair hearing. For should the SACB hold that the Party was not a Communist action organization as defined by the act, neither could there be Communist front organizations. Thus the board, by such a finding—the only finding a truly fair hearing could produce—would not only nullify the act but put itself out of business.

My position, and Marc's, was that we should take every opportunity and use every legal tactic to expose the nature of the act. The first tactic was to prolong the proceedings in hopes that the political atmosphere in the country would change and we would eventually win.

Our view prevailed, and it was decided that we would appear before the board and fight every inch of the way. The *New York Times* (January 5, 1951) reported Marc's and my being retained by the Party in its attempt to dismiss the attorney general petition to the SACB and to quash the proceedings. In explaining our decision, we told the *Times:*

> The issue is not communism; the issue is the Constitution of the United States. The constitutionality of the McCarran Act will be adjudicated in this first test of the law. . . .
>
> The act destroys the basic freedoms of a democratic nation. By legislative fiat, it outlaws a political party and an entire system of political thought, denies freedom of association to its adherents and creates the new crime of political heresy. The act imposes this system of thought control upon the whole people, proscribing every organization and penalizing every individual for deviating from the authoritarian standards of political conformity that Congress declares to be orthodox.

I remember the evening when Johnny Gates and Betty Gannett, two members of the Party's leadership, called upon me to take the case. Gates said that the whole business would be over in six months, implying that fascism was a certainty. I assured him that it would take at least a couple of years for the case to wind its way from the SACB through to the Supreme Court. I couldn't have known or even imagined that dismantling the McCarran Act would occupy my full time and energies for the next twenty-four years.

* * *

Vito Marcantonio died in 1954, but for me—as for anyone who knew Marc or worked closely with him—he remains a vital, living presence. The son of immigrants, Marc lived his entire life in East Harlem, an almost exclusively Italian neighborhood at the time of his birth. I met him during my New Deal days when he first came to Washington as a freshman Republican member of Congress, elected to replace his mentor and benefactor, Fiorello LaGuardia, who had become mayor. A Republican like Fiorello, not as a statement of preference but as a means of bucking the Democratic machine grip on city politics, Marc was always and only his own man. "My party," he liked to say, "caucuses in a telephone booth." Reelected in 1938 as the American Labor party candidate, he became the leader of the ALP for its entire seventeen-year existence. He was willing to run as a Republican or a Democrat as well, and frequently he did. When the

GOP and Democratic bosses combined to pass the Wilson-Pakula law in the New York legislature, prohibiting a candidate from running on a party ticket without the approval of that party's leadership, Marc simply ran on the ALP line alone and continued to be elected. The two major parties then gerrymandered his district to extend it from East Harlem into Yorkville, a predominantly German, Irish, and "silk stocking" district. Marc simply opened another district office in Yorkville and worked as diligently in servicing his new constituency as his old. He was still reelected. It was not until the Korean War and the McCarthyite frenzy, with the combined opposition of the Republicans, Democrats, and Liberals, that Marc was defeated.

A politician of unparalleled courage, Marc pushed to repeal the poll tax long before anyone else in Congress and when in some states it was a invitation to be lynched. For many sessions HR 1, the first legislation introduced, was Marc's anti–poll tax bill. He was the only member of Congress who spoke against the Korean War in its first months. Despite great pressures not to do so, Marc argued brilliantly on the question. Not until six months after the war began, when I. F. Stone began to give U.S. readers a different view, did many liberals and progressives begin to question the war. Marc didn't need a "Duclos letter" to know his own mind.

Mastering the rules of the House of Representatives, Marc became a parliamentarian without peer and was recognized as such by his contemporaries, however much they might despise his politics. One day during a break in the SACB hearings, Marc and I were walking along Fourteenth Street in Washington and bumped into, of all people, Richard Nixon, then a senator. Nixon, by every account a man not given to physical expressions of affection, gave Marc a big hug, expressed his great delight upon seeing him again, and told Marc how much he was missed in the Congress. Charlie Kramer, who served as our investigator and researcher, recalled an almost identical encounter while dining with Marc in an Italian restaurant. In this instance, it was Len Hall, the Republican national chairman, who expressed how sorely Marc was missed in Washington. When Marc died couple of years later, Rep. John Rankin of Mississippi—Marc's bitterest foe in the poll-tax battles but also the Democrats' foremost parliamentarian—delivered a eulogy for the man he believed was his most worthy adversary.

The reason for his enormous popularity at home was that no member of Congress ever serviced his constituents the way Marc did. As a former tenants' organizer, he never relinquished the grass-roots techniques he had developed, and of course he never forgot the grass

roots. When he wasn't in Washington, he was in his office helping get
kids back into school, dispossessed tenants back into their apartments, dismissed employees back into jobs. Short and squat, his powerful legs served him well as he spent weekends climbing the six-
floor tenements that dominated his district, to speak directly to "his"
people. Despite the conventional wisdom, Marc was never a Communist. When Bernie Sanders of Vermont was elected as an independent
socialist to the House in November 1990, the media reported that he
was the "first socialist elected to Congress since Vito Marcantonio."
But I'm not even sure Marc considered himself a socialist; certainly
he never talked about it. He had no theoretical foundation to his politics and had little patience with the very idea. But he was unrelenting in his opposition to any form of injustice, and this led him, if not
to the Communist party, then to working closely with Communists.

The consummate politician, he was extremely flexible on tactical
matters; what works, works. But on questions of principle, he was
absolutely unshakable. After his defeat in 1950, he wanted nothing
more than to return to Congress and begin planning for a 1954 election bid. One evening in Washington, Marc and I stayed at the Congressional Hotel on Capitol Hill—you could actually see the Dome of
the Capitol from our window—as we prepared for an SACB hearing.
I was complaining about how much Washington had changed from
those early, exciting days of the New Deal to the repressive atmosphere that now dominated. Marc turned to me and said, "But there
is one place I still love." And, pointing out the window, he said, "It's
under that Dome."

For years, he had had a love-hate relationship with the Communist party. He was fiercely independent and beyond anyone's control,
much to the chagrin of some comrades. Marc felt that the Party was
less than enthusiastic about independent political action, that it was
much too friendly with the Democrats and too accepting of the "lesser-evil" thesis, and that consequently the Party's support for him was
often ambivalent. When the Communists abandoned the Progressive
party and made a turn toward "the mainstream" in the early fifties,
Marc became disenchanted. Yet he didn't hesitate for a moment in
agreeing to represent the Party in the McCarran Act case.

For someone intent on returning to Congress, particularly at that
moment in history, this was hardly the most opportune means of in-
suring himself a reserved seat under the Dome. Those were days
when lawyers with inflated liberal reputations and far less at stake
than Marc would have nothing to do with representing the Communist party or its members in Smith and McCarran Act cases and pro-

tested, some with tears in their eyes, that they couldn't afford to do so. In those days, too, Attorney General McGrath publicly urged that lawyers who undertook the defense of Communists "be taken out to the woodshed and spanked." But neither considerations of political expediency nor a vendetta over tactical differences with the Party mattered to Marc when it came to this issue. While still a member of the House, he was its most steadfast and articulate opponent of the McCarran Act, speaking time and again against it. On the floor of the Congress and off, Marc argued that the defense of the constitutional rights of the Communist party was the first line of defense of the democratic rights of the entire people. It was impossible for Marc, given his temperament and his convictions, to even pause before acceding to the Party's request that he represent it in the matter.

Marc had his abrasive side. And, being the political loner, he harbored small suspicions of nearly everyone with whom he worked, fearing they would let him down at some point. Always aggressive in protecting his own turf, constantly worrying that he might not be receiving the necessary help in his reelection campaigns, Marc was not one to hide his thoughts or emotions. But I had worked alongside him for many years in the ALP and Progressive party, and he was convinced that I had no ulterior motives, no ambitions that might conflict with his own. His wife, Miriam, told me that I was one of the few persons he trusted. Still, when the Progressive party organized a fund-raising dinner on the occasion of my fiftieth birthday, Marc, who was still quarreling with the CP over its abandoning the IPP, refused to come. What some considered a form of paranoia on his part was not without foundation. All politicians guard their flanks, and no politician's flanks were more exposed than Marc's.

He also had a strong whimsical streak and loved to get under the skins of opponents with his provocations. He enjoyed giving people "heat waves," as he called them, via the telephone. He'd call someone up in the dead of night, wake them, scream at them, and then hang up. When the Supreme Court ruled against the Party leadership in the first Smith Act case, my former friend and boss Bob Jackson wrote a malicious concurring opinion in the decision. Jackson said that obviously communism wouldn't go to prison with the Communists, whom he vilified, but that it should. Marc asked me, "John, who is there in Washington that nobody, absolutely nobody, would refuse to talk to on the telephone?" I had no idea what he had in mind, but I suggested as a possibility Arthur Krock, head of the *New York Times* Washington bureau, perhaps the most widely accepted establishment journalist in those days. Marc said, "Great. Nobody would refuse to speak with Krock." After lunch, we went into a drugstore. Marc headed for a phone booth, dropped his coin in the slot, dialed the Supreme Court, and asked for Justice Jackson. Jackson's secretary came to the phone and asked, "And whom should I say is calling?" Marc replied, "Arthur Krock." Jackson picked up the phone and said, "Why hello, Arthur. How are you?" And Marc screamed in his ear, "You lousy, double-crossing, no-good son of a bitch," and banged the phone down. For days afterward, he was a happy man. Some time before this episode, Marc told me of another "heat wave." *New World Review,* my wife's magazine, each year on November 7 held a major event—usually a banquet—on the occasion of the anniversary of the Russian Revolution. This particular year, the event was covered by Murray Kempton, who wrote in the *New York Post* that Jessica's "speech was as phoney as her gardenia." As it happened, Jessica's gardenia was fresh and I myself had bought it for her that afternoon. I mentioned this to Marc the next day as he read Kempton's column over my shoulder. Marc was incensed and phoned Kempton around 4 A.M. the next morning, called him a dirty SOB, and slammed the phone down, quite pleased with himself.

The third member of our team was equally remarkable. We needed a Washington attorney, and I'd met Joseph Forer once before. The occasion was a breakfast conference at the home of Howard Fast, the writer, at which we discussed how to handle HUAC's contempt citation against Howard. What I remember most clearly from that breakfast was Joe's absolute contempt for New York lawyers, a characteristic that was never far from hand. A native of Trenton, New Jersey, he inveighed against New Yorkers' arrogance and incompetence without hesitation. Only when he found out that I was a Chicago boy did he change his initial assumptions about me. He accepted Marc because Marc was just something special.

Joe first went to Washington to work in the Office of Price Administration during the war. At war's end, he and another government attorney, David Rhine, set up a private firm with the intention of handling commercial cases. But after Truman's loyalty order was announced, theirs was the only firm in Washington that would undertake the representation of known or avowed Communists. In short order, they were overloaded—to the exclusion of any other kind of case—with accompanying clients before loyalty boards, HUAC, the Senate Internal Security Committee, deportation panels, and court trials, in the course of which they built up a remarkable record of successful defenses.

Joe was a terrific lawyer, perhaps the only one of my colleagues whom I considered my superior. A big difference between us was that Joe actually liked the law, and I never really did. With our joint disregard for most attorneys, we developed a great mutual respect that eventually evolved into a fast and lasting friendship. Joe wasn't explosive like Marc, but he had a rough-and-tumble demeanor and would never hesitate to let his thoughts be known. We collaborated on every brief. I wrote the drafts and Joe reviewed them, probing for weaknesses and omissions. We sweated every legal paper, and often got into terrible disputes, ending up screaming at one another, as we worked out the best arguments possible. My reputation for tranquility and calm under pressure was belied by my exchanges with Joe.

One day, Joe was in my office in New York and we were in the midst of one of our bitterest quarrels when Gene Dennis arrived to discuss a case. As he approached the outer door to my office, Gene heard us yelling at each other. He couldn't understand it and was quite frightened that this fine collaboration and partnership had broken up in a fight. We both had to reassure him that our professional and personal relationship was as secure as ever. On another occasion, this time in Joe's office in Washington, we were going through a similar battle when Joe's son-in-law came to pick us up to go home for dinner. While he sat in the outer office, he listened to our shouting through the door. When five o'clock came, we decided to knock off for the day, so we quit and walked out of the office together. Joe's son-in-law asked him, "You mean he's going home to dinner with us now?" That is how we worked. It was a combative collaboration. In rereading our briefs, I'm still impressed with how splendid they were, how everything that could possibly be squeezed out of an argument was squeezed. And this was precisely because of our give-and-take quarrels.

During the first years of the SACB hearings, Marc and I were generally in the hearing room, doing the examination and cross-examination of testimony. Joe worked in his office, researching prospective witnesses and preparing draft outlines of the next day's cross-examination. When we needed briefs or other written documents, I always prepared the first draft in New York then brought it to Washington for revisions, because Joe had a secretary and I did not. For a period of time Florrie, Joe's wife, was also his secretary, but Joe's male chauvinism, rarely below the surface, eventually made her quit the job. Florrie had earlier been a school teacher, and she resumed her former profession with great relief. As Joe later recalled, we came together solely to defend the Communist party in the first action brought against it under the McCarran Act. In 1950, the Justice Department had an eighteen-month timetable, at the end of which it would round up several thousand Reds and put an end to the Party. We had no idea we were committing ourselves to a quarter century of nonstop, full-time litigation. Normally, such a job would be a plum for a lawyer. But in this case our client was in somewhat dire financial straights, while our opponent—the government of the United States—had unlimited reserves. Yet, in the next twenty-four years—in the least desirable political atmosphere—Joe and I dismantled the McCarran Act piece by piece. At least six different provisions of the act were separately argued before the Supreme Court in that time, and each was declared, in the end, unconstitutional. And not a single Communist, or member of any of the other thirteen organizations that were cited as "fronts" by the SACB, ever went to jail under the act. Because of the complexity of the law, the longevity of the case, its importance to preserving American democracy, and of course the results, I consider my participation as co-counsel with Joe the outstanding achievement of my professional life.

Florrie Forer was an amateur musician of some accomplishment. She played the viola exceptionally well and performed in a string quartet organized by Abe Fortas, my old colleague from the Agriculture Department. Abe played the violin, poorly, to hear Florrie tell it. Fortas was on the Supreme Court through the largesse of his benefactor, Lyndon Johnson, at the time one of the McCarran Act provisions was struck down. Shortly afterward, at one of the quartet's recitals, Florrie reported, Abe came up to her to say how pleased he was "for John and Joe" that we won the case. This was more a sign of the times than an expression of principle on Fortas's part. Ten years earlier, in more difficult political times, Thurmond Arnold, Fortas's law partner and my former Justice Department colleague, turned me down when I asked their firm to represent the Party on a particular McCarran Act issue before the courts.

Happily, our problems in the office never interfered with our personal relationship, and the Forer household was, quite literally, my home away from home. After Marc died in 1954, I stayed at the Forers' whenever I was in Washington, which was often. When the case began, the Forers' daughter, Jane, was nine years old. One evening I was teasing her and said, "You know, Janey, one day I'm going to come down here and call your mom and ask her if I can stay at your house for a night. And she'll tell me, 'I'm sorry, John, but Jane is visiting here with her baby and there's no room.'" I thought it a pleasant little joke at the time, but eighteen years later it actually came to pass. I called and Florrie told me there was no room became Jane was there with her daughter. That's how long the case lasted.

* * *

Our work began in the winter of 1951, when we sought to enjoin the SACB from conducting its hearings into the Communist party on the grounds that the McCarran Act was patently unconstitutional from start to finish. To nobody's surprise, the Supreme Court refused to review the case. The SACB began its hearings in April, and they continued for the next fifteen months, four days a week. Marc and I flew down to Washington every Monday morning and flew back home to New York every Thursday evening for those fifteen months.

The first day, the hearing room was a virtual armed camp, with capital police stationed around the room and at its entrances. I can't imagine what they thought we might do, if they actually believed the nonsense about Communists and "force and violence," or if they were simply staging atmospherics to obtain the desired news coverage, following the examples of, say, Senator McCarthy or of Richard Nixon in the Hiss case. In any case, the hearings were anything but dramatic and soon settled down to outright banality. We had no attention from the media; we didn't even have an audience. The five members of the board, three or four Justice Department lawyers, and Marc, Joe, and I were the entire ensemble. The lead Justice Department attorney was Irving Shapiro, one of the prosecutors in the Smith Act trial of Foster, Dennis, and the others. A few years later, he left the government to become a lawyer for DuPont Chemical, eventually working himself up the greasy pole to become chair of the DuPont board of directors. Anticommunism meant a ticket to the promised land for any number of attorneys.

The government offered twenty-two witnesses, of whom twenty were either paid FBI informers or former Communists who made a career as professional anticommunist "experts" or both. The same witnesses the government used in the Smith Act prosecution of the Party leadership—most of whom had earlier auditioned before HUAC—later came to Washington for the SACB. Just as we eventually established new standards for longevity and the number of successful appearances over one law before the Supreme Court, so we set a new record for the aggregation of paid stool pigeons concentrated in a single government effort.

The Justice Department led off with Benjamin Gitlow, whom the Party expelled in 1929, twenty-two years earlier. Gitlow's testimony dealt with the relations of the Party to the Communist International (CI); i.e., in the Party's infancy in the twenties, the CI gave direction to the CP, if it didn't control the Party outright. Gitlow produced from his files some telegrams between the Party and Moscow up to his ouster from the Party, implying that the expulsion came at the insistence of Stalin himself. Now, the fact is that for a period of time in the twenties you practically had to ask permission of the CI to go to the toilet. But there is no evidence that Stalin even knew about Gitlow's existence, let alone cared so deeply about the man as to tell the CPUSA to give him the boot.

As it happens, Bill Foster, who was severed from the other Communist leaders in the Smith Act sentencing because of his severe heart condition, was completing his history of the Party at this time. Bill, who had no formal education, was a prolific writer if not a prosaic one, going about his research and writing with the same immense energy and organization that he brought to all efforts in which he was engaged. In the light of the SACB hearings, Gene Dennis asked me to look over Foster's manuscript, in particular the chapters devoted to the Party's early years. They actually confirmed much of what Gitlow was saying, insofar as the CPUSA's subservience was concerned. Foster, in poor health for many years, was then bedridden in his Bronx apartment. But Gene dispatched me to try to convince him to revise his manuscript. Bill was as stubborn an old fighter as he had been a young one; he insisted that, if anything, we should defend the role of the CI before the SACB. As an attorney, I thought this was absolutely the wrong approach, that we should argue that the CI was abolished in 1943 and was "ancient history," that whatever relationship the Party had with it a quarter century before was irrelevant. I sat at the side of Bill's bed, spending several hours explaining how difficult a position we would be in if William Z. Foster's book confirmed the testimony of the renegade Benjamin Gitlow. Bill was still a very tough guy and it was difficult to persuade him otherwise when he thought he was right, as he very often was. But at the end, he agreed to make some alterations.

In the months before the hearings opened, I did a good deal of homework, reading virtually everything that had been written by those whom we expected to be witnesses. I read Gitlow's *I Confess*, of course, and all of the books by Louis Budenz, a former *Daily Worker* editor and longtime FBI informer. I examined all of their previous testimony in earlier cases and before congressional committees. I perused records of deportation hearings in which these informers testified against Party members who were noncitizens and who, un-

der the McCarran Act, were liable to deportation because of their affiliation. We were well stocked with materials for cross-examination
of government witnesses and succeeded in showing that most of
them were abysmal liars, not that this made much of an impression
on the SACB.

One of the McCarran Act's points—then being investigated by the
board—was the extent to which the views and policies of the Party
were in compliance with those of the USSR. Philip Mosely, a Columbia University professor, was on the stand for a month, citing examples from Soviet publications addressing one or another issue, then
offering into evidence articles from CPUSA publications like the *Daily Worker*, showing the coincidence of positions. Mosely went into a
host of issues—attitudes toward Czechoslovakia, the League of Nations, whatever.

During the weeks Mosely was on the stand, Marc temporarily
withdrew from the hearings to defend William L. Patterson, the leader of the Civil Rights Congress who had organized the historic petition to the United Nations, *We Charge Genocide,* documenting the
pattern of lynchings and racist violence against African-Americans.
"Pat" had been indicted for contempt of Congress for refusing to cooperate with HUAC. (During the HUAC hearings, Rep. Latham, who
later brought the charges against him, ranted at Pat, calling him a
"black son of a bitch." Any contempt Pat might have exhibited was
not only justified but reasonable.) Marc's considerable skills as a trial lawyer were again demonstrated in his winning Pat an acquittal of
the contempt charge.

For the duration of Mosely's testimony, I faced him on my own. After his initial testimony, I spent several weeks offering counterevi-
dence. We sought to prove that many of the views in question were
widely held by noncommunists and anticommunists. For example,
one of Mosely's examples of "nondeviation" was the view that the
Chiang Kai-shek regime, before it was expelled from China, was corrupt and fascistic. We offered in evidence a State Department "white
paper," in which former Secretary of State Dean Acheson expressed
precisely the same opinion. The SACB rejected our evidence as "entirely immaterial." We also attempted to demonstrate that the forty-
five "nondeviationist" views presented by Professor Mosely were examples not of evil and sedition, but of acting in the interest of the
peace and well-being of the American people, that in fact, some had
been adopted by the U.S. government itself. Mosely, for instance, testified that in 1951, both Soviet Ambassador Malik and the CPUSA separately urged a conference to negotiate a cease-fire in Korea. In my

cross-examination, I asked Mosely whether the U.S. government had not adopted the Soviet view and, in fact, acted upon the Malik proposal. The Justice Department raised its usual objections to this question, and the board made its invariable ruling. Thus the act and the SACB evolved a new concept of heresy. Galileo was tried because it was charged that his view that the earth moved was false and wicked. In our case, an organization was condemned for views that concededly might have been true and good.

Under this test, the penalty of outlawry could be avoided only by adopting views that were demonstrably false, in the event that the USSR had adopted views that were demonstrably true, or, on controversial questions, by submitting to "domination and control" in reverse and rejecting any view, regardless of its merits, that happened to coincide with that of the Soviet Union. I showed several instances in which articles by the CPUSA introduced by Mosely on, say, support of opening up a second front during the war actually appeared before the articles Mosely offered from the Soviet side. We asked how that could be considered nondeviation from the Soviet viewpoint? If the Soviets didn't deviate from the American Party's views, that was another matter, but it was hardly proof of USSR control that the CPUSA articulated a point of view before the Soviet party did. Again, the SACB was unimpressed with our arguments. So we introduced, issue by issue, evidence that demonstrated an identical position by noncommunists. The president of the United States, Franklin Roosevelt, supported opening a second front and in fact did so. Did this indicate Soviet control of FDR? If the Soviets were anti-Nazi, was it incumbent on U.S. Communists to be pro-Nazi to differentiate themselves from their Soviet brethren? We knew of course that these were not hearings of a curious, impartial board, that no matter the undeniable logic of our arguments or the incontrovertible evidence we offered, the SACB was simply going through the motions before it ruled against us. For our part, we were building a record, knowing that we would be appealing the board's rulings through the courts.

After the government completed its case, it was our turn. One of our key witnesses was Johnny Gates, a veteran of the Abraham Lincoln Battalion in the Spanish civil war and of the European theater during World War II and former editor of the *Daily Worker.* After the first Smith Act trial, Gates was sentenced to five years in the Atlanta Federal Penitentiary. We informed the government that we wanted him as a witness. To help prepare his testimony, on our request, the government transferred Johnny to Danbury, Connecticut, driving distance for Marc and me. For Gates, this was a bit of a vacation from

the harsher conditions in Atlanta; and Jack Stachel and Irving Potash, two of his co-defendants, were in Danbury, so it was a chance to
catch up.

After a few weeks in Danbury, he was transferred to a District of
Columbia federal jail for the week of his SACB testimony. Each day,
we brought him lunch, the best food he would eat during his years of
incarceration. These were trying circumstances: each morning, he'd
be brought by marshals from his jail cell to the hearing, and in the
evening the marshals returned him to the cell. The SACB tried futile-
ly to order Gates to identify other Party members. The first time one
of the prosecutors asked him such a question, "Mr. Gates, who is so-
and-so? Is he a member of the Communist Party?" Johnny responded, "Don't ask me. Ask J. Edgar Hoover; he's the keeper of the rats."
This was the tone and character of John Gates under cross-examination. He wasn't exactly subtle, perhaps, but he was effective.

In *Story of an American Communist,* his book about his life in the
Party and his reasons for leaving it, Gates recalled his SACB appearance. He writes that the lack of disagreement with the Soviet party
did not mean that the CPUSA took orders, only that there was a
"shared belief in Marxism-Leninism as a universal science," that the
two parties arrived at the same conclusions. "We may have been
wrong," he says, "but we were not criminal." He also recollects that
one of the charges against the U.S. party was that its members took
an oath to defend the USSR. Gates testified that the only oath he had
taken in his years in the Party was in 1941, when, upon enlisting in
the army a week after the attack on Pearl Harbor, he led a large New
York membership meeting in the Pledge of Allegiance to the U.S. flag.
He told the board that he learned the oath in the New York public
schools, but its meaning was reinforced for him as an adult. "We
were not yet 'one nation, indivisible, with liberty and justice for all,'"
he informed the panel. Rather, we were a nation divided into "rich
and poor, Negro and white," and "there was a different justice for
capital and labor, for Communists and non-Communists." Later, a
congressional committee discussed Gates's testimony and concluded
that "something had to be done about the way Communists were taking advantage of the Pledge of Allegiance." The ultimate result of
Johnny's testimony was that Congress eventually added the phrase,
"under God," to the Pledge, figuring to make it impossible for "atheistic" Communists to invoke it.

* * *

At the end of the hearings, to no one's surprise, the SACB ordered the Party to register as a Communist action organization. The

board issued a lengthy report, reviewing the evidence that it claimed established that the Party fit the McCarran Act's definition of such an organization. Shortly after we filed the appeal, we received a break. We knew that most of the government's witnesses made their living moving from deportation hearing to HUAC appearance to Smith Act trial, picking up their paychecks and per diem from whichever government agency was employing their services at the moment. It came to our attention that three of these men—Manning Johnson and Paul Crouch, both early members of the Party, and Harvey Matusow, who joined for a brief period after the war—admitted to lying at various times, thereby discrediting the entirety of their testimony. The Justice Department, embarrassed by the admissions, released them from service in their troupe of witnesses-for-hire. But the severance notices weren't delivered until after their SACB appearances. In his book *False Witness*, Matusow called his testimony before the board a "step up the witness ladder," an excellent career move, so to speak. "This was my first experience under cross-examination," Matusow remembered, "and I loved it. I treated it like a game of chess. I respected both Marcantonio and Abt as lawyers. This was big-league stuff, I thought. And I didn't intend to strike out." He reminisced about his testimony regarding Alexander Trachtenberg, chair of International Publishers, the Party's publishing house, telling the SACB that in many cases "plates for printing books were received without cost, and that International Publishers was under the direction of Moscow." Commenting on this earlier testimony, Matusow wrote, "This was a lie on my part. I pieced together unrelated miscellaneous facts and, with the help of the attorney for the Justice Department in preparing my testimony, I made something sinister out of much that was innocent. I finished with the feeling I had done a good job."

We didn't need to wait for Matusow's book to appear, or even for the witnesses' acknowledgment of falsehoods, to know that they were lying on the stand. They had been lying for years. Hell, the entire cold war was premised on a Big Lie and the cold war institutions at home—the FBI, HUAC, the Smith Act, McCarran Act, loyalty oaths, etc.—had as a central purpose the fostering of lies and betrayals as acts of supreme patriotism. But with proof of perjury by Matusow, Crouch, and Johnson, we filed an affidavit with the Court of Appeals asking it to return the case to the SACB. The Justice Department responded that it did not deny the perjury of these witnesses, but argued that the point was irrelevant, that even if the SACB struck the testimony of Matusow, Crouch, and Johnson, it would have come to the same finding. As expected, the appellate court denied our motion.

All of this activity preceded our main argument before the courts.

We submitted that brief in January 1954. Turning the law on its head, the conclusion of our brief stated, "The Act, on its Face and as Applied, Is a Clear and Present Danger to the National Security." It read, in part:

> The Act advances a now-familiar justification for its suppression of democratic liberties. The legislation is necessary, according to section 2, to preserve the national security from the "clear and present danger" of Communism. This justification is false. It is a supreme illustration of Mr. Justice Jackson's aphorism: "Security is like liberty, in that many are the crimes committed in its name." . . .
>
> The Act does not promote, it undermines, the national security. For it annuls the fundamental liberties which are the basis of our security and the very things to be secured.

The brief was submitted in each of our names—Marcantonio, Abt, and Forer. It was to be Marc's final brief. In June 1954, as the court continued to deliberate, Marc was stricken by a heart attack as he was coming out of a subway and he died on the street. In the years since his death, it is still difficult to accept that nearly two generations of young people have grown to maturity without knowing the name of this man of legendary proportions. In another country, or at another time in our own, there would be streets named for him and movies made about his life. On the day he died, as a matter of fact, more than ten thousand persons spontaneously thronged the streets in front of his office to pay their respect, and is there another member of Congress in memory of whom there has been such an expression of love? (In 1970 the New York Board of Education named a new school in East Harlem after Marcantonio. Rep. Charles Rangel, former city council president Paul O'Dwyer, and others spoke at the dedication ceremony. I was the final speaker and I was disheartened that none of the others talked about who Marc really was, about the struggles he led, about the significance of the man for that community. The younger members of the audience, most of whom had never heard of Marc before, were hardly encouraged to learn more about him.)

The appellate court finally sustained, by a two-to-one vote, the SACB order to the Party to register. Judge David Bazelon, one of the most acute legal minds in the country, cast the dissenting vote, arguing that the Fifth Amendment protection against self-incrimination was in jeopardy. His position—which became an increasingly important issue as the case progressed through the courts—was that to require the Party to sign the registration statement that it had been ordered to file meant that the Party could comply only by having one of its officers sign. (An organization obviously cannot sign as such.) But to compel an officer of the Party to sign was to have that person identify himself or herself as a member and an officer of the Party, thereby being subject to the penalties Party membership carried under the act.

It was at this point that I called on Thurmond Arnold, with whom I'd had no contact since our days in the Justice Department, to ask him to represent the Party's appeal before the Supreme Court. Though our conversation was warm and friendly, Thurmond begged off with the familiar dodge of "having to consult his partners," Abe Fortas and Paul Porter. Two days later, he called with regrets that his partners decided against taking the case. We looked into other prominent constitutional experts to handle the Supreme Court representation, but could find none who would place devotion to the Constitution and defense of the rights of the country's least favored political organization over their devotion to a place in the established order and the lucrative fees that followed.

So Joe Forer and I were on our own. We submitted a 225-page brief to the Supreme Court, in which we argued all of the constitutional areas the McCarran Act violated—the First Amendment, Fifth Amendment, its denial of due process, its substance as a bill of attainder. In addition we argued the bias of the SACB, both in fact and in essence—the board could not rule against us without putting itself out of business. We also argued that the evidence did not support the finding of the board that the CPUSA's goal was the overthrow of capitalist governments by force, violence, espionage, terror, sabotage, etc. On the matter of Soviet control, the two judges in the appellate court majority could only say that the Party had an "ideological attachment" to the cause of communism. Well, obviously ideological attachment is not the same as control from abroad. One can modify an ideological attachment or abandon it or, for that matter, cling to it more fiercely than is healthy but, without control, there would be nothing the USSR could do about it.

We argued that the real purpose and intent of the act was to outlaw the Communist party by giving it the Hobson's choice of suicidal acts. The Party could register as ordered by the SACB and thereby acknowledge guilt as an organization engaged in a criminal conspiracy, directed from abroad. Or it could refuse to register, thereby subjecting itself, its officers, and members to the astronomical criminal and civil penalties the act imposed.

Of our 225 pages, we devoted 4 to the motion we had made for leave to adduce evidence that three of the government witnesses—Matusow, Crouch, and Johnson—had perjured themselves. When the Court finally handed down its decision, it disregarded all 225 pages of our brief except these 4, on which it based its decision exclusively. The Court's majority opinion, written by Felix Frankfurter, said it was limiting itself to this secondary question because it couldn't decide the difficult and complex constitutional questions with which the case bristled, on the basis of a record in which there was an unresolved question of perjury. First, the perjury matter would have to be resolved and the record purified in that respect, the Court held, before it could decide the other questions. In a dissent, Justice Tom Clark, one of the Court's most reactionary judges, made fun of the other justices. He pointed out that the majority was deciding this case on a matter that even the Party thought so unimportant that it would devote only 4 of its 225 pages of arguments.

Clark of course had a point. We understood that Frankfurter did not write the kind of opinion he did because he objected to deciding a case on a record that was sullied with unanswered charges of perjury. Popular mythology to the contrary notwithstanding, the judiciary is as political as the other two branches of the government, and the Supreme Court is the most political of all. It is subject to the pressures of the moment and will change as the pressures change. If the Court was not political, there would be no political debates over Court appointees. Frankfurter, as keen but also as politically shrewd a justice as we've had in this century, was responding to the existing political situation. By the time the opinion was handed down—April 30, 1956—McCarthyism was on the defensive. McCarthyite candidates took a beating in the 1954 elections. And after the army hearings, McCarthy himself quickly passed from the political scene. So, on the one hand, the country was retreating from the worst stages of the repression; on the other, we hadn't yet arrived at a point where the Supreme Court was prepared to repudiate the McCarran Act. In picking the question of possibly perjured testimony upon which to decide the case, the Court was simply sidestepping the question.

Soon thereafter, the Court handed down what is known as the *Jencks* decision, marking a long overdue and critical reform in criminal justice. At issue was the right of the defense in a criminal case to have access—to "make discovery"—to prior statements of prosecution witnesses. Before they ever take the stand in court, these witnesses have made statements to the police or FBI or prosecuting attorneys.

Defense lawyers need access to those statements to be able to show that a witness is lying, that prior statements don't correspond to those made in trial. Before *Jencks,* a kind of judicial catch-22 was operative. The courts had held that if you could show a witness's trial testimony didn't correspond to prior statements, you could have access to those statements for purposes of cross-examination. But of course you couldn't show this if you didn't first have the prior statements.

Clinton Jencks, an official of the Mine, Mill, and Smelter Workers' Union in New Mexico, was indicted under Taft-Hartley for allegedly filing a false affidavit that he was not a Communist party member. As in all such cases, the government presented an assortment of professional informers, most if not all of whom had made statements to the FBI before testifying in the case. Jencks's attorneys had asked for access to these statements, which the lower courts denied. The Supreme Court finally ruled that a defendant in a criminal trial must be given access to the written statements of prosecution witnesses to be able to test their credibility.

Prior to the *Jencks* decision, we made motions before the SACB to gain access to the reports and statements of government witnesses. We vigorously pursued these motions, particularly with regard to Louis Budenz. After he left the Party, Budenz had spent a good deal of time in the FBI's company telling his tales of life as a Communist. On the basis of *Jencks,* we were clearly entitled to those statements, but, predictably, the board denied us access to them. We returned to the Court of Appeals, which held that indeed we were entitled to access. The case again came back to the board and we received Budenz's statements, which showed the chief government witness to be a brazen liar.

We asked to recall Budenz to the witness stand to cross-examine him on the conflicts between his testimony and his earlier statements to the FBI. Budenz produced a statement from a doctor to the effect that he had suffered a heart attack and that undergoing cross-examination would endanger his life. We moved to have Budenz's testimony stricken from the record if he was too ill to be cross-examined. The board had no choice but to grant our motion. It struck Budenz's testimony, but asserted that the really important testimony was not that of the witnesses, but was contained in the works of Marx, Engels, Lenin, and Stalin. The SACB again reissued its report, although without the testimony of government informers. Again, the case went to the Court of Appeals, and again that court reaffirmed its prior ruling upholding the SACB registration order. This was in early 1959,

and we immediately asked the Supreme Court to review the Court of
Appeals decision.

* * *

In the nearly quarter century that the McCarran Act litigation
absorbed, I never received a single other case from comrades—not a
divorce, not a will, nothing. Presumably they feared that being represented by the lawyer for the Communist party wasn't in their best
interests. One friend, however, who did supply me with occasional
work was Hal Cammer, Nat Witt's partner, who represented me in my
appearances before HUAC. Even after their expulsion from the CIO,
Hal and Nat continued to represent the Furriers' Union and the Mine,
Mill, and Smelter Workers. They in turn hired me as an off-the-books
counsel, much like the blacklisted Hollywood screenwriters who
were hired to write movies for "fronts" whose names appeared with
the credits. I helped strategize in these cases and wrote briefs but of
course never appeared in court or in print.

As the Party's attorney at the time, I found myself in conflict with
my own feelings as a Party member. This was the period of the Party's "return to the mainstream," in which it abandoned the Progressive party and independent politics in general to immerse itself in the
Democratic party. The leadership was in prison, on trial, or underground, and the entire organization thrown on the defensive. Many
of the so-called "front" organizations—Party-initiated efforts in the
peace, youth, veterans', women's, and other social movements—were
dissolved. When the CIO and AFL began the process of merger, the
Party hailed it as virtually a revolutionary act, "uniting" the working
class. Independent Left-led unions, expelled from the CIO a few
years earlier, were encouraged by the Party to merge with Center-
led or even Right-led unions. The furriers eventually joined the meatpackers—today, after other mergers, they are part of the United Food
and Commercial Workers—and the Mine, Mill, and Smelter Workers
became much the junior partner of the United Steelworkers'. Party
pressure on Communists in the United Electrical workers to join the
International Union of Electrical workers resulted in the alienation
of those comrades from the Party. I was opposed to this entire direction but was clearly in no position to influence the Party's course. To
this day, the Party has never reexamined this experience, but then it
hasn't truly reexamined any of its history.

I continued to represent Communists qua Communists, however,
in other cases. In 1953 I handled the hearings on the Feinberg law
before the New York Board of Regents. One of the myriad repressive

acts of the period, the Feinberg law provided for such hearings to determine whether the Party advocated the violent overthrow of the government. It wasn't enough that virtually every agency of the federal government was doing the same; the New York school authorities wanted a piece of the action. If the hearings determined that the Party was violently and seditiously inclined, any member who was teaching in the New York public schools could be discharged. Thus, the hearings were the test of whether Communists could continue teaching in the public schools. In fact, the board of education had been firing one Communist after another, without reference to this provision of the law.

For nearly three weeks, a board of regents subcommittee conducted the hearings, giving many of the tried and true government informers yet another opportunity to perform for pay. The lawyer for the regents was Bruce Bromley, a senior member of Cravath, Swain, and Wood, one of Wall Street's most prominent firms. Governor Thomas Dewey had appointed Bromley to the New York Court of Appeals, the highest court in the state, and also appointed him to try the Feinberg law case. Bromley and I were actually old friends from when he had been the attorney for General Motors in the hearings I conducted for the LaFollette Committee. Contrary to that experience, in the present case, the Board of Regents held in his favor, not mine, and found that the Communist party advocated the violent overthrow of the government.

We were in no position to appeal. We didn't want yet another court decision that would inevitably condemn the Party as a subversive organization. And virtually all Party members who were teachers had already been fired, so an appeal would not have prevented further damage. I hated to forgo the appeal—the law was so vile and it was against my nature to do so—and it became the only case I handled throughout the cold war decades that we didn't take all the way to the Supreme Court. (Late in the seventies, the teachers who were fired and denied their pensions were finally reinstated—some posthumously—with back pay, after the Supreme Court reversed its decision of nearly thirty years earlier and ruled that the Feinberg law was unconstitutional.)

While I had been a backstage advisor and consultant to the Party during the three Smith Act trials of the national leadership in New York, it wasn't until 1955 that I conducted a Smith Act defense myself. The prior Smith Act prosecutions were conspiracy cases, i.e., the defendants were charged with conspiring to teach and advocate the violent overthrow of the government by force and violence. But the

Smith Act had another provision, making it a crime to belong to any organization that advocated the violent overthrow of the government. The first person indicted under this provision was Claude Lightfoot, a Party leader and African-American community activist in Illinois, who asked me to defend him. Shortly after Claude was indicted, the government brought the same charge against Junius Scales, a young white Party leader in North Carolina, whom I liked. When he was first indicted, Junius's wife called me for advice and I suggested that she ask Joe Forer's partner, David Rhine, to represent Junius.

Claude was indicted in Chicago, so the trial became something of a homecoming to me. When I arrived in Chicago, I first called my father's twin brother, Isaac, my "Uncle Doc." He remained the only member of my father's side of the family to maintain cordial relations with me. The others were repulsed beyond repair when I left Chicago to work with FDR's New Deal, but the Communist party was outside the pale. I exchanged greetings with Uncle Doc and told him why I was in town, explaining what the Lightfoot trial was about. He expressed his warm regards and love for me, but pleaded, "John, for God's sake, please keep your name out of the newspapers!" Of course, when the trial began a couple of days later, my name was all over the front pages.

Claude asked to be represented by a Black co-counsel, and I requested George Crockett to join me in trying the case. George was a junior associate of Maurice Sugar, the United Automobile Workers' attorney throughout its formative years (including during the Flint sit-downs and the LaFollette Committee investigations), but who had been fired by Walter Reuther in the latter's purge of the Left from the union. George received his early criminal trial experience in the first Smith Act trial in New York's Foley Square where he represented his fellow Detroiter, Carl Winter. In Chicago, George and I lived and ate together in the same hotel room during the weeks of the trial. I became extremely fond of this gentle man, one of the easiest people with whom I've ever worked. A dozen years later, George would preside over the entire Detroit court system and later was elected to Congress, where he served with distinction and great courage for five terms.

As it turned out, my first job in Chicago was not in defending Claude Lightfoot but defending George Crockett. At the outset of the trial, the U.S. attorney asked the judge to exclude George from the case because he had served six months in jail for contempt of court as a result of his representation in the New York Smith Act trial. In that case, Judge Harold Medina sentenced the entire team of defense attorneys for contempt. But in the Lightfoot trial, the judge denied the prosecutor's motion and George continued to work with me on every aspect of the case from designing a strategy to examining witnesses. James Parsons, the young assistant U.S. attorney who had moved to exclude George, was also Black and would win his spurs in this case and soon after be appointed federal district court judge. This was something of a common experience for Smith Act prosecutors.

Presiding over the trial was Philip Sullivan, who had been a state court judge before whom I'd frequently appeared in mortgage foreclosure cases in my early days as a corporate lawyer. I'm not sure Judge Sullivan remembered me, but he knew I was from Chicago, was acquainted with the Abt family, and we developed a warm relationship. He was a good judge—he had been so when I practiced before him a quarter century earlier—and a delightful man.

This was a vintage Smith Act case, with all the familiar witnesses and the familiar result. In my closing argument, I stated what I believed to be the importance of the case—"whether the American principles of liberty under law and equal justice for all will be preserved and strengthened, or whether we will take a step backward in the direction of some kind of a police state where all of us will live in fear." I repeated George Crockett's remark of a day earlier that "the immediate question that you are here to try is the state of mind of Mr. Lightfoot, his belief, his knowledge and his intent," and then I said, "the trial of a man's state of mind, ladies and gentlemen, is a most unusual trial to take place here in this land of ours."

I argued that the prosecution relied on a theory of guilt by inference and innuendo; that Parsons, the U.S. attorney, had said that "Marxism-Leninism is the nail on which this picture hangs" and that "Marxism-Leninism is a magic word" and by this statement was "attempting to turn back the clock of history by 300 years" to the trials of heretics and witches. I cited the prosecution's evidence on the meaning of Marxism-Leninism, a definition on which there was no evidence that Claude Lightfoot agreed. The government's eight witnesses, I argued,

> must have attended thousands of Communist Party meetings, conventions, open classes, closed classes, open meetings and socalled secret meetings; yet not a single prosecution witness testified that any American Communist, be he a member or a leader, at any time said or wrote anything advocating the overthrow of the government by force and violence.
>
> Now is it conceivable . . . that if an American Communist real-

ly believed that Marxism-Leninism equals force and violence, some of them, or at least one of them in that 20-year period, in a private meeting, wouldn't have let his hair down and said so, and said, "Boys, what we really mean is 'force and violence.'" Is it conceivable that that wouldn't have happened over that 20-year period? It didn't happen, ladies and gentlemen, from the prosecution's own evidence, and it didn't happen because Mr. Parsons' magic-word theory is a figment of Mr. Parson's imagination.

None of the government witnesses could conjure up even an inference to violent intent; nor could they, in interpreting Marxist writings, ascribe violence or sedition to the theories on which the CPUSA wished to base itself. I pointed out the irony of Claude Lightfoot being tried in a courtroom dedicated to the memory of Abraham Lincoln who, in his first inaugural address, had said: "This country, with its institutions, belongs to the people who inhabit it. Whenever they shall grow weary of the existing government, they can exercise their constitutional rights of amending it, or their revolutionary rights to dismember or overthrow it."

Finally, I called the jury's attention to the fact that while they numbered only twelve persons, when they began to deliberate upon their verdict, they would be accompanied by "a 13th juror":

> You won't be able to leave him behind, you won't be able to shut him out of the jury room, and the name of the 13th juror is "Anti-Communist Prejudice" and the 13th juror will make a number of powerful arguments . . . [such as] "Well, I don't care what the evidence in this case is, Claude Lightfoot is a Red and everybody knows that Reds are dangerous, and he ought to be locked up, evidence or not." And . . . "If you vote for an acquittal, you will be accused of coddling Communists, and that is a dangerous charge in this country today." Those are the kinds of arguments that the 13th juror will make. And it is because of the pressure of the 13th juror in the jury room that this case is so important, not only to my client . . . but to all of us.

When it came time to appeal, I again tried—as with Thurmond Arnold in the McCarran Act case—to obtain a prominent, noncommunist attorney to take the case to the U.S. Court of Appeals. This time I visited Laird Bell, a senior partner in one of Chicago's oldest and most prestigious law firms, chair of the board of trustees at my alma mater, the University of Chicago, and a great liberal, at least by reputation. I pleaded with Laird to take the case to the appellate court, which sits in Chicago, and told him why I thought it was so important. At the end of my urging his intervention, he put his elbows on his desk, head in his hands, then looked up, and, with tears in his eyes, explained why he couldn't take the case. Another profile in courage, another exegesis of the facts of "real" life in the United States in the fifties.

So it fell to me to argue the Lightfoot appeal. The Court of Appeals ruled against us, and we immediately petitioned the Supreme Court for a reversal. The Court set as the hearing date the same day it would hear arguments in the Junius Scales appeal. (Scales had been tried and convicted in North Carolina.) David Rhine, Scales's attorney, would join me for arguments before the Court. By the time the two cases reached the Supreme Court, it had already handed down its decision in *Jencks.* Even before the *Jencks* ruling, Rhine and I had separately made all the appropriate motions for the production of prior statements by the government witnesses against Scales and Lightfoot. This was fortunate, because the Supreme Court reversed both the Lightfoot and Scales convictions on the basis of the government's failure to comply with *Jencks.* In 1957, just before the government moved to retry Claude Lightfoot, the Supreme Court decided the *Yates* case. Oleta O'Connor Yates was one of the group of Party leaders in California who were tried and convicted under the Smith Act. Like all of the others, except Lightfoot and Scales, the California comrades were convicted under the conspiracy provision of the Smith Act. This was the first Smith Act case in which the high court had agreed to review the evidence. In the Dennis case, which involved the twelve members of the national board, the Court limited its review to constitutional questions and had refused to even consider whether the evidence was sufficient to support the convictions. In two subsequent cases—those of the "second-string" New York Smith Act defendants and the Baltimore defendants—the Court simply denied review altogether.

In the California case, the Court held that the evidence was insufficient to support the convictions. It didn't distinguish *Yates* from its earlier decisions, nor did it address the question of constitutionality of the Smith Act. But it held that where the Smith Act talks about advocacy of the violent overthrow of the government, Congress meant by "advocacy" not simply theoretical, abstract, or philosophical doctrine, but actually incitement to action, to real acts of violence. And the Court found that there was no evidence of such advocacy in the *Yates* case. Accordingly, a number of Smith Act cases were sent back to the lower courts for new trials; and some other defendants were acquitted outright.

Shortly after the Court ruled in *Yates,* the government moved to bring Lightfoot back to trial, a motion I opposed, of course. When we appeared before Judge Sullivan, the first thing the judge said to me was, "Tell me, Mr. Abt, why shouldn't I retry this case?" I found the judge's question encouraging, implying doubt on his part. I proceeded at length to explain why I thought he should deny the prosecution's motion, relying heavily on the *Yates* case. I argued that the evidence in the Lightfoot case was essentially the same as in the California case, indeed it was even weaker in Lightfoot. I hadn't even completed my presentation before Parsons, who had become the U.S. attorney in Chicago, agreed to withdraw his motion for a new trial. This ended the Lightfoot case, to both Claude's relief and my own. I believe the government decided to drop the matter, persuaded not so much by the eloquence of my argument as by Judge Sullivan's obvious lack of enthusiasm to pursue it. And the Justice Department thought it had a stronger case against Junius Scales, whom it decided to bring to a second trial, and figured there was no point in retrying both men.

* * *

Besieged by every form of government attack from the IRS to local school boards, from congressional inquisition to federal prosecutions, the Party was in great difficulty. Its leaders, from the National Board to local organizers, were in prison, on trial, or underground. In less than a decade, it went from being a major force in the trade unions and all of the important movements for social justice to a pariah status in the political life of the country. The Party's change of fortunes and circumstances was accompanied by shifts of policy—over questions as significant as creating an underground Party while those who remained "above ground" submerged themselves in "mainstream" organizations—that were not always easily grasped by its members and supporters. Given these circumstances, it was natural that the Party was also beset by internal disputes. The differences came to a head as a result of two crises over which we had no control, in which we were not even involved, and which occurred far from our shores.

In 1955, Nikita Khrushchev's report to the Twentieth Congress of the Communist party of the Soviet Union, detailing the crimes of the Stalin era, was made public. None of us could have imagined the extent of criminalization, and many of us continued to maintain a stance of disbelief and denial. The *Daily Worker* published the Khrushchev report as a special supplement, the only Communist party paper in the world to do so. This came largely as an individual initiative of the paper's editor, John Gates, who was looking to radically change the Party into an undefined formation of a social democratic character. A year later, Soviet tanks moved into Hungary to suppress what we believed was a counterrevolution in another socialist country. At that point Gates editorialized against the invasion, calling it antisocialist and antidemocratic, although again this was his personal position and not the Party's. Unfortunately, the paper did not provide a factual report on the Hungarian events or their background—for example, the role of that country as an ally of Hitler, under the fascist government of Horthy; the repressive, paranoid character of the Communist leadership of Rakosci, who had recently died; the different tendencies among Hungarian Communists; the uprising, which included democratic elements but also fascist ones, who had no compunction about, say, hanging Communist workers in the streets or turning broadcast facilities over to the primitivist Cardinal Mindzenty to call for the "return" of rural Hungary to the large land owners. In any case, the complexity of the issue, on top of the myriad problems confronting the Party, caused a serious division. The differences threatened to split the Party and, to avoid this, the national board issued a statement in which it said it could "neither condemn nor approve of the invasion" of Hungary.

A factional situation developed—in Party jargon, "factions" are groups within the Party to which its participants give their primary loyalty above that to the Party as a whole. Some, like Gates, wanted to dissolve the Party altogether. Another group played the role of "keepers of the flame" in which no mistake or crime was beyond justification. The Italian Communist leader Antonio Gramsci once wrote that the task of the Jesuits was to update dogma in such a way that only the initiated were cognizant of the changes while the faithful remained blissfully undisturbed. The Party has always had its share of such "Jesuits." Demoralization set in among the ranks of the organization, and significant numbers of members left in dismay or disagreement. In some cases, comrades left as "the better part of wisdom," seeking to preserve their livelihoods and careers.

Jessica and I found ourselves in a difficult position, although perhaps no more difficult than those of thousands of others. Jessica's whole life was changed by her experience in the newborn USSR in the twenties. She was an eyewitness to and participant in the infant socialist project, watching and working alongside a huge country of illiterate peasants transforming itself, under conditions whose adversity was without precedent in human history, into a major industrial giant. This experience validated her belief in the USSR to the last of her days. Even when she might have entertained doubts, she kept them within herself, determined not to give an inch. As the editor of a magazine devoted to promoting Soviet friendship to the American people, these were difficult days and presented very tough problems. Undoubtedly, Jessica went overboard in defending the Soviet Union but, in the cold war atmosphere where the use of nuclear weapons was openly contemplated, it was hard to make any concessions, no matter how warranted.

My own belief in all things Soviet did not come from such direct experience, but was more philosophical and intellectual, based in no small part on Jessica's influence, on Party doctrine, on the Soviet friends I'd acquired through Jessica, and on my admiration of the USSR for having borne the brunt of humanity's sacrifice to defeat fascism. As for Hungary, Pete and Anne Peters, among our closest friends in the world, were living there, and we took their view of events in that country. When the fight broke out within the Party, we opposed those who wanted to move the organization to a position more independent of the Soviets. But again, this was for me an intellectual position. I never belonged to a Party club and had no forum in which to participate in Party squabbles. My predicament, if one can call it that, was compounded by the fact that the leadership looked on me as something of a "technician," of great use and need to the Party but not as an equal in political terms. The organization, from its inception, being self-defined as a "party of the working-class," always had elements of anti-intellectualism and even distrust for its "petty bourgeois" members. Finally, as the Party's general counsel, I could only give legal representation to the organization as a whole if I remained above the fray, rather than identified with this or that group within the Party. Whatever thoughts I entertained, whether they were considered unquestioning or independent, remained unspoken.

In those years, as an attorney, I read through all the trial proceedings of Stalin's purge trials of the thirties and forties, the Slansky trial of the Czechoslovakian Communists, the Hungarian trials. Though it is now beyond dispute that the "confessions" of the defendants were either coerced or manufactured outright, I was thoroughly convinced of their truthfulness from my reading of the transcripts. To this day, I have yet to hear a viable explanation of what caused all of these people—without exception—to confess to crimes they didn't commit. Khrushchev had a simple explanation: they were terrorized. But I find this hard to accept. In most cases, they bore no physical evidence of beatings. The great majority of their trials were open to the public, or at least the press. A man like Joseph Davies, an experienced lawyer and ambassador to the Soviet Union, detected no evidence of physical coercion and accepted the confessions in the Soviet trials as bona fide. These men who confessed were not youngsters innocent in the ways of the world. For the most part they were Communists, hardened revolutionaries, who had demonstrated courage and perseverance their entire lives. While it is understandable that some might cave in under various means of physical and psychological pressure, they *all* yielded to coercion. I suppose this is not an important point, since it is now clear that they were all framed, but I still do not understand it.

After the Khrushchev revelations, Jessica, who was far better informed about Soviet life than I, told me that she suspected the frame-up nature of the trials, or at least some of them, at the time they took place. But she never mentioned these doubts even to me at the time she harbored them. When the doctors were arrested, shortly before Stalin's death, I raised no questions nor did Jessica, although I'm sure she had private doubts about the matter. I distinctly remember her rushing home not long after Stalin died, her face beaming, with the day's *New York Times* in her hand, shouting, "John, the doctors have been freed!" My own reaction to the Khrushchev report was not to question its accuracy in the least. But at the same time, the disclosures did nothing to undermine my belief in the superiority of socialism or to question the character of the Soviet state. I regarded Stalin's acts as distortions or perversions of socialism but they did not negate what I considered the enormous successes the Soviet peoples had achieved under socialism.

While we in the United States certainly did not suffer through anything like the incalculable terror that gripped the USSR, with millions imprisoned and killed under Stalin, the McCarthyite trauma was real and palpable, especially for us Communists who were its first targets and who faced imprisonment, blacklist, deportation, loss of career, ostracism, and, in no few cases, terrible personal tragedies. As the Party's general counsel, I had more than enough concerns about the turn our own country had taken.

On one of my infrequently quiet days in the office, I had a most curious visitor. This man walked, or more nearly crept, into my office as if sent from central casting for a part labeled "conspirator." I had no secretary, so there was no way of screening visitors. I'd never met the fellow before, but he introduced himself as Jack Childs. It turns out that I knew his brother Morris, who was active in the Party organization in Illinois. Now, Jack Childs sat down across the desk from me, looked around as if to spot anyone who might be listening, and whispered out of the side of his mouth, "Irving Potash wants to see you."

Irving, a Furriers' Union leader and member of the Party's national board, had been convicted in the first Smith Act trial and served several years in prison. He had first come to the United States as one of tens of thousands of immigrants who never took out citizenship, following the old socialist practice of being self-declared "citizens of the world." This was fine for self-gratification, but unfortunately the U.S. government holds folks to a different standard. When he came out of prison, the authorities ordered his deportation as an "undesirable alien." The Party decided that he would take what was called "voluntary departure," leaving the United States without contesting the deportation order. I have no idea what considerations entered into the Party decision. In many cases, deportation orders were vigorously challenged for years. But in Irving's situation, as earlier with my friend Pete Peters, the Party decided not to dispute the government decision. It was arranged for Irving to go to the Soviet Union.

He left the United States a little more than a year before, but decided that he could no longer live apart from his wife, children, and grandchildren. Now he was back and wanted to see me. I was completely submerged in the McCarran Act litigation, replete with innuendo about Soviet control of the Party here. The last thing in the world that I thought was appropriate was Irving returning illegally and asking to see me. But I obviously could not refuse his request. Jack Childs drove me in his car, first circling around the city to throw off any enterprising FBI agents who might be following. We wound up at a small hotel in Bronxville, about half an hour outside of New York City, where Irving was staying.

It turned out that he had come back via Windsor, the Canadian border town across from Detroit, entering the United States during the Christmas season when there was a good deal of back-and-forth traffic. He asked to see me because he knew he'd have to serve a sentence for illegal entry into the country, but before surrendering to the authorities, he wanted to visit Edith, his wife. He also asked about how, after meeting Edith, to arrange his arrest. Finally, he requested that I let Gene Dennis know of his whereabouts and his plans. I told him that in surrendering, he should follow the example of Henry Winston and Gil Green, who had recently come out of hiding by sending letters to the U.S. attorney and to the news media, saying that at such-and-such a time, they would be on the steps of the federal courthouse and the authorities should come and get them then.

As to getting the Party's agreement to his plan, I told Irving that I would talk to Gene and arranged to return to the hotel the next morning. I immediately went to speak with Gene. The Party was in the midst of preparing its national convention, which would be extremely tense and difficult in view of the atmosphere in the country and the political fights inside the organization. And of course, Gene was the central figure in organizing the convention. He was consumed with a host of problems, and the idea of Irving showing up unannounced was hardly welcome. When I told him of Irving's plans, Gene simply said, "Tell Irving to go back where he came from." This was not going to be pleasing news to Irving and it certainly wasn't pleasant for me to deliver it. The next morning, as I dressed, the top item on the radio news was that deported Communist leader Irving Potash had gone to dinner the evening before and, by the strangest coincidence, the FBI agent in charge of his case chose the same restaurant in which to dine, spotted him, and arrested Irving on the spot.

This seemed a bit peculiar, but the times were full of peculiarities and I didn't give this one too much thought. But a quarter century later, in 1981, the Childs brothers figured rather prominently in David Garrow's book *The FBI and Martin Luther King, Jr.* Garrow, relying almost entirely on FBI sources, revealed that Morris and Jack had been long-term employees of the FBI and that Morris had served as a courier for Gus Hall in communication with Moscow. I rarely saw Jack after that incident with Irving Potash, although once we were in the same fishing party off the Long Island Sound. I found Jack irascible and liable to go into a rage over the smallest matter, so kept my distance. But Morris was constantly around. It was commonly understood in the Party that he was one of Gus Hall's trusted confidants after Gus became general secretary, following Gene's tenure. For example, though not a member of the body, Morris was invited to attend every meeting of the Party's Central Committee, its highest governing body between conventions, where he was referred to, with a wink, as "the ambassador." When the Garrow book came out, I fully understood the circumstances of Irving's arrest.

When Garrow broke the story about the Childs brothers, Gus was away in the USSR. Henry Winston, the Party chairperson, immediately issued a statement denouncing the book and the FBI for trying to frame up Jack and Morris. I went to Winnie—as Winston was familiarly called by everyone—and told him my story about Irving Potash and Jack Childs. I hadn't a single doubt that the Childs brothers were stool pigeons, but Winnie dismissed my concerns. Meantime, Gus had some difficulty returning to the United States from Moscow—this was shortly after the Soviet intervention in Afghanistan, and the U.S. government had severed all flight connections between the USSR and the United States. Gus asked me to meet his return flight in Montreal, rent a car, and drive back to New York with him.

On the drive, I told Gus about my experience with Jack Childs and Irving Potash and said that I was convinced of the Garrow book's accuracy regarding Jack and Morris. Gus's response was not to respond. He said nothing and let the moment pass. Back in New York, nothing further was said about Jack and Morris, the Party issued no more statements, no charges were lodged against the FBI, but neither was there an acknowledgment that the two brothers were government informers. But with the appearance of the Garrow book, Morris and Jack were never again seen around the Communist party. They simply vanished and were not heard from again. Rather than using the moment to give the FBI a bloody nose for its methods of subverting a legitimate political organization, the Party let the matter die a quiet death. Gus, who held all the levers of power in the organization and who had a close personal relationship with Morris and Jack, could not admit to fallibility. To acknowledge that the brothers were police agents would imply acceptance of the rest of Garrow's story—that Morris was Gus's personal envoy to Moscow. It reminded me of the long-ago story we developed in the LaFollette Committee of Richard Frankensteen, the president of the Chrysler workers' local in Detroit, whose best friend turned out to be a police spy. But whereas Frankensteen was outraged and used the experience to publicly expose the government, Gus Hall's considerable vanity—and perhaps fear of closer scrutiny—prevented him from exercising a political judgment in the Childs matter.

* * *

When the first Smith Act trial of the Party's national board took place in 1949, the cold war atmosphere was reaching its most hysterical phase. The Soviet Union had developed and tested its first atomic bomb, the Chinese Revolution had taken power in the most populous nation on earth, two opposing states—with a divided Berlin—had been established on German soil. The loyalty hearings, blacklists, and deportations were in full force in the Land of the Free.

Divisions arose within the Smith Act defense team, not among the lawyers but between the defendants on the one hand and their lawyers on the other. The defendants saw the proceedings as a setting to emulate the performance of Georgi Dmitroff, the Bulgarian Communist who defied the Nazi courts, which accused him of setting fire to the Reichstag, the German parliament. Dmitroff, with great courage and eloquence, turned the tables on his captors and made the affair a "trial" of Hitler fascism. The Party leaders wanted to make the Foley Square proceedings a political trial, a defense of Marxism. In the United States, of course, we have de facto political trials all of the time, but the law books cite no political crimes. The lawyers, like the defendants, assumed that the Party leaders would be found guilty. But like all good defense attorneys, they also understood the need to prepare the legal basis at trial for a drawn-out appeals process. What a defense of Marxism had to do with rules of evidence, for example, was not always clear to the lawyers. Not that they were apolitical themselves; their readiness to go to jail and face disbarment proceedings—as they did for contempt—demonstrated their own commitment.

Addressing the jury on behalf of the defendants, Gene Dennis said:

> We defendants contend, and have proved, that our trial is in fact a most extraordinary trial, a political trial, a thought-control trial. The prosecution has tried to try the untriable, as the evidence and testimony prove. While contending that this is just an "ordinary criminal case," it has nonetheless put before a court and a jury a whole body of mind-readers and crystal-gazers. They presumed to tell the jury what we Communist leaders would do, would teach, would advocate—if and when. The prosecution could not bring us Communist leaders to trial for anything we have done, taught or advocated—individually or collectively. Yet it did not dare say frankly that it seeks to convict us for our political beliefs or for alleged hidden dangerous thoughts.

The Smith Act, violation of which was punishable by five years in prison, was never directed toward any *act* of political violence. There were already many statutes on the books punishing sabotage, espionage, and other criminal acts against the government. What the Smith Act made criminal was advocacy, i.e., mere speech. One needn't be a constitutional law professor to know that the Bill of Rights, specifically the First Amendment, expressly prohibits Congress from enacting any law abridging freedom of speech, press, or assembly. Any minimally informed high school student should know this. But in 1951, in *Dennis v. United States,* the Court refused to review the evidence and simply found that the Smith Act was constitutional. It wasn't until many years after Gene Dennis and his co-defendants served their prison terms—altogether 140 Communists were convicted in a long series of trials—that the U.S. Supreme Court finally reversed itself and ruled that the Smith Act was unconstitutional.

When that first Foley Square trial was held, I was counsel for the Progressive party and obviously in no position to serve as lawyer for the defendants. But I was constantly on call for informal consultation by lawyers and defendants alike, and continued to be so in subsequent Smith Act prosecutions. After three New York trials convicted the primary, secondary, and tertiary national leadership, local trials were held in Los Angeles, Pittsburgh, Boston, Baltimore, New Haven, wherever the Party was active. It wasn't until the Lightfoot trial—six years and several trials later—while the McCarran Act appeals were inching their way up to the Supreme Court, that I relinquished my off-stage role to become attorney of record in a Smith Act trial.

By the time the *Yates* decision was handed down, Gene Dennis and his co-defendants from the first New York Smith Act trial had served their five-year sentences and were back home. Bill Foster, of course, never went to prison because of his poor health. And Gil Green, Gus Hall, Bob Thompson, and Henry Winston remained in prison because of additional sentences stemming from their going underground instead of surrendering as scheduled. Early on, I considered the decision to avoid arrest a mistake. To my mind, it would only further stir up the anticommunist hysteria by confirming the stereotype of a conspiracy and, in effect, abdicate the struggle for the Party's legality. Furthermore, it would make it nearly impossible to obtain bail in future Smith Act prosecutions, which we knew would be plentiful. Gus was captured in Mexico eight months after the Party designated the four comrades to stay out of prison but inside the country in order to clandestinely run the organization. He was sent to Leavenworth. Bob was apprehended in the mountains of Oregon two years later and sent to Atlanta to serve his time. The authorities never did find Gil or Winnie, however, despite their "most-wanted" status. But with Gene and the others coming out of prison and the changes in the country evident by the wane of Senator McCarthy and his "ism," the Party decided that Gil and Winnie should surrender.

Upon their arrest, I became Gil's and Winnie's counsel. At that point, facing time for contempt over and above their five-year sentences, they were brought before a trial judge who gave them an additional three years. In appealing the sentences, I raised the constitutional provision that says that an infamous crime, defined as one punishable by more than one year—can only be prosecuted by an indictment. And there had been no indictment of Gil and Winnie. The lower court and the Court of Appeals both ruled against us and affirmed the defendants' three-year contempt sentences on top of their five-year Smith Act sentences. When we appeared before the Supreme Court, we still lost by a five-to-four decision. Justice Hugo Black wrote a long, scholarly, and brilliant dissenting opinion in which he cast aside my own arguments regarding an infamous crime requiring an indictment. Rather, he went back to the fundamental proposition that a criminal contempt case required a jury trial. A few years later, with some changes in composition, the Court, by a five-to-four decision, indeed held that criminal contempt cases require a jury trial. While in prison, Henry Winston lost his eyesight because of medical neglect of a brain tumor. Bob Thompson was set upon by a fellow prisoner, a Croatian fascist, who beat in his skull with a lead pipe, causing permanent injury. Soon after he got out of prison, Gil Green learned that his wife, Lil, was dying of cancer. I often think of the personal losses suffered and what might have been avoided or alleviated had the Court decided earlier rather than later on the justice of our arguments.

From the time I became the Party's general counsel in 1951, I made the rounds of the federal prison system, visiting most of the Smith Act prisoners. I saw Gene and John Gates in Atlanta, Ben Davis and later Winnie in Terre Haute, Gus and Gil in Leavenworth, Elizabeth Gurley Flynn in Alderson, etc. I was the one visitor the authorities allowed, in addition to family members, and I tried to see everyone at least twice a year. Often I bore messages and personal information from families. (In the cases of Winnie and Gil, they had been away from their families for five years *before* being sentenced to a combined eight years' imprisonment.)

In addition to this being just and essential to the prisoner's legal rights and morale, it helped me form some very close and lifelong friendships. Without exception, the Communist leaders were models of everything that a political prisoner should be. But even in this select company, Henry Winston was outstanding. Steeled—but not hardened—by years of poverty and difficult political activity, with a deep understanding of the system with which he was contending, I never once heard a word of self-pity or a personal complaint from this remarkable man. This was so even when standard prison indifference and bureaucracy combined with undisguised racism and anticommunism to deny him the medical care he so urgently required. It was characteristic of Winnie that throughout his imprisonment, he was concerned with his fellow inmates. After each visit with him, he would confront me with a long list of *their* problems, to the exclusion of his own. The Black prisoners never called him by name but always addressed him as "Pop," not in deference to his years—he was only in his forties—but as a mark of respect and an expression of appreciation for his solicitude.

I first met Gil during the Party struggle around the Duclos article, but didn't know him well until his prison days. Though he was formerly the leader of the Party in Illinois, I never knew him there. But our common Chicago background remained a bond. Because he successfully evaded the FBI for all of those years, despite the widest search for a fugitive up to that time, he became a particular target for the government's rancor. It had been my practice with the other defendants to visit them on the day of their release from prison, arranging to continue their bond because they were indicted not only on the Smith Act conspiracy for which they were convicted but for the membership clause of the act for which they had yet to be tried. I then accompanied each of them back to New York. Of course I was planning to do this with Gil but the U.S. attorney wouldn't give me his release date. Every time I'd call, the man was "unavailable," ironically the euphemism we used in referring to comrades who were underground. About the time I figured that Gil should be freed, I called the warden of Leavenworth, who informed me that actually he had been released a day earlier and was en route by car to New York where he would appear in court to ask for continued bond. The ride was made miserable for Gil, with local stops at county jails on the way to the decrepit old West Street holding facility on the Hudson River. Gil arrived in New York on a Friday, and the next day was his official release date. When we appeared in court, the U.S. attorney announced that this being a Saturday, the bond clerk was unavailable until Monday morning. Finally I raised hell with the judge, who ordered that the bail bond clerk be located and produced. I have always felt guilty about subjecting Gil to this humiliating treatment. Fortunately, he never held it against me. He remains one of my oldest friends. And though we have had political differences, he has always been and remains the most innovative and thoughtful leader of the Party.

I remember driving down to West Virginia to bring home Elizabeth Gurley Flynn, one of my very favorite people. Elizabeth was another of those brilliant American radicals—like Paul Robeson and Vito Marcantonio—about whom poems could be written and movies made, such were their charismatic personalities. Joe Hill immortalized the young Elizabeth in his song "The Rebel Girl." One of the greatest of all labor "agitators" in the most positive sense of that word, completely unselfish, passionately loyal, direct to the point of bluntness, Elizabeth was all the more endearing for her lovely face and sparkling blue eyes and a lively Irish wit that bubbled up on the most solemn occasions, even when the joke was on her.

She and my sister, Marion, were quite close, so Marion came with me to the prison as did Elizabeth's sister, Kathie. Elizabeth was the marquee name among the second-string Smith Act defendants and came out of the Alderson women's prison on May 23, 1957. She took umbrage, as the only woman on the national board, at not being indicted with the first group of leaders. "I felt quite embarrassed," she later wrote, "and at a loss to explain why I was not arrested with my co-workers. I felt discriminated against by Uncle Sam!" Coming out of prison, however, she was only on conditional release and had to ask permission whenever she wanted to go outside of the New York jurisdiction. Thus, when we invited her up to Kent, the parole officer had to first get permission from Washington, which finally agreed to let her visit on the July 4 weekend when her conditional release ended. Gene Dennis was also given permission to come to Kent that weekend, so we had a wonderful July 4 celebration.

Once Elizabeth visited Kent with Arnold and Aurelia Johnson. She spent a good deal of the time berating me for my male chauvinism in failing to put down the toilet seat after urinating. So powerful was Elizabeth's effect on me that from that weekend over thirty years ago to the present, I have carefully put down the toilet seat on each occasion that I've lifted it. Some years after Elizabeth's death, I was home at our apartment at 444 Central Park West and received a note, on embroidered stationary, that had been slipped under the door. It was from Jessica's and my next door neighbors, politely explaining that they were unable to sleep in the middle of the night because our toilet seat banged down with a sharp report and begging me to please refrain. Afterward, I still replaced the toilet seat but did so quietly. A couple of weeks after this incident, I received another piece of fancy stationary with but one word: "Thanks."

Elizabeth was a feminist but she used to complain about having to spend too much time with women. She loved the company of men and had a direct, earthy humor that stood her in good stead in any company. The greatest love of her life—during her pre-Party days in the Wobblies, the Industrial Workers of the World—was Carlo Tresca, the Italian anarchist who was killed by the fascists. One day Elizabeth arrived home to find him in bed with her sister, and she never completely got over it. Her only son, Fred, whom she had by another man, died of cancer at the age of forty. Elizabeth's was not an easy life by any means, but she lived every day of it with an uncommon zest and humor. I would have loved her in any case, but she truly won me over during the McCarran Act litigation by personally taking responsibility for raising the money to pay me, when nobody else did so.

* * *

Among Elizabeth's fifteen second-string Smith Act co-defendants was my sister Marion. "Second-string" was the news media's unflattering description, but the comrades adopted it in good humor. They were arrested by the FBI on a humid June morning and taken down to FBI headquarters at Foley Square to be photographed and fingerprinted, then shuttled off to a courtroom for arraignment. Israel Amter, another co-defendant, then well into his seventies, was dragged from an upstate nursing home, over the protest of the attendants. The judge allowed him to be released into the custody of his lawyer, but imposed stiff bail—ranging from $10,000 to $25,000 which, in 1951, was stiff indeed—on the others. Alexander Trachtenberg and Jacob Mindel, both in their seventies as well, were handcuffed and taken to the West Street holding facility with the other male defendants. Elizabeth and Marion were handcuffed together, as were Betty Gannett and Claudia Jones, the female second-stringers, and taken to the Womens' House of Detention. In *The Alderson Story,* Elizabeth writes about Marion that day: "She was our 'glamor girl.' She wore a pale purple summer suit, a little hat with purple flowers, and carried a square basketpurse with a nosegay on top. The inmates gazed at her and exclaimed, 'Isn't she cute!'" Our friend Phyllis Silverman remembered Marion as looking like Irene Castle, Fred Astaire's early partner.

I learned of the indictment when I was sitting in the Washington, D.C., hearing room arguing against the McCarran Act. I hurried back to New York to visit Marion in the Women's House of Detention, a high-rise eyesore set in the middle of Greenwich Village's busiest intersection. It was upsetting to be able to talk to my sister only by a static-filled telephone through thick sheets of glass. It would be a week before mother was able to raise her bail. (Because of the four defendants from the first trial who jumped bail, the amounts were much higher and money for bail scarcer.) George Charney, another defendant, was bailed out by his family. The others' money was put up by the Civil Rights Congress Bail Fund. The Civil Rights Congress (CRC) was led by William Patterson, a true pioneer in the struggle for human rights in the United States, who organized the petition to the United Nations charging genocide against African-Americans.

Marion affectionately referred to Pat as a "mad genius" for his au-
dacity. Pat was kind of suspicious of me for my conservative and cau-
tious legal approaches, but we eventually became quite close friends.
When the first Smith Act indictments were handed down in 1948, the
CRC set up a bail fund with four trustees—Dashiell Hammett, the
mystery writer; W. Alphaeus Hunton, a social anthropologist and
leading Africanist; Abner Green, an African-American journalist; and
Frederick V. Fields, a left-wing philanthropist (the *V* of his middle
name stood for his pedigree: Vanderbilt).

Shortly after bail was posted, the four bail fund trustees found
themselves in trouble with the federal government, which demanded the names of every individual who had loaned money to the fund.
Protecting their supporters from government retribution, the four
men refused to divulge the names and were themselves sentenced to
six months in jail for contempt. The government then canceled the
bail bonds, which meant that all the defendants except Marion and
George Charney were sent back to jail. Marion set about the task of
organizing a new Smith Act defense committee, asking Dr. Edward
Barsky, the noted surgeon and our family doctor, to serve as chair,
and Carl Marzani, an ALP activist, filmmaker, and publisher, to be
executive secretary.

In the course of pretrial motions, all the defendants received a
mandatory physical examination. For some time Marion had been
bothered by what she thought were hemorrhoids. The doctor didn't
take the trouble of a proctoscopy—a rectal exam—and gave her a
clean bill of health. Marion's "hemorrhoids" got worse, which she attributed to all the time she spent sitting on a hard courtroom bench.
She went to Eddie Barsky, who discovered a malignancy in the colon
and immediately operated to remove it. As a result of Marion's surgery, the judge declared a mistrial, dropping her as a defendant for
medical reasons. After the operation, the press somehow got hold of
the pathological report —which stated that she had lymph node me-
tastasis, indicating a real danger for a spread of the cancer—and this
was given publicity in the morning papers. Forty years ago, of course,
cancer was a subject of no little mystification and often went unmen-
tioned in polite company; even today, obituaries often use the euphe-
mistic "died after a long illness." So when the judge, Edward Dimock,
read the news reports of Marion's cancer, he sent two of his minions
to me to offer his personal apologies and assurances that had he
known this publicity was forthcoming, he would have tried to stop it.
For me, of course, it was the fact of the cancer and not the publicity
about it that was disturbing.

Two years later, in 1953, Marion was again ordered to stand trial in the third New York Smith Act prosecution. I reached Vin Hallinan, the Progressive party presidential candidate a year earlier, to ask him to represent her. Vin quickly offered his services but it took a week before he could get to New York. Hal Cammer, meanwhile, represented her at the bail hearing. Hal later recalled that as a result of this brief Smith Act appearance, every union client he had, except for the Furriers' Union, discharged him that week. "They loved me," he remembered, "but they couldn't take the heat." He also recalled that wherever he went with Marion that week, two FBI agents were right behind them. One day the four of them—Hal, Marion, and the two FBI men—were waiting for an elevator on the eleventh floor of the Foley Square courthouse. "Marion and I got in," Hal told me, "but there was no more room. 'Don't worry,' she told the agents, 'I'll wait for you downstairs.' And, ever the lady, she did."

Judge Bickes was a wealthy real estate attorney who was trying his first federal case. His rich relatives, replete in their furs and finery, visited the court to watch him preside. Vin Hallinan immediately moved to dismiss the charges against Marion on the basis of her illness. The court appointed a physician to examine her, and I'll never forget the words of the doctor's report. He said, of course, that Marion had had cancer and had undergone a colostomy, but concluded that she had "no residual disability" and was perfectly fit to stand trial. So Marion was compelled to endure yet another trial. As the case dragged on, mother was terribly concerned. I tried to mollify her by telling her, "Mother, don't worry, Marion is going to be acquitted." She asked me why I would say that. "Because there is no evidence to convict," I replied. "The FBI has nothing on her. Nothing, really." To which mother responded, "Well, the FBI doesn't know Marion as well as I do." As it turned out, at the end of the prosecution's presentation of its case, Vin moved for an acquittal. This was asking the judge, instead of sending the case to the jury, to rule that there was insufficient evidence to warrant a guilty verdict against Marion and to dismiss the case. After having put her through the rigor of another trial in her condition, the judge did just this.

Apparently Judge Bickes was troubled by the whole affair. Three years later, I'd finished arguing another case before him when he called me up to the bench. He wanted to explain that he really had no choice but to hold Marion for her second trial given the doctor's report that she had no residual disability. I told the judge that I understood, that my anger was not directed at him but at the doctor, who had violated his professional responsibilities in the interests of self-promotion. How, I asked, can someone have a colostomy and no residual disability?

For her part, Marion was by nature such an optimist and had such unbounded faith in Dr. Eddie Barsky that she was convinced he had cured her forevermore. She was hardly alone in her confidence in Eddie. His loyalists were legion, and Jessica and I could be counted among them. He and Jessica had initiated Russian War Relief during the war years. His wife, Vita, was Marion's co-worker on the short-lived *U.S. Week* in Milwaukee and Chicago in 1939 and 1940 and was at this time Jessica's right hand in organizing the annual banquets for *New World Review*. Eddie had a reputation, deservedly, not only as a brilliant surgeon but for having organized and administered the medical care for all of the International Brigades in Republican Spain during the civil war. He was a man of enormous energy and unreserved commitment. Upon his return from Spain after the war, Eddie organized the Joint Anti-fascist Refugee Committee to support the prisoners and other victims of Spain's military dictator, Francisco Franco. I remember some years later Eddie was recuperating from a mild stroke that had affected his arm. I went to visit him and Vita at their apartment. At some point in our conversation, the subject of retirement came up. I told Eddie, "I know I could easily retire. I'm a good loafer and I know Vita is too. I could be quite happy without work." Eddie was shocked at my attitude. "Not to work," he said, "that's immoral."

As a prominent surgeon, Eddie could move in money circles where others might be unwelcome or uncomfortable. He was fearless in approaching people for favors. During the Progressive party days, he convinced Charlie Goldman, the garment district's biggest manufacturer of moderately priced coats, that he should head up an IPP businessman's committee to raise money for the Wallace campaign. Eddie's persuasive ways would get people to do things for the movement they might not otherwise do. It wasn't so much that he articulated arguments in ways others couldn't, but people were drawn to his own selflessness. When he made the "pitch"—the fund appeal—at an affair to raise money, he would initiate the donations by giving, say, five hundred dollars of his own money and then asking others for one hundred dollars. Whatever the cause—Spanish democracy, U.S.-Soviet friendship, the Rosenbergs, the Smith Act bail fund— Eddie raised the money, while more often than not Vita was organizing the affair—putting together the mailing lists, setting up the committees, shopping for bargain salad greens in Little Italy, renting chairs, convincing a friendly restaurateur to donate the briskets. Vita said—and I certainly couldn't argue—that Jessica was Eddie's lone equal at fund-raising. But Jessica's methods were quite different. She had a mind for detail, leaving nothing to chance. She headed up no committee that she didn't check on constantly to make certain things were being done correctly. A woman with a cast-iron spine, her demeanor was so sweet and delicious that you ended up agreeing with her even when she said no to your request.

Eddie's gruffness was in distinct contrast. For those who didn't know him and what made him tick, he impressed as being extremely tough. Actually, he was so sensitive to the pain and suffering of others that he needed to disguise it with a rough exterior. During the McCarran Act hearings, when Marc and I returned to New York on Fridays, Eddie would drop in—he had been suspended from medical practice for having served a jail sentence for contempt of HUAC. He didn't come by for anything special, just to let us know that he was with us and to give us whatever comfort he could, which we needed after a week in Washington with the SACB.

One evening in 1951, Jessica came home in great pain. She was running a high fever. I called a doctor whose office was in our apartment building and whom we occasionally used. He diagnosed her ailment as flu and recommended that she stay in bed with a hot water bottle for the pain. Her condition grew worse, and after a couple of days, the doctor himself became worried and called in a surgeon, who briefly looked at Jessica and said he thought she might have appendicitis. I said that in that case, I wanted Dr. Barsky as her surgeon. I called Eddie at home—this was after 11 P.M.—and he told me to meet him at Beth Israel, his resident hospital. Early in our marriage, Jessica had a hysterectomy, and we were unsure if her appendix had been removed, a fairly common practice at that time. Eddie immediately took her into surgery after telling me, "Let's hope Jessica still has her appendix; otherwise, it must be something much more serious." A couple of hours later he came to report to me in the waiting room. Eddie put his all into whatever he was doing, and after a tough operation, it looked like it was him who had been the patient. He told me that Jessica had a ruptured appendix, and he had filled her up with penicillin. "She'll be all right," he told me and then, typical of tough Eddie, "unless she picks up pneumonia."

One late spring day in 1957, after we'd brought Elizabeth Flynn back to New York from West Virginia, Eddie called and asked me to come to his office. He told me that the cancer had spread to Marion's liver but that he hadn't informed her yet. I still have to remind myself that the fifties were "prehistoric" not only in political terms but even as regards personal health and maintenance. The list of taboo subjects ranged far beyond communism or even sex. *Cancer* was a word best spoken in a low whisper. I told Eddie that Marion, after her first operation, asked me not to conceal anything from her, that if she had something that appeared to be terminal, I should tell her. Eddie nevertheless strongly advised me not to tell her of the malignancy. "A lot of people talk bravely like Marion," he said, "but it is better that they not know." So I didn't tell her and I believe Eddie was right, that Marion never realized her illness was terminal.

She spent that last summer of her life, as she usually did, with Maxine Woods on East Blue Hill cove in Maine. She loved Maine as she loved her Green Mountains in Vermont, being happy "just watching the sky stay up," as she put it. Though she was obviously losing weight, Marion remained in good spirits. Lorraine Hansberry visited her and wrote a beautiful piece for *Playbill* about Marion and how she was coping. This was shortly before Lorraine discovered her own cancer.

When Marion returned to New York in the autumn, Eddie had her admitted to the hospital. Her natural optimism and confidence in Eddie convinced her that she was going to be okay. Phyllis Silverman said that Marion told her at Beth Israel, "I'm not able to eat but I'd love some lamb chops. Hide them from the nurses." In Maine, she had started to write her memoirs and wanted to use the time in the hospital to complete them. I bought her a tape recorder, which she kept beside her hospital bed, but she never was well enough to use it. She kept saying, "That tape recorder is sitting there mocking me."

On the night Marion died, mother stood guard by the bed as if she could somehow protect her precious daughter, unwilling to accept the worst of all tragedies—outliving her own child. Jessica and I convinced mother to go home and assured her we would remain. In a short while, Marion went into a coma. Eddie called and asked if we wanted him there. I said, "Eddie, there's no point in coming. There's nothing more you can do. Stay home with Vita." Of course he came anyway. As he entered the room, he went to the head of Marion's bed and held her hand for a few minutes. In the early morning hours, Marion died. (Three years later, when I was hospitalized while recuperating from a heart attack, Eddie dropped by after surgery to visit. He asked, "Do you remember the night that Marion died?" I said that I could never forget it. He said, "You know, John, I think she knew I was there." Three years and several hundred patients later, Eddie had never forgotten that night either.)

In the hospital, as letters poured in to her, Marion remarked, "Oh, how rich I am in friends!" And indeed she was. Her closest friends and countless admirers gathered for her memorial service, chaired by Louis Burnham. Paul Robeson sang the choral melody from Beethoven's Ninth Symphony and "Farewell, Beloved Comrade." Elizabeth Flynn talked about "her dearest friend, Marion." Nat Witt and Beanie Baldwin spoke, and Shirley Graham Du Bois read a message from W. E. B. Du Bois. Other messages came from Vin Hallinan and Governor Elmer Benson and from Vicente Lombardo Toledano, leader of the Mexican labor movement, who spoke of her years of work in building solidarity with Latin America. They all told of Marion's courage at a time when the country was in retreat from its best ideals and cowardice was honored. They spoke of her beauty and her brilliance for which, had she chosen a different path, as Dr. Du Bois put it, "America would willingly have paid large income and given glamorous publicity, which to her seemed trash."

An excerpt was read from remarks Marion made at a birthday party thrown in her honor two years earlier:

Fifty-seven years are nothing to boast about. But by my own reckoning, I'm not even that old. I'm really very young—only in my 20s. Mine was a sad case of arrested development. My mother says I talked very early. But I was mighty slow to open my eyes. It is only a little more than two decades since I began to see what was going on around me. . . .

Not long ago, I met a friend who has known me since childhood. He thoroughly disapproves of me now. And he finds me very puzzling. He says he can't understand what turned a cheerful person like me into a "dissenter." A dissenter. It is an honorable name; many fine men and women have borne it proudly. But I don't feel at home with it; somehow, it doesn't seem to fit. The truth is, I am not a dissenter. I am a yea-sayer. I was always a yea-sayer, by natural inclination. Therein lies the continuity. . . .

The right to dissent is a valuable right, and I respect it. Yet I would not see its abuse by murderers go unpunished. The right I claim for myself—the right I defend in court and out—is the right to assent, to affirm.

Marion ended her remarks by echoing Sean O'Casey: "Hurrah to life!"

I told of how Marion came to be the way she was, about our father, from whom Marion inherited an unquenchable zest for life and who, like her, died in life's fullness, and our mother, who always sustained us with her love and inner strength. We were proud to be the offspring of such parents, as they were proud of us, and so we—Marion and I—took deep pride in each other. Never, not once, did she and I exchange a word in anger, or even have a friendly disagreement, not quickly dispelled in conversation. For Marion, every moment of life, the sweet and the bitter, was high adventure to be savored. And people, really communicating with all kinds of people, was the highest adventure of all. With her keen sense of this adventure, she was incessantly curious. She invariably peeked at the last page of a new novel to see how it turned out. I told the memorial meeting that for Marion there was never a gap between grasping an idea and action to implement it. She often prodded me—her slow-motion brother—to make a phone call, visit an influential friend, arrange a meeting. I too admired her courage and only once saw her head bowed in surrender—to death itself.

The cold war repression took its toll on Marion, in one way much more even than the two Smith Act trials combined. Her son, Johnny, the youngest wartime captain of a merchant vessel, was screened off the waterfront by the Coast Guard during the loyalty purges. Virtually apolitical himself, Johnny was a wild kid who liked to drink a little too much and loved being master of his own ship. But he was his mother's son and that was all the government needed to blacklist him from his beloved merchant marine. He blamed Marion and cut himself off from all contact with her. In 1952, while hospitalized for her first operation, she asked me to contact her former husband, Artie Bachrach, to request that he inform Johnny of her illness and ask that he visit her in the hospital. I was in Chicago on Progressive party business and went to see Artie, then working as a docket clerk in his brothers' law firm. Artie was always terrified of Marion's politics and was reluctant to intercede, but agreed to do so, given the seriousness of her condition.

It turned out that Johnny was living in Staten Island, driving a tug boat, and married to a devoutly Baptist South Carolina woman. He came to Beth Israel Hospital to visit Marion and they had a delightful reunion. Marion, with her general gaiety, was tremendously buoyed by the visit. But Johnny was obviously not reconciled, for he never wrote or saw her again. When she died five years later, he called my mother, his grandmother—he was always fond of her and it was he who gave her the name "Mema," by which she was customarily known by all our friends—to ask that Marion's obituary not mention his name.

Johnny was my only nephew and named for me, but I never saw or heard from him again until my own mother died in 1960. On my recommendation, she had left Johnny twenty thousand dollars in her will, which I sent to him in stock. He called to thank me, knowing that I was likely responsible for the bequest. But it wasn't until the seventies, after Artie died, that I saw Johnny again. He and his wife had come to New York with his father's ashes, scattering them in Artie's favorite spots. They visited Jessica and me at our apartment. Johnny—he still called himself Captain Bachrach, dating from his days as ship's master—then lived in New Orleans, working as a marine insurance adjuster. He had converted to his wife's faith and was an upstanding "born-again" church member, a newfound teetotaler, and financially secure. He had also become quite reactionary and his racism was undisguised. His southern-born-and-bred wife was far more enlightened. We had always been in touch on May 1, our common birthday, and for a time I still sent him birthday cards but never received a reply. When Jessica died years later, I wrote to tell him and, much to my surprise, he called me from Washington, D.C., where he was visiting, and proposed to come to New York. Johnny had become every inch a Bachrach, like his father and all of Artie's brothers and male cousins. He was bald like them, and husky as ever, with the characteristic protruding nose, but he wore a wispy beard like a seaman who had been washed ashore. This was 1983, and Johnny was now anti-Reagan, antiwar, and living in Henderson, North Carolina, where he owned his own insurance business.

Our pleasant little lunch date led to a renewal of our relationship. His wife was in a nursing home with an advanced case of Alzheimer's, and Johnny was living with a woman whom I never met. In 1989, Johnny died of lung cancer, and his woman friend, who knew nothing of me, found my name in his address book. She didn't know what my relationship, if any, was to him but wanted to inform all of his friends and associates of his death. I wrote her to express my thanks and my shock at learning of Johnny's passing. I hadn't even known he was ill. Subsequently she sent me a photograph she had found of the entire Shire family, including my mother and father, from the late twenties.

I wonder what Marion, her incurable good cheer combined with her piercing intellect and literary gifts, might have made of this coda to her own story.

John seated at left, as Sidney Hillman speaks. Mayor Fiorello LaGuardia is seated at immediate right of Hillman.

Jessica at work on *Soviet Russia Today.*

The CIO delegation in Leningrad, USSR, 1945. *From the left*, James B. Carey, Albert Fitzgerald, Len DeCaux, Allen Haywood, John Green, Reid Robinson, Lee Pressman, John, Emil Rieve, and Joseph Curran.

General counsel for the Progressive
party, 1948.

John with Vito Marcantonio (*left*) and Joseph Forer (*standing*),
co-counsels in the McCarran Act litigation.

230:4

With one of the myriad Smith Act briefs.

Relaxing at Kent, circa 1965.

At Soviet Embassy reception with Jessica (*center*) and Ambassador Igor Troyanovsky in the early 1980s.

230.6

With Vita, 1989.

handwritten annotations:

See VITA FRIEND P. 95, 97

VITA BANSKY (NEE FRIEND)

See INDEX

See P. 225

AFTER AUTHORS 1ST WIFE (JESSICA) DIED he
MARRIED VITA BANSKY (NEE FRIEND) — P. 298

6

Victories

While Marion and Maxine Woods took their regular cottage in Maine that last summer, Jessica and I, together with Aurelia and Arnold Johnson, decided to join them for a couple of weeks. We found a little shack on an adjacent cove that was convenient for Arnold's and my fishing expeditions. One evening I received a phone call from a CBS television news producer informing me that the FBI had arrested a man named Rudolph Abel on charges of espionage and that Abel was asking me to represent him. I said I knew nothing about Abel, had never heard of him, but I'd look into it when I returned to New York.

The whole incident was preposterous. Obviously I was the last lawyer in the entire country to represent somebody accused of being a Soviet spy, since that same accusation had been leveled against me by Whittaker Chambers and in view of my position as counsel to the Party. Not only would it be absurd for me to accept but it was folly for any such defendant to ask me to represent them. Clearly, I would have nothing to do with the case. The CBS guy inquired as to where I was staying, how to get there, how long I'd be in Maine and such, and I did my best to be evasive. Next morning, we were packed and starting out of the driveway of our little shack, headed for the highway back to New York, when another car, loaded with television gear, drove up. The fellow behind the wheel opened the door and asked if I knew the whereabouts of John Abt. I pleaded ignorance and we drove on. We spent the day on the road, keeping our eyes out for anyone who might be following us. Rather than go directly to the city, we decided to head for Kent. We approached our house through the back side of the mountain so as not to be disturbed by any enterprising news reporters and stayed the night.

The next morning, I drove to the West Street facility, where Abel was being held, and introduced myself. He was a sweet, unprepossessing man living in the United States on a green card, issued by the immigration authorities to allow foreigners to work here. Abel's business card indicated that he had a photographer's studio in Brooklyn. Unfortunately, his unstated business was as a colonel in the Soviet intelligence apparatus. I asked him why in the world would he ask me to be his lawyer, given my reputation and my present clientele. He said, "Well, Mr. Abt, you are the only attorney whose name I know." I offered to try to find him legal representation and called an excellent criminal attorney who, after consultation with his partners, declined the case. I suspected this experience would be repeated no matter whom I called and urged Abel to ask the court to appoint a lawyer.

Abel had little legitimate defense. His one tenable point was that his arrest had initially come in a search of his premises in the absence of an arrest warrant. Eventually, he was convicted. It turned out that Colonel Abel was quite a significant officer in the KGB and became the central figure in the U.S. trade for Francis Gary Powers, the CIA pilot shot down in his U-2 spy plane over the USSR in the Eisenhower years.

It may have been that the federal government entertained some notions of labeling me a Soviet agent, beyond the failed efforts of Whittaker Chambers and Richard Nixon back in 1948. By 1959, of the eleven national board members first convicted under the Smith Act, only Gil Green and Henry Winston remained incarcerated. Years later, Gil obtained documents in his FBI file that were based on "audited" discussions between us while he was at Leavenworth. *Audited* is the FBI euphemism for wiretapped conversations, presumably privileged, between lawyer and client. The prison warden wrote to the director of the federal prison system: "Although we hesitate to infringe upon the confidential relationship of Attorney Abt and his client, the activities of these people are certainly not in the best interests of the country." Fictional fragments of alleged conversations appeared in Gil's file, in which he and I supposedly discussed people of whom neither of us had any knowledge and in which we used words like *cells*, which only the FBI and television dramas used to refer to Party clubs. The report in Gil's file, discussing "Abt," further alleges that I "was talking about a trip to Russia, where he [meaning me] was given rubles (he was sent there as a delegate of a union). Abt told Green that while he was in Russia, he conversed with Khrushchev. 'When they come to the United States, we will take care of them.'" It is unclear from this last reference to whom "we" and "them" refers, but it unmistakably alleges that I was the recipient of "rubles." The clumsiness of this particular falsehood was transparent, inasmuch as I had only been in the USSR once up to that time, on behalf of the CIO fourteen years earlier, and nine years before Khrushchev came to power.

If the purported conversations with Gil bordered on the farcical, the rather urgent messages I began to receive from Winnie, asking me to visit, were quite serious. His wife, Edna, had recently been to see him and called to tell me that he didn't seem well. I broke away from my work to travel to the Terre Haute Federal Penitentiary in Indiana, where he was being held. I was familiar with the facility because Ben Davis had also been imprisoned there.

Anyone who had even a casual relationship with Winnie knew that he was always concerned about others, asking after their health, their families, their well-being. And he had a smile that could light up even a dim jail cell. But when I saw him he wasn't smiling and his own difficulties preoccupied him. He was suffering from persistent headaches, having difficulty with his vision, and was unsteady on his legs. His repeated visits to the prison's sick line were rewarded with aspirin tablets and the suggestion that he was malingering. He hadn't been examined by an outside doctor, but his condition was sufficiently serious that he needed to be seen by one immediately. I went to the warden to demand an outside physician, but he refused to commit himself. I told him, "Look, I'm not leaving this prison until you arrange to get a qualified doctor in here to examine Henry Winston." He finally agreed, and a physician from Indianapolis was brought in.

The doctor suspected that Winnie might have a growth on his brain, which frightened the Terre Haute warden sufficiently that he had Winnie transferred to the federal prison hospital at Springfield, Missouri. Back in New York, I received a call from Springfield informing me that the medical staff had diagnosed a tumor on the cerebellum, which required surgery. We launched a letter and telegram campaign to urge the Justice Department to allow Winnie to be brought to New York for the operation. After several weeks, James Bennett, the federal prisons director who liked to brag about his membership in the American Civil Liberties Union, finally consented. I flew to St. Louis to bring Winnie home.

In the warden's office at Springfield, I was required to sign a receipt for the prisoner, with an agreement to return him after surgery to serve the balance of his sentence. I was shocked by the marked

physical deterioration in Winnie's condition since I'd visited him in
Terre Haute a month earlier. He could barely walk and was brought
to us in a wheelchair. His headaches had become excruciating and
he could no longer see. I said, "Winnie, I've come to take you home."
He looked disturbed. "John," he asked, "am I that badly off that
they're letting me out?" I explained that I had just signed for his release on the proviso that he again surrender as soon as he had recovered. At the assurance that the authorities expected him to survive, his face lit up with the beautiful Winston smile and he said,
"Well, that's all right, then."

We flew to New York, in the company of a federal marshal, and
went directly to Montefiore Hospital in the Bronx. The government
stationed an armed guard at the door of Winnie's room. For what purpose, God only knows. He couldn't see, couldn't walk, could barely
function at all with the pain he was in. I called the authorities to raise
hell and, small comfort, they agreed to remove the guard. Fortunately, the tumor turned out to be benign. But because of the pressure it
had exerted on his nerves for several months, Winnie's sight was per-
manently gone—"I have lost my sight but not my vision," he would
say—and for a long time he could not walk without difficulty.

On the day that I brought Winnie to New York, my mother died.
She had suffered from angina for a number of years, and the condition progressively worsened with chest pains that were quite severe.
One of my cousins had married a doctor, Roland Grausman, who became mother's physician. Once a month he visited her at her apartment at Lexington and East Fifty-sixth Street for an examination.
(For the edification of the younger reader, there really was a time in
the twentieth century when it was common for doctors to make
house calls.) But when Marion was indicted under the Smith Act, the
doctor dropped mother as a patient. Maxine Woods, Marion's friend,
was another of his patients, and once, upon entering his office, she
heard him scream at his receptionist, "Get that Communist out of my
office!"

Mother's new and last doctor was Louis Miller, who had gone to jail
with Eddie Barsky for having served on the board of the Joint Anti-fascist Refugee Committee. Lou was very attentive to mother, though she
wasn't infirm and lived alone, quite content and able to care for herself. Jessica said that mother's apartment was a haven of quiet and rest
from the troubles of the world. She was eighty-four years old when she
died. As she wished, we had only a small family service with a few
friends that were closest to her—Louis and Dotty Burnham, Aurelia
and Arnold Johnson, a couple of others. From mother and my grandparents I had picked up the German language as a child. In fact my

French is better than my German, but my German accent is far less faulty than my French. Before our family and friends, I recited mother's favorite poem by Goethe, inexactly translated:

Over all the hill tops is rest
Over all the tree tops, you scarcely hear a whisper
The birds are sleeping in the woods
Just wait, you too will soon rest.

* * *

On a Monday morning in April 1960, I traveled to Albany to argue a case before the New York Court of Appeals. A week later, I was to argue Winnie's case—our attempt to stop the authorities from sending him back to jail—before the U.S. Court of Appeals. A few days earlier, I had come to an agreement with the U.S. attorney to send Winnie to the Maritime Hospital on Staten Island but the court had yet to approve of the agreement. But as I worked in the library of the New York Court of Appeals, a peculiar feeling developed in my chest. It wasn't terribly painful but I was becoming dizzy. "Abt," I thought to myself, "you are having a heart attack. And you have certainly chosen a strange place to have it." A moment later, my case was called. I went into the court, presented my arguments, felt much better, and returned by train to the city that evening. I actually forgot about the episode in the law library. Jessica said later that I seemed tired and didn't perform my usual dishwashing chores, but that otherwise I behaved quite typically. I maintained my normal routine until Friday, when we drove up to Kent with Arnold and Aurelia. April was usually the time of year when we opened the country house for the summer. Going through our regular tasks of preparing the house for occupation, I again had chest pains. Jessica called a local doctor, who arrived with an electrocardiogram. He said that indeed I was having a heart attack. We called Morris Pearlmutter, Eddie Barsky's associate, who demanded we immediately return to New York. Arnold drove me directly to Beth Israel, where Morris and Eddie met us. They confirmed my heart attack, and Pearlmutter was convinced that the real attack had occurred not in Kent, but in Albany four days earlier. I was only fifty-six years old but had obviously been under strain. Mother had just died. Louis Burnham had just died. Henry Winston was in great difficulty. And we were awaiting a Supreme Court ruling on the McCarran Act. The doctors prescribed a month's stay in the hospital and another month at home, and I wasn't about to argue with them.

The federal appeals panel agreed with the U.S. attorney that, rather than return Winnie to prison, he be sent to the Maritime Hospital on Staten Island. After two months, he could again walk but, for reasons that remain unfathomable to me, Winnie decided that rather than stay at the hospital, he would return to prison. The Party comrades faulted me for permitting this but Winnie was not a man to be denied once he had determined a course for himself. Certainly it was not my place to do so. He was reassigned to Danbury Prison in Connecticut, a fortunate turn of events in that I was able to visit him frequently from Kent. In Danbury, Winnie began to study braille and made good progress up to the time of his release. But when he was freed from prison, he threw all of his energies into Party work and never became sufficiently proficient to enable him to use braille. This was unfortunate for several reasons, not least that he was a frequent public speaker but could not make notes or read them, so was unable to time himself.

While Winnie was at Danbury, the Party mounted a campaign to secure amnesty. Appeals came as well from abroad, and even Fidel Castro, after the Bay of Pigs invasion, offered to release some CIA-trained mercenaries if President Kennedy would release Winnie. Finally, Kennedy did commute his sentence, on July 4, 1961. The U.S. attorney's office called to inform me of Kennedy's action, telling me that Winnie was being transferred back to Staten Island and that I could pick him up the next day. Gus Hall, Ben Davis, Irving Potash, and I were the welcoming party. We drove out to Staten Island to bring Winnie home to a big celebration at the Chelsea Hotel, where we'd also gotten him a room.

When Marcantonio and I first undertook the McCarran Act case, Marc shared his office with the firm of David Freedman and Abe Unger, both of whom had done legal work for the Party. Abe was extremely rigid and dogmatic, almost Talmudic; he could give you an argument on any question, and usually did. He and David had been partners for years, which included a mandatory daily lunch date. When I came to work with Marc, David began to organize things so that I'd be the one who dined with Abe. It was impossible to be with Abe for any amount of time without his starting a quarrel. Naturally, this lunch arrangement landed me in more arguments than I care to remember. Abe had recently been expelled from the Party, the result of several disputes over legal tactics in the Smith Act defense. This was in 1951, about the same time that Winnie, Gil, Gus, and Bob Thompson jumped bail. A few months later, Abe was reinstated to the Party.

Now it was ten years later, and Abe had again been ejected from

the Party over factional disagreements. In anticipation of a negative
ruling from the Supreme Court in the McCarran Act case, he was
loudly and of course antagonistically advocating that the Party dissolve. "We will reorganize again in Macy's window," he announced.
Anyway, on the day we drove out to Staten Island to pick up Winnie,
after embraces all around, we got into the car. Winnie's first question was, "So what's new?" I replied, "The situation is just as it was
when you left. Abe has been expelled."

* * *

Gus Hall was elected general secretary of the Party in 1959 at
the culmination of the internal struggle over policy. Gene Dennis and
Ben Davis were in failing health, Elizabeth Gurley Flynn was too old,
and the other logical candidates, Henry Winston and Gil Green, were
still in prison. So Gus became the consensus choice. In Kent one day,
I revealed to Arnold Johnson my own misgivings about Gus's ascension to power. My sense was that he was far too bureaucratic for a
post that, above all and especially at this time, required a keen ear
and respect for others' thoughts.

My prior experience with Gus, subsequently renewed a thousand
times, was that he was always open to consulting with me as long as
he was assured in advance that there would be a unanimity of views.
But if he thought I was likely to give him advice he considered unwelcome, he avoided dealing with me directly, preferring to dispatch
a subordinate. For example, a news story circulated for years following Gene's death that, at his grave site in Chicago, Gus made some
bloodcurdling statement, at the core of which was a reference to as-
sassinating all Catholic priests. (Years later, another colleague, Si
Gerson, discovered that the remarks were actually delivered in a
quite different context by some antipapal Frenchman who had no
connection whatsoever to the Communist movement.) On four separate occasions, Gus raised the question of bringing a lawsuit against
those who published this falsehood. But he never discussed it with
me, preferring to send Arnold instead. Each time, I told Arnold that,
in my opinion, a libel suit would be a mistake. Libel is an injury to a
person's reputation, so when you sue someone for libel, you put into
question that person's reputation. If Gus sued, undoubtedly the defendants—the publishers—would take his deposition before a trial
and would ask questions that Gus would refuse to answer. For example, why he had failed to surrender in the Smith Act case and
where he had gone and whom had he seen while evading arrest.
And, upon his refusal to answer, the judge would simply dismiss the

suit. Thus, the only thing a suit would accomplish would be further publicity for the original libel. I patiently explained this to Arnold, who then presumably patiently explained it to Gus. A period of time would lapse and then Arnold would again be asked to visit me about the same matter.

I had a similar experience in the aftermath of President Kennedy's assassination. It had come to light somehow that over a year before the assassination, Lee Harvey Oswald, the accused killer, sent a letter to the Party inquiring about joining. The Party received such inquiries as a regular occurrence and certainly there was nothing out of the ordinary about it. On behalf of the Warren Commission, hundreds of federal agents were brought in to investigate the assassination. One day an FBI agent came to my office to ask what the Party knew about Oswald. The fact is that it knew nothing at all and wasn't even aware of Oswald's letter. I told Arnold that the chief counsel of the Warren Commission had asked me to produce Gus for a brief appearance to answer the commission's questions. Gus refused to cooperate. Whenever the FBI (or a congressional committee or any other official body) was conducting a repressive inquisition, I had of course advocated noncooperation as a matter of principle. But this was quite another matter, one that had nothing to do with the Party actually. In any case, Gus stated his adamant refusal to Arnold but never to me. I tried to prevail upon Arnold to persuade Gus to appear as any innocent and honest person would, and Gus and I went back and forth on the matter several times without any personal contact. In all my years as the Party's general counsel, I tried to get Communist leaders to behave like any normal people would, rather than like conspirators without a conspiracy.

In the more than thirty years I served as attorney for the Party, I never sought private clients, although I often could have used the money. Consequently, I never had any other clients. Ordinarily, this would not have been a problem. But money matters have frequently been a source of difficulties in my relations with the Party. Every Party treasurer I've known has thought it his personal and political duty to avoid payment of bills for as long as possible, and often even longer. And given the way the Party functions, its very structure, no treasurer operates except at the express will and behest of the general secretary. When we were first hired by the Party in 1951, it was agreed that Marcantonio would be paid $10,000 a year and I would receive $7,500. For over a year, we returned every Thursday evening from the SACB hearings in Washington and I spent the better part of each Friday at the Party office trying to collect on what was due Marc and me. Apart from the fact that I had very real financial needs, it was embarrassing to return empty-handed to Marc week after week. It was a personal humiliation and it severely harmed the Party's relationship with him. Finally, I went to Winnie, then the organizational secretary, who agreed with me and finally corrected the situation.

In the late fifties, the Party's treasurer was Sid Stein, a New Yorker who was allied with John Gates during the internal struggles of those days. An extremely officious man, Sid was also at political odds with Gene Dennis, the lone exception to the rule about the treasurer answering only to the Party general secretary. Marc had died some years before, but the same situation prevailed: Joe Forer and I had gone several months without being paid. I complained to Gene and he asked what I'd been living on during these months. I explained that when I was twenty-one years old, two of my well-to-do uncles took out a life insurance policy for $15,000 in my name, on which I'd been paying premiums all these years. Now, I was borrowing on my life insurance. Gene was absolutely horrified that I should be reduced to this. (My own skewed reaction to Gene's response at the time was mild surprise at such a bourgeois attitude on his part.) He said that he and Elizabeth Flynn would raise the money. First, however, he wanted a meeting with Sid, Joe Forer, and myself. So Joe came up to New York at the appointed time and we appeared in Gene's office. Sid never showed, sending word that he had another meeting, an obvious pretext and an extension of the factional struggle.

While I was in the hospital recuperating from my heart attack in 1960, I received a very warm get-well message from the political bureau, the Party's day-to-day top leadership, expressing many fine sentiments. At the time, the Party owed me eight thousand dollars in back pay, which I had been unable to collect. When I returned home for a month of rest, Gus came to see me on an unrelated matter. I took advantage of the opportunity to thank him for the nice get-well message but said that I would really appreciate being paid my eight thousand dollars. As usual, Gus was quick to agree: "Oh, don't worry, John," he assured me, "I'll get it to you immediately." And, also as usual, nothing happened, no money was forthcoming. After several weeks, I wrote a letter to Gus, expressing my unhappiness. I not only needed the money, I said, but the situation was humiliating, requiring me to make repeated demands. I indicated that apparently the Party put no real value on my services, that therefore I would resign. I would argue the impending McCarran Act case before the Supreme Court, but then the Party would have to find another attorney. When the letter arrived at Party headquarters, Gus was out of town. Ben

Davis received it and came to me immediately. He told me that this was the first he had ever heard of the situation and urged me to do nothing further until he had a chance to raise the matter with Gus. I don't know what was said but soon thereafter Gus took me to lunch to tell me I would have my money in a day or two, and I did. When I was appealing another Party case, I wrote the brief, had it printed, and sent the printer's receipt along with my own monthly bill to Phil Bart, yet another treasurer of the organization. Bart, in keeping with the deadbeat tradition, promptly forgot to reimburse me. After repeated billings and several conversations, I finally called Phil and told him, "Look, If I don't get reimbursed, I just won't argue the case. You can get another lawyer." It happens he was meeting with Gus at the very moment I issued my threat and could convey my sentiments on the spot. Reimbursement was soon forthcoming.

Working conditions for the Communist party general counsel were probably unique to the American Bar. Prior to this job, when I was in private practice, working for the government, the labor movement, the Progressive Party, I could dictate every document and correct drafts as needed. I always had a legal secretary and never learned to touch-type, being always a two-finger man. Now I had no secretary, no clerk, no research help, no law library. Without a secretary, and having lost a facility to compose on the typewriter, I could no longer write with creativity. I had to learn again, first scribbling out everything in longhand, then typing. To ask the Party to subsidize a secretary—who undoubtedly would have had a salary higher than mine—was ludicrous to contemplate. I also had no research assistant, and this period of course predated the personal computer by decades. I had access to the library of the New York County Lawyers' Association, only walking distance from my office, so I did all my own research as well. The circumstances were primitive by standards of the modern New York attorney perhaps, but they were gratifying, in their own strange way. While I never made much money, neither Jessica nor I were given to extravagances. In my entire life, I cannot remember having a craving for anything that I couldn't satisfy for lack of money. Aside from my politics, my tastes in life run to the traditional, modest, and conservative. Jessica was much the same. I satisfied all of her material wants with the occasional purchase of an ounce of Chanel No. 5. Our only serious concern was being able to provide for David after our deaths. His psychiatric care, schooling and hospitalization, and upkeep when he lived on his own were our only major expenses. Jessica earned Party-scale, subsistence wages, most of which went to pay a housekeeper, thereby enabling Jessica to spend all of her spare time at work. I knew mother was financially self-sufficient and that she periodically helped Marion. When mother died, I discovered that she had more money than I'd imagined. After paying the taxes on the estate and leaving a bequest to Johnny B., I inherited the remainder. This allowed me to continue working for the Party without worrying any longer about its ability or willingness to pay me.

* * *

In the midst of all the other litigation, I had a host of other, "minor" cases to deal with. Among these was a suit I brought on behalf of the Party against New York State. The case grew out of the Communist Control Act, passed by Congress as a companion piece to the McCarran Act. This law also pictured the Party as a conspiracy, not a legitimate political organization; from this, the state of New York got into the act by refusing to pay unemployment compensation to workers who left the Party's employ, saying, in effect, that the CPUSA was not a bona fide employer.

In 1960, the New York Court of Appeals held, in a five-to-two vote, that the Communist Control Act was constitutional and did indeed deny the Party's right to be an employer. I filed what is called a petition for certiorari, in which one asks the Supreme Court to review an appeals court decision. It takes four of the nine Supreme Court Justices to grant certiorari, i.e., agreement to review the lower court's stand. The Court can always, and usually does, deny a petition, thereby letting stand the lower court decision. In this manner, the Supreme Court sets its own docket.

The Court granted our petition, so I had two cases—the SACB appeal and the New York unemployment insurance case—pending before the Supreme Court. Then I acquired a third such case, all in the 1960–61 session of the Supreme Court. This third case was the defense of John Noto, a Party member in Buffalo who had been convicted under the membership clause of the Smith Act.

Gene Dennis and his co-defendants, except for Gil and Winnie, had served their sentences under the conspiracy section of the Smith Act but were still under indictment under the membership section. In fact, they were still under what is called "bail limits" and couldn't leave Manhattan, if that is where they lived, for Brooklyn without receiving permission from the U.S. attorney. One of my minor responsibilities, and a real pain in the neck when one considers that these were nine full-time organizers, was to secure consent whenever one of my clients wanted to go to another borough or another city. Some of the assistant U.S. attorneys were reasonable and decent and granted permission as a matter of course. Others would play games with me, refusing to come to the phone or making themselves unavailable for several days at a time. This went on for several years until I finally managed to have the courts dismiss the membership indictments in the midsixties.

John Noto was represented at trial by a local Buffalo ACLU attorney. Upon his conviction, the ACLU argued the appeal before the U.S. Court of Appeals and again lost. I was dissatisfied with the ACLU's handling of the appeal and undertook to take it myself to the Supreme Court. Meantime, Junius Scales was retried and again convicted, and the Supreme Court had granted certiorari, with my old friend Telford Taylor arguing Scales's appeal. On October 12, 1959, the opening day of its new term, the Court agreed to hear arguments for both the Scales and Noto cases on February 23. But on February 5, it agreed to review my SACB appeal, challenging the registration provisions of the McCarran Act. Because some constitutional and statutory issues of the three cases were interrelated, the Court consolidated them with the intention of hearing arguments and deciding them together. The Court set October 10, 1960, for argument. I would argue the unemployment insurance case in the spring.

I joined Tel Taylor in attacking the membership clause of the Smith Act as violating the First and Fifth amendments of the Constitution; but I also argued on behalf of Noto that, by the standards set in the *Yates* decision, the prosecution's evidence was "devoid of any statement by petitioner, or by anyone in his presence, advocating violent action, present or future, for the overthrow of the Government." The evidence was obviously inadequate to demonstrate that the Party advocated the forceful overthrow of the government or that Noto had any knowledge of its doing so. I pointed to the various cases the Justice Department had dropped in an oblique admission of its inability to meet the test the Supreme Court had established in *Yates*.

One could ponder the peculiarities of a Supreme Court that could uphold Junius Scales's conviction and overturn John Noto's under the membership clause of the Smith Act, with Justice Harlan writing the majority opinions in both cases. Harlan held in both cases that the membership clause of the Smith Act did not violate the First or Fifth amendments. But in *Noto*, he said, the government failed to prove that the Party incited the overthrow of the government by violence or did much more than teach an abstract doctrine. In his dissent in the Scales case, Justice Black pointed out that the contradictory decisions in the two cases made the liberty of a human being dependent on the inventiveness of the government's paid informers—all of the witnesses in the two cases were professional stool pigeons—and the gullibility of the juries. As a result of the *Noto* decision and the

How about "INVASION" you commie.

Court's reaffirmation of the *Yates* test of incitement to violence, all other pending membership indictments—including those against Gene Dennis and his ten co-defendants—were eventually dismissed by the government.

After the Soviet intervention in Hungary in 1956 and the subsequent internal struggle in the Party, Junius became disaffected and quietly severed his membership. Had he been less than principled, he might have struck a deal with the Justice Department and escaped prosecution. John, on the other hand, remained a Party member in good standing and was proud of it. It was a bizarre twist—perhaps owing to the fact that Junius was the only Smith Act defendant in the South, where notions of "justice" had a history of some severity—that he was given six years, the longest sentence of a Communist under the act. (The four leaders who jumped bail had longer sentences only because of the additional time for contempt of court.) A major clemency campaign for Junius was mounted by civil libertarians like Archibald MacLeish and Eleanor Roosevelt. Fifteen months later, at the urging of Attorney General Robert Kennedy, President Kennedy commuted Junius's sentence to time served, and he was home for Christmas 1962.

At a New York reception for him early in the new year, attended primarily by "exes"—former Party members—Jessica and I were chatting with friends over cocktails when a little old man whom neither of us recognized came up to effusively congratulate Jessica on her most recent book. It took some moments before we realized it was Earl Browder. The last time I'd seen Earl was ten years earlier, when he asked to meet with Marcantonio and me. He came to Marc's office to tell us that two Justice Department prosecutors visited him to ascertain his attitude should they subpoena him in the SACB hearings as a witness against the Party. As he later wrote in a letter to a friend, "I told them at some length that I would do everything possible to destroy their case, root and branch, that I would be a 'hostile witness' in the fullest sense." The prosecutors left in disappointment: "They had evidently been misled by reading the *Daily Worker*," to whom Browder was anathema. Fearing that he might be subpoenaed anyway, he came to us to tell us of the incident. As Earl described our meeting, "Marcantonio . . . was generally cordial. Abt was stiffly correct and courteous as he would be to any enemy."

* * *

On the same day it decided the *Scales* and *Noto* cases, the Supreme Court ruled against us in the McCarran Act case by a five-to-four decision. Justice Frankfurter wrote the 115-page majority opinion, which, in my judgment, was the single most dishonest opinion ever issued by the Court, with the exception of the Dred Scott decision upholding slavery a century earlier. Our appeal argued that the purpose of the McCarran Act was not to secure the Party's registration as a Communist action organization but to make it impossible for the Party to register. By imposing astronomical criminal penalties, its effect was to outlaw the Party. Looking at the Act as a whole and with all of its provisions, one couldn't avoid such a conclusion.

Frankfurter said in essence, no, you can't do that, you can't look at the act as a whole, the only issue before the Court was whether the act of registration was constitutional. Frankfurter argued that Congress "rejected the approach of outlawing the Party by name and accepted instead a statutory program regulating not enumerated organizations but designated activities." Thus, "the Act is not a bill of attainder." Frankfurter also quoted approvingly the district court's opinion that in designating Communist action organizations, Congress did not intend to restrict this to those "subject to enforceable demands" of the USSR. Rather, an "organization or a person may be substantially under the direction or domination of another person or organization by voluntary compliance as well as through compulsion. This is especially true if voluntary compliance is simultaneous in time with the direction and is undeviating over a period of time and under variations of direction." Such a description could of course as easily fit, say, the Anti-defamation League or most other Zionist organizations and their relations with Israel.

Frankfurter said that no other provisions of the act might ever be invoked, that there might not be an occasion for the Court to ever consider them. For example, Frankfurter contended, the act says that once the registration order becomes final, Party members can't apply for or use passports. But it remained a question whether any Party member would want to travel. If a member tried to use a passport and was indicted for doing so, there would be time enough for the Court to consider the constitutionality of the passport provision of the act. Similarly, with regard to the provision requiring the Party to label all of its mail as "issued by a Communist action organization," Frankfurter asserted that we couldn't project into the future, that we didn't know if the Party would ever use the mails again, and that if it did, it might well decide to label the mails according to the law. Only if the Party used the mails, failed to label it as prescribed by the act, and was indicted for this failure could the Court consider the constitutionality of the mail-labeling provision. And so on, with each separate provision of the McCarran Act.

In our brief, we argued that requiring the Party to register, which would entail signatures by the Party's officers, subjected the officers to self-incrimination, a violation of the Fifth Amendment. Frankfurter remained consistently cute: he replied that maybe the officers would register and never claim Fifth Amendment protection. Anyone can waive a privilege as well as claim it. There would still be time enough to consider the question of self-incrimination should the Party leaders fail to register and be indicted. Frankfurter said it was premature to consider this question, despite the fact that the act entailed a five-year prison sentence for each day the officers failed to register. Thus, the Party could challenge the constitutionality of the act's provisions only by subjecting its officers and members to indictment and unprecedented punitive criminal penalties.

The Court's majority held that the single question it needed to consider was whether the act of registration was in itself unconstitutional, whether requiring the Party to register with the names of all of its members violated the First Amendment. Frankfurter held that given the findings of Congress regarding the character of the Party, the requirement of registration did not violate the Constitution. It was not for the Court to judge the findings of Congress, but to accept them.

Of the four dissenting justices, Chief Justice Earl Warren held that he needn't address the constitutional arguments because the SACB had committed a host of errors outside the purview of the Constitution, including its failure to provide sufficient evidence on which to conclude that the Party was a Communist action organization, as defined by the act. Douglas and Brennan sided with Warren. Only Justice Black directly challenged the McCarran Act as a virulent abridgement of the First Amendment and as a virtual bill of attainder. He pointed out the obvious: the government's proposition that compelling the Party to register was little different than compelling, say, corporations to register as such, was belied by the fact that among all those institutions required to register in some way with the government, only the Party was "branded as being engaged in an evil undertaking bent on destroying this nation." Pointing to both the employment and the passport provisions of the McCarran Act, Black wrote that the law "makes it extremely difficult for a member of the Communist Party to live in this country and, at the same time, makes it a crime for him to try to get a passport to get out."

Justice Black eloquently concluded, "When the practice of outlawing parties and various public groups begins, no one can say where it will end. In most countries such a practice once begun ends with a one-party government. There is something of a tragic irony in the

fact that this Act, expressly designed to protect the Nation from becoming a 'totalitarian dictatorship' with 'a single political party,' has
adopted to achieve its laudable purpose the policy of outlawing a party—a policy indispensable to totalitarian dictatorships."

* * *

We needed to buy some time to plan a legal strategy. First, we
filed a petition with the Court for a rehearing. The petition went to
the justice who wrote the majority opinion, in this case, Frankfurter.
We assumed correctly that he wouldn't grant us a rehearing. Instead,
he referred our petition to the full Court, which was then in recess
until October. This meant that the decision could not become final
for several months.

Meantime, the Party leadership was debating three possible cours-
es of action, in something of a Smith Act redux, ten years later. Some
argued that the Party had reached the end, that the McCarran Act
was a decision of the government to outlaw the organization, that
there was nothing to do but again go underground. A second view
was that the Party should dissolve itself, to await a better day when it
might be reorganized in full legality. Both of these views, in my opinion—it hadn't changed from the earlier debate in 1950—amounted to
much the same thing, an avoidance of the struggle for the Party's legality. The third view was to continue functioning even at the risk of
incurring awesome criminal penalties, because the only way we
could fight and test the constitutionality of this Draconian law was
by violating it. My own strong conviction was that this was the only
viable option, realizing that it was not my own head—at least for the
moment—on the proverbial chopping block. Going underground
would simply confirm the view, held by even some natural and potential allies, of the Party as a conspiracy. But to dissolve the Party
would be no less than a surrender. The Party had a responsibility not
only to itself but to the American people as a whole to struggle for its
constitutional rights; in the process of vindicating the rights of the
Party, it would uphold the constitutional rights of the whole people.
This view prevailed in the end. But having arrived at the decision,
we still faced the immediate tactical question of contesting the Mc-
Carran Act provision by provision.

The first problem we would confront was an indictment of the Party for failing to register. We knew the primary defense against the indictment would be the Fifth Amendment privilege against self-incrimination to be invoked by the officers. But they themselves
couldn't come forward to assert the privilege, because by doing so

they'd identify themselves as officers, thereby surrendering the privilege in the very act of claiming it. We discovered the essential principles of catch-22, years before Joseph Heller revealed them to the reading public. Joe Forer and I concluded that we would have to file an anonymous claim of privilege. Some of our legal colleagues were shocked by our proposal, insisting that there was no such thing as an anonymous claim of privilege, that to claim a privilege, some human being has to do so. Ordinarily this was true, but ours was a most unusual, even unique, case that required an extraordinary response. We convened a meeting of perhaps a dozen or so Party lawyers from around the country to discuss the matter. Any gathering of attorneys is guaranteed not to reach unanimity, and in this meeting some of our colleagues scoffed at our idea of an anonymous claim of privilege.

In preparing the anonymous claim of privilege, we discovered to our surprise that the Party had a seal, like a corporate seal, in the form of a rubber stamp. So we prepared the anonymous claim of privilege with the indentation of the seal, rather than with signatures, stating that we were doing so because the Party's officers, were they to sign, would be relinquishing their privilege in the very act of asserting it. As anticipated, the first attempt to enforce the McCarran Act came in the form of an indictment of the Party for its refusal to register. The indictment was issued on December 1, 1961, twelve days after the registration order had become final. As indicated earlier, the penalty for refusal to register—you can't jail an organization, just its members—was $10,000 a day for each day of failure to register. So the indictment claimed a penalty, as of that time, of $120,000. Motions and other preliminary proceedings delayed the actual trial for a year, until December 1962.

Mundane in most every other respect, the trial was historic in that it was the first time in the history of the United States that a political party and its officers were put on trial for being so. In announcing the indictments, Attorney General Robert Kennedy had been less than forthright, contending that registration was a routine matter, that public relations firms and Wall Street law firms registered as a matter of course under the Foreign Agents Registration Act when representing foreign governments. Perhaps Bobby Kennedy simply hadn't read the act and understood the criminal penalties involved, that the indictment imposed $120,000 in fines on the Party for its first twelve days of refusal to register, that Ben Davis and Gus Hall faced thirty years in prison and $60,000 fines each for their first six days of refusal to register.

In seventeenth-century Salem, they tortured men and women in an attempt to make them confess that they were witches. If the victim refused to confess, he or she was put to death for refusing. If the defendant confessed, he or she was put to death as a self-confessed witch. Three centuries later, we had refined things. But essentially the McCarran and Smith Acts confronted people with the same kind of Hobson's choice that the Salem witch trials allowed. (Meantime, in Alabama and Mississippi, the state governments used the McCarran Act pattern to attack the NAACP, requiring that organization to register with the states and to supply a list of its members. Clearly the consequences for known NAACP members in the Deep South where, for obvious reasons, it operated semi-clandestinely in the fifties, would be no less disastrous than for Communists under the McCarran Act.)

The trial was largely pro forma, the government's entire case being that the law required the Party to register and the Party had failed to do so. My own closing argument couldn't have taken more than five minutes. I asked the jury to return a verdict of not guilty and wished them all a merry Christmas. To no one's surprise, they returned a guilty verdict. We promptly appealed. While the appeal was pending, the attorney general issued regulations providing for a registration form, saying that the registration should be signed by the Party's officers but, in lieu of that, could be signed by an attorney or another agent of the officers. The Court of Appeals seized on these new regulations to reverse the Party's conviction. The court held that requiring the officers themselves to sign the registration statement would violate their privilege against self-incrimination. But the judges suggested that perhaps an attorney or someone else would be willing to sign the registration document on behalf of the Party's officers. The court remanded the case for a new trial, if the government wished to prove that there was such an agent willing to sign. The government appealed the decision to the Supreme Court, which declined to review it. Consequently, the government brought the case to trial for a second time two years later.

* * *

In the meantime, I went before the Supreme Court in an entirely different matter, a suit for $1 million on behalf of Henry Winston. We charged that he was blinded as a result of negligence on the part of the prison authorities in not providing him with proper and timely treatment.

The case was tried under the Federal Tort Claims Act, which requires a bit of explanation. A tort is a wrongful act. It can be willful or the result of negligence. The law has always been that a sovereign, such as the United States, cannot be sued without its consent. As a result of legal theory, the government has passed laws that grant its consent to specified kinds of tort suits. If the suit falls within one of these specified classes, the government is liable for its actions. The Federal Tort Claims Act waives immunity of the United States for suit in all but thirteen specified classes of torts. Not included among these thirteen categories is the negligent treatment of federal prisoners. So, on the face of the statute, it appeared that the United States was liable for the negligence of its prison officers. However, a long series of cases in the lower federal courts held that the government was not liable for negligent injuries to prisoners. The basis of these decisions was the contention that Congress couldn't have intended not to exclude such cases and to make the government liable in such cases would undermine prison discipline and would inject the courts into an unintended supervision of the prisons.

These decisions were typical of the courts' attitudes toward prisons during that period. In the 1970s, an important prison reform movement—with the cases of the Attica Brothers, the San Quentin Six, the Soledad Brothers, and with Angela Davis and the ACLU Prison Project and other public advocates—developed a new consciousness. In the Winston case a decade earlier, I encountered the attitude that this was an impossible intrusion into the authority of prison officials to run their own institutions. This whole theory of law has been swept aside in recent years, and a salutary thing it is. Judges today hand down decisions limiting the maximum number of prisoners that can be kept in one cell and proscribing other prison conditions where it is proved that prisoners are kept in inhumane conditions.

But in 1960, this was far from the case, and I knew to expect trouble. We alleged that in 1959, Winnie began to experience headaches, dizziness, and difficulty with his vision and that the prison doctor diagnosed his case as borderline hypertension and prescribed a regimen to lose weight. As the symptoms progressively worsened, Winnie had difficulty standing up and began to experience falls and temporary losses of vision. Despite the obvious deterioration in his condition, Winnie received no further medical attention except for the doctor's giving him Dramamine, which was of no help. Until I visited him in January 1960, our complaint charged, both the warden and prison doctor were negligent in not having him examined by competent physicians.

The government moved to dismiss the case on grounds that there was no liability for prison negligence under the Federal Tort Claims

Act. The district court judge agreed and threw out our suit. We appealed to the Court of Appeals. The three-judge panel was comprised of particularly conservative judges, including Irving Kaufman, who presided over the trial of Ethel and Julius Rosenberg. (The Rosenbergs, of whose innocence I have no doubts, were defended by a friend of mine, Emmanuel Bloch. Because of the public paranoia, Manny was in an impossible position, forced to operate in isolation. Subjected to every conceivable pressure, he had nobody to turn to for help. From time to time in the course of the appeals process, Manny consulted with me. The Party took no public position in support of the Rosenbergs for fear of harming them, meanwhile informally encouraging the widest movement of defense. Because of my own notoriety and that of my clients, my meetings with Manny took place out of sight and earshot of the authorities. But I had become quite familiar with Judge Kaufman's arrogance, contempt, and biases.) To my surprise, the judges voted two to one, Kaufman dissenting, in our favor. Then, Judge Kaufman moved that all nine judges of the Court of Appeals hear the case. The nine also ruled for us, five to four, at which point the government appealed the decision to the Supreme Court.

In my brief, I set out the results of an exhaustive study of the legislative history of the Federal Tort Claims Act. This included hearings conducted by congressional committees, debates on the floor of Congress, and other indicia of what Congress intended in the act. This demonstrated that Congress did not intend to exclude cases of negligence toward federal prisoners from the scope of the act. I showed that in those states where statutes permitted negligence suits against prison officials, there was no evidence that prison discipline was undermined or that problems arose with respect to the supervisory discretion of prison officials. With Chief Justice Warren writing the opinion, the Court was unanimous in upholding our right to sue.

Next we had to prove our case. This could only be done through the testimony of competent doctors who, based on an examination of prison and hospital records, would say that had the prison warden and doctor not been negligent, Winnie's condition would have been diagnosed much earlier and that, as a result, he would not have lost his sight. I went to the surgeon at Montefiore Hospital whom Eddie Barsky had recommended and who had operated on Winnie. He was obviously a skilled surgeon, but just as obviously a callous human being. He refused to have anything to do with the case. Despite my best efforts to shame him into testifying, he turned a deaf ear. Today malpractice cases are commonplace, with verdicts often so enormous that insurance rates for doctors have soared. But in the early sixties, it was still considered a breach of professional courtesy for one doctor to testify against another. A colleague of mine who specialized in malpractice cases took me to meet a New York University Hospital neurosurgeon, in hopes that he could be persuaded to testify. But he too turned us down flatly. We could find no doctors to testify for us, and without a single doctor, our case was hopeless. We were compelled to drop it. Consequently, our suit and Supreme Court decision established an important precedent for other prisoners in the future but, in the end, was of no real value to Winnie.

Not long after this I had another unsolicited and unwanted moment in the sun. When Andy Warhol made his famous pronouncement that everybody eventually gets to be "famous for fifteen minutes" in this media-conscious society, he was obviously thinking of people of his own generation. Having lived twice as long as most of the Warhol group, I was given thirty minutes of notorious fame. The first "fifteen minutes" came when Col. Rudolph Abel of the KGB asked for my help. My second such "opportunity" came on November 22, 1963.

It was a Friday afternoon and I'd just returned to the office from a lunch break devoted to purchasing a hi-fi record player as a birthday gift for Jessica. The elevator operator in my building informed me that President Kennedy had just been assassinated. I left the office early, for Jessica and I were, as usual, driving up to Kent for the weekend. We heard on the car radio that the alleged assassin, Lee Harvey Oswald, was under arrest. The radio reported on Oswald's supposed left-wing sympathies and on his sojourn in the Soviet Union. The speed of this accumulation of background information was surprising, even given the nature of the crime and the presumption that the Dallas police, FBI, and Secret Service would leave no resources untapped to find the president's murderer. It occurred to me that they might try to tie the Party to the assassination.

Saturday mornings in Kent were usually lazy, relaxing periods. But not this time. The phone rang early. It was CBS-TV telling me that while Oswald was being transferred within the jail, he shouted to news reporters, "Get hold of Abt to be my lawyer!" The guy from CBS wanted to know if I'd represent Oswald. I told him that I'd have to be asked by the defendant, not by a television reporter. Also, I said that I had an extremely busy trial schedule right then and didn't know if I could manage a case of this magnitude and that I'd have to consider it. CBS, of course, was only the first caller. The phone rang constantly with calls of the same nature, as well as friends who wanted to know my thinking. A number of news organizations wanted to interview me, a prospect that didn't interest me in the least. Luckily, October Hill was far off the beaten track and difficult to locate without having been there previously. On Sunday morning I learned that several television crews had been to the village trying to find me. When I drove into town to pick up my Sunday *Times,* the owner of the newspaper store greeted me with, "Ah, here comes our TV star!" Back up at the house was a message waiting for me from Vin Hallinan in San Francisco, asking in on the case and volunteering to represent Oswald. Later that day, of course, Jack Ruby shot and killed Oswald in the jail, and I no longer had a potential client to represent.

When Jessica and I returned to New York on Sunday evening, we found that television crews and news reporters had surrounded our apartment building the entire weekend. A few days later, Arnold Johnson told me that the Party had received a letter from Oswald some months earlier, asking for information about how to join, and that Arnold had sent a reply of no consequence, enclosing some promotional brochures. I felt that there was still a possibility that the FBI might want to, at least through innuendo, imply a Party connection to the assassination, and I urged Arnold and Gus to inform the FBI about the letter from Oswald. When the president is shot and you have some piece of information that conceivably could be of some relevance, you don't withhold the information; if you're innocent, you act as any innocent person would. It took some argument to convince others for whom the FBI was pure anathema. But we never again heard from the FBI on the matter.

When Lyndon Johnson appointed Earl Warren to head up the official commission to investigate the assassination, Warren asked J. Lee Rankin to serve as counsel. Rankin had been solicitor general, and we had crossed swords in arguments before the Supreme Court. At one point, Rankin asked Arnold Johnson to appear before the Warren Commission and I accompanied him. We had little to say, for our small tale was barely worth the telling. The Party hardly enjoyed a beneficent relationship with the federal government, and we expected little charity this time around. But it quickly became obvious that neither the FBI nor the Warren Commission were interested in digging into the case, to really discover if there was a conspiracy. They certainly weren't interested in trying to show that the Communists were a party to the matter. We were pleased with this, of course, but it seemed somewhat unusual, given the unrelenting hostility federal agencies had heretofore shown to the Party. They were quite content to let it rest as they had started out: Oswald was alone responsible, an unfathomable lone assassin. Dozens of reputable journalists and investigators have sifted through the evidence and debunked this official "truth." And every public opinion poll taken then and since indicate that most people were not so accepting as the Warren Commission of the official findings.

* * *

The Winston torts claim and the Oswald episode were diversions from what was, for Joe Forer and me, an intense period of a wide variety of McCarran Act cases. Gus Hall and Ben Davis were indicted, as officers, for failing to register on behalf of the Party. Then, acting under the passport provision of the act, the State Department canceled the passports of Elizabeth Flynn and Herbert Aptheker.

While we prepared arguments in the passport case, Eslanda Robeson wrote to me and Ben Davis, concerned about her husband, Paul's, principled refusal to sign a noncommunist affidavit in applying for a passport. Paul's career as an actor and concert artist inside the United States had long been destroyed. On top of the Hollywood and television blacklists, the major concert halls and the recording studios had banned this great baritone from performing. He was only able to sing, and to make a living, beyond our borders. In the late fifties he lived in Europe. Without a passport, his career would be finished. But Paul was a man of great integrity and would not sign a noncommunist affidavit. He felt that this was matter of principle particularly now, when so many of his Communist friends were operating under considerable difficulties. Ben and I wrote to him "unanimously and emphatically" recommending he sign the affidavit. There would be no legal consequences for him; the affidavit asked him to swear he had not been a Party member for the past year and, whatever government informers might be dredged up to testify otherwise, he had been publicly living abroad for the past four years. Paul had given his life and career for the cause of peace, human rights, and social emancipation, we wrote. "Paul's strong right arm is still needed for a host of battles," we told him and Essie, "but the second round of the passport fight is not one of them." With Ben's and my assurances, Paul agreed to sign the affidavit, and he and Essie were promptly issued passports and returned abroad.

We argued the McCarran Act passport case before a three-judge court in the District of Columbia. We emphasized that the act was outdated, because Congress found that the world communist movement was a monolithic organization under the absolute control and domination of the USSR. But the act was passed in 1950, and it had by this time become obvious that that finding was wildly fallacious. The examples of Yugoslavia, China, and Albania clearly demonstrated that a Communist party could be not only independent of but also at odds with the Soviet party. There was clearly debate and discussion and dissent within the world communist movement, but one of the judges allowed as how "the Communist leopard could *never* change its spots." The panel as a whole upheld the cancellation of Elizabeth's and Herbert's passports. But in 1964, in an opinion written by newly appointed Justice Arthur Goldberg—who had generally joined the Warren-Black-Brennan-Douglas majority—the Supreme Court held that the passport provision of the act was unconstitutional. The ruling said that since the foundation for denying the passports was an assumption by Congress that any Communist who traveled abroad would endanger the national security, this presumption of disloyalty violated due process.

Meantime, beginning in 1961 when the Court upheld the constitutionality of the act per se, the attorney general had instituted a series of over twenty prosecutions of Communists under the membership provision. The hearings were little more than a catechism. The same informers appeared, repeated their testimony from earlier appearances; the board reached its foreordained conclusions and ordered the member to register.

The case of Dorothy Healey was typical. Dorothy was head of the Party in Southern California and had earlier been convicted and sentenced under the Smith Act. As one of Oleta Yates's thirteen co-defendants, her conviction was overturned by the *Yates* decision. In November 1962, the SACB sent three of its members and a battery of Justice Department lawyers to Los Angeles to conduct a hearing to ascertain whether Dorothy was a Party member and should be ordered to register as such. Dorothy was a public figure in California, widely quoted and willing to talk about herself and her membership even before the proverbial drop of a hat. But she refused to admit her Party membership before the SACB. This was hardly a coy gambit on her part, but rather a refusal to submit to a proceeding in which the verdict anticipated the trial. As Bertrand Russell wrote at the time:

When we consider the McCarran Act and the entire legislation of repression which has been enacted in the United States, we must consider it in the context of a whole range of activity. Paid informers, investigating committees, operating in conjunction with a slanderous press, subversive lists, a secret political police, loyalty oaths—all of these—have been part of an attempt to reduce the American people to a condition of servility and of hysterical fanaticism with respect to independence of thought. Professor H.H. Wilson has referred to this climate and this pattern of behavior and has called it the development of "a concentration camp for the mind."

In my opening statement as Dorothy's counsel at the hearing, I referred to her arrest and conviction under the Smith Act, for which she was held on $100,000 bail, spent four months in prison awaiting trial until her bail was reduced, then tried, convicted, and spent another month in prison until the Court of Appeals released her on bail. In *Yates*, the Supreme Court held that the government failed to prove that the Party or Healey had engaged in any criminal conspiracy. The Court, I argued,

> sent the case back for retrial, to give the government another bite at the cherry, to permit them to prove what they had failed to prove in the original trial, and six months later the United States Attorney for this district walked into the courtroom and moved to dismiss the indictment on the grounds, as he said, that the evidence in the Government's possession was insufficient to meet the standard of proof which the Supreme Court had laid down in the Yates case. And what have we then today? A proceeding by the Attorney General to compel Mrs. Healey to confess to what the United States Attorney stated in open court, that the Government was unable to prove against her.

Dorothy herself testified that "no Communist can register under the McCarran Act because the very act of registration would be an act of perjury, because the McCarran Act has a built-in verdict, stating that Communists are guilty of being foreign agents, are guilty of espionage, subversion, and treason and so forth. We are not guilty of these things.... We cannot and will not register under this law because to do so would be to violate not only our rights but the rights of all Americans ... to free association."

Like the others, Dorothy was ordered to register. We took all of these cases—Betty Gannett, Arnold Johnson, Mickey Lima, William Patterson, Louis Weinstock, Florence and Sam Kushner, Miriam Friedlander, Bill Albertson, Roscoe Proctor, and a dozen others—on appeal. The Department of Justice agreed to consolidate all of them into one case, using the orders against Albertson and Proctor as the test in the appeals process. Bill Albertson was the organization secretary of the New York district, the Party's largest component; Roscoe

Proctor was a leader in Northern California. Both were elected members of the Central Committee, the Party's highest leadership body. The Court of Appeals upheld the orders to Albertson and Proctor to register, taking its lead from the Frankfurter opinion that the defendants couldn't claim the Fifth Amendment protection against self-incrimination until they failed to register and the government indicted them.

One morning in 1964, shortly before we were to argue the appeal before the Supreme Court, a comrade in Brooklyn, who drove Bill Albertson home from a meeting the night before, found a peculiar document on the front seat of his car. On a sheet of yellow-lined legal-sized paper was what appeared to be a note, in Bill's handwriting and signed by him, addressed to the FBI, reporting on what had happened at a recent Party meeting. At the end of the note was a request for an increase in payments. The fellow who found the note turned it over to the Party leadership. The Party's constitution provides for hearings before a trial committee in cases of violation of the organization's norms. A trial committee was quickly established in Bill's case and recommended his expulsion by the Central Committee. The Central Committee acted with dispatch and expelled him.

I read about the expulsion order in *The Worker*, the bi-weekly successor to the *Daily Worker*. In the turgid prose typical of Party bureaucratese, Albertson was proclaimed a police agent: "With callous and malicious intent, he violated the confidence entrusted in him to perform the role of stool pigeon and informer against those whom he called his comrades, his friends, men and women who are devoted fighters for peace, freedom and equality. Albertson lived a life of duplicity and treachery—posing as a dedicated defender of the workers' interests while in actuality betraying them." Even had I been convinced of his guilt, I would have been bound as an attorney to continue to represent him in his Supreme Court appeal, unless he wanted me to withdraw from the case. Actually, the government at that point moved to dismiss the case against Albertson, on the grounds that the order for him to register was moot since he had been expelled from the Party. But Bill insisted on his innocence and had initiated an appeal of his expulsion order through the Party machinery. Since his appeals within the Party hadn't yet been exhausted, he successfully fought the government's motion, and the registration case remained before the Supreme Court.

After reading of his expulsion, I asked if he wanted me to continue to represent him. He did, and I carried his fight against the government to the Court. Personally, I had reservations about Bill, but they were in the nature of criticisms of his own bureaucratic ways. I did not believe then, and still do not, that he was ever a government informer. He was in the Party for thirty years. His mother and wife were both Communists. He had been convicted under the Smith Act in the Pittsburgh trial and also served a sixty-day contempt sentence for refusing to name names. Of course people can change with circumstances. But the sole evidence against Bill was the "FBI report" in question. The Party leadership never really tried to investigate the matter before expelling him. There had been no serious checkup, no interviews with friends, comrades, and co-workers, no attempt at surveillance. There had only been an immediate denunciation, which greatly disturbed me. *Only after it had already expelled him* did the Party leadership begin to investigate the evidence against Albertson, hiring several handwriting experts, all of whom confirmed that the writing on the FBI report matched Bill's.

Albertson himself researched and discovered that newly developed computer techniques made it possible to manufacture an exact replica of a person's signature that would be undetectable even by experts. But what convinced me that Bill was the subject of a frame-up was the "FBI report" itself. In the course of my career, I have seen hundreds, even thousands, of reports, letters, and affidavits of paid informers, and this one conformed to none I had ever seen. It was addressed to "Joe" and signed "Bill," an absolute violation of all known procedure. Stool pigeons are invariably given false names or code numbers. The "report" was also undated and worded so that a change in the date of its discovery would not affect its timeliness. In my experience it was also unheard of for an informer to ask, in writing, for a raise in pay. This was simply earmarked to give a motive to Albertson's "turn" to the government. This was a classic effort at what the FBI calls "putting a snitch jacket on," that is, framing someone to appear to be an informer.

Bill visited me while I labored on the Supreme Court appeal. I never told him whether I thought he was innocent or guilty and didn't think that was part of my legal representation. But he asked, "John, what can I do? How can I prove that I'm not a stool pigeon." And I told him, "Frankly, Bill, you're in an hopeless position. You can't prove a negative. Someone might be able to prove that you are something, but it is impossible to prove you are not." In any case, Bill continued to press his appeal, which went before the Party's 1966 convention. The Central Committee established a subcommittee to consider his appeal and, in the end, recommended finding neither that he was guilty nor that he was innocent, but what we lawyers called a "Scottish verdict"—not proved. (In Scotland, there are three possible verdicts: guilty, not guilty, and not proved.) The evidence was not enough to prove Albertson was an informer, but neither was the Party leadership ready to recommend his reinstatement, and he remained an outcast.

In 1965, the Supreme Court reversed the lower courts on the registration orders to Albertson and Proctor. The Court held, with us— the majority opinion written by Justice Brennan—that the membership clause of the McCarran Act was unconstitutional because it violated the privilege against self-incrimination. Regrettably, Bill didn't fare as well before the "high court" of the Party. His wife and mother were expelled shortly after he was—for anyone who is a lifelong member, this is no less traumatic than excommunication for a lifelong Catholic—and the reputation of being a government informer followed him the rest of his life. In the circles in which he was known, nobody wanted to hire him. In a tragic irony, he was blacklisted from the food and hotel industry, where he had worked as a younger man, because of his Smith Act conviction. And, still considering himself a Communist, he spurned subsequent efforts by the FBI and IRS to actually enlist him as a spy.

In February 1972, Bill Albertson died in a car crash. Three years later, in a lawsuit on another matter brought by NBC television newsman Carl Stern, the FBI opened up some of its files under the Freedom of Information Act. Among the papers subsequently revealed about the FBI's COINTELPRO operations, aimed at disrupting and destroying the Communist Party and other radical movements, was a five-page report, dated January 6, 1965, which contained this admission:

> [Name deleted], the most active and efficient functionary of the New York District of the Communist Party USA and leading national officer of the Party, through our counterintelligence efforts, has been expelled from the Party. Factors relating to this expulsion crippled the activities of the New York State Communist organization and the turmoil within the party continues to this date. Albertson's exposure as an FBI informant has discouraged many dedicated Communists from activities and has discredited the Party in the eyes of the Soviets."

Subsequent efforts by the ACLU and others, on behalf of the Albertson family, eventually secured other documents and finally posthumous exoneration for Bill. The FBI ultimately made a cash payment to the family to settle a lawsuit. The Party leadership still denies its own culpability in the Albertson case. Unquestionably the FBI is the culprit and the Party itself—not only the Albertson family—the victim. So it is shameful that instead of giving the FBI the bloody nose it deserved the Party leadership preferred to bury the case rather than acknowledge fallibility and simple human error. After so many years, the Party can no longer salvage whatever slight honor and integrity it might once have had in the matter.

* * *

It would be a mistake to think that legal issues of great political moment are determined only by competence of counsel or the understanding of the courts, even given changing political climates. I have always thought that political cases are won politically, hence, that time was on our side if we could act to delay litigation for a better day. But it takes people to organize outside the courtroom. My sister, Marion, had a genius for this in the days of the Smith Act trials. In 1961, the Hall-Davis Defense Committee was extremely fortunate to bring Clara Colon on board as its secretary. One of the very few who mastered the constitutional and procedural intricacies of the litigation, Clara understood the relation of this "legal-schmegal"—as we called it—to the basic freedoms that were at stake. She could speak and write about our cases in simple terms that anyone could understand, a task beyond most lawyers. Clara, who had been the target of the Florida witch-hunt, knew the desolate, overwhelming sense of isolation that such an experience can bring.

Even as we challenged the membership clause of the McCarran Act, we picked apart the other provisions. One made it a crime for a member of an organization that has been ordered to register to seek employment in any enterprise designated as a defense facility by the secretary of defense. Beginning in 1962, Robert McNamara designated several thousand factories and production plants as defense facilities, with notices to this effect posted on their premises.

In 1963, Eugene Robel, a Party member and for ten years a skilled machinist in the big Todd Shipyards in Seattle, was indicted for doing the same thing he'd been doing for the past decade before the posting of the Pentagon's notices—working, as the Supreme Court would eventually find, "apparently without incident and apparently without concealing his Communist Party membership." The shipyards were organized by the International Association of Machinists, to which Gene belonged. A few years earlier, after pleading the Fifth Amendment in declining to answer questions before HUAC, he was expelled by the IAM. At the time, the union prohibited Communists from membership, under a provision in its constitution that was deleted only in 1979 when the IAM came under the progressive leadership of William Winpisinger. Still, Gene continued to work in the shipyards though victimized by both the government and the union. After being indicted, he filed a bond and went back to work as he had every day for ten years.

The federal district judge dismissed Robel's indictment on technical grounds, and the government appealed the decision. In a remarkable opinion written by Chief Justice Warren, the Supreme Court, by a five-to-four majority, dismissed the case, holding that the provision of the McCarran Act under which Robel was indicted was unconstitutional as a violation of the First Amendment. Warren said that it was "guilt by association alone" for the government to prohibit a person from working in a so-called defense facility solely on the basis of membership in the Communist Party. If a person had been accused of no personal wrongdoing but was simply a member of an unpopular organization, he or she was protected by the constitutionally guaranteed freedom of association and could not be fired. Moreover, the Court made no exceptions as to the sensitive or security nature of the place of employment. "The phrase 'war power,'" wrote the Chief Justice, "cannot be invoked as a talismanic incantation" for bypassing the Bill of Rights.

On the same day that the Robel case was decided, the Supreme Court refused to enjoin the SACB from proceeding with hearings against the W. E. B. Du Bois Clubs under the Communist front provisions of the McCarran Act. The Du Bois Clubs were a nationwide socialist youth organization initiated in large part by the Party. The Court avoided what it called the "important and difficult constitutional issues" on the ground that consideration of these questions was premature. Writing for himself and Justice Black, Justice Douglas dissented. His opinion contains such an unbiased view of the Communists and such an unequivocal statement of the reach of the First Amendment—and says much about the effect of the changing times on Douglas himself—that it merits quotation at length:

> I see no constitutional method whereby the Government can punish or penalize one for "being a Communist" or "supporting Communism" or "promoting Communism." Communism, as an ideology, embraces a broad array of ideas. To some it has appeal because the state owns the main means of production, with the result that all phases of national life are in the public sector, guaranteeing full employment. To some Communism means a

See also p. 281

medical care program that reaches to the lowest levels of society. To others the communal way of life, even in agriculture, means a fuller life for the average person. To some the flowering of the dance, music, painting, sculpturing, and even athletics is possible only when those arts and activities move from the private to the public sector. To some there can be no equivalent of the unemployment insurance, old age insurance, and social security that obtain in a socialized state. To others Communism is a commitment to the atheistic philosophy and way of life. To still others, adherence to Communism means a commitment to use force and violence, if necessary, to achieve that kind of socialist state. And to some of course it means all of the projects I have enumerated plus perhaps others as well.

The word "revolution" has of course acquired a subversive connotation in modern times. But it has roots that are eminently respectable in American history. This country is the product of revolution. Our very being emphasizes that when grievances pile high and there are no political remedies, the exercise of sovereign powers reverts to the people. Teaching and espousing revolution—as distinguished from indulging in overt acts—are therefore obviously within the range of the First Amendment.   //

After a jury convicted the Party officers of refusing to register—the "evidence" consisted of three paid government informers who testified that they volunteered to Party leaders to register on their behalf—we appealed once more. Again the Court of Appeals reversed the conviction, ruling that to require the officers of the Party to incriminate themselves to paid government informers by authorizing them to sign the registration documents was the equivalent of incriminating themselves by signing the documents directly. At this point, Attorney General Ramsay Clark announced that he was terminating the case, that the government would not even apply for certiorari. The Supreme Court had, one by one, struck down all of the criminal sanctions of the McCarran Act—the passport sanction, the job sanction, the membership provision, the registration requirement—but one. Only the provision requiring the labeling of mail remained.

But the act had served much of its purpose in weakening the Party and destroying the constellation of left-wing organizations and institutions it had helped to build. Together with the Smith Act prosecutions and the whole array of inquisitions, the McCarran Act undoubtedly drove tens of thousands of members and sympathizers away from the Party, greatly weakening it and diminishing its influence. Moreover, these years of persecution and court cases had the effect of intimidating and discouraging others from starting or joining similar progressive organizations. This is not to minimize the Party's self-inflicted wounds—its internal strife, bureaucratic centralism, and inability to allow democratic debate, particularly insofar as it included an independent view of the USSR, etc.

By 1968, with the McCarran Act largely dismantled piece by piece, the SACB had little to do anymore. Its members had among the softest jobs in Washington, collecting their $25,000 annual pay—quite a nice sum for that time—for doing virtually nothing. Fortuitously for them, their jobs were saved through the largesse of President Johnson, who was not motivated by a recharged anticommunist zeal, but by matters of the heart. In 1966, LBJ quietly whisked through the appointment to the SACB of Simon F. McHugh, Jr., a young accountant whose only qualification for the job, according to the *Wall Street Journal*, was his marriage to the president's former personal secretary, whose relationship to the Oval Office was said to extend beyond the purely professional. The paper described her as "a particular Presidential favorite." To preserve McHugh's job, the man needed some tangible work to perform. Johnson and GOP Senate minority leader Everett Dirkson collaborated to amend the McCarran Act to adapt to the new conditions. Dirkson in turn secured an SACB appointment for one of his cronies, John S. Patterson.

Since the registration requirement floundered on the rock of the privilege against self-incrimination, LBJ and Dirkson proposed to eliminate the registration requirement. Instead they would substitute the SACB's simply finding an organization to be a Communist action organization, or an individual to be a member of the Communist Party, but not require them to register, thereby erasing our Fifth Amendment defense. The organizations and individuals would be listed in the Federal Register, open for public inspection. In December 1969, the U.S. Court of Appeals ruled that the revised act, substituting SACB findings of Party membership but eliminating the registration requirement, was still unconstitutional. The court held that to officially identify a person as a Party member, without evidence that he or she was guilty of any criminal act, would abridge the First Amendment protection of freedom of association. The government appealed the decision to the Supreme Court, but in the improved atmosphere of 1969, the high court refused to review the Court of Appeals's ruling.

At this point the SACB was completely without a reason to exist. But the newly elected Nixon administration, hoping to salvage the board, raised its members' annual salaries by 44 percent to $36,000. To give the board at least the appearance of purpose, Nixon asked it to administer the attorney general's list of subversive organizations. Authorized by President Truman in 1947, the list established the principle of guilt by association to determine the "loyalty" of applicants for federal jobs and set a pattern for similar action based on this list by private employers and public agencies. Countless thousands of women and men were victimized by this device. (In 1974, President Ford's attorney general, William Saxbe, finally abolished the list, describing it as "a sort of vestigial tail" that "no longer serves any useful purpose.") By 1973, Congress was no longer willing to appropriate funds for the SACB—not only the salaries plus expenses for its members but the overhead, including secretaries, phones, supplies, travel—and the board was allowed to die for lack of funds.

Still, the act remained on the books, and although nearly all of its provisions had been ruled unconstitutional, one had yet to be tested. This was the section requiring all of the Party's mail and all radio and television broadcasts to be labeled as those of an organization found to be a Communist action organization. For years I had been looking for a way to challenge this provision, and I finally found it during the 1974 congressional election campaign. The Party in Pennsylvania had purchased some time on a local CBS radio affiliate for one of its candidates, and CBS insisted that the McCarran Act required that the broadcast be preceded by a disclaimer saying that "the following broadcast is paid for by the Communist Party, an organization found to be a Communist action organization." I took the opportunity to file suit against CBS and the Justice Department to have this provision of the act declared unconstitutional.

CBS actually had no particular interest in defending this case; it was only doing what it thought the law required of it. And after long negotiations, the attorney general agreed to have the federal district court enter an order which said that the SACB's finding that the Party was a Communist action organization no longer had any "force, validity or effect." Interestingly, it was Judge John J. Sirica, who presided over the Watergate trials of Richard Nixon's White House staff, who entered the order on May 30, 1974. Thus, the U.S. government finally surrendered the McCarran Act, ending twenty-four years of litigation, including seven separate Supreme Court decisions.

7

Changes

The political climate in the seventies had obviously greatly changed from that in 1951, when we first undertook to challenge the McCarran Act. To cite but one measure of the difference, opposition to the Korean War had been largely confined to Communists and those who followed the Party's leadership, whereas the movement against the Vietnam War cut across the political spectrum and had, by 1973, come to embrace a majority of the country. Over the same period, anticommunism as a pretext for repression had worn razor thin. Justice Douglas's dissent in the *Du Bois Clubs* case, quoted earlier, took note of this change. He wrote that the *Dennis* decision, ruled on in 1951, was made "at the peak of the notorious witch-hunt in this nation." Douglas added: "It is not conceivable that the Court [as constituted in 1966, when he was writing] would approve *Dennis.*"

When the McCarran Act litigation first began, the chief justice then was Fred Vinson, who also wrote the majority opinion in *Dennis.* Upon his death, President Eisenhower appointed Earl Warren to head the Court, a propitious turn of events, though we hardly understood it as such at the time. I certainly had no enthusiasm for Warren's ascension. His record as governor of California had hardly distinguished him as a liberal. Early on, as district attorney of Alameda County, his only established credentials were those of a headhunter of trade unionists and radicals, in particular, of Communists. When Eisenhower appointed Brennan, I again took no encouragement, recalling his role on the New Jersey Supreme Court in upholding the barring of Communist candidates for public office under the Communist Control Act. Similarly, when Lyndon Johnson appointed Arthur Goldberg to the Court, I could scarcely rejoice knowing as I did Arthur's background in the Amalgamated Clothing Workers and the CIO as leader of the anticommunist purges in the labor movement.

But these three justices—and Abe Fortas, appointed when Goldberg left the Court to become ambassador to the United Nations—with Douglas and Black, became the core majority of perhaps the most progressive Supreme Court in the history of the United States. This changed composition was essential to our ultimate victory in overturning the McCarran Act. But a compelling case can be made that the changes in the world, and in our own domestic politics, propelled or at least allowed the Court to take the direction it did; that in 1951, Warren, Goldberg, and Brennan may have voted no differently than Vinson and his colleagues. In any case, the Court did change, and the changes validated our original strategy of participating in the SACB hearings and using every opportunity to contest the government's position, thereby prolonging the case until more favorable conditions developed.

For me, the Supreme Court was always the most pleasant and easiest Court before which to argue. Joe Forer and I had some background in constitutional law from the start of the McCarran Act litigation, but our understanding and argumentation deepened as the years passed. As indicated earlier, we divided up the drafting of the briefs, then battled one another until we agreed on the final product. Before the Supreme Court, we usually split the oral argument, although I handled one or two cases in their entirety. Today, the justices rush attorneys through their oral arguments, but in those days, they would give us at least an hour and sometimes even an hour and a half. Whatever their political views, however much they might have been opposed to my own, the justices of the Supreme Court were, almost without exception, very knowledgeable lawyers. If you are well prepared, know and believe in the case you are arguing, your dialogue with the justices can be most stimulating and an often profitable intellectual exercise. Almost always, they have read the briefs beforehand so are also knowledgeable about the case before you begin your argument. For me, it was far more frustrating to argue before a witless judge on a lower court who couldn't grasp the arguments. Not all the Supreme Court justices were equally argumentative. Douglas, for example, rarely interrupted an argument to ask a question. Frankfurter was Douglas's polar opposite, a little terrier pursuing you with questions, always making clear his own position. Warren and Black were my personal favorites, Black not least of all because while he liked to argue with me from the bench, he almost always sided with my arguments when it came time to issue an opinion.

During my oral argument in the Robel case, Justice Brennan interrupted me to ask if there was not an improper delegation of authority given to the secretary of defense to designate "defense facilities" in which it would be illegal for a Communist to be employed. The McCarran Act lacked a definition of "defense facilities," and what Brennan was asking was, didn't this latitude violate the Constitution by delegating Congress's legislative authority to the executive branch? This had been the basis on which the Court held unconstitutional FDR's National Recovery Act in the *Schecter* decision over thirty years earlier, while I was still in the Agricultural Adjustment Administration. In *Schecter*, as I discussed earlier, the Supreme Court held that Congress cannot delegate its authority to any other branch of government, that this was "delegation run riot." But no other case discussed these issues in the three decades since *Schecter*, despite the vast growth in the federal bureaucracy and the creation of huge federal agencies with broad authority. We had not argued this question in our brief—it was probably the only pertinent question we didn't argue—and I told the Court that it seemed to me that *Schecter* was obsolete. Black took great umbrage with my writing off *Schecter*. In the New York state unemployment compensation case, Black also became upset when I made a slighting remark about the sole question of due process. But Black was the one justice who directly challenged the constitutionality of the McCarran Act in the first decision in 1960. And in the five decisions that we lost by five-four majorities, before the Court changed with the majority in our favor, Black was the only dissenter who framed his opinions on principled grounds rather than technical or secondary questions.

As with Brennan and the *Schecter* argument, another case from my distant past came back to haunt me. As I discussed earlier, in 1935 I was on loan from the WPA to work with Bob Jackson in preparing the *Electric Bond and Share* case for the Securities and Exchange Commission. Our position was that the only issue before the Court was the validity of the Public Utility Holding Company Act's registration requirement. This dictated that holding companies, like Electric Bond and Share, register with the SEC, and we argued—successfully—that all other questions be reserved until the SEC ordered the breakup of the companies. Back then we said that there would be plenty of time to decide the constitutionality of the other provisions when the order came to disaffiliate.

Twenty years later, when I was arguing before the Court of Appeals, the young lawyer who was litigating the McCarran Act on the government's behalf argued that registration of the Party under the act should be treated like registration in the *Electric Bond and Share* case. The appellate court decided against her, but when we got to the Supreme Court, Justice Frankfurter resurrected this point, basing his entire decision on limiting the issue to that of the registration requirement, as in the *Electric Bond and Share* case. One journalist at the time pointed out the irony of my being hoisted by my own petard.

* * *

Arnold Johnson, my old friend and fishing instructor, also became my client in 1970. At the time, he chaired the Party's peace commission, and as such was the Party's representative on the steering committee of the New Mobilization against the War in Vietnam. For ten years, beginning in 1965, a vast coalition of organizations, churches, civil rights groups, student groups, and such came together to mount massive demonstrations in Washington, New York, San Francisco, and around the country against the war. The coalition's character and membership varied little during that decade, but its name changed from time to time. By 1969 it had generally become known as the New Mobe and was headed by the venerable pacifist leader A. J. Muste, then in his eighties. Though not a pacifist, Arnold was a sweet and gentle man and was himself well into his sixties, and the mostly younger antiwar activists referred to him affectionately as "A. J., Jr."

The House Internal Security Committee (HISC) adopted a resolution to conduct what it called "an in-depth study" of the coalition. HISC was established a year earlier as the successor to the House Un-American Activities Committee, which was simultaneously dissolved. Under its charter, HUAC was able to range far afield, investigating nearly anything it wanted to, and it had a large appetite for inquiry. But the HISC resolution confined the new committee's investigations to organizations that advocated sabotage, the violent overthrow of the government, or other criminal activity. In June 1970, pursuant to its "in-depth study" of the New Mobe, HISC subpoenaed Arnold to testify.

He asked me to meet him for lunch at the Prince George Hotel to discuss what legal tactics might be employed before the committee. I expressed my opinion that there were really only the same two options unfriendly witnesses had who appeared before HUAC—to plead the Fifth Amendment or not to plead the Fifth. Somewhat to my surprise, Arnold told me that he wasn't going to plead the Fifth Amendment this time, that the political climate had changed sufficiently that it wasn't any longer imperative to take refuge in the Fifth. He wanted to rely solely upon the First Amendment. I pointed out the hazards of this, that if he refused to answer questions solely on the basis of the First Amendment, all case law went against him; he would wind up with a contempt citation and risk a jail sentence for six months to a year. It hadn't been so many years since Arnold served a prison sentence under the Smith Act, and his health was not so vigorous as it had once been. But I had known and loved Arnold for many years, long enough to know that he was quite stubborn once he had determined a course for himself. He decided that there would be no Fifth Amendment for him this time around, that he wanted to retain the respect of his colleagues on the New Mobe steering committee, that he couldn't do that by pleading the Fifth and he wasn't going to do so.

The hearing was held on a balmy June day before a subcommittee chaired by Rep. Edwin Edwards, who would later become governor of Louisiana. When Arnold was called to the witness stand, I moved to quash the subpoena on the grounds that HISC had no jurisdiction to investigate the New Mobe, that its right to investigate was limited to organizations advocating criminal activities. There was no evidence before HISC that New Mobe advocated violent or criminal activities, hence the committee had no jurisdiction to investigate. Representative Edwards claimed that the committee possessed such evidence, taken in earlier hearings. I asked if these hearings had been published. Well, Edwards answered, one such hearing had been, others hadn't, some hadn't yet been transcribed. I demanded to see the evidence, agreeing that my motion would be invalid if the New Mobe had in fact advocated criminal activities. Edwards posed a bargain: he would make the earlier testimony and evidence available to us if we would agree to let Arnold testify. I asked how I could agree to have my client testify before I saw the evidence that might compel him to do so. Edwards beamed at his own cleverness, telling me, "I thought you'd say that, but I wanted to make my offer anyhow." He refused to quash the subpoena and again called Arnold to the witness stand. Arnold refused to be sworn and was threatened with a contempt citation by Edwards. After the hearing, HISC asked the entire House of Representatives to cite Arnold for contempt, and he was indicted in October 1970.

Joe Forer joined me in the defense. We moved to dismiss the indictment because it didn't allege that the New Mobe was of a character that gave the committee jurisdiction to investigate. Judge G. L. Hart ruled that while he wouldn't dismiss the indictment, he would require the government to produce evidence that the organization fell within the committee's purview. After some time the government supplied its "evidence," which any disinterested party would have labeled trash. But Judge Hart—who had presided over the Party's challenge to the McCarran Act's passport provision and declared that "the leopard of Communism would never change its spots"—found the evidence sufficient to deny our motion.

In the hundreds of district court appearances I have made over the years, I had been before Judge Hart on a number of occasions. We were quite familiar with one another. As with virtually all of the judges before whom I have argued—and this is a long list in a long life—I have never had a problem with Judge Hart on a personal level. Many of these judges were tough, and many shared Judge Hart's anticommunist passions. They decided cases against the Party, they have often been quite nasty in deciding which evidence to admit or not, and on this lowest level in the federal judiciary, they have pretty consistently ruled against me. I have always treated them as befits an attorney's conduct before a judge and so, on a purely personal basis, I have gotten along with them. Now, as he denied our motion, Judge Hart was cordial and again welcomed me before his bench.

We introduced a second motion, together with an affidavit in which I stated my belief that Arnold Johnson had for many years been the subject of extensive electronic surveillance, by wiretapping and microphone installations, on the part of the FBI. I asked for the tapes and transcripts of this surveillance. The motion rested on the Fourth Amendment, which protects against unreasonable search and seizure. It is unconstitutional for governmental authorities to make a search of one's home or office or person, or to seize anything they might find there, without a warrant. The warrant must be issued by a judge, after the authorities demonstrate that there is probable cause to believe that the person is guilty of a criminal act.

Of course the authors of the Fourth Amendment could not have foreseen telephones, let alone telephone wiretapping. But in 1928, a case before the Supreme Court raised the question of whether bugging a phone fell within the scope of Fourth Amendment protections, whether in fact a government agency needed a court-ordered warrant to engage in the practice. Over the vigorous dissent of Oliver Wendell Holmes, the Court held that wiretapping was neither searching nor seizing, but only listening, and was constitutional. It wasn't until the sixties and the Warren-led Court that electronic surveillance was prohibited, except by court-ordered warrant, by the Fourth Amendment. Consequently, Congress moved in 1968 to allow the government, after demonstrating probable cause and receiving a court-ordered warrant, to engage in wiretapping. But the statute also required that the government provide tapes or transcripts to a defendant in a criminal case who submitted an affidavit that he or she thought they were the subject of warrantless electronic surveillance. This allowed the defendant to determine if the results of the surveillance afforded the government evidence or gave it clues to evidence to be used in prosecuting the case.

It was under that provision of the statute that we demanded the tapes of Arnold's conversations. Before we made the motion, John Mitchell, President Nixon's attorney general of ill repute and himself soon to become a convicted felon, took the position that this provision of the statute was inapplicable to national security cases, that the FBI needn't obtain warrants where suspected subversion was at hand. And of course the Watergate ordeal demonstrated the extent to which Nixon and Mitchell were engaged in extensive and arbitrary wiretapping. A local case in Michigan—in which Communists had no part—challenged Mitchell's assertion, contending that internal security cases were no different from any other criminal matter insofar as laws on electronic surveillance were concerned. The Supreme Court had not yet acted on the challenge when we made our motion on Arnold's behalf.

The government responded to our motion by acknowledging that it had bugged Arnold. Actually in one of our conferences before the judge, a government lawyer said, "We'd have to back up a truck to the FBI office to load up all the wire-tap material we have on Arnold Johnson." But the government argued that under the Mitchell doctrine, this was an internal security matter exempt from the warrant provisions of the law. We agreed to postpone the matter until the Supreme Court had acted in the Michigan case. Finally in June 1972, the Court ruled that Mitchell was wrong, at least in solely domestic security cases that didn't involve foreign governments, that the statute applied and warrants were required. We renewed our motion for the tapes and transcripts from electronic surveillance of Arnold Johnson.

Initially, the government agreed to produce all of the material we demanded. But it also said that some of the material was related to foreign organizations or governments, that the Supreme Court had withheld judgment on such matters, and that it would take time to separate them from the tapes of purely domestic matters. Judge Hart agreed to give the Justice Department sufficient time to collate the materials. Before the time expired, however, the government attorneys said that on further consideration, it would be prejudicial to the national security to produce any of this material. Further, since the Justice Department had the choice of producing it or having the case dismissed, it consented to the dismissal of the case against Arnold. As it turned out, this was the last contempt case of any of these congressional witch-hunts. HISC was itself abolished in 1974.

* * *

A Scythian philosopher named Anarcharis once compared laws with cobwebs: they are too weak to impede the strong, but strong enough to ensnare the weak. Frederick Engels brought Anarcharis up to date in his *Origins of the Family, Private Property, and the State,* in which he demonstrated, among other theses, that all the mechanisms of the capitalist state, including the judiciary, are erected to keep the poor in their place and the rich in theirs. Unfortunately, there is no legal requirement that arresting officers give criminal suspects the Anarcharis and Engels "warnings" in addition to the *Miranda* warning to remain silent until an attorney is present. My career until 1970—and I was then of normal retirement age—had been in corporate law, government practice, antitrust law, labor law, and constitutional law. At the age of sixty-six, I was about to acquire a quick apprenticeship in criminal law as well.

After the 1967 and 1968 ghetto rebellions in Watts, Detroit, Newark, Washington, D.C., and elsewhere, it was becoming clear that the civil rights movement that had, at great sacrifice, been so successful in the Deep South, would need a different agenda for the urban North. The causes of the riots remained long after the riots were suppressed. In the late sixties, the Black Panther party (BPP), with its ability to grab the public's attention albeit often with provocative swaggering, began to build a real following among disaffected youths in the urban African-American communities. Local police and federal authorities were swift to respond with their own shows of force. Virtually the entire Panther leadership in every community found themselves under indictment on one charge or another. In more than a few instances, "justice" was summary, as Panther members were killed by police gunfire.

The Communist party had many internal debates about a policy toward the BPP, reflecting both honest differences and contradictory experiences. In some places, Party members worked closely with the BPP. There were serious disagreements over tactics—experienced

Communists tried to politicize the inexperienced Panthers, often
without an invitation to do so—but the CP always believed in the right
of the BPP to exist and was active in its legal defense. There were
even a few cases of comrades holding membership in both groups.
My old friend Bill Patterson constantly impressed upon me the importance of the Panthers as a national development. Communists
played a significant role in organizing the Emergency Conference on
the Right of the Black Panther Party to Exist, held in Chicago in 1969.
At Pat's urging, I worked with the organizing committee, chaired by
Angie Dickerson. I had, after all, some experience defending against
government attempts to put a small party out of existence. And Charlene Mitchell, a member of our Party's political bureau, served on its
executive committee.

    One Communist who enjoyed a particularly close relationship with
many Panthers was Angela Davis. After being fired from her teaching job at UCLA because of her Party membership, at the public urging of Governor Ronald Reagan, Angela threw much of her energy
into organizing support for the Panthers, particularly those who were
in prison. I had heard Angela speak once in New York at a fund-raising event but had never met her. With tens of millions of others, I
was aware of her being the first woman ever placed on the FBI's Ten
Most Wanted list and of the huge federal hunt, following the shootout at the Marin County Civil Center in August 1970. In what was presumably an attempt to free George Jackson, who, because of his published writings, was perhaps the country's best-known prisoner, his
younger brother Jonathan Jackson and some companions took Judge
Harold Haley prisoner. The judge, Jonathan, and two others were
killed in a hail of gunfire. And Angela was accused of aiding and
abetting the alleged kidnapping and murder of the judge. Conviction
would bring a mandatory death sentence or life in prison.

    I was hardly prepared to receive a phone call from Bill Patterson
on October 13 telling me that the FBI had arrested Angela in New
York and that the Party wanted me to represent her. He suggested
that we both go downtown to the Women's House of Detention and
try to see her that evening. The last time I'd visited that jail—which,
with its high-rise sooty brick, resembled nothing so much as a medi-
eval fortress—was when my sister, Marion, was incarcerated there.
It was not my favorite place but of course I went with Pat in the middle of the night to try to meet with Angela. To the surprise of neither
of us, the authorities would not allow our visit. I left my business
card, with a note asking Angela to call if she wanted legal help.

    I had to figure out a creditable way to get myself designated as

Angela's attorney. I called my friend Dorothy Burnham, who, together with her late husband Louis, were neighbors of the Davis family in Birmingham when Louis was running the Southern Negro Youth Congress. Dottie agreed to call Frank Davis, Angela's dad, to tell him of my offer to represent her. After Dorothy's call, I telephoned Mr. Davis myself and obtained his authority to serve as legal counsel. When I returned to the Women's House of Detention the next morning, the guards informed Angela that her "father's attorney" was waiting outside. Of course Angela didn't know me, didn't know about her father's and my talk, didn't know if this was another trick of the authorities. She thought perhaps I was a friend using a ruse to get in to see her. It was my good fortune that at that moment Margaret Burnham—Louis and Dorothy's daughter and a childhood friend of Angela's—also showed up. Then a lawyer for the NAACP Legal Defense Fund, she came to see her friend in a personal capacity. Because I had also known Margaret since her infancy, she became my good conduct pass to Angela, who greeted me warmly. Angela told me that when she'd seen my business card the night before, she assumed I was a high-priced Wall Street lawyer retained by her family and was suspicious of my motivations. Angela agreed that I should represent her in her extradition fight, but asked that Margaret join me in the representation, a proposal I was pleased to accept.

As a child, Margaret, with her sisters and brother, were frequent weekend guests at Kent. For a kid growing up in Birmingham and Brooklyn, our country log cabin with its great stone fireplace was indeed an adventure. These visits extended through her college years. When Margaret began to entertain the possibility of becoming a lawyer, I tried to dissuade her. I questioned whether her gentleness and lack of aggressiveness suited her for the profession. But also I questioned the profession itself. I have never recommended that anybody become an attorney, because of my own lack of enthusiasm for the vocation. Happily, Margaret overruled me and became a very fine lawyer and, for a time, an excellent judge. I monitored her progress as a student at the University of Pennsylvania Law School, and in 1968, Margaret organized a seminar on labor law and invited me to speak on the CIO. I don't believe I saw her again—she graduated in 1969 and immediately joined the NAACP Legal Defense Fund—until we came together almost two years later on that October day at the Women's House of Detention.

I was Margaret's senior by forty years, and I supposed this would be something of a learning experience for her. She was very young and quite shy, this being her first real case. I intellectually engaged her in the legal issues before the court, and on several occasions I urged her to speak up in court on one or another question, though she was invariably reluctant to do so. Because I enjoyed the confidence of the Party, I took Margaret with me to meet with Winnie, Gus Hall, and Jim Jackson (another old family friend of both Margaret's and Angela's) to discuss Angela's legal status and the courtroom and political options available for fighting extradition and to get a handle on the enormous publicity barrage that greeted her capture. My own presence reinforced the Party's relationship with Angela, as she desired. Margaret recalled all of this as "a step into a new world."

I should say that Margaret's and my relationship was mutually beneficial. As a warm and trusted friend of Angela's, with some legal ability, she became the interpreter, both explaining to her the options she faced and explaining Angela's concerns and interests to us. As it was for Margaret, this was also a learning experience for me, as I tried to get up to speed on the issues, personalities, and contradictions within the African-American movement at that time. As someone who is quite conventional and traditional, I was not always comfortable with the confrontational style of the seventies. (Margaret recalled Angela urging me to argue at the bail hearing that her treatment was akin to that of a runaway slave and my resistance to this tactic.) Moreover, heretofore nearly all of my colleagues in the bar, even within the left-wing National Lawyers Guild, were white, and in large part, Jewish. A natural offshoot of the civil rights movement was the development of significant numbers of young, militant, socially conscious Black attorneys, many grouped together in the National Conference of Black Lawyers.

One of our tasks was to help identify counsel for the trial that would eventually take place. Most lawyers enjoy bathing in publicity, and this case was certainly awash with that. Scores of attorneys wanted into the case, to "touch the garments," so to speak. I was unfamiliar with a number of the younger Black lawyers, and many naturally called Margaret rather than me. For her part, Angela insisted on having a Black attorney as her lead counsel at trial. She felt it imperative to demonstrate that African-American lawyers were every bit the equal of the Charlie Garrys and William Kunstlers and the other publicized white defense counsels for the Black Panthers and kindred movements. (When Angela's trial finally took place in California much later, she obtained the services of Howard Moore, an experienced criminal attorney from Atlanta, and Leo Branton, a brilliant Los Angeles lawyer who, fresh out of law school, first cut his teeth in the Smith Act trial of the California Communist leaders. Margaret continued throughout the trial as an essential part of the defense team. They were aided by white co-counsel, including my longtime colleague Doris Bryn Walker.)

On meeting Angela that first time with Margaret, I explained what little I knew about extradition law, how she was arrested under the Federal Interstate Fugitive Act, giving the federal authorities jurisdiction to arrest someone for the crime of fleeing across state lines to avoid prosecution. The law is used mainly as a pretext for involving the FBI in what would otherwise be a local police case. I explained that it was unlikely she'd be prosecuted on this charge; more probably she'd be turned over to New York State to be extradited to California and tried on the murder and kidnapping charges awaiting her there. We then went before a federal magistrate for arraignment. The courthouse was crowded with security people of various local, state, and federal agencies. The magistrate ordered her held on $250,000 bail and adjourned the case until a decision was made to prosecute her on the flight charge or turn her over to New York for extradition.

At 8 P.M., Margaret and I were called back before the magistrate who, on motion of the U.S. attorney, graciously released her from the bail he had fixed and turned her over to the tender mercies of two burly New York City detectives to be held without bail pending extradition proceedings. As they took Angela from the courtroom, the detectives condescended to inform us that she would be booked at the Seventh Precinct station. When Margaret and I arrived at the Seventh Precinct, the desk sergeant told us he knew nothing about Angela's whereabouts, she hadn't been there, there was no plan that she be there, and he suggested we try other precincts. It was then nearly 10 P.M., and I urged Margaret to go home and rest. During the next couple of hours, it appeared that the police department had mislaid our client, for, after visiting four more precincts, no one in authority could tell me where to find her. I finally learned that she had been brought to night court for arraignment. I found the Criminal Courts Building guarded by some two hundred police—it was nearly midnight—denying admission to the court to all but lawyers and reporters, all of whom were frisked. When I suggested that given the lateness of the hour and my long search for my client, an adjournment until next morning was in order, the prosecutor countered with the question, "Have you any idea how much money tonight is costing the City of New York?"

In the morning's wee hours, Angela was finally arraigned, pleaded not guilty, and returned to the Women's House of Detention. That evening I received my first indication of the possibilities of the mass

movement that subsequently arose in Angela's defense. Before I left
the courtroom, the clerk of the court, a Black man, said to me, "Mr.
Abt, don't you think I should give you a card identifying you so that
you can get in to see Ms. Davis tomorrow morning?" For a New York
City court clerk to offer such a proposal was unprecedented in my
experience. Moments later, another clerk told me, "They would never have done anything like this to her if she hadn't been Black."

At the Women's House of Detention, Angela was placed in a cell
block for psychiatric cases, where she was awakened in the middle
of each night by a white inmate screaming obscenities at Blacks. Virtually all of her companions were doped on Thorazine, rendering
them incapable of communication. Our protests resulted, after a
week, in Angela's transfer to a normal cell block. However, twenty-
four hours later, she was placed in solitary confinement. We lodged
complaints that elicited a reply from the Department of Corrections
that there was no such thing as solitary confinement in the House of
Detention. How solitary can confinement be? Angela was locked in
her cell twenty-three hours a day, under the constant scrutiny of a
guard, forbidden to communicate with other prisoners. The twenty-
fourth hour was spent in solitary "recreation" on the jail roof, like-
wise under guard and incommunicado. Our further protests were
met by contradictory inventions: first, that Angela would stir up re-
bellion if allowed to mingle with the other prisoners, and second, that
isolation was essential for her safety. It was only as a result of her
two-week hunger strike, and a lawsuit instituted by the National Conference of Black Lawyers under the leadership of Haywood Burns,
that a federal judge finally ordered her released from solitary. During this period I received another indication of Angela's popular impact on the community at large when I went to a Western Union office to send a telegram protesting her confinement in solitary. The
telegraph operator, after reading the message for legibility, looked at
me and said, "I hope you win."

                              * * *

Extradition required that the governor of California, Ronald
Reagan, request of the governor of New York, Nelson Rockefeller, that
the defendant be returned. To supply the legal basis for the request,
Bruce Bales, the Marin County district attorney, swore out a complaint and affidavit indicating there was "probable cause" to believe
that Angela was guilty of an extraditable offense. Reagan, who had
personally instigated the proceedings to fire Angela from UCLA, took
less than a day to sign the extradition request. The former actor nev-

er acquired a reputation for deliberation or study, but this speed was unprecedented. Under New York law, the governor has thirty days to study any such request and to secure the opinion of legal advisors on whether to act upon it. In Angela's case, Rockefeller issued an extradition warrant within twenty-four hours of Reagan's request. And those hours were not spent in weighing the legality of the request, but in campaigning for reelection on the sidewalks of New York. Had Rockefeller given the Bales affidavit the scrutiny that the law requires, he would have been forced to conclude that it was hopelessly defective in furnishing "probable cause" to believe Angela was guilty of the crimes with which she was charged. Nobody saw Angela engaged in the commission of any crime. The evidence was, at best, circumstantial; and that evidence tended to prove her innocence, not her guilt. The DA's affidavit failed to even fix responsibility for the death of Judge Harold Haley at the Marin County courthouse shootout. It stated merely that "one of the prisoners shot and killed" him, without identifying the kidnapper or even the name of the witness (if there was one) who supplied this information. The DA's silence on the subject of ballistic tests left the inference that the judge was killed not by his alleged abductors but by the deputy sheriffs and correction officers responsible for the deaths of Jonathan Jackson and his companions.

Other than her leadership in the George Jackson defense campaign, the only fact in the affidavit that connected Angela with the events at the San Rafael courthouse was that the guns Jonathan Jackson carried into the courtroom had been openly purchased and publicly registered by her, as shown by registration statements she filled out and signed in compliance with state and federal law. The affidavit did not claim that Angela gave Jonathan the guns, let alone that she knew what he planned to do with them or intended to aid him in accomplishing his purpose. Thus, the affidavit omitted the essential ingredients of the offense of aiding and abetting. In their absence, Angela's purchase and registration of the guns evidenced innocence, not guilt, especially in light of the surrounding circumstances. The fact was that after Reagan had her fired for being a Communist, Angela received a series of threats on her life. She purchased guns as a means of self-protection, and Jonathan Jackson was her bodyguard. Of course he had access to the guns. The obvious inference was that this young man, in frustration at the failure of the years-long legal efforts to free his brother George, whom he considered innocent, resorted to an act of desperation to free him by his own hand.

On November 5, Margaret and I filed a petition for a writ of habeas corpus in the Supreme Court of New York, challenging the extradition order on the ground that the Bales affidavit was wholly insufficient to satisfy the requirement of probable cause that the Fourth Amendment to the Constitution makes prerequisite to a valid arrest. Habeas corpus (literally, "produce the body") is the legal instrument by which one secures the release of someone held unconstitutionally in prison. Our petition evidently alerted the prosecution to the fact that the Bales affidavit was fatally deficient. Five days after we filed it, a grand jury convened in Marin County and indicted Angela on counts of murder, kidnapping for ransom, and conspiracy to commit these offenses.

The strategy of this move was obvious. The law assumes that a grand jury, supposedly made up of twelve unbiased and disinterested men and women, would not vote an indictment without legally sufficient evidence. So the law presumes that every grand jury hears enough evidence to give it probable cause to believe the accused guilty of the crime for which it indicts him or her. On this ground, an indictment need not recite the evidence on which it was based. The murder count in Angela's indictment, for example, simply stated that on August 7, 1970, in Marin County, she "did murder a human being, to wit: Judge Harold Joseph Haley." The theory of grand jury objectivity is the purest fiction. Every lawyer knows that a district attorney can go before a grand jury anywhere in the country and get an indictment for the asking. Yet the presumption that grand juries act only on legally sufficient evidence is universal.

But California is one state that at least provides a procedure for overcoming this presumption. A California statute requires that an accused be furnished with a stenographic transcript of the grand jury proceedings within ten days after the indictment is issued. A related statute permits an accused to secure a dismissal of the indictment upon showing, from this transcript, that the evidence was insufficient to satisfy the probable cause requirement. It seemed obvious that an accused who is apprehended outside of California should be entitled to defeat extradition on the same grounds, and there had never been a court decision to the contrary. Accordingly, I asked a San Francisco colleague to pick up a copy of the transcript of the grand jury proceedings against Angela for use in opposing her extradition. He found that Marin County Chief Judge Wilson had entered an unprecedented order when the indictment was returned. Contrary to the explicit mandate of the statute, the order provided that Angela should not receive the grand jury transcript until she appeared in person before the Marin County Court. The effect of this extraordinary order was to furnish her with the documents she required to defeat extradition only if she gave up the extradition fight and voluntarily returned to California.

We filed an amended petition for habeas corpus in the New York court challenging extradition on two related grounds. First, we argued that the unprecedented and illegal order of the California court withholding the grand jury transcript violated due process of law and denied Angela the equal protection of the laws, both guaranteed by the Fourteenth Amendment. Second, we argued that the indictment was returned in bad faith to cover up the lack of a case against Angela and that the grand jury transcript was withheld because, like the Bales affidavit, it was devoid of incriminating evidence. The petition concluded by asking, as a minimum, that extradition be deferred until the California authorities produced the transcript so that New York could determine whether the evidence satisfied the probable cause requirement.

At the hearing on December 3, Judge Thomas Dickens tried to stifle argument of these constitutional points, then listened with ill-tempered impatience and immediately ruled against us. His single concession was to stay extradition for five days to permit an appeal. The Appellate Division granted a further stay to December 16, the date it set to hear the appeal. There followed the fastest Cook's tour of the appellate courts that I have ever been given in over sixty years of practice. On average, it takes well over a year to exhaust the appellate process in a New York extradition proceeding—and this where the defendant's points are insubstantial to the point of frivolous. In Angela's case, our constitutional arguments received a brush-off by *five courts in five days*. And the five days included a weekend when the courts were closed.

The Appellate Division heard arguments on December 16, decided against us an hour later, and gave us until 6 P.M. the next day to seek a stay from the Court of Appeals, the highest state court. At 9:30 the next morning, I appeared before Chief Judge Fuld, who denied a stay at 11 A.M. At noon, we filed a petition for a writ of habeas corpus in the U.S. District Court. Judge Marvin Frankel heard arguments that afternoon and, next morning, denied the petition but granted a stay for the next ten minutes, or until the fastest elevator could take me to the seventeenth floor to apply to the U.S. Court of Appeals. Within the hour, three judges of that court were convened—headed by Judge Irving Kaufman, who had condemned the Rosenbergs and with whom I had clashed during my attempt to obtain care for Henry Winston—heard the arguments and affirmed Judge Frankel. It being a Friday, the court stayed extradition until 4 P.M. the following Monday to permit us to seek relief from the U.S. Supreme Court. I presented the application to Justice John Harlan, who was in charge of the courts in the New York circuit, at 10 A.M. on Monday morning. He was our final recourse, and by 1 P.M. I received his denial and returned to New York too late to visit Angela that evening.

I had an understanding with the assistant district attorney that he would give me notice before they actually moved Angela, and he now informed me that she would be taken to California by commercial airliner on Tuesday afternoon. But at 3:30 Tuesday morning, I was awakened by a reporter with news that Angela had just left the Women's House of Detention and was evidently bound for the West Coast. We didn't get the full story until Margaret and I saw Angela in the Marin County jail a day later. She had been awakened at 3 A.M. on Tuesday by a prison matron who said that her lawyer was downstairs to advise her about extradition. Instead of her lawyer, she encountered two policemen and two policewomen. When she refused to accompany them, a policeman threw her to the floor, bruising her arms and legs. The four then forcibly took her to a car and, after a short ride, transferred her to another, where the California authorities took over. Then, escorted by twenty police cars, she was driven through the Holland Tunnel (closed to all other traffic for the passage of this dangerous woman) to a military airport in New Jersey, whence she was flown by National Guard plane to San Francisco. Margaret and I followed her by plane the next morning and saw her in her cell at San Rafael that night. It should be added that on her appearance for arraignment before the Marin County Court Thursday morning, with three hundred news reporters present, the grand jury transcript was delivered to us and confirmed our charge that the evidence it contained was as barren of incrimination as the Bales affidavit—a point that was grasped by millions of supporters the world over and eventually by twelve members of the jury who witnessed her trial in San Jose, California, and returned a resounding verdict of not guilty.

I spent the next ten days in the Bay Area, visiting Angela every day, helping her and Margaret put together a defense team to represent her on the pretrial motions in the case. My direct involvement in Angela's legal defense ended upon my return to New York, but of course I kept up with the case and consulted with Margaret and the other attorneys on a regular basis. Despite the flimsiness of the evidence, there is no question that this Black female Communist—so despised by Ronald Reagan, Nelson Rockefeller, and President Richard Nixon, with all the weight of state power at their disposal—was in great danger. But complementing the lawyers who worked on her defense was the greatest outpouring of national and international public opinion ever organized for any U.S. political prisoner. The extralegal defense campaign was coordinated by the Campaign to Free Angela Davis and All Political Prisoners, chaired by Ossie Davis and organized by Charlene Mitchell. I was pleased to serve as counsel to the campaign and to the Angela Davis Legal Defense Fund, which raised the enormous sums of money necessary to underwrite the costs of her courtroom defense.

* * *

After more than three decades as general counsel of the Communist party, I know as well as anyone the extent and extremes of repression to which this mightiest of all governments in history has gone to destroy a small Party of modest means because it sought to fundamentally alter the existing relations of economic and political power. In its seventy years, the Communist party was compelled to accept the forced deportation of many of its most dedicated members because they were foreign-born. Its leaders have repeatedly been imprisoned, often for years, without having committed a criminal act. Congressional headhunters have intimidated the country and corrupted the political culture for decades at a time while driving tens of thousands of Communists out of their jobs and often out of the Party. News reporters and commentators have either been paid outright or quietly fed information from the FBI and other agencies to vilify, slander, and engage in calumny against what has been, in the first place, a party largely of working people, idealistic and humble, seeking a world of peace and social justice. As a result, the government has been able to reduce the Party to, at best, a marginal factor in American political life. Unquestionably the Communist party has made horrendous mistakes and, in its zeal, justified enormous crimes in other countries. Its own acts of self-destruction have been extensively catalogued. But it has also committed great acts of heroism, perhaps none more heroic than to simply remain alive and active in the face of the unrelenting repression.

When I suggest that I know perhaps the extent of the repression as well as anyone, I must also acknowledge that what I know may not be the half of it. For when, through a lawsuit by NBC newsman Carl Stern, we inadvertently learned about the FBI's fabrication of a "report" to place Bill Albertson in the role of an informer and divide the Party, we also discovered that it was only part of the Bureau's COINTELPRO-CPUSA operation. The FBI used COINTELPRO plans to disrupt and provoke the Socialist Worker's party, the small Trotskyist grouping; "New Left" organizations like Students for a Democratic Society; and many of the organizations of the African-American community, with particular attention to the Black Panther party (the FBI called this operation "COINTELPRO—Black Nationalist Hate Groups—Internal Security"). But the COINTELPRO-CPUSA began in 1956, preceding the others by a decade, lasted longest—fifteen years—and generated the greatest number of actions—1,388 out of a total of 2,370 approved and implemented. That is to say, nearly 60 percent of COINTELPRO actions were vented against the Party. These are the most lawless actions ever undertaken by the U.S. government against a political organization, attempting to punish and destroy, *in secrecy,* a party it could not convict of a crime. It was well established that the Party eschewed violence as a tactic, hence the only "crime" of the Party was its revolutionary theory. (And, in the thirty-seven years that the Party existed before COINTELPRO, not a day went by that it was not subjected to other government programs under other code names.)

Of the 1,388 COINTELPRO actions the FBI acknowledges it undertook against the Party, only two have come to public light. One is the Bill Albertson case. The other is Operation Hoodwink, the code name for an attempt to provoke a clash between the Party and the Mafia and thus, according to an FBI memo, "cause disruption of both groups by having each expend their energies, time and money attacking each other." Late in 1966, a bomb damaged the Party offices. For several years, pipe bombs and other incendiary devices were placed at the building, usually the handiwork of ultrarightist groups. On this occasion, the Party called upon the FBI to apprehend the criminals. As the COINTELPRO files later revealed, the FBI's New York office got agreement from Washington to forge three letters on Party letterhead to leaders of the city's Mafia families, blaming the godfathers for the bombing and promising retribution. Fortunately the forgeries produced no response from the Mafia. J. Edgar Hoover, still the FBI director, vetoed a proposal from his New York office to plant rumors in the columns of friendly journalists about Party plans "to take on local hoodlum elements." But he okayed another forgery, this a letter to *The Worker* attacking the Mafia, signed by a "long time Jewish reader." Luckily nothing came of this provocation, unlike the operation against Bill Albertson. We still don't know of what the remaining 1,386 COINTELPRO "actions" directed against the Party consisted.

In the seventies, I attempted to obtain the Party's FBI files, but was told this would be impossible for there were *26.5 million* pages on the Party. In a supreme though unintentional irony, the FBI said that for us to demand our files was "oppressive." The incident arose in connection with a 1976 lawsuit we instigated against the government in attempting to secure ballot status. Beginning in the midsixties, after we successfully challenged the most repressive aspects of the McCarran Act, the Party again began to engage in electoral work, to run candidates for public office, particularly in national elections. After its formation in 1919, the Party ran candidates for president and vice-president every four years, from 1924 to 1940. But that had been the last time; in 1944, in the midst of the war, the Party supported FDR's fourth election campaign; in 1948, it supported Henry Wallace; and in the years following, with the intense anticommunist hysteria, it fought for its very existence. Party members were reluctant, if not downright fearful, to engage in any kind of open political work that would cost them their jobs and perhaps much more. In the early sixties, the *Milwaukee Journal* circulated, as a test, a petition endorsing the Declaration of Independence. It found that, with rare exceptions, most people were afraid to sign such a petition. Obviously in such an atmosphere people were not going to sign petitions to place the Communist party on the ballot. And few Communists were themselves willing to circulate such petitions.

In 1989 and 1990, with the collapse of Communist governments in eastern Europe, newspaper columnists and other pundits hailed the emergence of multiparty systems in those countries. Actually multiparty systems are the norm in most countries that conduct elections. Were that it were so in our own, where the Democratic party more nearly resembles a coalition partner than an opposition to the Republican party and where, beyond the two of them, there is no party worth speaking of. The Communist Party USA was never a huge party, counting at its peak perhaps one hundred thousand members, with a Young Communist League of equal size, although the membership was somewhat overlapping, and with a considerable following particularly in the trade unions. By the sixties, after the cold war abroad and repression at home, exacerbated by its own internal problems and errors, the Party had largely been crushed, reduced to a tiny albeit cohesive band of a few thousand members. This was hardly the instrument to challenge the dominant two parties for political power. But by running for office, it could make a legal challenge to the array of restrictive laws that all but eliminated minority parties from the electoral arena, Fourth of July rhetoric about democracy to the contrary notwithstanding.

State election laws made it difficult or virtually impossible for minority parties to qualify for a place on the ballot. As the history of these laws shows, every potential threat to the two-party monopoly of the political system has been countered by legislation imposing more stringent requirements for access to the ballot. This was the case after the Eugene V. Debs Socialist party campaigns during and after World War I, after the LaFollette candidacy on a Farmer-Labor ticket in 1924, and again following the Progressive party campaign for Henry Wallace in 1948. Twenty years after that, the possibility that Eugene McCarthy might bolt the Democratic party and run as an independent was enough to provoke a new round of restrictive legislation. Yet the courts only rarely and reluctantly intervened to preserve what the Supreme Court declared, in 1968, one of "our most precious freedoms."

The obstacles to ballot status took many forms. One device was to increase the number of signatures needed for the petitions of minority parties, often accompanied by shortening the period allowed for gathering signatures. Most states required the signers to be registered voters and many invalidate the signatures of those who have voted in a major party primary. In California, for example, 100,000 signatures of registered voters who failed to vote in the primaries had to be produced in a period of twenty-five days. (A rule of thumb in signature-gathering is to acquire 50 percent more than the requirement since up to a third will be discounted for illegible writing, abbreviated addresses, or other bases for invalidation. Thus, the California signature requirement was a de facto minimum of 150,000.) Some states required county quotas in addition to statewide quotes. For example, in Illinois, as we discovered during the Progressive party campaign in 1948, 25,000 valid signatures were required, including 100 from each of fifty counties, thus giving the sparsely populated rural counties veto power over the nomination of independent candidates by the urban majority. After the Supreme Court invalidated this provision as a violation of the one person, one vote principle, the state legislature promptly enacted a new law retaining the rural quotas in a disguised form. Then no more than 13,000 signatures could be gathered from any one county. And of course, over and above the restrictive laws aimed at all minority parties, the statute books were packed with legislation specifically directed against the Communist party. In 1968, twenty-nine of the fifty states explicitly denied ballot status to Communists, many laws the products of the cold war period, others of an earlier vintage. Some states made it illegal to contribute to the Communist party, making untenable any election campaign. Some statutes were simply ludicrous, for example, the Texas law barring a Party member from becoming a licensed pharmacist. These were over and above the federal laws—the Mc-Carran Act and others I've discussed at length—which denied constitutionally guaranteed rights, privileges, and immunities to Communists on the basis of their allegedly violent, conspiratorial, and insurrectionist nature.

For the next several presidential elections, the Party made meager efforts to break through the plethora of laws, advertising costs, and media biases that make the two-party system so formidable. With one exception, Gus Hall was the standard-bearer, each time increasingly campaigning from his office, with a phone bank tuned into various radio talk shows across the country. Claims of "influencing the thought patterns of millions" notwithstanding, the Party's vote was never more than minuscule. The campaigns did give me a good deal of work, challenging rigged election laws in various states. In 1976, I engaged in my last major litigation, in a suit we brought against the Federal Election Commission. The case arose around the Federal Election Campaign Act, passed by Congress in the wake of the Watergate scandals. Meant to reform the election process, the act had exactly the opposite result, polluting the political arena with corporate political action committees. One provision of the act required campaign committees to keep records of the names and addresses of any contributors of fifty dollars or more and the names, addresses, and places of occupation of contributors of one hundred dollars or more and to turn these over to the Federal Election Commission for open public inspection. The stated purpose of this aspect of the act was to allow "sunshine" into the financing of political campaigns, and although it made sense in general, for the Party it posed an insurmountable problem. If it asked supporters for more than token contributions, it had to explain that their names would be subject to FBI investigation and be made public.

Soon after passage of the act, James Buckley, the conservative New York senator, and Gene McCarthy, the progressive Minnesota senator, certainly an unlikely couple, teamed up to file suit challenging almost every provision of the act, including the one on financial record-keeping and reporting. The case was expedited and the Supreme Court ruled early in 1976. On the question of reporting names of contributors, the Court held that the plaintiffs offered no proof that these requirements would seriously hinder their ability to raise funds; therefore the Court could not hold the provision unconstitutional. But the Court also recognized the potential harm of the provision for minority political parties, and if such a party offered evidence of a reasonable probability that its contributors might suffer if their names were reported to the government, the Court would listen to the complaint. Further, the Court recognized the difficulty of obtaining proof; therefore it would be sufficient for a party to demonstrate past threats, reprisals, or harassment.

The ruling was ready-made for the Party. If the record-keeping requirements of the Federal Election Campaign Act weren't unconstitutional in their application to Communists, they couldn't be unconstitutional for anybody. I wrote an opinion to this effect, citing the Smith Act, the McCarran Act, the Communist Control Act, the vast number of anticommunist statutes in the fifty states, the various revelations of FBI harassment. I concluded by advising the Party campaign to assure potential contributors that their donations could be anonymous. When the campaign filed its first report with the Commission, it indicated that, on my advice, it withheld the names of contributors who wished to remain anonymous.

The commission responded that if the Party wanted an exemption, it should file affidavits from people who said they were afraid to contribute. To which I replied that we certainly would not file any affidavits, that this was precisely what the Supreme Court said we couldn't do. I added a summary of the conclusions of the Senate Intelligence Committee, under the chairmanship of Frank Church, which identified a systematic pattern of illegal acts by the FBI and other agencies directed against the Party and other radical organizations. Included among these was COINTELPRO. My summary also listed anonymous letters to employers and to spouses of targeted persons to provoke their discharge from jobs or to destroy their marriages; anonymous letters falsely labeling targeted persons as government informers, exposing them to disgrace and possible physical violence, provoking IRS tax investigations of targeted persons; warrantless FBI electronic surveillance in fifteen "target categories" ranging from "Communist Party headquarters" to "Communist Party apologist"; warrantless break-ins of homes and offices—what the FBI calls "black bag jobs"—to steal mailing and membership lists; widespread use of undercover informants; the compilation of lists of persons to be apprehended in a national emergency because of their "subversive associations and ideology"; and a mail-opening program targeted against citizens professing "pro-Communist sympathies." The Election Commission rejected as insufficient these findings of the Church committee, holding that they still didn't prove that potential donors were afraid to contribute because of possible public exposure. It was at this point that I decided to subpoena the FBI records on the Party. In fact, I never really expected to obtain the records. The subpoena effort was a tactic based on our experience with the Arnold Johnson contempt case. I was confident that the FBI would claim executive privilege and fail to produce its extensive files on the Party, thereby resulting in an exemption for the Party from reporting its contributors.

The FBI surprised me. Rather than claim executive privilege, the bureau moved to quash the subpoena on the grounds that it was "unreasonable and oppressive," an irony worth savoring. Just think: we were oppressing the FBI by asking for its records on the Party. To support its contention, the FBI submitted an affidavit claiming that its Communist party files contained an approximate 26.5 million pages of records at the J. Edgar Hoover Building in Washington, another 9.5 million pages at FBI headquarters in New York, and untold millions more in FBI field offices around the country. Processing the files would cost the bureau some $36 million and require a special congressional appropriation. Furthermore, the FBI said that such a process would paralyze it from carrying out any other duties, given the numbers of agents that the job would require.

I told the court that I really wasn't interested in adding to the federal deficit and would be willing to settle—rather than stretching back to 1936 when the FBI says it began keeping files (although I'd wager it began back in 1919 when the Party was founded)—for the records dating back only to 1972. It was now 1978. The FBI, after some consideration, reported to the court that just since 1976 it had accumulated over 90,000 pages of records on the Communist party. Still the FBI equivocated, neither turning over the records nor claiming executive privilege. It finally became clear to me why it hadn't made such a claim. If the government refuses to produce relevant documents on grounds of executive privilege, the head of the concerned department, in this instance the attorney general, is required to personally examine each page of the records in question to certify that, in his or her opinion, they would injure the national defense. For the attorney general to personally examine each page in the Party's FBI file would mean that there would be no time for anything else for a period of some years.

Finally, after many circuitous legal maneuvers, I filed a motion for summary judgment. A summary judgment is issued when the contending parties do not dispute the facts in a case but only the legal effect of the facts. Instead of conducting a trial to establish the facts, the parties swear out affidavits of the facts upon which they agree and move for a summary judgment. With my motion I submitted the twelve affidavits, the summary of the Church committee's findings, and a survey I made of the anticommunist laws of the fifty states and the federal statutes.

The motion was filed in September 1981, but it was another year before the judge rendered an opinion in our favor, saying that the Federal Election Campaign Law was unconstitutional as applied to us. The Election Commission appealed the decision to the U.S. Court of Appeals for the Second Circuit, which assigned the case to a three-judge panel headed by my old antagonist Irving Kaufman, with whom I'd collided on a number of cases, including those seeking Henry Winston's release from prison and preventing Angela Davis's extradition to California. This was one judge from whom I'd never gotten any leeway, and I was concerned on the morning we went to court. There were two cases scheduled for argument ahead of us. As chief judge of the panel, Kaufman introduced the audience of lawyers to a British lord, a judge of England's High Court, who was in attendance. Then, presuming it would be interesting for His Lordship, Judge Kaufman announced, "We'll start this morning with the *Federal Election Commission* case." The commission's lawyer wasn't two minutes into his argument when Kaufman interrupted him, making it clear that he was now in my corner, and with both feet. "Look," he asked the commission counsel, "if you decided that you would like to make a contribution to a Communist election campaign, would you do so unless you could get absolute assurance of anonymity?" The lawyer swallowed hard and answered, no, he wouldn't. I knew the case was won, and this was confirmed when the judges handed down their ruling, with Kaufman writing the opinion. Not only did they decide in our favor, but Kaufman criticized the Election Commission for even bringing the case. He wrote that "for the Federal Election Commission to pursue so vigorously its demand for the names and addresses of the contributors to the committee in the face of the clear chilling effect this activity will inevitably have, is to exhibit an appalling disregard for the needs of the free and open political process safeguarded by the First Amendment."

Whether Kaufman was swayed for the moment by the presence of the British Peer or was perhaps reaching the point in years when he hoped for a favorable judgment upon meeting his Maker, I couldn't guess. I wasn't the only one surprised by his ruling. Roy Cohen, New York's preeminent political fixer, former junior aide to Senator Joseph McCarthy, and a prosecutor of the Rosenbergs in the trial over which Judge Kaufman presided, publicly took the jurist to task. In a letter to the *Law Journal,* read by every lawyer in town because it contains the daily court calendars, Cohen upbraided Kaufman on his ruling, charging that it favored the Communists over the Democrats and Republicans because the two major parties have to list their contributors. This set off a flurry of letters from different lawyers—mainly from Kaufman's friends and those who wished to be regarded favorably when they next appeared before him—blasting Cohen, which dominated the *Law Journal's* letters column for weeks. On top of Kaufman's ruling, the controversy was cause for some small gratification.

8

Losses

On the sixtieth anniversary of the USSR in 1977, Jessica and the staff of *New World Review* decided to compile a special issue, in book form, titled "Six Decades that Changed the World." The idea was to ask a couple of dozen "experts" from both the United States and USSR to contribute articles on various aspects of Soviet life and culture. Jessica asked me to write about the new Soviet constitution, just completed and adopted under the leadership of Leonid Brezhnev.

I read through the document, which was actually quite appealing, until I came to the provision on freedom of speech, which made an exception for "slanders against the Soviet state." It appeared that the Soviet criminal code contained two separate kinds of such violations—slanders against the Soviet state "with intent" (which brought a harsher punishment) and slander "without intent." I told Jessica, "I've spent the best part of my life doing my very best to enforce the First Amendment to our own Constitution in its fullest sense. How can I defend a constitution which expressly permits the kind of repression involved in the Smith and McCarran Acts?"

Jessica understood my viewpoint. She asked me to think through how I might comment on what was positive in the Soviet constitution while expressing my disapproval on this particular question. In the end I indicated my disagreement "with the extent of Soviet restraints on freedom of expression as excessive and lacking justification in any actual or threatened injury to the fabric of socialist society." My criticism was tempered with the knowledge that since its birth, the Soviet Union had been subject to invasions, quarantine, subversion, discriminatory trade practices, cold war, "containment," and of course

the massive invasion and occupation of the western third of its terri-
tory by Hitler's best divisions, resulting in the deaths of 20 million of
its people. I also noted the absence of a democratic tradition or of civil liberties in the previous forty generations of Russian history and
Soviet life.

A year after the article appeared, Jessica and I visited Moscow,
where I met one of the leading lights of the Soviet Institute of Law
and the State. We were discussing Soviet law and I was frank in my
criticisms of the prohibition of "slanders" against the state. I told him
how I had spent my life defending Communists against similar laws
in the United States. He countered by defending the Soviet laws and
how fair they were, saying that the slander law that brought stiff pun-
ishments required proof of intent. I told him that I was familiar with
such laws, that the Smith Act required proof of intent to overthrow
the government, but any prosecutor knows how easy it is to prove intent with professional informers as witnesses. After considerable discussion along these lines, the Soviet expert finally sighed and agreed
that it might be better if the Soviet constitution had omitted this provision. If nothing else, I considered this a moral victory. But a week
later in Leningrad, I had the same discussion with a group of practicing attorneys and failed to budge any of them in their defense of
the slander laws. This was seven years before the beginning of *glas-
nost* and eleven years before the election as mayor of Leningrad the
former Communist and then anticommunist Anatoli Sobchek, himself a practicing attorney.

* * *

Throughout the McCarran Act tribulations, we found refuge and
solace in Kent. Early on, when I first took the case, an old man, with
whom I had a nodding acquaintance but never a conversation, approached me in the village. He grew some beautiful Siberian irises,
which I noticed in his garden, and he invited me to his home to offer
me some flowers. I said that I'd be delighted to visit and pick some of
his irises. It turned out that his offer was a pretext. The old man had
something to tell me. He had noticed news photos of Stalin, thought
the Soviet leader didn't look well, and asked if I thought Stalin would
be interested in a cure for whatever ailed him. I asked what was the
cure he had in mind. "Well," he explained, "most people when they
dream, just dream in black and white. But I dream in color. All I have
to do is dream of Stalin and change his sickly pallor to a healthy col-
or and he'll recover." I confessed that I wasn't in touch with Uncle
Joe, had no way of being so, and wouldn't be able to ascertain his

interest in the man's formula for good health. But I was happy to relieve him of a Siberian iris. That was my only conversation with this particular man, but it brought home to me that through the good offices and many inquiries of the FBI, the entire village of Kent—the village then consisting of little more than a general store and newsstand, tackle shop, liquor store, and a few other shops for basic necessities—knew who I was.

In general, I was accepted by the townsfolk, the shopkeepers, and the farmers from whom we bought milk and corn and other produce. They were traditional New Englanders, and if you didn't make a nuisance of yourself and paid your bills on time, your politics were your own business. Occasionally there was an exception, like James Burnham, who was no more a Yankee than I but who also had a place not far from ours. Burnham, a former Trotskyist turned publisher of William Buckley's *National Review,* noted my presence with disfavor in one of his books, having watched me drive around the area in my jeep.

Judy and her kids, Dorian and Bouj, who have become my granddaughters, spent vacations with us at the house. Jessica, Judy, and David loved to read Dickens together, *David Copperfield* being a particular favorite. Jessica and David enjoyed trouncing the rest of the family in poker. I played grandpa, teasing the girls, who loved our giant frog pond, about having frogs legs for dinner. I took them trout fishing, taking on the role of Ahab trying to catch a "legendary" fish that always got away. I only wore beat-up clothes in Kent, and Bouj recalled that it wasn't until she was eleven years old that she discovered I was a lawyer, not a fisherman. Jessica, gourmet cook and maker of coffee supreme, ruled the kitchen as a benevolent dictator. Her grandmotherly aspects were revealed when she lectured the girls on the benefits of social activism: "Not only is it the right thing to do," she would say, "but you also get to meet a lot of good men."

Bouj recalled David always being in Kent when she visited. Her memories of him were of a young man, always kind, sweet-tempered, and whimsical, given to old-fashioned manners and good graces. That he was quite troubled never made itself felt until she was a teenager. In his own youth, he demonstrated a real talent for music. He had perfect pitch and was an outstanding pianist, but he was unable to stay with anything requiring discipline. By the end of high school, he developed exquisite taste in design and decided to study architecture. He was admitted to the Massachusetts Institute of Technology and by all appearances seemed to be doing well. Jessica and I visited him there on occasion. But then, when I returned from my visit to Moscow with the CIO delegation in 1945, I discovered that David had left MIT.

He told me that he needed to see a psychiatrist. He let me know that he was a homosexual, which, a quarter century before the bare beginnings of the gay rights movement, was considered a subject best left unspoken. On top of his developing schizophrenia or manic-depressive personality (he was diagnosed as each by different therapists), David's sexual orientation left him quite unhappy. In my own ignorance of such matters, I didn't understand how serious his situation was becoming. Of course we arranged for him to get treatment, but he never returned to school. Our household was host to unrestrained family rows, as David vented his fury at Jessica over anything or nothing. Jessica was miserable, both because the son whom she deeply loved was so troubled and because her own feelings of guilt were exacerbated by the inadequacy of her answers to the devastating question "What have I done wrong?" But in Kent, with the extended family and friends, David remained the "perfect English gentleman," in Bouj's words, perhaps reclusive at times but not explosive as he was when alone with Jessica and me.

The Connecticut countryside remained as gorgeous as ever. We continued to spend nearly every weekend and most of our vacation time at the house. The solitude provided me not only with sanctuary from work, but also, when I chose, a much needed retreat for preparing the McCarran Act appeals. It was a godsend, but also a lot of work. With no heat except that provided by a fireplace and wood stove in the kitchen, much of my time was spent sawing. It wasn't until 1970 or so that I invested in a newfangled invention called the chainsaw. Until that time, I exploited our weekend guests to join me in cutting up the dead chestnut poles that remained standing from a recent blight. Our flower garden was Jessica's pride, but it remained turf contested by the resident woodchuck population.

At the foot of October Hill flowed the Housatonic River, where Arnold Johnson first taught me to fish. It was always loaded with bass, and when I graduated to fly casting, I discovered it was equally well stocked with trout. I found that when I fished—this was hardly a novel discovery on my part—I thought about nothing else. Such a lovely escape from our troubled times, but even in such a haven, the times came upon us. The Housatonic flows down to Kent from the Massachusetts Berkshires, through Pittsfield, Stockbridge, and Great Barrington. And we learned that the huge General Electric plant in Pittsfield was using the river to dump its waste, which was filled with PCBs. This sharply decreased the fish supply and made them unfit for eating if you were able to catch those that remained.

With my bad back, driving became increasingly difficult. Jessica was in her late seventies, and keeping up the place became a burden. Moreover, neither of us felt that we could keep a country home without a regular stream of weekend guests, and the political problems and the aging process took their toll on our circle of friends. Reluctantly, in 1975, we placed the house on the market. I thought we'd do well to get $15,000, but Beanie Baldwin urged me to ask $60,000, which we finally got from an airline pilot named Smith. The day of the closing was a traumatic experience for Jessica. At one point, in a friendly gesture to Mrs. Smith, Jessica said, "You know, in the spring, if you open the kitchen door and just look across the driveway, you'll see the most beautiful yellow ladyslippers." Pink ladyslippers were plentiful on our property, particularly in the woods, but the yellow ones were quite rare. To which Mrs. Smith replied, "What are ladyslippers?" Jessica was devastated. Ever afterward, she would permit me to drive no closer than five miles from the house.

* * *

Back in 1951, when I teamed up with Marcantonio to defend the Party, he had an office on Park Place, which he shared with Abe Unger and David Freedman. I moved in for what I thought would be a temporary assignment, and for the next thirty-seven years, until his death in 1988 at the age of ninety, David and I were office mates. David was the most knowledgeable generalist I ever knew. In his nearly seven decades at the bar, there was almost no field of law in which he had not practiced: commercial, real estate, tax, wills and estates, elections, libel, marital, personal injury, immigration—he had done it all. His name is not associated with any landmark or highly publicized cases, but in his quiet, unassuming way, David made important contributions to the ability of his clients to survive and function in a hostile political environment. A law office association has much in common with marriage. And lawyers being contentious fellows by nature and profession, the divorce rate for associates is about the same as for spouses. But in our thirty-seven years of association, David and I never had a serious disagreement, let alone an argument, except when I found that he, who acted as office manager, was underbilling me for my share of expenses.

I suppose when one has been around as long and reached into ripe old age as I have, it is natural that one begins to lose friends to the

facts of nature. In my fifties, I lost Marion and mother, Louis Burnham and Marc. It has been my terrible fate for three decades to preside over or speak to funeral and memorial services for the most generous, courageous, and loveliest collection of friends one man could
ever hope to gather—Eddie Barsky, Henry Winston, Joe Forer, Nat
Witt, Harry Freeman, Beanie Baldwin, Bill Patterson, Clara Colon,
Elizabeth Gurley Flynn, George Murphy, Paul Robeson, Mortie Silverman, Ann and Pete Peters. I have been truly blessed by their friendships and those of their families.

My most devastating loss by far, quite naturally, came with Jessica's
death. Up to the end of her life, she continued to work. She loved to
help other people, spending countless hours doing research for them
to help them understand and use material about the USSR. Over the
years, I learned to hesitate to ask her questions of my own, knowing
that if I asked she would spend endless time finding the sources and
putting them together, even though my query was of little importance.

In 1957, she developed a chronic kidney condition that almost ended her life. Fortunately, we were able to bring it under control with
antibiotics, but it troubled her for the next twenty-five years. Then,
in the late 1970s, she began to suffer terribly from shingles, which
appeared on her face, particularly around her mouth. Sometimes
shingles disappear, or come and go, but in Jessica's case, they
wouldn't go away. The pain was unbearable—often preventing the
intake of food—yet Jessica never complained to anybody else and
very seldom to me. She tried innumerable cures but nothing worked.
It was rumored—we learned this from some American doctors—that
the Soviets had developed a cure for shingles. We anticipated our
1978 visit to Moscow with some degree of optimism, hoping that perhaps Jessica's ordeal would be ended.

She was just shy of her eighty-fourth birthday when we arrived. We
stayed at the October Hotel, reserved for Party guests, and the day after our arrival, we were given a physical examination. Upon taking
Jessica's blood pressure, the doctor became greatly agitated. "Too high,
too high," he muttered and ordered us bundled into an ambulance to
be taken to a hospital that serviced the Kremlin. Neither of us was
much concerned; we knew that each time Jessica arrived in the USSR
was an experience of great excitement for her. Undoubtedly, her high
blood pressure was the result of this raised stimulus. Our problem became how to spring her from the hospital where the doctor continued
to detain her. After several days, I called on Nikolai Mostovitz, the Central Committee staff secretary responsible for relations with the
CPUSA, to tell him of our problem. He agreed to call the doctor, but

later informed me that the doctor insisted on keeping Jessica in the hospital. Nikolai told the doctor that he knew Jessica and me well, that we were greatly attached to one another, and that the separation was deleterious to both of us. To which the doctor replied, "In that case, I'll make arrangements for John to stay in the hospital." It was several more days before Natasha, our lovely, young interpreter, went to the hospital and all but kidnapped Jessica and brought her back to the hotel. We didn't say as much at the time, but both of us were cognizant that John Reed, Bill Haywood, Bill Foster, Elizabeth Flynn, and Pettis Perry had died in the hands of Soviet doctors.

Jessica was, above all, a fighter, certainly tougher and probably more emotionally self-reliant than me. In the midst of her toughest battles, she never lost her good humor. Once, late in life and about to undergo surgery, she told her anesthetist, "Now I don't want you to do anything to jeopardize my sex life." She was the great romance of my life since the time, as I told the story, she lived in New York, I lived in Washington, and we compromised—I moved to New York. With my arm around Jessica, I used to tell my granddaughters, Dorian and Bouj, that "a woman should be a great armful." Soon my "great armful" was fighting for her life. One morning shortly before her eighty-eighth birthday, she woke up feeling extremely weak, unable to rise out of bed. At first her symptoms indicated that she might have flu. I called Dr. Pearlmutter, our family physician. By then—this was 1983—American medicine had achieved the "advanced" state in which house visits were shunned by virtually all who swore to the Hippocratic oath. Pearlmutter wanted me to bring Jessica to the New York University Hospital. When I explained that she couldn't move out of bed, he ordered an ambulance. Upon examining her, his diagnosis was pneumonia. That evening, Pearlmutter awakened me to say that Jessica had been transferred to intensive care. When I arrived at the hospital, I learned that she had choked on a chicken bone and suffered cardiac arrest, which they were able to bring her out of.

Jessica was placed in a respirator and fought to stay alive. After a couple of weeks, she began to weaken, to turn inward. I sat at her side, her hand in mine, and told her, "Just give me your beautiful smile." Her ordeal in the respirator lasted five weeks until she lost all strength to fight off the infection and died. We had been lovers, as well as husband and wife, for forty-six years. At her memorial service a few weeks after her death, our granddaughter Dorian spoke on behalf of her sister, Bouj, and herself:

> Not only was [Jessica] our beloved grandmother, she was also
> a woman of strength and smiles, of purpose and wit, of vibrancy

and compassion: she taught us that fighting the battle does not mean forsaking a joy of life.

She was born in an era that did not look kindly upon the woman who took an independent point of view and pursued her path with a life-long dedication. But no one could dismiss Jessica by saying that she was somehow misfit and had to lead a different kind of life. She could have done and she could have been anything she wanted—the most glamorous social butterfly, the most competent of all wives dedicated solely to her husband's career . . . or numerous other choices open to someone of her intelligence, beauty, charm and wit. So when Jessica decided to devote herself to an all-important but unpopular battle, she did not provide the world with an excuse with which to belittle her words and actions. What Jessica had to say was always taken seriously—Jessica was too important for anyone to do anything less. . . .

[Our days in Kent] were filled with conversations about life, values and truths, literature and fresh baked cookies, fishing and the politics of nations, catching frogs and reading the newspaper from cover to cover. . . . We will always remember Jessica . . . with her hair touched with amber, her eyes and smile radiant with laughter, beaming with the vision of a better world.

* * *

Before Jessica died, I decided to legally adopt David. I had no near heirs; Johnny Bachrach, Marion's son, was the closest. If Jessica died, I would have no heirs at all, and also I wanted to assure David's financial well-being. David rather liked the idea and entered the adoption process in the courts with an enthusiasm that was rare for him. He was then fifty-nine years old. In earlier years he had worked at a number of jobs—selling books at Gimbels, editing investment surveys, proofreading translations from Russian scientific papers—even while living with us. Each job was short-lived, invariably ending in disputes when David let it be known in no uncertain terms that he knew how the work should be done better than his employers. This was the same reason that his therapy at the hands of various psychiatrists never lasted for long. He thought (and said) that he knew better than they, and I believe he was often correct in his assessment.

In the early sixties, after his release from Gracie Square Hospital, he lived on his own. The doctors at Gracie Square made this a condition of his release. From then on, he lived in a series of apartments, filling up one until it was no longer habitable, and he received a court

summons at the instigation of an angry landlord, then moving on. He
never again held a job and became increasingly reclusive. Usually he
lived alone, although on occasion he would have a boyfriend who
lived off of him and what we provided. He preferred to live in Queens
and had little to do with us beyond receiving his weekly check. David never showed resentment toward me, but was quite outspoken in
holding Jessica responsible for his problems. While Jessica lay dying
in the hospital, he reluctantly overcame his understandable dislike
of hospitals to say a final good-bye. He made another rare sojourn
into Manhattan for Jessica's memorial service but by then was so
consumed with his own troubles that he seemed not to be deeply affected by the death of his mother.

I missed Jessica dreadfully. I was miserable in her absence and
suffered from depression. At one point, Vita Barsky came to visit me
and probably saved me from giving in to my misery. I had known her
for many years, back when she worked in Milwaukee on that ill-fated magazine in 1940, even before she married Eddie. She is one terrific organizer and became Jessica's primary fundraiser at *New World
Review*. Like Eddie, she has a tough "act" and, like him, is quite soft
underneath. When she first visited me to express her sympathy after
Jessica died, Vita said, "You know, John, it doesn't get any easier. As
a matter of fact, it gets harder all the time." Eddie had already been
gone for eight years.

To comfort each other in our loneliness, Vita and I began to go out
together to dinner and to movies. And she took it upon herself to organize an eightieth birthday banquet in my honor. I suppose I am
somebody who needs to be with someone I love, to share experiences and laughter. My stepdaughter, Judy, and granddaughters Dorian
and Bouj have remarked that romantic love is a big part of my life.
Perhaps they saw this more clearly than I, but in any case I soon discovered that Vita and I were in love. I briefly became scared and
pulled away, but I couldn't pull very far or for very long. I asked her
to marry me and, happily, she agreed.

I called David to join us at city hall to witness our wedding. Later
he phoned me to tell me of a dream he had in which Jessica told him
how happy she was for Vita and me. I can say without hesitation that
Vita has saved my life. Soon after we were married, I had, at the age
of eighty-one, a second operation for a slipped disk. The operation
itself was successful but I developed a bone infection. The doctors
confined me to a hospital bed for a few months while they poured
antibiotics into me. When I was finally able to get out of bed, I found
that I couldn't walk. My convalescent period and relearning to walk

would take several more months. Without Vita's love, care, and buoyancy, I would never have survived.

David lost interest in his earlier avocations—art, science, music—and we rarely saw him. He preferred to keep his distance, and our relations narrowed to financial matters, his pressing me for money as he needed it. In 1989, he was hospitalized for pneumonia, and Vita and I went to visit him. Always a heavy drinker and smoker, David had also developed emphysema. After a week, the hospital released him with the understanding that he return within fourteen days for further tests and treatment. A couple of days later, his roommate called to inform me that David had died in his sleep. He was sixty-one. It seemed such a tragic waste of a life. David was bright, witty, talented, funny, but he was deeply troubled. And a deeply troubled society could not deal with him. Coming of age as a homosexual in an age when nonconformist sexual preferences brought only fear and loathing, on top of having a psychiatric history that made most therapists throw up their hands in frustration with their own inabilities to treat him, David could only see himself as a misfit and withdraw into himself. His death was terribly sad and there was no solace except that Jessica was no longer around to suffer his loss.

* * *

For the past forty years, since my heart attack, my doctor has been Morris Pearlmutter. I first met him when he was Eddie Barsky's associate. Morris has constantly reminded me that when I was hospitalized for my coronary, I told him that I held him responsible to keep me alive because I wanted to be around long enough "to see how things turned out." Four decades ago, I would never have suspected that by this time things would turn out as they have. In fact "things" never do turn out; they just keep turning. This experience has made me more than a bit wary about predictions as to how they will turn in the near or distant future or what might be done to make them turn as I would like.

For myself, whose entire career was devoted to protecting the rights of working people and extending democracy in the United States, the crisis of socialism internationally is certainly unsettling. It is difficult for me to say this, but *in this sense only,* I'm glad that Jessica is not around to witness it. It would have simply broken her heart. She was not a naive person. She was perfectly aware of the stultifying bureaucracy in the USSR. She was intellectually conscientious and didn't accept at face value whatever was told her. In 1968, neither of us were enamored with Gustav Husak, who was installed in the presidential palace in Prague by Soviet troops, replacing Alexander Dubcek, the reform-minded leader of the Czechoslovak Communists. Husak and his group were inflexible bureaucrats who obviously enjoyed no popular support. I remember Jessica agonizing for weeks over what to do or say at that time. Typically, she was extremely hard on herself. In the end, she wrote in her magazine of her doubts but concluded that given the international situation—the United States had massively invaded South Vietnam while carrying on the most intensive bombing campaign in history in North Vietnam—and faced with making a choice, she would side with the Soviets. That such a choice was unnecessary would never have occurred to Jessica, who had devoted fifty years to promoting Soviet socialism, nor to me, for that matter.

She used to say, "What I write in the magazine is my record on which I can stand, by which my life can be judged." It turns out that at least part of that record was just wrong, a complete misjudgment of events. Jessica was so extremely honest, particularly with herself, that I just don't know how she would have reconciled this. Having dedicated her entire being to the defense of the socialist system as practiced in the Soviet Union, it would have been dreadful for her to discover how much of what she believed in and fought for was wrong, mistaken, indefensible.

At the same time, I have little patience for those who argue that Soviet socialism was a ghastly mistake from the beginning and who belittle its contributions to humanity. Whatever its errors, mistakes, and crimes, the USSR's enormous achievements cannot be erased at will. In three-quarters of a century—a mere wink, in human history—socialism was able to transform an underdeveloped, semifeudal country occupying one-sixth of the earth's land surface and bring it into the modern age. This is a staggering accomplishment, especially when one considers the depth of the crisis now gripping the developing countries. The Soviets made education available as no other country ever had to more than 200 million illiterate peasants, creating perhaps the most highly schooled population the world has ever seen, with more doctors, scientists, cultural workers, and engineers than any other country. It built a vast modern industry, achieving feats of science, technology, and production in a brief span of time, far shorter than it took our own country to accomplish similar deeds.

And it did so against incredible odds and the fierce hostility of a capitalist world that was determined, in Winston Churchill's memorable phrase, "to strangle the Bolshevik baby in its cradle." Foreign

> EXCEPT FOR The PRIVILEGED COMMUNIST
> BEAURACRACY

intervention, armed and otherwise, civil war, sabotage, famine, forced isolation, war—this was the lot of the USSR for the entirety of its existence until 1985. At the unfathomable price of 20 million lives and ten thousand cities and towns, the Soviets bore the brunt of humanity's defeat of fascism—and was credited for as much by the same Winston Churchill—while our own country escaped remarkably unscathed. Through the entire ordeal, the USSR was able to abolish exploitation—the profiting of the few from the labor of the many—to a large degree, providing the world's third-largest population with full employment, social security, and free health care. Finally, one cannot underestimate the enormous diplomatic, material, political, and military help rendered by the USSR—not to mention the positing of an alternative vision—to the Third World in bringing an end to classical colonialism in our time.

Paradoxically, it was the absence of democracy in the USSR that provided Western capitalism with its trump card in the ideological struggle between the two systems. In no small part, this struggle compelled the United States to abandon McCarthyism and Jim Crow or to be shown up as hypocritical before international public opinion. In a speech before the American Bar Association, Earl Warren once made much the same point, that the extent to which we lived up to our own Bill of Rights would have a determining effect on the competition between the two social systems. If this be the case, it might be one of the contemporary world's great ironies that the lifelong effort by myself and other U.S. Communists to defend and expand democracy in our country in effect strengthened American capitalism in its contest with Soviet socialism.

I realize in hindsight that there is no way to square the equation between my lifelong work for democracy and civil rights and liberties at home and defending governments abroad that didn't put much stock in such things. My work will have to speak for me. The sociologist C. Wright Mills once wrote that the entirety of bourgeois social science since Karl Marx has been devoted to refuting him. If Mills's point has merit, as I believe it does, it is because Marx's critique of capitalism is irrefutable. But as I am impatient with those who refuse to recognize the contributions the USSR has made to humanity's welfare, I am equally indignant with those who believe that life has taught us nothing about the problems of socialism, that the Soviet model—really the Stalinist model—is in no need of radical revision. If eighty-seven years of this life has taught me anything, it is the pitfalls of arrogance and dogmatism.

I admit that with all the reading and study I've done on the subject, I've yet to find anything that gives a satisfying account of what is needed to make socialism work. Joe Slovo, the leader of the South African Communist party and a major figure in the African National Congress, made an outstanding contribution to the discussion of democracy and socialism in his pamphlet *Has Socialism Failed?* He argues that without the workers and farmers actually participating in the governing process, socialism is undermined. The Bolsheviks took power in the USSR with the call, "All power to the Soviets." But under Stalin and since, this was distorted to mean "all power to the party and its general secretary." Still, the question remains, can socialism provide complete economic security to its people—full employment and satisfaction of basic needs—and still get the maximum productivity essential to building and maintaining an advanced technological society? What is the nature of economic planning—and how will it work?—that provides production for human needs rather than private profits, and at the same time assures the kind of competition that is necessary to make the system function at a satisfactory level?

Sometimes I've thought—perhaps it is an affliction of the aging process—about the what-might-have-beens. Friends who have been generous in their praise have on occasion suggested that given the "pedigree" into which I was born and the legal abilities I developed, I might have risen to the top of the profession, even to the Supreme Court as did some of my colleagues, had I chosen a different path for myself. Perhaps it is a basic flaw in my character, but I have never been personally ambitious. I never had any interest to be anything other than what I was. The question has been asked of me in recent years if, knowing what I now know, I regret my choices. I've reflected on this and have answered without hesitation, no, I made the right choices for me. With a bit more ambition and aggressiveness, I might have "achieved" more in traditional terms, but I wouldn't have been as nice a person as I like to think I am.

Besides, I start with the proposition that our capitalist system is rancid to its very core: it needs racism and its attendant brutality to keep natural allies divided against one another; it breeds corruption of the individual and of the culture as a whole; it results in an unfettered concentration of wealth, and therefore of *real* power in increasingly few hands, and a growing impoverishment of tens of millions, and is thus profoundly undemocratic. Moreover, much as attention has been paid to the errors and crimes of socialism, they are dwarfed by the crimes of capitalism. If Stalinism was sustained by the gulags and the murder of Kulaks, was not our own U.S. capitalism built on

→ MARX'S PREDICTION THAT THIS WOULD OCCUR IN A CAPITALIST SOCIETY PROVED WRONG.

the slave trade, the genocide of Native Americans, the annexation of half of Mexico, the plunder of other lands? And are not the shanty towns of Peru, the bloated stomachs of the children of Senegal, the corpses found in the streets of the Indian subcontinent each morning, not to mention the millions of homeless of our own people, more typical of the capitalist experience than the Long Island suburbs or the Manhattan high-rises? Stalin was a brute and a murderer, but it was not socialism that killed two million Vietnamese, trained death squads in El Salvador, and imposed apartheid on South Africa. I ask myself: If the U.S. government can resort to the terrorism of McCarthyism when there is no internal threat to it, if it can carpet-bomb Iraq when there is no external threat to it, what might it be prepared to do to our people if they ever took it in mind to fundamentally restructure the order of things, to actually threaten the power and the treasure of capitalism? I wonder if we would have a "velvet revolution" like Czechoslovakia or a peaceful transition to a different system as in Hungary? Or would we have a unrelenting blood bath?

Clearly the end of the twentieth century is far different than I would ever have imagined. The cold war is at an end and that is to the good. (And the Nobel Committee, in awarding its 1991 Peace Prize to Mikhail Gorbachev, justly recognized who was primarily responsible for bringing it to a conclusion.) New threats to human survival loom: environmental catastrophe, nuclear and high-tech warfare, the monopolization of communications, and the resultant crisis of democracy, a crisis of survival for the impoverished and the racially and nationally oppressed, here and abroad. If the socialist models in other countries have been discredited, all the more reason why we U.S. radicals have to create our own. My own spell in government at the point of its greatest economic crisis taught me that it is incapable of resolving the crisis short of going to war. And if a new way is to be found, it can only be through a people united in action, through organization. Our loyalty, however, must be to the objectives of socialism—to making life for the majority more livable, more peaceful, more fruitful, more free—rather than to an organization per se.

I must still say that for all its many flaws and weaknesses, the Communist party allowed me to acquire knowledge I could never have gotten in any other way. I was raised to be a bourgeois intellectual. I had no experience in the class struggle. I was never bound by chains. In a material sense, I stood only to lose by being a Communist. But in a human sense, I was greatly enriched. The Party was involved, and consequently I was involved, in every struggle for decency and social progress for a half century, usually before they became acceptable. If the Party operated by command, if in trying to pattern itself after a foreign model it created blinders, I acknowledge my own complicity in following it. It was a chosen path, not a forced march. We may not have built a new society with a new human personality, but I could count among my friends and comrades some of the most heroic, idealistic, and selfless figures of our time.

I look around me and remain unprepared to compromise my commitment to a better way of life to achieve a few more accolades, honors, or luxuries. I could not be other than I am. The old union song poses the key question of our time in its refrain "Which side are you on, / Which side are you on?" This is a question each of us has had to answer, not once but at each turn of history. And in my lifetime, history has taken many turns. And the question cannot be avoided. The failure to answer is itself an answer. Whatever my own failures, I've always known which side I was on.

Index

ARTIE BACHRACH, JOHN APT'S BROTHER IN LAW
P. 94

Hollywood Ten -p.152 [handwritten]

NATION, The [MAG] p. 105

MAILER, NORMAN, 155

117, 163,
171, 172
220, 236, 238,
294,

MOSTEL, ZERO, 162

PICTURE ON P. 230.3; WAS A FRIEND OF THE COMMIE BUT NEVER A MEMBER P. 117, 189; HE REPRESENTED THE COMMUNIST PARTY IN THE McCARRAN ACT CASE—P. 189, 238, 294,

SMITH ACT- p.150

WELLES, ORSON —p. 1 05,

Michael Myerson's books include *These Are the Good Old Days, Memories of Underdevelopment, Watergate: Crime in the Suites, Nothing Could Be Finer,* and *Stopping World War III.* He has worked as a writer and editor for various publications and as an organizer in political campaigns and the civil rights, labor, and peace movements. He presently lives in New York City, where he teaches and writes about labor and politics.